T0388554

Comfort in the Eighteenth-Century Country House

Country houses were grand statements of power and status, but they were also places where people lived. This book traces the changes in layout, the new technologies, and the innovations in furniture that made them more convenient and comfortable. It argues that these material changes were just one aspect of comfort in the country house: feeling comfortable was just as important as being comfortable. Achieving this involved the comfort and solace to be found in daily routines, religious faith and, above all, relationships with family and friends. Such emotional comforts, and the attachment to things and places that embodied and memorialised them, made country houses into homes.

Jon Stobart is a Professor of History at Manchester Metropolitan University.

Routledge Studies in Eighteenth-Century Cultures and Societies
Series Editors: Elaine Chalus and Deborah Simonton

The long eighteenth century sits as a pivotal point between the early-modern and modern worlds. By actively encouraging an international focus for the series over all, both in terms of wide-ranging geographical topics and authorial locations, the series aims to feature cutting-edge research from established and recent scholars, and capitalize on the breadth of themes and topics that new approaches to research in the period reveal. This series provides a forum for recent and established historians to present new research and explore fresh approaches to culture and society in the long eighteenth century. As a crucial period of transition, the period saw developments that shaped perceptions of the place of the individual and the collective in the construction of the modern world. Eighteenth-Century Cultures and Societies is a series that is globally ambitious in scope and broad in its desire to publish cutting-edge research that takes an innovative, multi-vocal and increasingly holistic approach to the period. The series will be particularly sensitive to questions of gender and class, but aims to embrace and explore a variety of fresh approaches and methodologies.

Sartorial Practices and Social Order in Eighteenth-Century Sweden
Fashioning Difference
Mikael Alm

Daily Lives and Daily Routines in the Long Eighteenth Century
Edited by Gudrun Andersson and Jon Stobart

Comfort in the Eighteenth-Century Country House
Jon Stobart

At Home in the Eighteenth Century
Interrogating Domestic Space
Edited by Stephen G. Hague and Karen Lipsedge

For more information about this series, please visit: www.routledge.com/ Routledge-Studies-in-Eighteenth-Century-Cultures-and-Societies/book-series/RSECCS

Comfort in the Eighteenth-Century Country House

Jon Stobart

Routledge
Taylor & Francis Group

NEW YORK AND LONDON

First published 2022
by Routledge
605 Third Avenue, New York, NY 10158

and by Routledge
2 Park Square, Milton Park, Abingdon, Oxon, OX14 4RN

Routledge is an imprint of the Taylor & Francis Group, an informa business

Library of Congress Cataloging-in-Publication Data
Names: Stobart, Jon, 1966– author.
Title: Comfort in the eighteenth-century country house / Jon Stobart.
Description: New York, NY : Routledge, 2022. | Series: Routledge studies in eighteenth-century cultures and societies | Includes bibliographical references and index.
Subjects: LCSH: Dwellings—Environmental engineering—History—18th century. | Country homes—England—History—18th century. | Country homes—United States—History—18th century.
Classification: LCC TH6057.A6 S76 2022 (print) | LCC TH6057. A6 (ebook) | DDC 728.80941/09033—dc23
LC record available at https://lccn.loc.gov/2021013334
LC ebook record available at https://lccn.loc.gov/2021013335

ISBN: 978-1-032-07291-3 (hbk)
ISBN: 978-1-032-07292-0 (pbk)
ISBN: 978-1-003-20636-1 (ebk)

DOI: 10.4324/9781003206361

Typeset in Sabon
by Apex CoVantage, LLC

For Jane

Contents

Figures

Tables

Acknowledgements

This book is one of the principal outputs of a Marie Skłodowska-Curie Fellowship 'House and home: physical and emotional comfort in the country house, England and Sweden c.1680–1820', awarded in 2015. My particular thanks go to Cristina Prytz, the Fellow on this award, who has contributed much of the material on Sweden that is included here and helped to shape the analysis. I would also like to thank Johanna Ilmakunnas and Daniel Menning for assistance with translations and for their helpful feedback; Kate Retford for advice on illustrations; Dale Townshend and Andrew Crome for comments on earlier drafts, and Deborah Simonton and Elaine Chalus for their invaluable editorial input. Earlier versions of chapters have been presented at conferences and seminars in Antwerp, Belfast, Groningen, Leeds, Manchester, London, Oxford, Tübingen, Uppsala, Valencia, Wolverhampton, Wrest Park and York. My thanks go to the organisers of these events and to all who participated and helped to shape my ideas and arguments.

Introduction

Visiting England in the 1820s in search of a wife, the German prince, Hermann Pückler-Muskau stayed briefly at Guy's Cliffe in Warwickshire. A great fan of the informality he found in English country houses, he painted an idyllic picture of the house. In the drawing room, 'burnt a comfortable fire; exquisite pictures adorned the walls, and many sofas of different shapes as well as tables covered with curiosities and furniture standing about in agreeable disorder made everything appear homely and charming'.[1] Three decades earlier, in 1792, Lady Caroline Dawson wrote to her sister Lady Louisa Stuart about the illness suffered by their father, the Third Earl of Bute: 'Oh, my dear Louisa, how I feel for you, and how I wish I could partake in the melancholy employment of giving comfort to my dear mother'. His health was deteriorating rapidly, with little prospect of him recovering. In these unhappy circumstances, Lady Dawson told her sister:

> it gives me great comfort to hear he suffers very little pain, and that my mother is so calm and resigned; indeed, if we consider the advantage it is to him to be delivered from a life in which he has appeared to have very little happiness or comfort for some time, we ought to rejoice instead of grieving.[2]

Mrs. Mary Delany, describing in 1745 the arrangements made by her husband to set up his nephew with a small estate, expressed her satisfaction with his plans. She wrote that: 'The Dean *gives* them a very comfortable farm about twelve miles off, and they are to supply us with all farming affairs. When this is done the Dean has not a relation left that he has *not portioned* or *settled* in some comfortable way'.[3]

As the correspondence of these three very different individuals makes clear, both country-house owners and visitors were alive to the idea and ideal of comfort in their lives and homes. However, it held very different meanings in each context. For Pückler-Muskau it was associated with a warming fire and with a sense of relaxed informality; for Dawson, it had more to do with the consolation given or received during times of

DOI: 10.4324/9781003206361-1

difficulty, and for Delany, it was shorthand for a general sense of material and financial well-being. Across these varied interpretations, comfort clearly mattered to people in the eighteenth century and it matters to how we understand their lives and the broader social and cultural processes which shaped them. It is surprising, then, that comfort has gained limited traction in the historiography and, when it does feature, the focus is squarely on its physical manifestations.[4]

This book addresses this lacuna by analysing comfort in all its various guises: the materiality and technology that provided a comfortable domestic environment; the arrangements of furniture and people that made people feel comfortable, and the comfort that was derived from personal and familial relationships and from sentimental attachment to things. This takes us beyond a narrow focus on physical comfort, important though this was to many householders, and links histories of the country house (often preoccupied with architecture and aesthetics) with histories of family, religion, memory and emotions. This serves to animate the country house by populating rooms with people who were concerned with keeping warm, creating a relaxing atmosphere, maintaining caring relationships with friends and family and feeling at home. It also means drawing together a broad range of human activities and experiences and thinking about how these were interrelated in the context of comfort. This book is therefore concerned with buildings and things, but above all with people: how the owners of country houses both large and small sought to shape their domestic environments and how they described their thoughts and feelings towards their homes and their families. These interrelationships are fundamental to how we understand the complexities and importance of comfort in the long eighteenth century, and what we understand by the word and the idea(s) of comfort. They are also crucial in looking beneath the grand surface of the country house and uncovering the complex behaviours, motivations and concerns of their owners.

Country House and Home

Styled as mansion, hall, house, manor, castle, park, abbey, priory and even palace, the English country house brings to mind a clear image, both of the structure and its setting, and the lifestyle enjoyed by its occupants. They have been variously described as 'the houses of the ruling class' and 'the creation of large landowners'; their construction in the eighteenth and early nineteenth century was of 'national significance', and they became 'treasure houses', filled with costly art, furniture and decoration.[5] Although quintessentially English, the country house found its equivalent throughout the British Isles and across Europe. In Ireland, it was the 'big house', as at Moore Hall; in France, the *chateau* (for example, Vaux le Vicomte) or *maison de plaisance* (Petit Trianon at Versailles);

in Germany, the *schloss* (Glücksburg stein or Schwetzingen); in the Netherlands, the *kastell* (Merckenburg or Middachten); in Sweden, the *slott* (Ljung) or *herrgård* (Stola); and in Italy, the *palazzo* (Ducale, Lombardy). Many of these houses shared important characteristics with their English counterparts, from the key connection between the house and the surrounding estate, to the adoption of fashionable architectural styles and the construction of lavish interiors, to their variation in size and grandeur.

As residences of the landed elite, these chateaux, schlosser and herrgårdar were frequently overshadowed by the town houses owned by the same families, most notably the aristocratic hotels in Paris and palazzi lining the squares and streets in Italian cities.[6] In many German states, schloss were often located in towns, forming the seat of the government for the Duke or Prince, as at Rastatt and Nymphenburg in Munich. English aristocrats also built grand town houses; Northumberland House, Devonshire House and Somerset House, amongst others, were important in marking the presence and power of their owners in London. However, in Georgian England, the balance of attention and spending was shifting towards the country house as a residence, the location of collections and sometimes a political base. This is not to say that the English country house was inhabited throughout the year. Like its continental counterparts, it often formed the family's summer residence, although this was a practice much more common for those with deeper pockets or with political or social ambitions; the gentry, in particular, were often in their country houses all year round.

The English country house has generated a huge body of literature, the focus of enquiry gradually shifting from the economic and architectural to the social and cultural. Early studies were concerned with the economics of estate ownership and the balance sheet of income and expenditure, attention gradually broadening to encompass the use of marriage and estate settlements, mortgages and credit.[7] The emphasis was mostly on understanding the mechanisms underpinning continuity in status and wealth of early-modern elites, and particularly the role of land in these processes. This was complemented by the work of F.M.L. Thompson, Gordon Mingay and later John Beckett who sought to understand as a whole the various social groups making up the gentry and aristocracy, and the ways in which they exercised social and political power.[8] The country house played a major part in this projection of power, as Mark Girouard captured beautifully in his conception of the 'power house'. For him, the English country house was: 'the headquarters from which land was administered and power organised. It was a show-case, in which to exhibit and entertain supporters and good connections . . . It was an image maker, which projected an aura of glamour, mystery or success around its owner. It was visible evidence of his wealth'.[9]

The country house thus had both a practical and symbolic function; it formed an index of the owner's social and political ambition, with some laying out huge sums on building and decorating halls, and on landscaping parks.[10] Spiralling costs brought serious financial difficulties on some occasions as ambition ran ahead of wealth, but many landowners were able to spread the costs and thus finance building programmes from their income. This was especially true of the smaller and numerous seats of gentlemen and minor aristocrats. Men like Thomas Coke, 1st Earl of Leicester, and William Beckford capture the imagination with their huge building projects at Holkham Hall and Fonthill Abbey; but more typical of the landed classes were the hundreds of gentlemen living very comfortably on a few hundred a year in houses that cost just a few thousand to build.[11] This means that 'country house' encompasses a huge variety of properties, from the grandeur of Blenheim Palace or Welbeck Abbey, with frontages extending 300 feet or more, to the modest villas occupied by the gentlemen-clothiers studied by Stephen Hague.[12]

Regardless of their size, these houses represented a significant investment in cultural and symbolic capital, architecture forming a key measure of the taste and character of the owner. Architectural histories have traditionally taken a linear approach to stylistic development in country house architecture—a tendency seen most clearly in the seminal work of John Summerson and John Harris.[13] They outline a basic four-stage progression, from Baroque, through Neo-Palladianism and Neo-Classicism, to neo-Gothic styles.[14] Again, however, the tendency to foreground the houses of the wealthiest and most ambitious landowners—places like Blenheim Palace, Holkham Hall, Kedleston Hall and Fonthill Abbey— simplifies the often hybrid nature of many houses and obscures the extensions and remodelling frequently undertaken where money or preference precluded major rebuilding.[15] Moreover, different architectural styles gave landowners choice about what they built, the process being played out in dialogue with architects. Reading these choices as symbols of their tastes, preferences and allegiances, country house architecture can tell us much about the political, cultural and aesthetic values of the owners.[16]

Investment in the country house as cultural capital spread to the interior, seen as an integral part of the overall architectural scheme in the grander houses designed by prominent architects.[17] Here again, the focus is often on the grand patron and the most famous craftsmen and artists. It is the Thomas Chippendale furniture at Nostell Priory and the wall paintings of Louis Laguerre at Blenheim that attract attention, rather than, for example, the furniture of William Gomm and the unattributed but still noteworthy stuccowork at Stoneleigh Abbey.[18] More importantly, the key concern is with these as works of art: how the furniture was used; how the paintings, murals and stuccowork that adorned walls and ceilings impacted on people living in these houses, and how these things formed part of the wider material culture of the country house have only recently begun to receive the attention they deserve. I have referred to this elsewhere as the '*Country Life* view of the house: an assemblage of unique and precious objects brought together by discerning owners who were noted aesthetes and key patrons of the arts'.[19] It has the effect of presenting the country house as preconceived and stable, rather than contingent, fluid and changing.

Recent studies have begun to open up the country house to a wider range of perspectives. The rise of global history has helped to focus attention on the position of the country house in global as well as European systems of supply. Many of the materials used in high-quality furniture came from the West Indies (mahogany), India and the East Indies (rosewood, burh, satinwood), or Africa (ivory), and China remained a key source for lacquer work, porcelain and wallpaper, whether bought new or via house sales. Moreover, the return of newly rich East India Company officers or West Indian planters, along with retired naval and army officers, not only swelled the ranks of the land-owning elite (and threatened the established social order) but also tied the English country house firmly into the cultures and material cultures of imperialism.[20] As Stephanie Barczweski argues, British country houses abound with the 'physical representations of empire'.[21] Yet the focus largely remains on the luxurious and the permanent, with relatively little attention being given to the full breadth of the elite's changing material culture and patterns of consumption, even in the form of colonial groceries which have excited so much attention amongst historians of consumption and retailing.[22]

A more rounded picture of the country house as a site of consumption is starting to emerge, often through studies focusing on the management of the household. In this respect, recent work by Amanda Vickery and by Jane Whittle and Elizabeth Griffiths is particularly important, both in adding detail and colour to our picture of elite material culture and spending and in linking this to gender identities and gendered divisions of labour within the country house.[23] My own research on consumption and the country house has developed these ideas further, refining our understanding of the ways in which elite identities were shaped through consumption, and exploring the processes of decision-making and systems of supply through which goods were chosen and brought to the country house.[24] Importantly, this work was concerned with the mundane as well as the magnificent—the everyday spending necessary for maintaining and cleaning, and feeding the household—and paid attention to the positioning and repositioning of goods within the house. In this, my analysis built on the approach, pioneered by Girouard, of considering the country house as a lived space.[25] Girouard himself was concerned with the ways in which the architecture and especially the layout of the house reflected and facilitated changes in modes of living, from the formality of the late seventeenth and early eighteenth century, through the so-called social house of the early Georgian era, to the growing informality of the decades either side of 1800. Others have focused on more utilitarian aspects of the country house, especially the service areas and domestic offices, and the ways in which changing technologies impacted modes of behaviour and ways of living.[26] Servants have attracted less attention than might be expected, especially given their centrally to making the country house function in a way that made it a liveable space. They eased the lives of their employers by fetching and carrying, cooking and cleaning, whilst being increasingly pushed to the spatial margins in rooms that occupied basements, garrets and separate wings.[27]

Different room arrangements, the deployment of new technologies—from stoves to water closets—and the labour of servants were all intended to make the country house more convenient and more comfortable as a place in which to live. This could be quite a challenge given the size and architectural form of many houses: building lofty entrance halls, installing grand staircases and arranging rooms enfilade might speak of wealth and taste, but they did not make for easy living environments. Rather knottier is the issue of what made a country house feel like home, if this is, indeed, a useful and meaningful idea for a place sometimes occupied for only a few months during the summer. The difficulties start with identifying exactly what distinguished a house from a home.[28] Early lexicographers struggled with this: Edward Phillips, in his *New World of Words* (1706), defined Home as 'house, or place of abode', and House as 'Home, Place of Abode'. John Kersey's *New English Dictionary* (1713), escaped from this tautology by redefining house as a 'building to live or dwell in'.[29] Samuel Johnson added notions of privacy and possession, so that home became (amongst other things) 'His own house; the private dwelling'; but it was only in the early nineteenth century that the affective nature of home was explicitly identified. Whilst Charles Richardson, in his *New Dictionary of the English Language* (1839) reproduced the old definition of home as a place of dwelling, residence or abode, he identified a second meaning: home was the locus of 'our feeling or affections; our own hearts, our interests or concerns, our pursuits or aims'.[30]

This emphasis on the sentimental associations of home is apparent in literature from the late eighteenth century onwards. Whereas writers from Daniel Defoe to Fanny Burney had mostly used home to denote a place of abode, Hannah More characterised it as a place of virtue that could afford comfort and happiness. In her 1796 moral tale *Mr. Bragwell and his two daughters*, she contrasts Mr. Worthy's 'neat and pleasant dwelling' with that of Mr. Bragwell: 'it had not so many ornaments, but it had more comforts', including a 'good old-fashioned chair in a warm corner'.[31] These sentiments align closely with the ways in which historians have sought to understand home as both a social and material construct and a lived experience. Clive Edwards notes that the idea of home is 'rooted in a number of different aspects, including privacy, security, family, intimacy, comfort and control, as well as personal input, the nature of relationships, the surroundings'.[32] This lengthy list is helpful but requires some unpacking. Comfort, control and personal input all feature in Vickery's exploration of the 'nest of comforts' wrought by women's active engagement in the domestic production of artefacts and in the construction of homes that had emotional resonance.[33] Things that they made as well as bought were important in making their houses into homes.

In a similar vein, Judith Lewis and Helen Metcalfe have shown how emotional attachment to specific objects—often old or with particular familial associations—was central in the ways that not only women but also men made houses into homes by providing them with sentimental meaning for their occupants.[34] As Ian Woodward puts it, objects may play a very public role in communicating taste, wealth or power (very much in the tradition of country house studies), but they might also 'do very private psychological work for the viewer, which revolves around the object serving as a focus for managing self-identity, family relations or self-esteem'.[35] This was very much the case for the various women studied by Lewis, although the title of her article—'When a house is not a home'—hints at the difficulties they faced when seeking to give personal and emotional meaning to dwellings they had inherited or occupied through marriage. For Karen Harvey, it is these emotional, imaginative and representational dimensions that distinguished home from house, but Roderick Lawrence also emphasises the home as a place of shared values and rituals that create or mould relationships between people.[36]

These studies pick up on older arguments, advanced by Witold Rybcynski and others, concerning the ways in which home was a place of emotional well-being and belonging; it was associated with family, intimacy and personal attachment, all of which could be symbolised, cemented and memorialised through material objects.[37] This process of remembering and memorialising is developed more fully by Gaston Bachelard in his account of the ways in which people's relationship with things are central both to their construction of home and their construction of self.[38] Home, then, was a place of memories, objects and people; it was also a place of physical and psychological comfort: a haven from the outside world.

Comfort: Meanings and Materialities

In early modern England, comfort was firmly associated with emotional well-being, a feeling of being comfortable and offering comfort (or consolation) to others. John Kersey's *New English Dictionary* (1713), for instance, defined it as a noun that meant 'help, ease or relief in distress'; in its verbal form, 'comfort' meant 'to afford comfort, to encourage'.[39] It is in this sense that Daniel Defoe used the word most frequently. In *Moll Flanders* (1722), the eponymous heroine worries that 'in this distress I had no assistant, no friend to comfort or advise me'.[40] Little, it seems, had changed by the time Samuel Johnson compiled his *Dictionary of the English Language* (1755), though he added nuance to both noun and verb, offering three definitions: 1. Support, assistance, countenance; 2. Consolation, support under calamity or danger; 3. 'That which gives consolation or support'.[41] However, Johnson was clearly aware that comfort carried other meanings too. In his *History of Rasselas* (1759), he compares the situation of Europeans and Africans from the perspective of a fictional African traveller who observes that 'in enumerating the particular comforts of life, we shall find many advantages on the side of the Europeans'. Such advantages, it soon becomes clear, include medical care, transport and houses—material rather than emotional benefits.[42]

It is this shift in the meaning of comfort that John Crowley places at the centre of his analysis; for him, comfort meant physical ease and a focus on the corporeal body. This set of changes was also mapped by John Cornforth in his study of country house interiors, which he explicitly saw as a quest for comfort in a physical sense.[43] For Crowley, this 'invention of comfort' was manifest in changing attitudes among householders and in a related set of changes in domestic material culture: technological developments aimed at making the house warmer, lighter and better ventilated (through the use of lamps, stoves and chimneys); an array of different and especially upholstered furniture (most notably easy chairs and sofas), and shifts in the organisation and setting of the house, with a growing emphasis on privacy.[44] Such changes were by no means culturally specific, as Joan DeJean has demonstrated in her study of late seventeenth- and early eighteenth-century Paris, where she also touches on water closets, bedrooms and even dress.[45] Indeed, these two contexts can be seen as part of a longer trajectory of change in domestic environments which, for some, reached their zenith in the cosy parlour of Victorian Britain, crammed as it was with upholstered furniture.[46] For other scholars, such tendencies have continued well into the twentieth century, with its proliferation of labour-saving domestic devices such as vacuum cleaners and electric fires.[47]

Comfort as improvement applied to society as well as to the individual. Growing physical comfort signalled material and societal progress, and helped to defuse moral debates about luxury by offering a more morally neutral language of comfort and convenience.[48] Marie Odile-Bernez suggests that comfort in the eighteenth century allowed contemporaries to critique foreign and especially French luxury, along with its overtones of waste, excess and inequality, with virtuous English comfort, available to all as a consequence of economic and social development.[49] Indeed, the extent to which the population enjoyed some measure of comfort and convenience was increasingly taken as an index of northwestern Europe's move from barbarism to civilisation: they became part of the rhetoric of progress.[50] As was so often the case, travellers often found the places they visited falling short of their own country's higher standards. For instance, in a visit to the Swedish town of Karlstad in 1838, the Scottish travel writer, Samuel Laing, noted that there was 'a want here of those little outward signs and tokens of a spirit of comfort [. . .] from which I infer an inferior state of well-being among the rural population here'.[51]

Crowley goes further, arguing that, alongside this growing perception of comfort as progress, there was a fundamental shift in mindset as comfort became a key goal for elite and middling householders by the closing decades of the eighteenth century. For the first time, he argues, bodily comfort was being prioritised over considerations of fashion, taste or gentility.[52] Despite DeJean's assertion of the origins of comfort in early-eighteenth-century Paris, writers in the early nineteenth century saw domestic comfort as something that was new and noteworthy. In *Ivanhoe* (1819), Walter Scott gave expression to the opinions of many when he claimed that domestic comfort was a thoroughly modern construct, tellingly interrupting his description of the visually sumptuous chamber of the twelfth-century Saxon Princess Rowena with the following claim: 'Yet let not modern beauty envy the magnificence of a Saxon princess . . . Magnificence there was, with some rude attempt at taste, but of comfort there was little, and, being unknown, it was unmissed'.[53]

Scott's view of the past and present is somewhat teleological, but the importance of material comfort rapidly worked its way across Europe in the early years of the nineteenth century. In an English-German dictionary from 1784 comfort as a noun is translated as '*trost, bergnügen*' and as a verb it is '*trösten, stärken*'; both signified consolation. Around the same time, the French word '*confort*' was translated as 'solace' and was described as being old and no longer in use.[54] To describe feelings of physical ease, Pückler-Muskau might have opted for *bequemlichkeit* (convenience) instead of *behagliche* (pleasure). The former was often used in the *Journal des Luxus und der Moden*; for example in October 1788 readers were told of the importance of building according to the rules as well as with comfort and elegance (*Regelmäsighkeit, Bequemlichkeit und Eleganz*).[55] The Swedes used the very similar word *bekvämlighet*, which carried the same connotations of convenience, whilst notions of discomfort were generally expressed as *obekväm* or *unbequem* (respectively, inconvenience and uncomfortable). Thus, the writer Johan Oxenstierna noted in his diary that 'Sahlman arrived here from Regensburg, and as he stays here, I invited him to share my chamber. I am now paying for this hasty courtesy with my inconvenience and discomfort [*besvar ock obeqvamlighet*]'.[56]

The lack of a word with the same nuanced meanings as the English 'comfort' was bemoaned by another Swedish commentator as a sign that his was a barbarous country. This is striking because it attaches the rhetoric of progress as much by the presence in the language of a specific (English) word as to improvement in a population's well-being.[57] Moreover, when it did appear in Swedish, Dutch and German dictionaries, comfort was shorn of its original meanings of solace and consolation: only its modern connotations of physical well-being were given. Equally, having reintroduced the term from England in the early nineteenth century, the French deployed *confort* in ways that were very different from its traditional meaning of consolation and soothing, and it obviously communicated something different to *aise* and *agréments* (easy and amenities). As late as 1872, a French dictionary tied *confort*/comfort explicitly to the English, noting that 'the English have a great love for comfort' (*Les Anglais ont un grand amour pour le confort*).[58]

In this light, the sentiments of Jane Austen's heroines would have resonated well beyond England. Speaking of Colonel Brandon's home in *Sense and Sensibility* (1811), for example, Mrs. Jennings observes that Delaford Parsonage—the sort of house sitting at the bottom rung of country-house status—'is a nice place, I can tell you; exactly what I call a nice old fashioned place, full of comforts and conveniences'.[59] This pairing of comfort and convenience is telling: the two went hand in hand for Mrs. Jennings, making this a physically comfortable home and also one that was suited to current modes of living. In *Pride and Prejudice* (1813), Charlotte Lucas remarks, when contemplating marriage to Mr. Collins, 'I am not romantic, you know; I never was. I ask only a comfortable home'.[60] This vision of comfort was no doubt based around the provision of warming fires, soft furnishings, ample lighting and the convenient arrangement of rooms—the hallmarks of the new domestic environment described by Crowley, DeJean and others.[61] However, as is clear from the comment from Pückler-Muskau with which we started, it would also have involved arranging rooms and furniture in a manner that was in keeping with the increasingly informal modes of living found in well-to-do households from the later decades of the eighteenth century.

This is an idea that ties in with Mark Girouard's characterisation of the later eighteenth century as marking the rise of the 'informal house' in England, something which Cornforth explores through the growing plethora of interior domestic paintings produced from the 1810s onwards. For both, the English country house became more a place to live, the ideal of the Great House being replaced by that of the villa in terms of scale, organisation of rooms, and arrangements of furniture.[62] This linking of informality and physical comfort has a longer history, Joan DeJean finding abundant evidence of relaxed seating and clothing in early eighteenth-century Paris.[63] Yet it was in early nineteenth-century England that this combination came to fruition in the form of a restrained and more accessible material culture that was very different from the excesses of luxury. Or perhaps more correctly, it was more in step with Jan de Vries' notion of bourgeois 'new luxury', with its emphasis on inclusive sociability and restraint, than the exclusivity and excess of aristocratic 'old luxury'. Certainly, Christine Adams saw the emphasis on comfort and status in the Lamothes family of eighteenth-century Bordeaux as essentially bourgeois in nature.[64]

This domestic ideal was central to foreign perceptions and appreciation of 'English comfort': a combination of convenience, informality and good cheer captured by Pückler-Muskau. His enthusiasm for the comfortable fire, inviting sofas and agreeable disorder is quite apparent. In this passage, he uses *ansprechend* (appealing) and *behagliche* (comfortable/pleasurable), but elsewhere in his letters, he employs the English word 'comfort', always in its modern sense of physical well-being. Such arguments offer a compelling narrative of material change and cultural diffusion—part of the Anglomania that gradually spread across much of Europe through the late eighteenth and early nineteenth century, often at the expense of a taste for French fashions and practices. These were seen as aristocratic and decadent in comparison with English moderation and restraint.[65]

To reduce comfort to a set of material objects and spatial arrangements would be to miss its important mental and social dimensions. Crowley argues that one of the things that limited the spread of physical comfort was that 'people acquired goods more often to display . . . gentility than they did for purposes of personal comfort'.[66] This overlooks not only the fact that many household objects could display gentility as well as affording personal comfort (clean bed linen, table forks, lighting, etc.) but also the ways in which what we might call social comfort could be derived from things that were physically uncomfortable. Feeling properly dressed in an itchy wig, sitting correctly on an upright chair or entertaining in a large dining room that was difficult to keep warm could make the individual *socially* comfortable by conforming with social norms and acting with propriety. The rather stiff and formal poses struck by the subjects of Arthur Devis' many portraits of country-house owners should be seen in this light: their posture, dress and surroundings linked to this different matrix of comfort.[67] More importantly, older meanings of comfort were by no means swept away in a rush to embrace new visceral experiences. Even in the early nineteenth century, Jane Austen may have written about the comfort and elegance of a cottage, but she most often used comfort to refer to emotions and expectations rather than physical attributes, as did Elizabeth Gaskell in the middle decades of the nineteenth century.[68] Comfort meant consolation received in times of trouble; the enjoyment of social interaction; the emotional support of family and friends, and especially a contented marriage.

Scope and Themes

In exploring comfort in its various guises, this book draws on material from a wide range of country houses and families. They include both the magnificent residences of titled and wealthy nobility, such as Stoneleigh Abbey in Warwickshire, home of the Barons Leigh whose estate was worth £19,000 *p.a.* by the early nineteenth century, and more modest gentry houses, like Whetham House in Wiltshire, occupied by Revd William Money. Some were home to the families of notable statesmen, such as the Marquess of Bute's Luton Hoo in Bedfordshire, or career politicians like Sir Roger Newdigate of Arbury Hall, Warwickshire. Elsewhere, the owners had little interest in participating in national politics—the Huddlestones of Sawston Hall in Cambridgeshire, for instance. At Colworth House in Bedfordshire, the wealthy William Lee Antonie spent handsomely on improvements in the early nineteenth century; at Canons Ashby in neighbouring Northamptonshire, the Drydens made few material changes to their house after the 1710s. Most households were headed by men, but Mary Delany spent her later life in the company of other women at Bulstrode in Buckinghamshire, and both Canons Ashby and Stoneleigh Abbey were in the hands of women in the later decades of the eighteenth century. Some of the correspondence analysed came from famous men and women whose letters have been published—Horace Walpole and Mary Delany, for instance—but much of it was produced by less prominent figures and exists only in manuscript form. This includes the letters of the Revd William Money, Elizabeth Dryden of Canons Ashby, and Philippa Hayes, the mid-eighteenth-century housekeeper at Charlecote Park in Warwickshire.

In taking this broad view of the country house, the analysis is mostly focused on England, but this is not a book about English exceptionalism: it locates processes, practices, motivations and emotions within a broader European context. The book is organised into two parts. In the first part, *Physical and Social Comfort: The Materiality of the Country House*, spaces and objects are brought into sharp focus, and comparisons with country houses elsewhere in Europe are frequently drawn in terms of room organisation and layout, technologies, furniture and fittings, and social practices. In the second part, *Emotional Comfort: Feelings, Letters and Home*, attention centres more fully on England and switches to the emotions and relationships of country-house owners, their families and visitors. The house itself does not disappear from view, but rather forms a frame for interpersonal relationships and the object of emotional attachment.

Within this broad structure, four broad themes can be identified. First is the *relationship between comfort and convenience*, particularly in terms of the spatial arrangements that made the country house a place that was organised in a manner that made it a place that accommodated social practices and the growing demand for privacy. Such ideas link closely to Girouard's interest in the social life of the country house, developed here by exploring how architects and owners planned their houses with regard for the practicalities of daily life as well as the aesthetics and strictures of architectural rooms.[69] Chapter 1 thus focuses on the layout of rooms and their growing specialisation, paying particular attention to growing requirements for privacy. Of concern here is how the villas and cottages of country-house owners were viewed as a mechanism through which greater privacy could be achieved and the extent to which they facilitated the growing informality of social practices from the middle decades of the eighteenth century. In focusing on the growing spatial convenience of country houses, there is a need to recall its other functions, both practical and symbolic. Chapter 1, therefore, explores and questions the extent to which country-house owners and architects saw ornamentation and convenience, or status and comfort, as competing priorities.

Growing physical comfort lay at the heart of Crowley's notion of comfort as an invention of the Anglo-American world in the eighteenth century. It also informs DeJean's analysis of late seventeenth- and early eighteenth-century Paris.[70] For both, it was the emergence of improved heating and lighting technologies, easy seating, and the provision of better ventilation and plumbing that was crucial in a transition to more modern attitudes to comfort. Changing technologies went hand in hand with changing attitudes. Chapters 2 and 3 engage critically with these ideas, which form the second key theme: *the imperative for being comfortable.*

Chapter 2 focuses on heat and light, often key challenges for country-house owners, in terms of both the effectiveness and efficiency of existing technologies. Challenging the functionalist arguments that portray new types of stoves and lamps as transformative, it examines the array of choices available to house owners. Viewing each as a viable option puts greater emphasis on understanding both the attractions of new technologies and the reasons why apparently less efficient technologies were frequently retained. Central in this is a consideration of the level of heat and light seen as necessary or desirable: more heat and light may have afforded greater comfort and convenience, but this attraction needs to be tempered by asking whether it was possible to be too hot and for lighting to be too bright—ideas that have been explored very little to date. Also overlooked in the emphasis of new technologies are the array of related furniture and fittings required to allow stoves, candles and lamps to be used to best effect—a set of object-associations that links into assemblage theory.[71] As with the country house as a whole, it is important to consider how this furniture might display wealth and status as well as augmenting comfort and convenience.

This is also true of the growing range of comfortable seating examined in Chapter 3. In tracing the development of easy chairs and sofas, it is possible to see this as the progressive advance of comfort, but such a teleological viewpoint needs to be tempered by considering the choices available to householders and, for example, the complicated physical and semiotic distinction between settees, couches and sofas. In tracing the spread of such furniture, the chapter again considers the array of other furniture necessary for the use of sofas and easy chairs and the ways it was grouped and arranged in rooms. This links back to Girouard's and DeJean's notion of informality, both in social interaction and posture, and considers the role of this in creating the kind of relaxed social and spatial practices that many foreign visitors admired as English Comfort. This process is discussed in terms of the ways in which furniture could facilitate *feeling* comfortable as well as being comfortable.

This twin conception of comfort is continued in Chapter 4 which links together the discussion of the body and the mind. Bodily comfort is discussed through a focus on fresh air and cleanliness, both of which were critical to how contemporaries assessed their domestic environments. Building on the arguments of Woodruff Smith and others, these physical considerations are linked to psychological concerns about virtue and respectability.[72] Of particular concern here is the extent to which both were addressed through the language of comfort and how this was expressed as a social as well as physical ideal. These ideas are brought together through analysis of the problem of bed bugs and the ways in which these might render an otherwise welcoming bed thoroughly uncomfortable for the body and destructive of mental ease through the anxieties they caused. Again, the use of language is a key concern: how did householders conceive bodily and mental comfort in light of these infestations?

The same is true when it comes to *emotional and spiritual comfort* which form the third broad theme of the book. The second half of Chapter 4 explores this in terms of religion and the comforts to be derived from personal faith. A key question here is the extent to which there was congruence between the ideas expressed by the writers of religious pamphlets and the faithful themselves. How far was trust in God the ultimate comfort in this world and the next, and how did this square with the kinds of material or worldly comforts discussed in earlier chapters? These emotional aspects form the focus of Chapter 5 which explores the comfort derived from friends and family. Engaging with Barbara Rosenwein's idea of emotional communities as well as the literature on parenting, the discussion focuses initially on the nuclear family.[73] It assesses idealisations and experiences of marriage and parenthood, exploring how both were conceived and expressed through the language of comfort. This brings the discussion into dialogue with the history of emotions, broadening the focus to encompass not only intense and powerful emotions such as love but also gentler emotions like contentment, which have hitherto attracted less attention. Language is important here, not just in highlighting comfort as a word used to describe the experience and feeling of close family relationships, but also in capturing the nuances of what comfort meant and communicated in emotional terms. What was the comfort that parents sought from children, for example, and what does this tell us about their mutual relationship? Exploring this aspect of comfort through the correspondence and journals of country-house owners and their families adds an important new dimension to what comfort meant to them, and how they sought out and offered such comfort to others. It also offers important insights into the ways in which letters could afford comfort both to the recipient and the writer. Letter writing is well recognised as a key leisure activity for the social elite; Chapter 5, therefore, concludes with a sustained analysis of what made a letter comfortable and comforting.

The fourth key theme extends the idea of emotional comfort by exploring the *relationship between comfort, objects and memory*, and how their mutual interaction served to construct notions of home. Conceptually, Chapter 6 draws on Bachelard's notion of the house-home as a receptacle for and construct of memories; practically it links to the emotional attachment to things and places explored by Lewis and, in a modern-day context, by Amber Epp and Linda Price.[74] The central questions here are: firstly, how household objects—from paintings and miniatures to textiles to chinaware—took on sentimental and emotional meanings; secondly, how such things were used to curate family to create particular constructions of kin relations and emotional bonds, rather in the manner studied by Grant McCracken; and thirdly, how they were bound up with memories of other people and other places.[75] In some ways, this moves the overall discussion away from an explicit focus on comfort, but the final part of Chapter 6 returns to the core concern of the book by exploring the role of memories and emotional bonds in creating home as a place of contentment and comfort.

In drawing the extensive literature on the country house into constructive dialogue with the rather more limited historiography of comfort, this book offers a different way of approaching and animating the English country house. It is brought alive with people making choices about the character of their domestic environment, voicing their concerns about health and happiness, and doing their best to sustain meaningful relationships with friends and family; in short, being comfortable and feeling at home. It also offers fresh insights into the sentiments and emotions underpinning relationships between people and between people, things and spaces. Here, ideas of agency are important, but so too are the contingency of individual circumstances and the impact of individual priorities and preferences. Comfort was something that did not simply happen: it involved considerable investment in time, resources and emotion.

Notes

1. Herman Pückler-Muskau, *Briefe eines verstorbenen: Ein fragmentarisches Tagebuch aus England, Wales* (Halberger, 1831), 242–3: 'Im Zimmer selbst brannte ein behagliches Kaminfeuer. Ausgezeichnete Gemälde schmückten die Wände, und viele Sophas von verschiedenen Formen, so wie Tische mit Curiositäten bedeckt, und in angenehmer Unordnung zerstreute Meubles ließen Alles auf's wohnlichste und anmuthigste erscheinen'. I am grateful to Daniel Menning for this translation, which lends the passage a rather different gloss from that given in John Cornforth, *English Interiors, 1799–1848: The Quest for Comfort* (London: Barrie & Jenkins, 1978), 65.

2. Alice Clark (ed.), *Caroline, Countess of Portarlington and Other Friends and Relatives*, vol. 2 (Edinburgh, 1895), 176: Lady Caroline Dawson to Lady Louisa Stuart, 14 March 1792.
3. Sarah Chauncey Woolsey (ed.), *The Autobiography and Correspondence of Mrs Delany*, vol. 2 (Boston: Roberts Brothers, 1879), 296: Mary Delany to Anne Dewes, 31 January 1745. Patrick Delany was Dean of Down in Ireland.
4. See, for instance: Cornforth, *English Interiors*; John Crowley, *The Invention of Comfort: Sensibilities and Design in Early-Modern Britain and Early America* (Baltimore: Johns Hopkins University Press, 2001), 171–200; Joan DeJean, *The Age of Comfort: When Paris Discovered Casual and the Modern Home Began* (New York: Bloomsbury, 2009), 93–101; Marie Odile-Bernez, 'Comfort, the Acceptable Face of Luxury: An Eighteenth-Century Etymology', *Journal for Early Modern Cultural Studies*, 14:2 (2014), 3–21; Alan Wilson, *Comfort, Pleasure and Prestige: Country-House Technology in West Wales, 1750–1930* (Kibworth Beauchamp: Matador, 2016).
5. Mark Girouard, *Life in the English Country House: A Social and Architectural History* (New Haven: Yale University Press, 1978), 2; Richard Wilson and Alan Mackley, *Creating Paradise: The Building of the English Country House, 1660–1880* (London: Hambledon Continuum, 2000), xvii; Christopher Christie, *The British Country House in the Eighteenth Century* (Manchester: Manchester University Press, 2000), 4; Gervase Jackson-Stops (ed.), *The Treasure Houses of Britain: Five Hundred Years of Private Patronage and Art Collecting* (New Haven and London: Yale University Press, 1985).
6. See, for example, Mark Girouard, *Life in the French Country House* (London: Cassell & Co., 2000), chapter 7: 'Were they ever there?', 163–96.
7. See, for example: John Habakkuk, 'Marriage Settlements in the Eighteenth Century', *Transactions of the Royal Historical Society*, fourth series, 32 (1950), 15–30; B. English and J. Saville, 'Family Settlement and "the Rise of the Great Estates"', *Economic History Review*, 33 (1980), 556–8; J. Beckett, 'The Pattern of Landownership in England and Wales, 1660–1800', *Economic History Review*, 37 (1984), 1–22; John Habakkuk, *Marriage, Debt and the Estate System: English Landownership 1650–1950* (Oxford: Oxford University Press, 1996).
8. F.M.L. Thompson, *English Landed Society in the Nineteenth Century* (London: Routledge & Kegan Paul, 1963); Gordon Mingay, *English Landed Society in the Eighteenth Century* (London: Routledge & Kegan Paul, 1963); John Becket, *The Aristocracy in England, 1660–1914* (Oxford: Blackwell, 1986).
9. Girouard, *English Country House*, 3.
10. Christie, *British Country House*, 4–25; Wilson and Mackley, *Creating Paradise*.
11. Wilson and Mackley, *Creating Paradise*, 242–3; Beckett, *Aristocracy in England*, 26–42.
12. For a rare exception, see Stephen Hague, *The Gentleman's House in the British Atlantic World, 1680–1780* (Basingstoke: Palgrave Macmillan, 2016).
13. John Summerson, *Architecture in Britain 1530–1830* (1953; New Haven: Yale University Press, 1993); John Harris, *The Design of the English Country House* (London: Trefoil Publications, 1985). See also Howard Colvin and John Harris (eds.), *The Country Seat: Studies in the History of the British Country House* (London: Allen Lane, 1970).
14. Summerson, *Architecture in Britain*, esp. 296, 384–409, 452–4.
15. On the way that gothic architecture was integrated into many other architectural styles see Peter Lindfield, *Georgian Gothic: Medievalist Architecture,*

Furniture and Interiors, 1730–1840 (Martlesham: Boydell and Brewer, 2016). For examples of extended and remodelled houses, see Dana Arnold, *The Georgian Country House: Architecture, Landscape and Society* (Stroud: Alan Sutton, 2003), 12; Christie, *British Country House*, 32.

16. Joan Coutu, Peter Lindfield and Jon Stobart (eds.), *Houses of Politicians* (Montreal: McGill University Press, forthcoming 2022); Girouard, *English Country House*, 180; Arnold, *Georgian Country House*, 40; Rosie MacArthur, 'Material Culture and Consumption on an English Estate: Kelmarsh Hall 1687–1845' (Unpublished PhD thesis, University of Northampton, 2010), 10–11.

17. See, for example: Geoffrey Beard, *Georgian Craftsmen and Their Work* (London: Country Life, 1966); Michael Wilson, *The English Country House and Its Furnishings* (London: Batsford, 1977); Charles Saumarez Smith, *Eighteenth Century Decoration: Design and the Domestic Interior in England* (London: Routledge, 1993); John Cornforth, *Early Georgian Interiors* (New Haven: Yale University Press, 2004).

18. Christie, *British Country House*, 179–231; Francis Russell, 'The Hanging and Display of Pictures, 1799–1850', in Jackson Stops et al. (eds.), *The Fashioning and Functioning of the British Country House* (New Haven: Yale University Press, 1989), 133–53; Kate Retford, *The Conversation Piece: Making Modern Art in Eighteenth-Century Britain* (New Haven: Yale University Press, 2017). For analysis of Stoneleigh Abbey's stuccowork, see Andor Gomme, 'Stoneleigh After the Grand Tour', *The Antiquaries Journal*, 68 (1988), 265–86.

19. Jon Stobart and Mark Rothery, *Consumption and the Country House* (Oxford: Oxford University Press, 2016), 5.

20. Stephanie Barczewski, *Country Houses and the British Empire, 1700–1930* (Manchester: Manchester University Press, 2014); Jonathan Eacott, *Selling Empire: India in the Making of Britain and America, 1600–1830* (Chapel Hill: University of North Carolina Press; Margot Finn and Kate Smith, *The East India Company at Home, 1757–1857* (London: UCL Press, 2017); Stephen McDowall, 'Imperial Plots? Shugborough Chinoiserie and Imperial Ideology in Eighteenth Century British Gardens', *Cultural and Social History*, 14:1 (2017), 17–34.

21. Barczewski, *Country Houses and the British Empire*, 137. See also Finn and Smith, *East India Company at Home*.

22. James Walvin, *Fruits of Empire: Exotic Produce and British Taste, 1660–1800* (New York: New York University Press, 1997); Sydney Mintz, *Sweetness and Power: The Place of Sugar in Modern History* (London: Routledge, 1985); Woodruff Smith, *Consumption and the Making of Respectability, 1600–1800* (London: Penguin, 2002); Brian Cowan, *The Social Life of Coffee: The Emergence of the British Coffeehouse* (New Haven: Yale University Press, 2005); Jon Stobart, *Sugar and Spice: Grocers and Groceries in Provincial England, 1650–1830* (Oxford: Oxford University Press, 2013); Markman Ellis, Richard Coulton, and Matthew Mauger, *Empire of Tea: The Asian Leaf That Conquered the World* (London: Reaktion Books, 2015).

23. Amanda Vickery, *Behind Closed Doors: At Home in Georgian England* (New Haven: Yale University Press, 2009); Jane Whittle and Elizabeth Griffiths, *Consumption and Gender in the Early Seventeenth-Century Household: The World of Alice Le Strange* (Oxford: Oxford University Press, 2012).

24. Stobart and Rothery, *Consumption and the Country House*. For similar studies of other houses, see J.D. Williams, 'The Noble Household as a Unit of Consumption: The Audley End Experience, 1765–1797', *Essex Archaeology*

and History, 23 (1992), 67–78. Two important recent studies are: MacArthur, 'Material Culture and Consumption', and Hannah Chavasse, 'Material Culture and the Country House: Fashion, Comfort and Lineage' (Unpublished PhD thesis, University of Northampton, 2015).

25. Giroaurd, *English Country House*.

26. Pamela Sambrook and Peter Brears (eds.), *The Country House Kitchen, 1650–1900* (Stroud: Sutton, 1996); Peter Barnwell and Marylin Palmer (eds.), *Country House Technology* (London: Paul Watkin Publishing, 2012); Marylin Palmer and Ian West, *Technology in the Country House* (Swindon: Historic England, 2016).

27. On the changing lot of servants, see: Pamela Sambrook, *Keeping Their Places: Domestic Service in the Country House* (Stroud: Alan Sutton, 2009); Jeremy Musson, *Up and Down Stairs: The History of the Country House Servant* (London: John Murray, 2009).

28. For a discussion of some of the difficulties, see Karen Harvey, *The Little Republic: Masculinity and Domestic Authority in Eighteenth-Century Britain* (Oxford: Oxford University Press, 2012), 8–13.

29. Edward Phillips, *The New World of Words or Universal English Dictionary* (London, 1706); John Kersey, *A New English Dictionary* (London, 1713).

30. Samuel Johnson, *A Dictionary of the English Language*, vol. 2 (London, 1755–56); Charles Richardson, *New Dictionary of the English Language* (London: William Pickering, 1836).

31. Hannah More, *Mr Bragwell and His Two Daughters* (1797), 11.

32. Clive Edwards, *Turning Houses into Homes: A History of the Retailing and Consumption of Domestic Furnishings* (Aldershot: Ashgate, 2005), 4.

33. Vickery, *Behind Closed Doors*, 207–30.

34. Judith Lewis, 'When a House Is Not a Home: Elite English Women and the Eighteenth-Century Country House', *Journal of British Studies*, 48:2 (2009), 336–63; Helen Metcalfe, 'The Social Experience of Bachelorhood in Late-Georgian England, c.1760–1830' (Unpublished PhD thesis, University of Manchester, 2017), chapter 5. See also Hague, *Gentleman's House*, 95–115; Chavasse, 'Material Culture and the Country House', chapter 4.

35. Ian Woodward, 'Domestic Objects and the Taste Epiphany', *Journal of Material Culture*, 6:2 (2001), 121.

36. Harvey, *Little Republic*, 12; Roderick Lawrence, 'What Makes a House a Home?', *Environment and Behaviour*, 19:2 (1987), 154–68.

37. Witold Rybcynski, *Home: A Short History of an Idea* (New York: Viking, 1986). See also Grant McCracken, *Culture and Consumption: New Approaches to the Symbolic Character of Consumer Goods and Activities* (Bloomington and Indianapolis: Indiana University Press, 1988), 44–53.

38. Gaston Bachelard, *The Poetics of Space* (London: Penguin, 1964).

39. Kersey, *A New English Dictionary*.

40. Daniel Defoe, *The Fortunes and Misfortunes of the Famous Moll Flanders* (1722; Oxford: Oxford University Press, 1971), 191.

41. Johnson, *Dictionary of the English Language*, vol. 1.

42. Samuel Johnson, *The History of Rasselas, Prince of Abissinia* (1759; Oxford: Oxford University Press, 1988), 30.

43. Crowley, *Invention of Comfort*.

44. Crowley, *Invention of Comfort*; Cornforth, *English Interiors*; Cornforth, *Early Georgian Interiors*, 209–12; Girouard, *English Country House*, 245–66.

45. DeJean, *Age of Comfort*.

46. John Gloag, *Victorian Comfort: A Social History of Design from 1830–1900* (Basingstoke: Palgrave Macmillan, 1961); Deborah Cohen, *Household Gods: The British and Their Possessions* (New Haven, CT: Yale University Press,

2006); Jane Hamlett, *Material Relations: Domestic Interiors and Middle-Class Families in England, 1850–1910* (Manchester: Manchester University Press, 2010).

47. Frank Trentmann, *Empire of Things* (London: Allen Lane, 2016), 222–71.
48. Paul Slack, *The Invention of Improvement* (Oxford: Oxford University Press, 2015), 215–28; Odile-Bernez, 'Comfort, the Acceptable Face of Luxury'.
49. Odile-Bernez, 'Comfort, the Acceptable Face of Luxury'.
50. Crowley, *Invention of Comfort*, 151–3.
51. Samuel Laing, *Journal of a Residence in Norway, During the Year 1834, 1835 and 1836; Made with a View to Inquire into Moral and Political Economy of That Country, and the Condition of Its Inhabitants* (London: Longmans, 1839), 32–3. For fuller discussion, see Mark Davies, *A Perambulating Paradox: British Travel Literature and the Image of Sweden, c.1770–1865* (Lund: Lund University, 2000), 150–1.
52. Crowley, *Invention of Comfort*, 147.
53. Walter Scott, *Ivanhoe* (1820; Oxford: Oxford University Press, 1996), 73.
54. Theodor Arnold, *A Compleat Vocabulary, English and German* (M. Johann Bartholomäus Rogler, Züllichau, 1784); Chretien. F. Schwan, *Nouveau Dictionnaire de la Langue Francoise* (Mannheim, 1787).
55. *Journal des luxus und der Moden*, October 1788.
56. Gustaf Stiernström (ed.), *Dagboks-anteckningar åren 1769–1771* (Uppsala: Svenska Litteratursällskapet, 1881), 187. My thanks to Cristina Prytz for her assistance in assessing the Swedish use of comfort.
57. Martina von Schwerin, *Småsaker af en nybegynnare*, 4 (1840), 58, 7 January 1833.
58. E. Littré, *Dictionnaire de la langue francaise* (1872–77).
59. Jane Austen, *Sense and Sensibility* (1811; London: Penguin, 1995), 166, 322.
60. Jane Austen, *Pride and Prejudice* (1813; Oxford: Oxford University Press, 2004), 96.
61. Crowley, *Invention of Comfort*; DeJean, *Age of Comfort*; Christine Adams, *A Taste for Comfort and Status: A Bourgeois Family in Eighteenth-Century France* (Philadelphia: Penn State University Press, 2000).
62. Girouard, *English Country House*, 213–44; Cornforth, *English Interiors*, 11–14.
63. DeJean, *Age of Comfort*, 102–30, 186–204.
64. Jan de Vries, *Industrious Revolution: Consumer Behaviour and the Household Economy, 1650 to the Present* (Cambridge: Cambridge University Press, 2006), 44–5; Adams, *Taste for Comfort and Status*.
65. See, for example: Michael North, 'Fashion and Luxury in Eighteenth-Century Germany', in Johanna Ilmakunnas and Jon Stobart (eds.), *Taste for Luxury* (London: Routledge, 2017), 100–15; Kristof Fatsar, 'Enjoying Country Life to the Full—Only the English Know How to Do That!': Appreciation of the British Country House by Hungarian Aristocratic Travellers', in Jon Stobart (ed.), *Travel and the Country House* (Manchester: Manchester University Press, 2017), 147–67.
66. Crowley, *Invention of Comfort*, 147.
67. DeJean, *Age of Comfort*, 18–19; Retford, *Conversation Piece*. The "wooden" nature of the figures is also linked to his practice of using dressed wooden mannequins to paint from. See also chapter 4.
68. Kenneth Phillipps, *Jane Austen's English* (London: Deutsch, 1970), 74–5; Norman Page, *The Language of Jane Austen* (Oxford: Oxford University Press, 1972), 30, 38–9.
69. Girouard, *English Country House*, esp. 213–44.
70. Crowley, *Invention of Comfort*, 111–200; DeJean, *Age of Comfort*, 67–101.

71. Gilles Deleuze and Félix Guatarri, *A Thousand Plateaus: Capitalism and Schizophrenia*, trans. Brian Massumi (London: Continuum, 1987); Manuel DeLanda, *Assemblage Theory* (Edinburgh: Edinburgh University Press, 2016).
72. Smith, *Consumption and the Making of Respectability*, esp. 105–38.
73. Barbara Rosenwein, *Emotional Communities in the Early Middle Ages* (Ithaca: Cornell University Press, 2006); Joanne Bailey, *Parenting in England, 1760–1830* (Oxford: Oxford University Press, 2012).
74. Bachelard, *Poetics of Space*; Lewis, 'When a House Is Not a Home'; Amber Epp and Linda Price, 'The Storied Life of Singularized Objects: Forces of Agency and Network Transformation', *Journal of Consumer Research*, 36:5 (2010), 820–37.
75. McCracken, *Culture and Consumption*, 44–53.

Part 1

Physical and Social Comfort

The Materiality of the Country House

1 Convenience and Privacy
The Architecture of Comfort

Eighteenth-century architects had little to say about comfort, being more concerned with loftier and more abstract aesthetic concerns such as the character, proportion and expression of a building, and the meanings and associations that derived from particular styles.[1] Architects were, first and foremost, artists who were primarily concerned with the beauty and external aesthetics of their designs; they were, in general, less concerned with the practicalities of building. However, this is not to say that they were disinterested in how a house operated, both as a showpiece and a place to live. The Duchess of Marlborough complained bitterly that Vanbrugh's grandiose Blenheim Palace was impossible as a place to live, but the problem was more one of scale than organisation.[2] Indeed, architects were increasingly interested in the idea of convenience—a term which in some sense was deployed as a synonym for comfort. Samuel Johnson defined convenience as fitness and propriety; commodiousness, ease, freedom from difficulties; cause of ease, and fitness of time or place.[3] For architects, the key element of this was the idea of fitness and propriety: a convenient house was one where the spatial organisation was rational and functional, answering to the needs of the owner both for display and everyday living. However, there was a tension between aesthetics and practicalities, external appearance and internal organisation, which was never fully resolved by eighteenth-century architects, with their preoccupation with classicism, proportion and style. As we shall see, however, the practicalities of the house became a matter of increasing concern to a growing number of architects who published treatises and pattern books in ever larger numbers.

The realisation of spatial and domestic convenience was appreciated by owners and visitors alike. David Hume, when discussing the role that sympathy played in the appreciation of beauty, used an architectural metaphor:

> A man, who shews us any house or building, takes particular care among other things to point out the convenience of the apartments, the advantages of their situation, and the little room lost in the stairs,

DOI: 10.4324/9781003206361-3

anti-chambers and passages; and indeed'tis evident, the chief part of the beauty consists in these particulars.[4]

On a more practical level, Mary Delany was struck with the arrangements at Cornbury, which she visited in 1746. She purred about her own apartment, describing it as being 'so neat and so elegant that I never saw anything equal to it', but it is her summing up that is particularly telling: 'upon the whole I think the house the *most comfortable and pleasant fine house* I ever saw, for it is not only magnificent and elegant but *convenient* and *rational'*.[5] Delany thus articulated the growing understanding, clearly shared by architects, political economists and country house visitors, that convenience meant a rational layout and practical arrangement of rooms. Importantly, this was quite compatible with the house being fine, elegant and fashionable.

These are the ideas that are discussed in this chapter. It begins by exploring this conception of convenience in terms of the location, form and layout of the house, drawing on architectural treatises and pattern books to examine how architects attempted to make elite houses convenient places in which to live, in keeping with modern domestic life. It shares with these architects an interest in the growing specialisation of room use and the increasing use of corridors and back stairs which link closely to ideas of privacy from both servants and visitors. But it is also attentive to the voices of owners and guests who speak of the ways in which country houses worked—or failed to work—as lived spaces. Here, diaries and letters supplement the rhetoric of treatises, vocalising compliments and complaints about the convenience and inconvenience of domestic arrangements. The perspectives of architects and occupants often coincided in an appreciation of villas and cottages—domestic forms which historians have also lauded as the epitome of comfort and convenience.[6] This was, in part, connected to scale as both cottage and villa offered more intimate and easily managed space. It was also a reflection of different modes of living and greater control over access: being able to determine who entered made these more private and convenient places in which to live. In exploring the villa as a building type and domestic arrangement, the analysis remains attentive not only to all of these arguments but also to the continued importance of status in shaping the house or villa and in moulding what convenience meant in practical terms. Here, the chapter argues that space and scale were critical considerations that pushed in the opposite direction: bigger was, in some ways, better, and certainly gave greater scope for both displays of status and the kind of room specialisation that was increasingly a part of elite lifestyles, even if the result was less convenient in other ways. Overall, the concern is with exploring the idea and ideal of convenience as a way of assessing the suitability of a house for comfortable modern life, and with how these imperatives changed over time.

Architects and the Convenient House

Notions of convenience were something that preoccupied the architects and owners of country houses in the late seventeenth and eighteenth centuries. William Halfpenny, an architect and prolific writer of builders' patterns books in the first half of the eighteenth century, noted in the preface of his *New and Complete System of Architecture* (1749) that: 'As necessity was the parent of building, convenience should the architect's first view'. He asserted that convenience was, therefore, the 'principal and foundation' of the designs he presented; but he continued: 'as to beauty and magnificence, they are schemes inexhaustible, simplicity is the basis of beauty; as decoration is of magnificence; harmony is the result of the first, and proportion elegantly compos'd is the certain effect of the latter'.[7] In other words, his designs would be both convenient and tasteful. This ambition reflected the well-established principles of Renaissance architectural treatises by Vitruvius, Serlio, Palladio and others. These were *firmitas, utilitas and venustas*: the material and technical; the functional and social (with a goal of comfort and convenience); and the beauty and aesthetics of a building.[8]

These ideas were prominent in Sir Henry Wotton's *The Elements of Architecture* (1624), in which he asserted that 'well building hath three conditions—Commoditie, Firmness and Delight', and in the work of German and Dutch contemporaries, such as Joseph Furttenbach and Hendrick de Keyser.[9] They were guiding principles for French architects through the second half of the seventeenth century, most famously in Jacques-François Blondel's five-volume *Cours d'Architecture* (1675–83), but more practically in Augustin Charles D'Aviler's *Cours d'Architecture* (1691), which went through numerous editions and was still being used well into the eighteenth century.[10] The published texts were also an inspiration for new publications, and sometimes parts of them were 'borrowed', translated and published under new names.[11] Their influence spread across Europe, carrying with it these three guiding principles. They were embodied in the family crest of the Swedish architect Nicodemus Tessin the younger when he was ennobled in 1714, the same year that he published his *Observations on both public and private houses, their strength, comfort, and beauty.* For his crest, he chose a lion to symbolise strength (*starkheten*), a lily for beauty (*skiönheten*) and a shell for convenience and comfort (*commoditeten och beqwämligheten*).[12]

Creating a convenient house was by no means straightforward. One persistent problem in living up to these ideals was ensuring that architectural and aesthetic priorities were in step with the local climate: Italian and French principles did not necessarily travel well. This was commented on by Joseph Furttenbach, who presented his work as 'a model combination of German and Italian customs', and was made explicit by Nicodemus Tessin in his *Observations on both public and private houses, their strength, comfort, and beauty, designed in accordance with our Swedish climate and economy* (1714).[13] Despite this, and the practical guidance given in a collection of architectural plans published by Captain Carl Wijnbald in 1755, Tessin's son, Carl Gustaf Tessin, struggled to make his new house at Åkerö a satisfactory blend of French taste and Swedish practicality.[14] He noted in his diary in June 1757 that one should 'never plan one's rooms *à rez de chaussée*' (on the ground floor) in Sweden, since 'our snow, our cold and our damp will make the ground floor uncomfortable'.[15]

The suitability of fashionable Italian styles for inclement British weather also troubled architects and landowners in England. Writing in the late seventeenth century, Roger North emphasised the need to modify classical architecture because the climate was very different from that in Italy—a point brought out by William Hanbury, who visited numerous houses in the 1720s when planning his new house at Kelmarsh in Northamptonshire. He was unimpressed with Lord Burlington's work at Tottenham Park, Wiltshire, of which he wrote:

> Ld Bruces house in Savernack forest a seat lately built (Ld Burlington being ye architect) who has mistaken ye english for ye Italian climate he has made ye windows small & ye walls thick consequently ye house is dark and damp it is also cumbred Wth entries [passages] & dark rooms wch ye air having but little vent from are stinking.[16]

For Hanbury, an inappropriate design in terms of windows and passageways produced a house that was inconvenient and poorly ventilated. Henry Home, Lord Kames, went further, arguing that:

> A colonnade along the front of a building, hath a fine effect in Greece and Italy, by producing coolness and obscurity, agreeable in warm and luminous climates. The cold climate of Britain is altogether averse to this ornament. A colonnade therefore, can never be proper in this country, unless when employ'd to communicate with a detached building.[17]

This observation formed part of a broader discussion of the importance of utility and convenience in any architectural design. The paradox of marrying these with regularity had long troubled architects and was neatly captured by Alexander Gerard in his *Essay on Taste* (1759):

> *Utility*, or the *fitness* of things for answering their ends, constitutes another species of beauty, distinct from that of figure. It is of so great importance that, though *convenience* is sometimes in lesser instances sacrificed to *regularity*, yet a degree of inconvenience generally

destroys all the pleasure, which should have arisen from the symmetry and proportion of the parts.[18]

The problem was particularly acute with classical designs, in which external (and internal) symmetry was all important. Blondel, D'Aviler, Le Blond and others grappled with this problem and presented plans and descriptions of how rooms could be laid out in a convenient manner—usually involving matching apartments either side of a central *salle* or hall—whilst maintaining a symmetrical facade.[19] This was possible when building on a grand scale. Indeed, Kames thought that it was only in 'palaces, and other buildings sufficiently extensive to admit a variety of useful contrivance' where 'regularity justly takes the lead'.[20]

Combining regularity and convenience was more challenging in smaller houses. Kames felt that utility ought to prevail in such dwellings, but most English architectural pattern books continued to offer essentially classical designs. In the early 1750s, William Halfpenny published books on Chinese and Gothic architecture, but all of the 'convenient and decorated' designs in his 1749 *New and Complete System of Architecture* were in the classical style. So too were the seventy 'convenient and ornamental' designs published by John Crunden in 1767.[21]

In one sense, this is understandable, given the conservative and genteel rather than aristocratic market being targeted by these writers. Nonetheless, it is quite striking since gothic forms of architecture were becoming increasingly fashionable in the middle decades of the eighteenth century and released the architect from the need for regularity and symmetry.[22] Moreover, Kames felt that the 'old Gothic form of building seems well suited to the rough uncultivated regions where it was invented', suffering none of the problems identified with neo-classical colonnades, and the like.[23] Yet most commentators were convinced that classicism equated with convenience. It is perhaps telling that even William Gilpin, a champion of the picturesque, could argue in his *Observations on the Western Parts of England* that:

> Nor are the conveniences, which the Grecian architecture bestows on private buildings, less considerable, than the beauty of its decorations. The Gothic palace is an incumbered pile. We are amused with looking into these mansions of antiquity, as objects of curiosity; but should never think of comparing them in point of convenience with the great houses of modern taste, in which the hall and the saloon fill the eye on our entrance; are noble reservoirs for air; and grand antichambers to the several rooms of state that divide on each hand from them.[24]

In part, Gilpin's criticism of the gothic was directed at ecclesiastical buildings being turned into private dwellings, the form and scale of which made them difficult to render convenient in terms of the layout and arrangement of rooms. The solution arrived at by many advocates of Gothic architecture was to combine a Gothic exterior with a more 'convenient' Grecian interior. This was seen at Richard Payne Knight's house at Downton Castle in Herefordshire and at Sandleford Priory in Berkshire built for Elizabeth Montagu by James Wyatt.[25] In embracing gothic styles both for the interior and exterior of Strawberry Hill, Horace Walpole declared that 'In truth, I did not mean to make my house so Gothic as to exclude convenience, and modern refinements in luxury. The designs of the inside and outside are strictly ancient, but the decorations are modern'.[26]

As Gilpin indicates, architectural convenience meant a spacious and airy house with specialised rooms arranged in a systematic manner. Such ideas were being developed in France through the late seventeenth and early eighteenth century in the work of D'Aviler, Le Blond and most notably Jacques-François Blondel.[27] But they were also being put into practice elsewhere, for example in the writings of Roger North—a one-time successful lawyer and MP who retired to rural Norfolk after the 1688 Revolution and the fall of the Tory interest. Of particular note are his lengthy treatise *Cursory Notes of Building* (1698) and his much shorter *On planning a country house* (c.1696).[28] Both were based on his experiences in remodelling his own house, Rougham Hall, Norfolk, as well as his knowledge of a wide variety of houses owned by friends and family, and his reading of the architectural texts of the day. North was not necessarily the first and certainly not the most influential writer, but his ideas form a roadmap through the architecture of convenience. For North, convenience was a complex idea that required careful planning and execution to achieve in a domestic setting. Its achievement was predicated on three broad concerns: the orientation, setting and form of the house (which impacted on heat, light and ventilation); the separation of internal space into specialist rooms and their integration through corridors and staircases; and the importance of privacy, most clearly seen in the distinction between public and family rooms.

Location, Form and Convenience

North argued that a house should be built facing south because the winter sun would warm the rooms and make them 'comfortable', whilst in summer the noon-day sun would be too high to shine into the house. An east or west orientation would mean 'the summer sun every shining morning or evening makes the chambers furnace-hot'.[29] Writing in the 1720s, the German architect Leonhard Christoph Sturm was more specific, recommending a gendering of space: the 'male rooms'—the study, the library and office—should be 'on the morning side' of the house, with its light and its fresh, dry air. This was also where a dining room should be situated, especially for eating during spring and autumn. The evening sun was more important for the mistress's apartment, where warm air was more important than early light.[30] Related to this, North makes recommendations about the number and size of windows and, perhaps surprisingly, warns that 'it is an error, to affect much light, and wee confess it, by darkening o' lights againe with curtaines'. The dangers of 'over lighting an house' were clear: it was 'both cold, and bad for the eyes'. The problem of insufficient lighting, North argued, was occasioned by 'walls, buildings, and trees, which taking away the sky's light, darken a room'.[31]

These problems were exacerbated by building around a courtyard, which 'dulls the light, and hinders the prospect'. Building on a hilltop addressed these issues, but North did not recommend 'lofty scituations'.[32] In part, this was linked with the need to secure a good water supply— something which also concerned William Hanbury. In his travels around southern England, he recorded the position of the house relative to water at Longleat, Wilton and Ampthill, noting that the last of these was 'well watered' despite its bold situation.[33] At Tottenham Park, Hanbury commended the arrangements, there being 'a pretty trout river whereon is a engine for supply water to the house'. He regretted not being able to see the mechanism but reckoned one could be made for considerably less than the £1400 apparently spent by the owner.[34] Such arrangements were already in place in the late seventeenth century and were observed by Celia Fiennes during her visit to Broadlands in 1695.[35]

North's other concern about building on hilltops was that this left the house exposed to wind. The same sentiments were echoed over a century later by John Byng, Lord Torrington, who complained about 'modern hill-top gazeabouts' which were, in contrast with earlier dwellings, 'exposed to every tempest and distant from every comfort'.[36] Byng was very much of the old school, with a natural distrust of change, but Jane Austen also viewed such exposed locations as problematic. In her unfinished novel *Sanditon* (1817), she has the heroine, Charlotte, remark of a house in a sheltered dip that they pass on their journey: 'And whose very snug-looking place is this? . . . It seems to have as many comforts about it as Willingden' (the house in which she has been staying).[37] Her host, Mr. Parker, replies that it is his old house, given up in favour of a 'better situation': a house on the brow of a hill with fine views rather than 'pent down in this little contracted nook, without air or view'. Yet his wife seems less convinced, looking at the house through the back window of the coach in which they were travelling and noting that 'It was always a very comfortable house . . . And such a nice garden, such an excellent garden . . . it was a nice place for the children to run about in. So shady in summer!' The virtue of sheltered position was especially important in bad weather, Mrs. Parker continuing her reverie by noting that: 'The Hilliers did not seem to feel the storms last winter at all. I remember seeing Mrs. Hillier after one of those dreadful nights, when *we* had been literally rocked in our bed, and she did not seem at all aware of the wind being anything more than common'. Her husband's response mixes the sublime with the medical:

> *We* have all the grandeur of the storm with less real danger because the wind, meeting with nothing to oppose or confine it around our house, simply rages and passes on; while down in this gutter, nothing is known of the state of the air below the tops of the trees; and the inhabitants may be taken totally unawares, by one of those dreadful currents which do more mischief in a valley when they *do* arise than an open country ever experiences in the heaviest gale.

The storm is grand whilst the dangers of a valley location lie in the settling out of bad air, laden with disease. When they arrived at their new hilltop house he exclaims 'Now, for our hill, our health-breathing hill'.

There was a certain romanticism in the avowed attractions of this windy hilltop, one which also appears in Goethe's *Die Wahlverwandschaften* (1809). The main characters of the novel, Charlotte and Edward, are joined at Edward's ancestral home by Charlotte's niece, Ottilie, and Edward's friend, Otto. Together they plan to build a new cottage within walking distance from the country house. At first, they think to place the cottage so that it can be seen from the castle, but Ottilie suggests otherwise:

> 'I would have the house built here' she said, as she pointed with her finger to the highest point of the slope on the hill. 'It is true you cannot see the castle from thence, for it is hidden by the wood; but for that very reason you find yourself in another quite new world; you lose village and houses and all at the same time. The view of the ponds, with the mill, and the hills and mountains in the distance, is singularly beautiful—I have often observed it when I have been there'.[38]

Edmund's old friend Otto, a Captain and a land surveyor, agrees. He finds that Edward's family has chosen a good spot for their country house 'for it is sheltered from the wind, with the conveniences of life close at hand'. He continues by observing that a 'place, on the contrary, which is more for pleasure-parties than for a regular residence would do very well there [on the hilltop]'.[39] It is telling that a residence should be placed conveniently, whereas a pleasure house could be set in a more dramatic location.

In terms of the house itself, North thought that a dwelling just one room deep was 'very inconvenient; for heat and cold are troublesome in a single building, and there is no retiring from either'.[40] A double pile (i.e. two rooms deep) might resolve some of these issues and was certainly favoured by later architects when discussing the ideal format for a convenient house. David Laing, for instance, argued in his *Hints for Dwellings* of 1800 that 'the nearer the Building approaches to a Square, the greater are its Conveniences, and the Cost proportionately less'.[41] A double row of rooms also made the house warmer and the chimneys could be situated centrally in the house—an arrangement which quickly became common in Germany and Scandinavia. There were disadvantages of such compact designs, however. They lacked the grandeur of a house with wings and were thus less effective in communicating status. More practically, noise and smells pass too readily because, as North put it, 'the proximity of the rooms gives a tinct of the same air throut, which I could scarce have believed if I had not proved it'.[42] Moreover, closets could only be included at the expense of other rooms, and the different ceiling heights needed for formal and family rooms were hard to accommodate. Yet there were also 'inconveniences of too much spreading', including 'the great charge of walls, and roof' and the necessity of long passageways or, still worse, having to go outside to access other parts of the building.[43]

In France, architects such as D'Aviler, Jean Mariette and Jacques-François Blondel were concerned with houses at an altogether grander scale and mostly in an urban setting, although Blondel's 1737–38 treatise *De la distribution des maisons de plaisance* laid out a model for country houses 'in the modern taste'. With cost less of an issue, they favoured a layout in which a courtyard was enclosed by the main part of the house and two wings set at right angles. In D'Aviler's plan, these wings contained a private apartment and a long gallery; in Blondel's design for a *grand hôtel* (which formed part of his entry on architecture, produced for the *Encyclopedie* edited by Diderot and d'Alembert and published 1751–65), they were considerably larger than the main part of the house. Each enclosed private gardens and courtyards and were split between private apartments (towards the house) and service areas (closest to the road or public square).[44]

Specialist Rooms and Convenient Corridors

Roger North's own house, Rougham Hall, was a compromise between compactness and spreading. Its organisation also highlights another of his concerns: that of the specialisation of rooms and their integration into a convenient whole through the use of corridors and staircases. These were concerns that were also discussed by D'Aviler and further developed by Le Blond and Blondel. D'Aviler laid out a double apartment system, but the key distinction was between the *appartement de parade* (state apartment) and the *appartement de commodité* (private apartment), distinguished not only in their scale and decoration, but also—as we have seen—by their location within the house. The use of *commodité* is significant and reflects the more relaxed atmosphere in these private apartments. In Sweden, Nicodemus Tessin drew on the same language: writing about the best way to arrange rooms, *la distribution*, to give convenient access between different rooms and floors, and the kind of rooms that were needed, he refers to *bekvämlighet* (comfort/convenience).[45] In Germany, Johan Friedrich Penther took a similarly pragmatic approach, discussing how the balance between structural strength, beauty and convenience could shift and be negotiated in a house.[46] And such concerns were not solely the business of architects: they also struck those who occupied or visited these houses. As we saw at the outset of this chapter, Mary Delany appreciated Cornbury as '*comfortable and pleasant*' because it was 'not only magnificent and elegant but *convenient* and *rational*'.[47] In short, it was laid out in a manner that made life easy.

Blondel's designs for *maisons de plaisance* and *grand hôtels* thus crystallised a set of ideas and ideals that were circulating widely in France and the rest of Europe. His particular contribution was to formalise a triple system, in which rooms were arranged in suites according to their function as formal rooms of parade, which formed showy public spaces designed to impress with their magnificence; societal rooms in which a more intimate circle would be received, and private spaces, for family and the closest friends.[48] Within these were a series of specialist rooms, including everything from a state bedroom to private toilets. Just as important in making this arrangement convenient and the house 'liveable' were the *degagements*, which allowed the owner private access into and between rooms by means of passageways and small staircases, and removed servants to separate service corridors. For example, in his ideal *maison de plaisance*, spiral staircases on either side of the *Grand Salon à l'Italienne* allow the servants to move between floors without undermining the cleanliness and status of the grand staircase. Moreover, service corridors connected to stairs leading up to the servants' rooms and down to the cellars, facilitating direct movement between the two and ensuring that servants remained marginal to the main thoroughfares of the house.[49]

These ideas resonated across Europe. In Sweden, for example, Wijnblad's collection of plans for country houses offered an array of possibilities in terms of size, form and spatial arrangement.[50] As Johanna Ilmakunnas notes, they introduced many of Blondel's innovations, including small specialist rooms, corridors, and back staircases, but adapted these to local circumstances, for example by moving principal rooms to the first floor.[51] In Britain, the designs of men like William Halfpenny and John Crunden followed similar principles but generally scaled down to the proportions of a gentleman's seat. Plate 17 in Halfpenny's *New and Complete System of Architecture* (1749) shows a large villa with a hall leading to a lobby containing the main staircase and a cross corridor with a door out to the garden; the backstairs are set to the left of this central axis.[52] Crunden's designs were generally for larger houses. A substantial town house was provided with a central corridor which gave access to the common parlour and eating parlour, whilst a cross corridor gave access to the back stairs and the housekeeper's room. His 'Plan and elevation of a country house in the modern taste, & would be convenient & elegant' (Figure 1.1) has a T-shaped corridor giving access to all rooms on the ground floor: both the parlour, library and saloon,

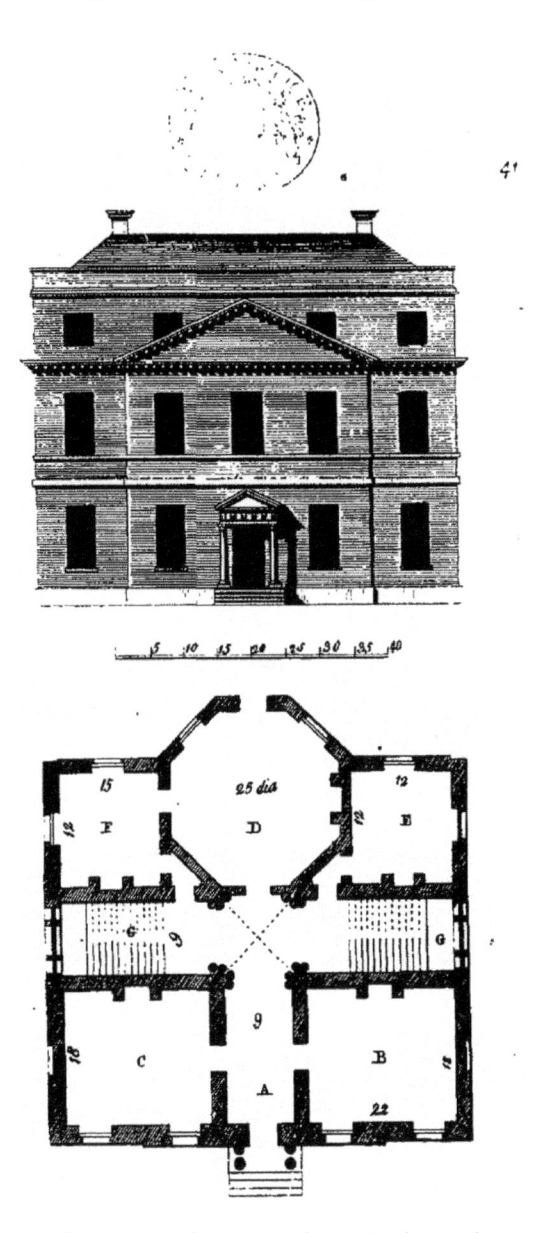

Figure 1.1 'Plan and elevation of a country house in the modern taste, and would be convenient and elegant', John Crunden, *Convenient and Ornamental Architecture* (London: Isaac Taylor, 1767): Plate XLI

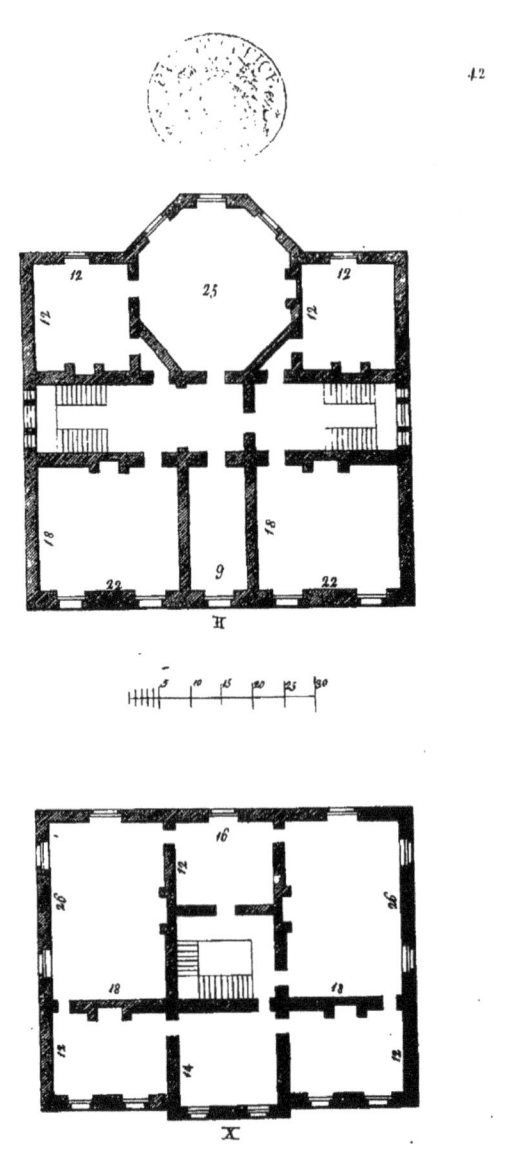

Figure 1.1 (Continued)

and the more private china closet and housekeeper's room, tucked into the corners at the rear of the house. Two staircases lead to a cross corridor on the first floor which connects the bedrooms and a drawing room. The staircases are not differentiated on the plan, but that to the right is presumably the backstairs as it leads to a section of the upper corridor closed off by a door.[53]

These practical considerations were being put into place well before they appeared in these pattern books. William Hanbury may have been sceptical about the suitability of strict Palladianism, but built his own house along symmetrical lines, to a design by James Gibbs.[54] Two pavilions housed the stables and the indoor servants, the latter connected by an enclosed service corridor; the central block contained a double-height hall and six other rooms on the ground floor, all connected by a corridor running across the full width of the house and incorporating two staircase halls at either end. This was a significant departure from Gibbs' original plan, as it appeared in his book of architecture (1728), and involved a radical rethinking of the interior space. It also meant that all rooms on the ground floor could be reached from this central axis, limiting traffic through individual rooms.[55] The provision of a separate back staircase and the repetition of the corridor on the first and second floors assured convenient and separate passage through the house for the owner and servants. As John Bold notes, such an arrangement meant that 'progress through the house is rapid and effective' and that 'the chance encounter in the through room is no longer encouraged'.[56]

This was the kind of arrangement that provided the private domestic space that Mary Delany enjoyed at Bulstrode. Her bedroom and closet were filled with her famous collection of shells: 'I have a new cabinet with whole glass doors and glass on the side and shelves within, of whimsical shapes, to hold *all my beauties*'. But this was an intensely private space that she would only share with intimate friends and family. 'How blest should I be', she wrote to her sister, 'could we have a tête-à-tête in it with you! it is calculated for that purpose, being retired from all interruption and eaves-droppers'.[57] A closed door and a separate corridor were essential to this privacy. Indeed, Bold argues that these architectural measures formed part of a 'defensive strategy against unwelcome and unpredictable territorial encroachments'—a strategy that was further augmented by the introduction of bell-pull systems which meant that servants could remain below stairs until required by their employers.[58]

These measures were relatively easy to incorporate when building from scratch, but many more houses were extended or remodelled than were built from first principles. Whilst this made it more difficult to incorporate all of the various aspects of convenience, owners invariably tried to make their houses more liveable as well as more up to date. Canons Ashby in Northamptonshire is a fairly modest country house that gradually expanded from its origins as a farmhouse to form a quadrangle of varied styles arranged around a central cobbled courtyard. When Edward Dryden inherited the house in 1701, he set about modernising the architecture and decoration, including sash windows and an enfilade running along the south front. However, access between the different parts of the house remained problematic. Whilst an open gallery on the first floor could be enclosed to create a corridor between the front and back of the house, moving between the kitchen and dining parlour meant passing through the hall. Part of the problem was a lack of capital to make radical changes, which meant that successive generations had to put up with the disorder that came with a house that had grown organically. That said, there were clear distinctions between the public rooms along the south front and private apartments elsewhere in the house, most notably the pair of rooms labelled in an 1819 inventory as Lady Dryden's breakfast closet and Lady Dryden's sitting room and room adjoining.[59] By this time, there was also a dining room, billiard room, drawing room and small family sitting room as well as the great hall.[60]

In France, a similarly modest house, the early-sixteenth-century chateau of Kernault in Brittany, was extended and altered in the mid-eighteenth century to create a more modern and convenient arrangement of rooms.[61] The original *grande salle* was divided to make a vestibule and a *salle de compagnie* for entertaining, and the former kitchen was converted into a dining room, accessed from the newly created vestibule. An extension at the back of the house comprised a new kitchen (complete with larder, washroom and *piquerie*), a *petite couer* and a bedchamber with closet. The last of these was accessed via a new corridor cut through a cabinet and had its own private staircase. Although the overall plan has little resemblance to Blondel's ideal, there was clearly an attempt to create distinct spaces connected by corridors and staircases. Elsewhere, the architect had less success in creating even this modest level of convenience. Designs for a small house in the country for an aristocratic family, drawn up in 1794 by the architect Friedrich Schmidt, include separate apartments for the husband and wife, but the former is bisected by the corridor and a grand dining room upstairs must have been two floors away from the kitchen. Moreover, there is only one staircase and a single central corridor on each floor, meaning that servants, guests and family shared the same routeways through the house—altogether, a rather inconvenient arrangement.[62]

An alternative to this horizontal reorganisation of space was the insertion of additional floors that split high-ceilinged rooms vertically to produce additional rooms, albeit with much lower ceilings. This entresol system was most common in France, where it was initially created in existing room arrangements to provide additional space; by the early eighteenth century, however, they were also being included in newly designed houses.[63] These small rooms could be aesthetically pleasing and part of the scaled-down and intimate living that was fashionable at the time, but they were above all practical arrangements, sometimes used not only to create additional bedrooms for servants (as a Vaux-le-Vicomte in 1661) but also to offer warmer accommodation for the owner or his wife during the winter months. As Blondel highlighted, such arrangements required additional staircases and corridors, both to link them into the rest of the house and to create more private suites of self-contained rooms. Differentiation of space necessitated these integrating routeways.

The dichotomy of grand and back stairs modelled by Blondel is now a cliché of the social separation of master and servants, but the distinctions were far from binary. Roger North had three separate staircases at Rougham Hall (Figure 1.2). The great stairs linked the hall to a first-floor corridor and afforded direct access to guest bedchambers and the gallery, the most public rooms on the first floor. A second set of stairs led from the suite of family rooms on the ground floor to a library and chamber on the first floor, keeping this more private suite of rooms separate from the public parts of the house. The third staircase linked the service wing of the house to North's own bedchamber. Such private staircases were increasingly necessary given the growing desire to remove servants from the public spaces of the house unless and until they were needed. North himself noted that 'it is no unseemly object to an English gentleman . . .

Figure 1.2 Floor plan of Rougham Hall, c.1690 (ground floor and first floor): author's own drawing

to see his servants and business passing at ordinary times'.[64] But a concern for privacy and for the kind of separate access that allowed families to remove themselves from both servants and guests was a growing concern, on which North placed particular emphasis:

> For if wee consult convenience, wee must have severall avenews, and bolting holes, for such as are in the family and undrest, or for any other reason, to decline passing by company posted about by accident. This doth not seem to be of any great moment, but in the course of living will be found wanting, and be much desired. For it is unpleasant to be forc't to cross people, when one has not a mind to it, either for avoiding ceremony or any other reason.[65]

These were essentially the arguments deployed by Blondel in his grand designs, and which underpinned the creation of the entresol system discussed earlier.[66] Remarkably, North is not just suggesting that the country-house owner might want to have routes through the house that allow them to avoid their guests, but that this is something that he has learnt from experience. It is an architectural innovation born of living in a house, not one that results from the principles of taste or design: it belongs to the owner, not the architect.

Much the same is true of the little parlour, which North places next to the service rooms, but separated from them by a passageway that links to the back stairs and the outside. This was expressly a room for business: a place where someone who comes to the door might wait until the master of the house can see them because, as North notes: 'it is troublesome passing to and againe by them'.[67] Yet this is more than simply a waiting room; it is also a place where business can be transacted. The inclusion of a closet for the master of the house (corresponding with that for his wife, situated above it on the first floor) provides a space to interview the visitor and store papers relating to the estate. Another closet for the bailiff or steward provides a space 'where the books of entrys may be allwais open, and files of papers disposed, so as ready recourse is had to them'.[68] This went further than the need to allow 'proper space for offices', which many architects saw as one of the 'objects of comfort' in a properly planned country residence.[69] For North, it was a convenience that would easily repay the space it occupied because 'it must needs make a man's domestick affairs both pleasing, and thriffty', in part because there was no need for 'kitchening very fellow that comes to an house'—that is, having him sit and no doubt take some refreshment in the kitchen.[70] It was both a mechanism for and symbol of a sound domestic economy, allowing the master of the house to keep his business in order and to run the estate efficiently and effectively. Just as importantly, all of this business could be transacted without disturbing the spaces and routines of family life. The advantages of this were psychological as well as practical. Since this room was dedicated to business, it would focus the mind of the gentleman; if this work was transacted in one of the family rooms, it would be: 'all blended with his other concernes'; the result would be 'not only a confusion without a carefull method of economising his materials, but also an unsteddyness of thought, which the objects appertaining to different concerns brought into his mind'.[71]

A very similar sentiment was articulated over 50 years later by Mary Delany. Writing to her sister about her house at Delville, she noted that:

> I am going to make a very comfortable closet;—to have a dresser, and all manner of working tools, to keep all my stores for *painting, carving, gilding,* &c.; for my own room is now so clean and pretty that I cannot suffer it to be strewed with litter, only books and work, and the closet belonging to it to be given up to prints, drawings, and my collection of fossils, petrifactions, and minerals. I have not set them in order yet; a great work it will be, but when done very comfortable. There is to my working closet a pleasant window that overlooks all the garden, it faces the east, is always dry and warm. In the middle of the closet a deep nitch with shelves, where I shall put whatever china I think too good for common use.[72]

The nature of her busy-ness is different from North's, but the intention is very similar: a room in which her things can be kept in order and to hand, separate from the main run of things in the house.

Public and Private

For North, as much as Blondel, a convenient house was one that worked on a practical level: a place in which the family could live and from which the business of the estate could be transacted, a place that combined privacy and practicality. But it was also a place for entertaining guests, displaying status and demonstrating taste. Fundamental to his arrangements at Rougham was the distinction between public and private space—a central tenet of Blondel's triple system. North had a smaller and more intimate private parlour, withdrawing room and closet at one end of the house whilst the hall and great parlour form the representational rooms and occupy the grander space immediately accessible from the entrance portico.

In France, newly designed houses in the late seventeenth and especially the eighteenth century contained many of the features included in Blondel's model for a *maison de plaisance*. At Champs-sur-Marne, near Paris, for example, Paul Poisson de Bourvallais took possession of an unfinished chateau in the 1690s and completed its construction in 1706. It had rooms of parade in the form of two salons; that on the ground floor was flanked by large billiard and dining rooms, the former leading to a *Grand*

Cabinet or *lieu d'Assemblée*. On both the ground and first floors, there were series of apartments comprising a bedchamber, cabinet and *garde-robe*, which provided more private space for the owner and his guests. This privacy was underscored by the inclusion of an *escalier derobé*, which gave separate access to the first floor on one wing of the house, and three other sets of stairs in the other wing, one of which is marked on the plan as a *degagement*.[73] A similar arrangement can be found in Ragley Hall in Warwickshire, completed by the widow of Lord Conway around 1690. The scale of building was more modest, but the same principles of zoned public and family/private space and distinct routes of passage through the house were just as evident. As at Champs-sur-Marne, the main public rooms occupied the central part of the house, here comprising a large double-height Great Hall with a large saloon beyond. These gave access to four pavilion apartments in the French style, each with a withdrawing room, bedchamber, closet, servant's room and private staircase (Figure 1.3).[74] The architect Robert Hooke highlighted the advantage of this arrangement, which allowed the apartments to be self-sufficient 'without all intermingling or running through one another'.[75]

A different and arguably more modern solution was affected at Stoneleigh Abbey, originally a Cistercian monastery where the Leigh family had, for generations, lived in rooms constructed within the structure of the old building. Following his Grand Tour of 1712–13, Edward, Third Baron Leigh, clearly felt that his ancestral home needed upgrading both

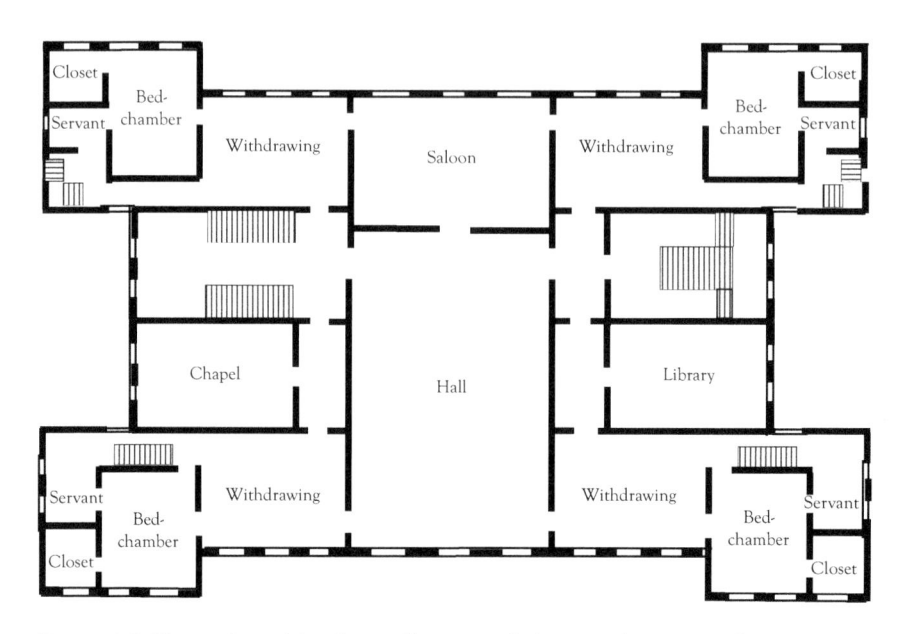

Figure 1.3 Floor plan of Ragley Hall, Warwickshire: author's own drawing

architecturally and functionally, and he commissioned the Warwick-based architect Francis Smith accordingly. Smith's designs were not particularly fashionable, forming a kind of provincial baroque: grand without achieving the bravura of Hawksmoor or Vanbrugh.[76] However, they provided his patron with nine new rooms on the principal floor, plus offices below and two floors above for bedchambers.[77] This additional space made Stoneleigh Abbey a much more convenient house. The Great Apartment, furnished by Edward Leigh in the 1730s, comprised the most formal public rooms, including a state bedchamber, whilst the Plaid Parlour and Plaid Drawing Room (later renamed the dining and breakfast rooms) provided space for entertaining guests. These rooms were arranged in an enfilade but were also linked by a corridor running down the spine of the West range. On the other side of this corridor, and facing into a courtyard formed with the original part of the house, were two family rooms: the Back Parlour and the Common Dining Room, which may have been used for conducting estate business.[78] This version of the triple system allowed the family to occupy and furnish different rooms for different purposes. The central corridor, replicated on all four floors of the West range, allowed easy movement between rooms and the provision of back stairs kept the main staircase free from servants. In this sense, it conformed closely to the ideals of convenient living. The original abbey buildings remained largely untouched by these improvements. However, an undated plan from the 1760s—when Edward Leigh's grandson, also called Edward, was making further improvements to the house and its furnishings—marks a succession of servants' bedchambers along the north range, linked by a corridor and served by four separate staircases (Figure 1.4).[79]

More radical in its demarcation of separate types of space, but in some ways less convenient as a dwelling, is Kedleston Hall in Derbyshire. Built as a venue in which Sir Nathaniel Curzon could display both his art and his love of ancient Rome, the entirety of the central block comprised rooms of parade. The main axis comprised an impressive marble hall and a round saloon, modelled on the Pantheon. To one side of these showpiece rooms were a music room, drawing room and library; on the

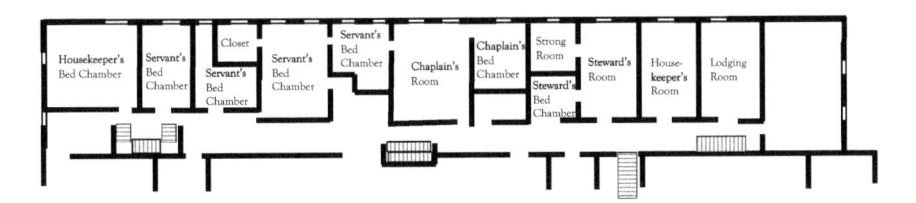

Figure 1.4 Floor plan of the original east range at Stoneleigh Abbey, first floor: author's own drawing, based on SCLA, DR671/33 Designs for Stoneleigh Abbey c.1765)

other a dining room and state apartment (bedchamber, anteroom and dressing room). Visitors, of which there were many, were taken around all these rooms to view the art and admire Curzon's taste. The offices were situated on the ground floor and the kitchen in a large separate wing, accessed by a long, curved corridor. Most striking, though, is the location of private family rooms in a corresponding wing, the corridor to which was described by the Duchess of Northumberland when she visited in 1766 as 'not only a pretty but very convenient communication'.[80] Convenience came from the separation of public and family space, which meant that the Curzons could occupy manageable and liveable rooms distinct from the main house. That said, Kedleston certainly suffered from what Roger North termed 'too much spreading',[81] not least in the enormous cost involved: it took over 10 years to complete, and even then two further wings remained unbuilt. As Horace Walpole remarked, Curzon's house was 'in the best taste, but too expensive for his estate'.[82]

The separation of public from more private space was always partial and contingent but was clearly manifest in the shifting location, organisation and use of bedchambers.[83] In large houses, those of the owner and his wife had traditionally formed part of the state apartment, arranged enfilade and marking increasing status and privacy as one progressed from antechamber to cabinet.[84] Whilst these arrangements were retained in grander houses, and even incorporated into new projects, such as Kedleston Hall, they were increasingly supplemented or supplanted by less formal arrangements that gave greater privacy. This was central to Blondel's triple system but was already apparent in John Vanbrugh's designs for Blenheim Palace (1705–20), where twin state apartments ran along the whole of the south front and were complemented by private family apartments for the Duke and Duchess on the east front. The latter included a bedchamber, dressing room, plus wardrobes and closets. Such suites of private rooms were seen in a refined and intricate form in the French system of bedchamber, cabinet de toilette and cabinet avec niches, or boudoir—an arrangement perfected by the middle of the eighteenth century.[85]

Maria Edgeworth was very struck by the arrangement at chateau de La Celle, once owned by Madame de Pompadour. The bedroom was 'high, comfortable, but not large'; off this led a 'pretty little dressing room and that onto a pretty little cabinet' with 'low sofas in tent stitch'; each of these three rooms had 'exquisitely contrived private exits and little dens of closets and antechambers'.[86] What pleased Edgeworth was both the organisation and decoration of the rooms, and the thought of the intrigues acted out in them. These associations were based partly on the decoration of certain aristocratic boudoirs (that of Madam de Pompadour's brother was decorated with paintings of nudes) and partly on them being the setting for sexual liaisons in many novels. Underpinning both was the privacy of the boudoir and its place as a retreat from the formality of the salon de compagnie.[87] In doing so it offered separate and private spaces in which to sleep, dress, beautify oneself and sit and read, daydream or simply relax.

Mark Girouard sees this arrangement and specialisation of rooms as being peculiarly French, especially when it included entresol rooms, often used to accommodate servants. However, the concept caught the imagination in England where the idea of a boudoir as an extension to or variation on the dressing room gained currency around the turn of the nineteenth century. The OED dates the first reference to a 1781 poem by William Hayley called *Triumphs of Temper*:

> As the French boudoir to the Gothic tower,
> Such is the peer, whom fashion much admires,
> Compar'd in person to his ancient sires[88]

Boudoirs are seen here as something fashionable and modern, a point reinforced in the anonymous *Letters of Miss Riversdale* (1803) in which the eponymous correspondent visits an aristocratic house recently fitted up with 'pretty little *boudoir* recesses'—part of a more general makeover of the house in a modern and tasteful manner.[89] Given this, it is perhaps surprising that boudoirs are only occasionally listed in the inventories and auction catalogues of country houses in the early decades of the nineteenth century. When they do appear, as at Colworth House in Bedfordshire, they have a rather different character. In the 1816 inventory, it lies between the library and the drawing room and thus formed part of the extensive series of alterations and improvements made by Samuel Reynolds on behalf of William Lee Antonie.[90] This rather unusual location also indicates its use as a retreat from the more public rooms on either side: one that could even be used for restorative sleep during the day, a use facilitated by the presence of a couch with a mattress, pillows and squabs. However, there was also an ornate gilt ink stand with 'three sconces and pedestal elegantly mounted with best cut glass stands', two glazed china cupboards and two satinwood stands 'with handsome china dishes'.[91] These link back to an earlier tradition of cabinets, whilst the backgammon and draft board table argue for shared rather than solitary leisure.

Although they lacked the nomenclature, spatial intricacy and frisson of the French arrangement, the private apartments at Blenheim, Bagley and elsewhere offered a corresponding privacy. The arrangements at Rougham Hall are again instructive. As noted earlier, the bedchamber shared by North and his wife was situated in the service wing of the house, accessible via a separate staircase. Leading from their bedchamber was Mrs. North's closet which gave onto a dressing room that could also be accessed from a corridor shut off from the rest of the house by a door (Figure 1.2). Seclusion from guests was less apparent in houses like

Stoneleigh Abbey, where all the rooms, including that of the owner, were arranged along a single corridor on each floor. Privacy here came from their vertical removal from the living rooms on the ground floor; their horizontal separation from servants' rooms, which were located in the old part of the house, and the provision of a separate dressing room or closet with each bedchamber. Closing the door to the corridor rendered each suite a separate and private space. Something of this can be seen at Highcliffe in Hampshire, as described by Lady Louisa Stuart. Writing to her sister about recent improvements, she first described the arrangement of her parents' rooms and then added 'My bedchamber and dressing-room are over their bedchamber—the prettiest little rooms you ever saw, as much retired as if I were in another house'.[92] The attraction of the rooms lies not only in their decoration but also in their seclusion from the rest of the house.

Privacy, of course, is a relative term; the furniture provided in each of these suites made them suitable for sleeping and dressing, and for the toilette or shaving, as appropriate. In the early 1760s, Edward, fifth Baron Leigh, ordered beds, commodes, dressing fables, chests of drawers and shaving stands en suite from London craftsmen: the furniture maker William Gomm and the upholsterer Thomas Burnett.[93] But these men also supplied sets of chairs—usually six or eight for each bedroom, upholstered to match the bed hangings, and a further one to four in the dressing room—plus Pembroke tables and occasionally portable writing desks. These made the rooms suitable for private entertainment, a use underlined by their ornamentation with porcelain and flower pots arranged on chimney pieces and pedestal tables. Fifty years later, William Lee Antonie had fitted all the principal bedrooms at Colworth with easy chairs or couches and their respective dressing rooms with sofas, complete with squabs and cushions.[94]

That such rooms were used by groups of people is apparent from the account left by the Reverend Stotherd Abdy of a gathering at Welford in Berkshire in 1770. The days were generally occupied with outdoor pursuits—hunting or walking in the garden—but small groups also assembled in dressing rooms, passing the time in conversation.[95] Mary Delany wrote from Bulstrode in November 1754 describing a similar mix of indoor and outdoor pursuits. Her afternoon and evening routine was focused around the Duchess of Portland's dressing room: 'After dinner our Duchess and I hold a tête-à-tête in the dear dressing-room till five; then all hands to work till between six and seven, then tea, and we return to the dressing-room, and I read whilst the rest work'.[96] The privacy of the dressing room was thus contingent on the time of day: after tea the entire company of women—numbering at least five—gathered there; in the afternoon, however, it was a more intimate space, suitable for private conversations. This is certainly how the dressing room is deployed in Fanny Burney's *Evelina*. Assembled for dinner at the house of Lady

Howard, Mrs. Duval is being goaded by Captain Mirvan and Sir Clement Willoughby when she receives a distressing letter. Lady Howard 'begged to know the cause of her uneasiness, and whether she could assist her'. Not wishing to divulge the contents of the letter to the whole group, she asks for a private interview, upon which 'Lady Howard then invited her into the dressing-room, and I was desired to attend her'.[97] The dressing room is thus used as a retreat from company and from the more public space of the dining room. At the same time, it was rendered a wholly female space—much as that of the Duchess of Portland.

The gendering and use of dressing rooms were reflected in their decoration. Many of those encountered by Mrs. Lybbe Powys in her visits to country houses in the middle decades of the eighteenth century were decorated with green wallpapers or hangings (a feminine colour, associated with Venus and thus with love) or in a Chinese style, which again was associated with femininity, albeit complicated with more general statements of taste and fashionability.[98] She also noted that many contained numerous decorative items. At Fawley Court in Buckinghamshire, for instance, the dressing room to best bedchamber 'is prettier than 'tis possible to imagine, the most curious India paper as birds, flowers, &c., put up as different pictures in frames of the same, with festoons, India baskets, figures, &c., on a peagreen paper'; that of the owners' wife, Mrs. Freeman, was 'ornamented with pictures and a thousand other curiosities'.[99]

More important to our present discussion, it was in the dressing room of the apartments in which she was accommodated when she stayed as a guest of the house owners that she wrote her diaries—a common practice, especially amongst female correspondents. Thus, when visiting Bulstrode in 1738, Mary Delany wrote to excuse the delay in replying to letters, noting how she was detained in the drawing room, drinking coffee and sitting with the Duchess whilst she worked on her netting, and then disturbed in her dressing room, first by visitors and then by a call down for tea. Finally, she was able to start writing at about eight o'clock.[100] This idea of the bedroom and dressing room as a retreat is repeated in Jane Austen's mock-gothic novel, *Northanger Abbey*; Catherine Moore retreats to the security of her bedchamber during moments of crisis and it is in there that she has the privacy to peruse the hidden manuscript which she supposes holds some dark secrets, but which turns out to be nothing more than a laundry bill.[101] This, then, was a personal and private space, even for the guest in a house—a space where one could expect to be alone and undisturbed, but into which others might be invited.

The Villa and the Cottage: Comfort and Privacy

The physical removal of family rooms from rooms of parade could involve moving into a separate dwelling altogether, as Lady Oxford did at Welbeck Abbey. Tiring of the constant stream of company that came to the house, she built a small cottage on the estate to which she could retreat. It comprised a modest hall, dining room, a drawing room, a bedchamber and dressing room; she lived there for part of each week, attended by just two servants.[102] Lady Oxford sought privacy. In Sweden, Carl Gustaf Tessin was perhaps more interested in keeping warm: in winter, he decamped to a separate wing of the house at Åkerö. On the ground floor were a large and small living room, a book room and rooms for resident and visiting footmen. Upstairs was a library and paper room, plus separate bedrooms for the count and countess, and one for guests. Significantly, whilst this was a desirable and convenient move for Tessin, it clearly did not work for his wife, who remained in the main house throughout the winter.[103]

These dwellings provided much of the comfort, convenience and privacy often associated with villa residences. Traditionally, the villa was a private rural retreat for the urban elite, set in a country estate away from the city and with unwanted visitors excluded to create a particular social milieu. Pliny had his Tuscan villa where he could escape public ceremony and the merchant princes of Renaissance Italy did the same—a practice formulated by Palladio.[104] This practice was picked up by the burghers of the Dutch Republic during the golden age, who bought land and built houses in the countryside as an escape from the city.[105]

In the late seventeenth and eighteenth centuries, German, French and English aristocrats built villas and palaces in the environs of their respective capitals. Perhaps the most famous example is that of Sanssouci, the summer palace of Frederick the Great built in the 1740s at Potsdam on the outskirts of Berlin. Its purpose as a place of relaxation and escape from some of the formalities of court is apparent both from its name and its scale. Whilst imposing, it contains just 12 principal rooms, arranged as a single-storey enfilade with a service corridor behind. Visitors would enter via the central hall or vestibule and pass into a grand marble hall with its domed ceiling, which formed the principal room for entertaining guests. Turning east, the visitor passed through the audience room and the concert or dining room before gaining access to the King's study and bedroom. Beyond this, and accessible only via a narrow passage was his private library. West of the marble hall were a set of five private bedrooms, each with its own entrance from the corridor running behind. Sanssouci thus represented both an escape and a rational organisation of internal space: increasing privacy within the public rooms in the east wing and private bedrooms in the west wing.

Sanssouci was exceptional in its magnificence and in its mixture of public and private rooms. Most villas offered much greater seclusion, as Roger North understood, noting in 1690 that 'A villa, is quasy a lodge, for the sake of a garden, to retire to injoy and sleep, without pretence of enterteinement of many persons'.[106] This is how Lady Lucas viewed her villa in Putney; it was a half-way house between the bustle of London and the grandeur of the family seat, Wrest Park in Bedfordshire, which she inherited in 1797. The summer months were mostly spent at Wrest, but from December to June she generally split her time between Putney and London, sometimes making day trips out of town to her suburban villa.[107] The villa offered Lady Lucas an escape from the heat of London and a place where she could enjoy time with her family and away from the bustle of London society and its obligations of polite visiting and formal entertainment.

Her close contemporary, the Honourable Mary Leigh, had a grand country house in Stoneleigh Abbey, but no town house; instead, she had a villa in Kensington Gore: Grove House.[108] Like Lady Lucas, she did not engage in regular entertaining at Grove House and appears to have discouraged casual visitors. Her most frequent guest was Mrs. Hill, the wife of her lawyer and also a close friend with whom Mary Leigh regularly exchanged small gifts. Hill came over from their house on Queen Street, Lincolns Inn Fields, generally on a day trip, similar in nature to those described by Lady Lucas who 'went after dinner to Putney, drank tea with Lady Grantham. Return'd to Town'.[109] This kind of small-scale entertaining is reflected in the contents of Grove House. An inventory of china taken on 19 July 1806, shortly after Leigh's death, lists a good variety of tea, chocolate and coffee cups, breakfast plates, tea chests and caddies, slop basins and sugar basins; but there are no dinner plates, serving dishes or the like.[110] Similarly, her Grove House silverware comprised candlesticks, spoons and cork stoppers rather than the tureens, epergnes and waiters bought for Stoneleigh Abbey.[111]

The convenience of location and privacy was underpinned by that of living in a modestly proportioned and well-maintained house. The precise arrangement of rooms at Grove House is unknown, but the five-bay structure, which had been extended during the middle decades of the eighteenth century, included living space for Mary Leigh, plus a suite of service rooms, several servants' bedrooms, stables, two coach houses, gardens and three closes of land. Early in her tenancy, Leigh engaged a variety of tradesmen to restore and repair various parts of the house. In the principal rooms, this chiefly comprised repairing some plasterwork and windows, and repainting the woodwork; but work on the service areas was more extensive: replacing plasterwork, repairing and cleaning windows, repointing brickwork, replacing guttering, digging drains, retiling floors, fitting pipework and repairing skirting, roof timbers, doorcases and floorboards.[112] This kind of work was essential in maintaining the house as a convenient place in which to live. However, what was particularly important in making Grove House so agreeable for Mary Leigh were the gardens and closes. The latter were productive spaces, helping to provide produce for the house. The daybook notes payments for washing and shearing sheep, mowing and haymaking, building and thatching hayricks, and spreading dung across the fields; and Leigh also writes about her cows.[113] Yet these fields and agricultural activities also served to remove the house from the town, conforming with traditional notions of the villa as a rural retreat, set in a productive agricultural world.[114]

This desire for a retreat is seen in Goethe's *Die Leiden des jungen Werthers* (1774), where the young Werther writes to his friend about his living arrangements: 'You know of my old ways of settling anywhere, of selecting a little cottage in some cosy spot, and of putting up in it with every convenience. Here, too, I have discovered such a snug, comfortable place, which possesses peculiar charms for me'.[115] Here, it is the cottage that offers comfort on a modest scale, whilst linking to a taste for the picturesque that was growing across Europe. Crowley draws on contemporary architectural treatises to situate cottages and villas on a continuum of comfort, privacy and aesthetics.[116] Cottages were picturesque and the epitome of comfort because they were, as one writer put it, 'unincumbered with the forms of state and troublesome appendages. The leading feature of this style of building is to appear in every respect a dwelling calculated for comfort and convenience, without minute attention to the rules of art'.[117] Their aesthetics may have been rather different, but their function and convenience were essentially the same as those of the villa. Indeed, the connection is readily apparent in the comment made by Robert Ferrars in Jane Austen's *Sense and Sensibility* (1811), when viewing the living accommodation of the Miss Dashwoods:

> I am excessively fond of a cottage; there is always so much comfort, so much elegance about them. And I protest, if I had money to spare, I should buy a little land and build myself within a short distance of London, where I might drive myself down at any time and collect a few friends about me and be happy.[118]

This was not merely a sentimentalisation of the picturesque and rustic; it was also a place of privacy and intimacy with close friends—precisely the attractions of Mary Leigh's villa and surely at the heart of her assertion that 'it is impossible for me to have so agreeable and suitable a place as is the Grove House in every particular'.[119]

The cottage and the comfort imagined by Ferrars was very different from that conceived by Nathaniel Kent and John Wood as befitting rural labourers. Kent's *Hints to Gentlemen of Landed Property* (1775) was intensely pragmatic, arguing that decent housing was essential to maintaining a healthy and productive workforce: 'His situation then should be considered, and made at least comfortable, if it were merely out of good policy'.[120] Comfort in this context comprised a warm room, and a place to cook food and store provisions, but it also meant separate sleeping quarters for parents and children. Given spatial form by Wood's designs in his *Series of Plans, for Cottages or Habitations of the Labourer*, this meant four rooms, each bedroom having a separate door leading off a small landing.[121] This distinction between the basic comforts of the labourer's cottage and those of the picturesque retreat of the elite were as much to do with function as form: one was a decent place to live; the other an attempt to achieve privacy and removal from society.

Status and Distinctions of Convenience

The comfort and convenience of a house were not absolute; rather, they were often conceived relative to the status of the individual concerned. Indeed, the notion that a country house was the ultimate expression of wealth and power is central to Mark Girouard's reading of its architecture and decoration; it was equally important to how contemporaries conceived, imagined and constructed their houses. Again, Roger North put his finger on the importance of the owner's status when he wrote:

> Consider well your owne ambition, that is what sort of housing you desire, which I must allwais allow to be more than is strickly needful according to your circumstances, else a farme is equall to the best. But the distinction of well borne and bredd, is by elegant and neat living.[122]

This need to augment what was strictly necessary, both in size and ornamentation, is central to the myriad designs offered in architects' pattern books. David Laing is explicit in his preface:

> In the Designs for Dwelling in the Cottage Style, I have attended to a Simplicity to the Character of the Structure; rejecting all Superfluity of Ornament, as inconsistent with the Building: in the Plans on a larger Scale, and in the Designs for Villas, I have indulged in more Ornament and Variety of Contour, as allowable in such Buildings, whose Inhabitants may be considered of some Rank in Life, and entitled to more Show as well as Conveniences.[123]

In short, those of higher social standing might expect their houses to be more comfortable and convenient as well as more ornate, so practicalities were as important as show.[124]

John Crunden's designs are fairly typical and show these gradations very clearly.[125] They range from a 'small house, to be built near town for use of a tradesman' and with a frontage of about 40 feet, through a 'country house 85 feet in front' and a villa some 147 feet across, to a 'mansion for a person of quality', which was 177 by 96 feet. These differences in size are underpinned by a similar variation in ornamentation and, just as telling, in the internal arrangement of rooms. The plain front of the small house is relieved only by a projecting bay in the centre; inside are just two parlours, a kitchen and pantries, with four bedrooms and a single dressing room above. The country house enjoys modest wings and an ornamented main entrance and the greater space allows for more specialist rooms: a library, eating parlour and withdrawing room for the family and a servants' hall, kitchen, pantries and washhouse for the servants, all with separate access outside; upstairs, there are seven bedrooms and two dressing rooms, with separate access via a back staircase. Up another notch, and Crunden offered the prospective owner a broadly neo-Palladian pile with a portico entrance and substantial wings containing stable and coach houses on one side, and a laundry, bake house and storeroom on the other. On the ground floor of the main block, we find the kitchen, steward's room, butler's and housekeeper's apartments and so on. Above these, on the principal floor, are a breakfast room, dining room, withdrawing room and library, along with the principal bedroom and dressing room. Up a further flight of stairs are another drawing room, seven bedrooms and two dressing rooms. Finally, the mansion has external columns along the first floor, an ornamental balustrade and a large marble hall. Inside, the extra space gives scope for considerable room specialisation and an arrangement that broadly matches the triple system deployed by Blondel in his design for a *maison de plaisance*.[126] Along the front of the house, Crunden placed the large marble hall with an anteroom and parlour on either side; at the back of the house were the more formal public rooms—a circular saloon, linked to the marble hall via a 'grand staircase' and flanked by a dancing room and a withdrawing room. Down one side of the house was a statue and picture gallery comprised of three rooms and down the other were the gentleman's and lady's libraries linked by the principal library.

Similar distinctions can be seen in the designs offered by Halfpenny, Plaw, Laing and dozens of other architects. In all of them, the extra space afforded by bigger houses offered the convenience and comfort of specialised rooms and suites organised by function and/or relative privacy. Such considerations were in the mind of Elizabeth Dryden when she was searching for a suitable London house following the inheritance of the Canons Ashby estate by her son Henry, with whom she had a very poor relationship. In January 1819, she expressed a desire for a 'comfortable house in town', but later refined and amplified this considerably.[127] April saw her writing to her sister-in-law, Mrs. Steele, asking for her to seek out 'a moderate residence with a good garden', preferably on Gower Street. In June, she itemised her requirements as: 'a good sized House with garden & backhouse & stables adjoining; the House three rooms on a floor or light Closet at least . . . I want also a large dining Parlour many feet long'. Comfort clearly meant a good amount of space, both inside the house and in terms of outbuildings, as this afforded convenience and bolstered her status. Indeed, she later added that a coach house and stables were 'indispensible as I mean to drive my own horses'.[128] At the same time, she was concerned with location, echoing the snobbishness of the *Beau Monde* nearly 100 years earlier identified by Hannah Greig.[129] One house was rejected because it was in 'the worst part of Gower Street', but her prejudices were often framed in terms of her health: Gower Street, Conran Street and Tavistock Square were places where the air would be good—they were, of course, also desirable though not exclusive neighbourhoods.[130] Significantly, there is no mention of the particular physical features that are generally seen as defining physical comfort and discussed in the following chapters, but she was happy to reject possible houses as 'much too small', suggesting that her ideals for comfortable town life revolved status as well as warmth, cleanliness and sociability.

What made Elizabeth's ideal house comfortable was therefore linked with what it would communicate about her and her social standing as well as what it might offer in terms of physical well-being. But not everyone felt comfortable in expressing their status through grand and convenient housing. In 1850, at the very end of the period under focus in this book, the author Elizabeth Gaskell wrote to her friend Eliza Fox about the house that she and her husband—a Unitarian minister in Manchester—had recently acquired at the southern edge of the town. She was clearly excited, exclaiming that 'we've got a house. Yes! We *really* have'. But then came her reticence: 'And if I had neither conscience nor prudence I should be delighted, for it certainly is a beauty'. The problem was that she felt it too grand and too expensive—an unwarranted extravagance when there was so much poverty all around her. This, she explained, was:

> the haunting of me; at least one of my 'Mes', for I have a great number, and that's the plague. One of my mes is, I do believe, a true Christian . . . another of my mes is a wife and mother, and highly delighted at the delight of everyone else in the house . . . Then again I've another self with a full taste for beauty and convenience which is pleased on its own account.[131]

The convenience of the large house outweighed her doubts and the problems created by taking a house that was a little beyond their means— Roger North's advice about always allowing more than is strictly necessary was clearly easier for those of considerable means. Writing to another friend in September the following year, Elizabeth confessed that 'Our house is proving rather too expensive for us' and that they were not going to furnish the drawing room because of the need to be economical. Nonetheless, the house offered the family the great benefit of space, it being 'such an addition to the children's health and happiness to have plenty of room'.[132]

Conclusions

Elizabeth Gaskell was unusual in struggling over the rights and wrongs of taking a large and convenient house, but her weighing up of status, taste, convenience and economy was far more common. We can see this in the writings of Roger North and the improvements rendered at Stoneleigh Abbey, Canons Ashby and many other houses. It is also apparent in Humphrey Repton's *Sketches and Hints on Landscape Gardening* (1794) where he focuses on the need to balance aesthetics with practicalities:

> I may here observe, that it is unnecessary to retain the Gothic character within the mansion, at least not farther than the hall, as it would subject such buildings to much inconvenience; for since modern improvement has added glass sashed windows to the ancient Grecian and Roman architecture, in like manner the inside of a Gothic building may, with the same propriety, avail itself of modern comforts and convenience.[133]

For Repton, then, aesthetic compromise was both necessary and desirable to achieve domestic comfort; but the focus was on the internal spaces of the house. We have seen how architects across Europe were increasingly attentive to such concerns and how their shifting sensibilities tuned into the changing requirements of elite householders for more flexible and rational arrangements of space, built around domestic routines and sociability rather than simply the stylistic dictates of aesthetics and taste. This shift involved the growing specialisation of room use, from Roger North's private parlour to the boudoirs of French chateaux, but above all the reorganisation of space and the growing deployment of corridors and back stairs. These articulated different flows through the house and, as John Bold puts it, formed 'enabling devices in the pursuit of convenience, comfort and privacy'.[134]

Privacy was by no means a new ideal and can be found in the closet or cabinet as a space for devotion, private study or intimate meetings; but its spread to many different parts of the house was characteristics of the age. Importantly, it meant not just the spatial separation of servants but also the creation of rooms and routes that were for family use, and the creation of spaces for personal privacy. This was perhaps most widespread in the emergence of the dressing room as a place of escape and of social intimacy, not only furnished for the kind of tête-a-tête enjoyed by Mary Delany but also equipped for writing and sometimes—in a throwback to earlier cabinets—for collections of china or knick-knacks. In some ways, the villa formed an extension of this: a private space for self and intimate friends—away from unwanted visitors and affording psychological as well as material comfort.

Of course, convenience did not march unopposed across domestic life and architectural treatises. Both elite householders and their architects remained concerned with what the house said about taste, status and wealth. When these were successfully combined with rational and convenient arrangements of space, the result was lauded, as we saw in Mary

Delany's praise of Cornbury, with its perfect marriage of convenience, elegance and magnificence. Yet they did not always work together. This was partly due to the constraints of external aesthetics, but also because of the difficulties of keeping the large rooms, lengthy corridors and multiple staircases of the large house warm and well illuminated.

Notes

1. See John Archer, *The Literature of British Domestic Architecture, 1715–1842* (Cambridge, MA: MIT Press, 1985), 33–118; Dale Townshend, 'Convenience, Utility and Comfort in British Architecture of the Long Eighteenth Century', in Jon Stobart (ed.), *The Comforts of Home in Western Europe, 1700–1900* (London: Bloomsbury, 2020), 19–38.
2. Judith Lewis, 'When a House Is Not a Home: Elite English Women and the Eighteenth-Century Country House', *Journal of British Studies*, 48 (2009), 342–3; Mark Girouard, *Life in the English Country House: a Social and Architectural History* (New Haven: Yale University Press, 1978), 154.
3. Samuel Johnson, *A Dictionary of the English Language*, vol. 2 (London, 1755–56).
4. David Hume, *A Treatise of Human Nature: Being an Attempt to Introduce the Experimental Method of Reasoning into Moral Subjects*, vol. 3 (London: John Noon, 1739–40), 154–5. My thanks to Dale Townshend for this reference.
5. Sarah Chauncey Woolsey (ed.), *The Autobiography and Correspondence of Mrs Delany*, vol. 2 (Boston: Roberts Brothers, 1879), 339: Mary Delany to Anne Dewes, 30 October 1746.
6. John Crowley, *The Invention of Comfort: Sensibilities and Design in Early-Modern Britain and Early America* (Baltimore: Johns Hopkins University Press, 2001); Dorian Gerhold, 'London's Suburban Villas and Mansions, 1660–1830', *The London Journal*, 34:3 (2009), 233–63; Ian Gow, 'The Edinburgh Villa Revisited: Function Not Form', in Dana Arnold (ed.), *The Georgian Villa* (Stroud: Sutton, 1996), 144–55.
7. William Halfpenny, *New and Complete System of Architecture* (1749). Similar sentiments are expressed by William Chambers in *A Treatise on Civil Architecture* (London, 1759) in which he argued that 'Architecture, by furnishing Men with convenient habitations, procures them that ease of body, and vigour of mind, which are necessary for inventing and improving Arts' (p. ii).
8. Hans-Georg Lippert, 'Das Haus in Architekturtraktaten zwischen 1450 und 1950', in Joachim Eibach and Inken Schmidt-Voges (eds.), *Das Haus In Der Geschichte Europas* (Köln: Böhlau, 2015), 703; Bo Vahlne, *Frihetstidens inredningar på Stockholms Slott: Om bekvämlighetens och skönhetens nivåer* (Stockholm: Balkong Förlag, 2012), 23–8. My thanks to Johanna Ilmakunnas and especially Cristina Prytz for highlighting some of the early Swedish and German literature on architecture, referenced here in the following footnotes.
9. Henry Wotton, *The Elements of Architecture* (London, 1624), 1; Joseph Furttenbach, *Architectura Civilis* (Ulm, 1628); Joseph Furttenbach, *Architectura Privata* (Ulm, 1641); Salomon de Bray and Cornelis Danckerts, *Architectura moderna ofte Bouwinge van onsen tyt* (Amsterdam, 1631).
10. Peter Thornton, *Authentic Decor: The Domestic Interior, 1620–1920* (London: Weidenfeld and Nicolson, 1985), 17, 48–50.

11. Konrad Ottenheym and Krista De Jonge (eds.), *The Low Countries at the Crossroads: Netherlandish Architecture as an Export Product in Early Modern Europe (1480–1680)* (Tournhout: Brepols, 2013), 220.
12. G. Lindahl, 'En arkitektkarriär i maktens följe', in M. Snickare (ed.), *Tessin: Nicodemus Tessin d.y. Kunglig arkitekt och visionär* (Stockholm: Nationalmuseum, 2002), 12.
13. Furttenbach, *Architectura Civilis*, prefaces; Nicolas Tessin, *Observationer angående så wähl pubiqve som priuate huus byggnaders starkheet, bekqwämligheet och skiönheet, in rättade, efter wår Swänska climat och oeconomie* (republished, Stockholm: Byggfölaget, 2002), 44–5. My thanks to Cristina Prytz for this reference.
14. C. Wijnblad, *Ritningar på fyratio våningshus* (Stockholm 1755). For further discussion of this and the work of Carl Hårleman, see Johanna Ilmakunnas, 'Northern Comfort and Discomfort: Spaces and Objects in Swedish Country Houses, c.1740–1800', in Jon Stobart (ed.), *The Comforts of Home in Western Europe, 1700–1900* (London: Bloomsbury, 2020), 46–53.
15. Carl Gustaf Tessin, *Framledne riks-rådet, m.m. grefve Carl Gustaf Tessins dagbok, 1757* (Stockholm: Gustaf Adolf Montgomery, 1824), 126: 'aldrig bygger sina rum *à rez de chaussée*. . . vår snö, vår kyla, vår vätska, gör nedra våningen gemenlingen'. My thanks to Cristina Prytz for translating this passage.
16. Howard Colvin and John Newman (eds.), *Of Building: Roger North's Writings on Architecture* (Oxford: Oxford University Press, 1981), 62; Northamptonshire Record Office (NRO), H(K) 183, correspondence between Scattergood and Hanbury, early eighteenth century, 122.
17. Henry Home, Lord Kames, *Elements of Criticism*, vol. 3 (London, 1762), 327. For a fuller discussion of Kames's writing, see Townshend, 'Convenience, Utility and Comfort'.
18. Alexander Gerard, *An Essay on Taste* (London, 1759), 38. These sentiments were echoed in Homes, *Elements of Criticism*, vol. 3, 326.
19. Thornton, *Authentic Decor*, 50–1.
20. Home, *Elements of Criticism*, vol. 3, 322.
21. William Halfpenny, *Rural Architecture in the Chinese Taste* (1750); William Halfpenny, *Rural Architecture in the Gothic Taste* (1752); Halfpenny, *New and Complete System of Architecture*; John Crunden, *Convenient and Ornamental Architecture* (London, 1767).
22. See Peter N. Lindfield, *Georgian Gothic: Medievalist Architecture, Furniture and Interiors, 1730–1840* (Woodbridge: Boydell, 2016).
23. Home, *Elements of Criticism*, vol. 3, 349.
24. William Gilpin, *Observations on the Western Parts of England* (London, 1798), 127.
25. Lindfield, *Georgian Gothic*, 144–5.
26. Horace Walpole, *Description of the Villa of Mr Horace Walpole* (London, 1784), iii.
27. On the latter, see Aurélien Davrius, *Jacques-François Blondel, architecte des Lumières* (Paris: Classiques Garnier, 2018).
28. These are both reproduced in Colvin and Newman, *Of Building*, from which quotes are taken.
29. Colvin and Newman, *Of Building*, 89.
30. Leonhard Christoph Sturm, *Vollständige Anweisung Innerer Austheilung der Gebäude* (Augsburg, 1720), 3. My thanks to Cristina Prytz for her translation.
31. Colvin and Newman, *Of Building*, 53.
32. Colvin and Newman, *Of Building*, 89, 28.

33. Rosie MacArthur, 'Material Culture and Consumption on an English Estate: Kelmarsh Hall, 1687–1845' (Unpublished PhD thesis, University of Northampton, 2010), 181.
34. Northamptonshire Record Office (NRO), H(K) 183, correspondence between Scattergood and Hanbury, early eighteenth century, 123.
35. Girouard, *English Country House*, 250.
36. C. Bryun Andrews and John Beresford (eds.), *The Torrington Diaries: Containing the Tours Through England and Wales of the Hon. John Byng (later Fifth Viscount Torrington) Between the Years 1781 and 1794*, vol. 4 (London: Eyre and Spottiswoode, 1934), Part I, p. 147, July 6, 1784.
37. Jane Austen, *Sanditon* (1817; Oxford: Oxford University Press, 1998), 335.
38. Johann Wolfgang von Goethe, *Die Wahlverwandtschaften* (Tübingen, 1809), 138: ' "*Ich würde", sagte Ottilie, indem sie den Finger auf die höchste Fläche der Anhöhe setzte, "das Haus hieher bauen. Man sähe zwar das Schloß nicht, den es wird von dem Wäldchen bedeckt; aber man befände sich auch dafür wie in einer anderen und neuen Welt, indem zugleich das Dorf und alle Wohnungen verborgen wären. Die Aussicht auf die Teiche, nach der Mühle, auf der Höhen, in der Gebirge, nach dem Lande zu ist außerordentlich schön; ich habe es im Vorbeigehen bemerkt"* '.
39. Goethe, *Die Wahlverwandtschaften*, 138–9: '*Das Schloß haben die Alten mit Vernuft hieher gebaut, denn es liegt geschützt vor den Winden und nah an allen täglichen Bedürfnissen; ein Gebäude hingegen, mehr zum geselligen Aufenthalt als zur Wohnung, wird sich dorthin recht wohl schicken und in der guten Jahrzeit die angenemsten Stunden gewähren*'.
40. Colvin and Newman, *Of Building*, 64.
41. David Laing, *Hints for Dwellings* (London, 1800), vi.
42. Colvin and Newman, *Of Building*, 69.
43. Colvin and Newman, *Of Building*, 69.
44. These plans are reproduced in Thornton, *Authentic Decor*, 50; Joan DeJean, *The Age of Comfort: When Paris Discovered Casual and the Modern Home Began* (New York: Bloomsbury, 2009), 53.
45. Vahlne, *Frihetstidens inredningar på Stockholms Slott*, 24–5.
46. Johann Friedrich Penther, *Ausführliche Anleitung zur bürgerlichen Bau-Kunst* (Augsburg, 1745), 3–4.
47. Chauncey Woolsey, *Correspondence of Mrs Delany*, vol. 1, 339: Mary Delany to Anne Dewes, 30 October 1746.
48. DeJean, *Age of Comfort*, 50–1. See also, Mark Girouard, *Life in the French Country House* (London: Cassell & Co., 2000), 129–45; Aurélien Davrius, 'Masters and Servants: Parallel Worlds in Blondel's *maisons de plaisance*', in Jon Stobart (ed.), *The Comforts of Home in Western Europe, 1700–1900* (London: Bloomsbury, 2020), 39–44.
49. See Davrius, 'Masters and Servants'.
50. Wijnblad, *Ritningar på fyratio våningshus*.
51. Ilmakunnas, 'Northern Comfort and Discomfort', 47.
52. Halfpenny, *New and Compleat System of Architecture*, Plate 17.
53. John Crunden, *Convenient and Ornamental*, Plates 13, 41–2.
54. See MacArthur, 'Material Culture and Consumption', 95–112.
55. MacArthur, 'Material Culture and Consumption', 137–44.
56. John Bold, 'Privacy and the Plan', in John Bold and Edward Chaney (eds.), *English Architecture, Public and Private: Essays for Kerry Downes* (London: Hambledon Press, 1993), 115.
57. Chauncey Woolsey, *Correspondence of Mrs Delany*, vol. 1, 350: Mary Delany to Anne Dewes, no date, believed to be 11 July 1747.

58. Bold, 'Privacy and the Plan', 115. Marilyn Palmer, 'The Social Impact of Technological Innovation in the English Country House', in Peter Barnwell and Marilyn Palmer (eds.), *Country House Technology* (London: Paul Watkin Publishing, 2012), 6–9.

59. NRO, D(CA) 904, Schedule of Furniture . . . of the Mansion of Canons Ashby, 1819.

60. For more detailed discussion of the furnishing of these rooms, see Jon Stobart, 'Inventories and the Changing Furnishings of Canons Ashby, Northamptonshire, 1717–1819', *Regional Furniture*, XXVII (2003), 1–43.

61. Girouard, *French Country House*, 138–9.

62. Thornton, *Authentic Decor*, 139.

63. Girouard, *French Country House*, 149–51.

64. Colvin and Newman, *Of Building*, 129.

65. Colvin and Newman, *Of Building*, 137.

66. See Dejean, *Age of Comfort*, 52–3.

67. Colvin and Newman, *Of Building*, 138.

68. Colvin and Newman, *Of Building*, 139.

69. See, for example, John Plaw, *Sketches for Country Houses, Villas and Rural Dwellings* (London, 1800), 5.

70. Colvin and Newman, *Of Building*, 139.

71. Colvin and Newman, *Of Building*, 139.

72. Chauncey Woolsey, *Correspondence of Mrs Delany*, vol. 1, 385: Mary Delany to Anne Dewes, 6 October 1750.

73. Girouard, *French Country House*, 139.

74. Girouard, *English Country House*, 135–6.

75. Quoted in Geoffrey Tyack, *Warwickshire Country Houses* (Chichester: Phillimore, 1994), 167.

76. Andor Gomme, 'Abbey into Palace: A Lesser Wilton?', in Robert Bearman (ed.), *Stoneleigh Abbey: The House, Its Owners, Its Lands* (Stratford-upon-Avon: Shakespeare Birthplace Trust, 2004), 83.

77. See Gomme, 'Abbey into Palace'.

78. Jon Stobart and Mark Rothery, *Comfort and the Country House* (Oxford: Oxford University Press, 2016), 63–6.

79. Shakespeare Central Library and Archives (SCLA), DR671/33/25: General Plan of the House. See also DR671/33/11, The Chamber Plan.

80. Quoted in the National Trust, *Kedleston Hall* (London: National Trust, 1999), 11.

81. Colvin and Newman, *Of Building*, 69.

82. Quoted in the National Trust, *Kedleston Hall*, 4.

83. On privacy and the home, see Amanda Vickery, 'An Englishman's Home Is His Castle? Thresholds, Boundaries and Privacies in the Eighteenth-Century London Home', *Past and Present*, 199:1 (2008), 274–301.

84. See Girouard, *English Country House*, 126–8, 144, 154–60.

85. Girouard, *French Country House*, 147–61.

86. Quoted in Girouard, *French Country House*, 148.

87. Girouard, *French Country House*, 153–5.

88. For the full poem, see http://spenserians.cath.vt.edu/TextRecord.php?action=GET&textsid=34965.

89. Anon., *Letters of Miss Riversdale* (London, 1803), 92.

90. James Collett-White (ed.), *Inventories of Bedfordshire Country Houses, 1714–1830* (Bedford: Bedford Historical Record Society, 1995), 40–1.

91. Collett-White, *Inventories of Bedfordshire Country Houses*, 54–5.

92. Alice Clark (ed.), *Gleanings from an Old Portfolio Containing Some Correspondence Between Lady Louisa Stuart and her Sister, Caroline, Countess*

of Portarlington and Other Friends and Relatives, vol. 2 (Edinburgh, 1895), 102: Lady Louisa Stuart to Lady Caroline Dawson, 2 April 1788.

93. SCLA, DR18/3/47/52/15, bill from Thomas Burnett; DR18/5/4408, bill from William Gomm. For further discussion of the nature of these bedchambers, see Jon Stobart, 'Making an English Country House: Taste and Luxury in the Furnishing of Stoneleigh Abbey, 1763–1765', in Johanna Ilmakunnas and Jon Stobart (eds.), *A Taste for Luxury in Early Modern Europe* (London: Bloomsbury, 2017), 143–60.

94. Collett-White, *Inventories of Bedfordshire Country Houses*, 61–3.

95. Alice Houblon, *The Houblon Family: Its History and Times*, vol. 2 (Edinburgh: Archibald Constable & Co., 1907), 119.

96. Chauncey Woolsey, *Correspondence of Mrs Delany,* vol. 1, 457: Mary Delany to Mrs Dawson, 24 November 1754.

97. Fanny Burney, *Evelina: The History of a Young Lady's Entrance into the World* (1778, London: Harrison, 1861), 153.

98. For a fuller discussion of relationship between chinoiserie, gender, taste and social status, see Stacey Sloboda, *Chinoiserie: Commerce and Critical Ornament in Eighteenth-Century England* (Manchester: Manchester University Press, 2014), 108–58.

99. Emily Climenson (ed.), *Passages from the Diaries of Mrs Philip Lybbe Powys* (London: Longmans, Green and Co., 1899), 147–8.

100. Chauncey Woolsey, *Autobiography and Correspondence of Mrs Delany*, vol. 1, 164–5: Mary Delany to Mrs Anne Granville, 29 December 1738.

101. Jane Austen, *Northanger Abbey* (1817; Oxford: Oxford University Press, 1998), 137.

102. Arthur Turberville, *A History of Welbeck Abbey and Its Owners*, vol. 1 (London: Routledge, 1938), 399.

103. G. Selling, *Svenska Herrgårdshem under 1700-talet* (Stockholm: Stockholm College, 1937), 110–38 (125). My thanks to Cristina Prytz for this reference.

104. Deborah Howard, 'The Italian Renaissance Villa: The Reconciliation of Nature and Artifice', in Dana Arnold (ed.), *The Georgian Villa* (Stroud: Alan Sutton, 1996), 1–10. See also David Coffin, *The Villa Life of Renaissance Rome* (Princeton, NJ: Princeton University Press, 1979).

105. For fuller discussion, see Yme Kuiper, 'The Rise of the Country House in the Dutch Republic: Beyond Johan Huizinga's Narrative of Dutch Civilisation in the Seventeenth Century', in Jon Stobart and Andrew Hann (eds.), *The Country House: Material Culture and Consumption* (Swindon: Historic England, 2016), 11–23.

106. Quoted in Gerhold, 'London's Suburban Villas', 234.

107. Gerhold, 'London's Suburban Villas', 253–6.

108. For fuller discussion, see Jon Stobart, ' "So Agreeable and Suitable a Place": A Late Eighteenth-Century Suburban Villa', *Journal of Eighteenth-Century Studies* (2016), 89–102.

109. SCLA, DR671, Mary Leigh to Joseph Hill, 28 January 1792; quoted in Gerhold, 'London's Suburban Villas', 256.

110. SCLA, DR18/4/46, Inventory of china, 19 July 1806. The large quantities of china purchased from Josiah Wedgwood in the 1780s (SCLA, DR 18/5/5684) were presumably for use at Stoneleigh Abbey or less likely were moved between houses as Mary herself went from town to country for the summer months.

111. SCLA, DR18/4/47, plate sent down by Mr Hill from Grove House; SCLA DR18/5809.

112. SCLA, DR18/5/6125, bill from Thomas Watts, glazier; DR18/5/6126, bill from John Weston, plasterer; DR18/5/6130, bill from Joseph Naylor, painter; DR18/5/6129, bill from James Fisher, carpenter; SCLA18/5/6122— bill from Barnet & Mason, masons; DR18/5/6123, bill from M. Storer, plumber; DR18/5/6124, bill from Thomas Poole, bricklayer.

113. SCLA, DR18/31/656, Day Book for Grove House, 1793–98; SCLA, DR18/671, letter to Joseph Hill, 11 February 1791.

114. Gow, 'The Edinburgh Villa', 146–7.

115. Johann Wolfgang von Goethe, *The Complete Works of Johann Wolfgang von Goethe*, vol. 3 (New York: International Publishing Company, 1901), 15–16.

116. Crowley, *Invention of Comfort*, 203–29; John Crowley, 'From Luxury to Comfort and Back Again: Landscape Architecture and the Cottage in Britain and America', in Maxine Berg and Elizabeth Eger (eds.), *Luxury in the Eighteenth Century: Debates, Desires and Delectable Goods* (Basingstoke: Palgrave Macmillan, 2003), 135–50.

117. William Fuller Pocock, *Architectural Designs for Rustic Cottages, Picturesque Dwellings, Villas,* & *C.* (London, 1807), 8–9.

118. Jane Austen, *Sense and Sensibility* (1811; Oxford: Oxford University Press, 1970), 219. For a fuller discussion of this idealisation of the cottage, see Adrian Tinniswood, *Life in the English Country Cottage* (London: Weidenfeld Nicholson, 1995), 104–33.

119. SCLA, DR18/671, Mary Leigh to Joseph Hill, 27 March 1791.

120. Nathaniel Kent, *Hints to Gentlemen of Landed Property* (London: J. Dodsley, 1775), 228. For a fuller discussion of the comfort of the labourer's cottage, see Townshend, 'Convenience, Utility and Comfort', 25–32.

121. John Wood, *A Series of Plans, for Cottages or Habitations of the Labourer, Either in Husbandry, or the Mechanic Arts, Adapted as Well to Towns, as to the Country* (Bath: Hooper and Keenes, 1788), Plate XXVII.

122. Colvin and Newman, *Of Building*, 31. The idea of the comfort of a house being linked with status is something that we return to in chapter 4.

123. Laing, *Hints for Dwellings*, v.

124. By the late eighteenth century, there was a growing move in England to make workers' cottages more comfortable which linked to arguments about productivity as well as decency. See Townshend, 'Convenience, Utility and Comfort'.

125. Crunden, *Convenient and Ornamental Architecture*.

126. Davrius, 'Masters and Servants'.

127. NRO, D(CA)/361, Elizabeth Dryden to Mrs Steele, 8 January 1819.

128. NRO, D(CA)/361, Elizabeth Dryden to Mrs Steele, [no date] April 1819; 2 June 1819; [no date] November 1819.

129. Hannah Greig, *The Beau Monde* (Oxford: Oxford University Press, 2013), 37–45.

130. NRO, D(CA)/361, Elizabeth Dryden to Mrs Steele, [no date] October 1819, [no date] November 1819.

131. John Chapple and Arthur Pollard (eds.), *The Letters of Mrs Gaskell* (Manchester: Manchester University Press, 1966), 107–8, April 1850, 107–8.

132. Chapple and Pollard, *Letters of Mrs Gaskell*, 159, 1 September 1851.

133. Humphry Repton, *Sketches and Hints on Landscape Gardening* (London: Printed for W. Bulmer and Co., 1794), 15.

134. Bold, 'Privacy and the Plan', 115.

2 Warmth and Light
Technologies of Comfort

In the working-class homes depicted in Elizabeth Gaskell's 1848 novel, *Mary Barton*, physical comforts are in short supply. When they do appear, they are basic and visceral: coming from her cellar dwelling, the old washerwoman, Alice Wilson, basks in 'the delicious glow of the fire, the bright light that revelled in every corner of the room, the savoury smells, the comfortable sounds of a boiling kettle, and the hissing, frizzling ham'.[1] It is bodily comfort that dominates this vision of domestic bliss: food, drink and especially warmth and light. These are basic human requirements but made the domestic environment more comfortable when experienced at an enhanced level. Conscious attempts to make such improvements are frequently highlighted by historians as symbols of an increasing prioritisation of physical ease in the eighteenth century.[2] This had two closely related elements: the desire for houses to be lighter and especially warmer, and the ability to render them so. In analysing broader changes to domestic material culture and consumption, Daniel Roche emphasises the growing expectations of householders. He quotes the famous dramatist and writer, Sebastien Mercier, who noted that:

> Our fathers, more thrifty or more inured to cold, did hardly anything to keep warm. Three fires, including the one in the kitchen, were enough for a house in which resided eighteen or twenty masters, and what masters! Men who occupied the highest posts in the state. With their legs enclosed in a bearskin they braved with equal courage the sharpest cold and the Royal Academy of Architecture.[3]

Whilst no doubt overplayed for rhetorical effect, this suggests a clear shift in the level of warmth—of comfort—that householders might expect to enjoy. This cultural change was matched by improvements made to the efficiency and effectiveness of fireplaces, stoves and lamps: innovations that offered technological solutions to age-old problems. Viewing comfort in this way means taking a functionalist approach: cold and darkness were problems that could be addressed through the application of

DOI: 10.4324/9781003206361-4

science, and comfort was conceived and addressed as a product of (new) domestic technologies.[4]

The marrying of shifting priorities and developing technology lies at the heart of John Crowley's argument that comfort was reconceptualised or (re)invented in the eighteenth century. The 'enlightened comfort' of stoves and lamps was all about scientific endeavour harnessed to practical concerns.[5] Yet his analysis focuses on what was rendered possible by men like Franklin and Argand, rather than the uptake of the new or enhanced technologies they created. In this context, country-house owners are particularly important: they had the money to lay out on such things and a strong incentive, particularly in terms of the perishing cold that bedevilled many grand houses, with their large rooms and draughty corridors. Writing in the winter of 1695, the Marquise de Sévigné, for example, complained that her inkwell was frozen and that she found holding the quill difficult because her fingers were numb with cold.[6] Nearly 150 years later, Barbara Charlton wrote in her memoirs about the cold and dampness at Hesleyside in Northumberland. She noted that 'the long passages had no heat, the outside doors were never shut, the hall and corridors were paved with flagstones', whilst the windows on the grand staircase were so warped with damp that they 'contrived to make the downstairs space a cave of icy blasts'.[7]

This chapter attempts to bring together technological possibility and the priorities and actions of country-house owners by assessing the desire for and importance accorded to improved heat and light, and the ways in which this was addressed through the deployment of (new) technologies of heating and lighting. It begins by exploring the problem faced by householders—that their dwellings were cold and dark—and then traces the development and uptake of technologies that sought to mitigate these discomforts. In focusing on England, the discussion is also attentive to the ways in which these varied across Europe and how this related to the local and cultural milieu. Taking the perspective of the householder wherever possible, the chapter also examines how contemporaries viewed both the problems of cold and darkness and their technological solution in terms of comfort and conversely the extent to which their domestic comfort was defined in terms of warmth and light. Building on this, it emphasises that improvements to physical comfort were not purely technological: sets of related goods helped to make rooms warmer and better lit, from screens and carpets to polished sconces. Importantly, as well as providing functional enhancements, these offered the opportunity for displays of taste and wealth. Comfort and gentility went hand in hand. Woven through this discussion of technology and its deployment is a concern with people's reactions to and feelings about the merits (or otherwise) of new technologies and about the issues they addressed and sometimes the problems they created. Determining the right level of warmth and light and how this could best be achieved and enjoyed were human judgements, impacted by cultural norms and systems of taste.

The Comforts of a Warm and Well-Lit Room

For most householders, being physically comfortable meant being warm. Writing from Strawberry Hill in May 1774, Horace Walpole complained that:

> We are almost freezing here in midst of beautiful verdure with a profusion of blossoms and flowers: but I keep good fires, and seem to feel warm weather while I look through the window, for the way to insure summer in England is to have it framed and glazed in a comfortable room.[8]

A decade or so later, he recommended to Hannah More that she remove herself to her house in Richmond 'where you will as comfortable as in a hot-house'.[9] Both here and in his own situation, the warmth of the room gave protection from the cold weather and afforded comfort. This contrast between warmth and cold; inside and outside is echoed in the sentiments expressed by Mr. Elton in Jane Austen's *Emma*. The group is on its way to a house party, travelling in a carriage whilst the snow falls outside. Mr. Elton first commends the travelling arrangements, exclaiming: 'What an excellent device . . . the use of a sheep-skin for carriages. How very comfortable they make it; impossible to feel the cold with such contrivances . . . One is so fenced and guarded from the weather, that not a breath can find its way unpermitted'. Seeing the weather deteriorate, he then recalls a time when he was snowed in at a friend's house and looks forward to what awaits them at Mr. and Mrs. Weston's: 'We are sure of excellent fires . . . and everything in the greatest comfort'.[10]

For Walpole and Austen, fireplaces were the key source of heat. Indeed, most English country-house owners would have agreed with the poor milliner Mary Barton in thinking that her home was 'dingy and comfortless' without the 'dumb familiar home–friend, a fire'.[11] However, the technology of domestic heating took divergent paths in different parts of Europe depending on the availability of fuel, the climate and regional traditions. Concerns were regularly voiced about the effectiveness of the chimney in drawing up smoke and of the fire in heating the room. Roger North hints at the extent of published material in his treatise *Of Building* (1698), in which he determines not to 'medle in the common rules about chimneys extant in books'.[12] His chief concern is with the aesthetics and practicalities of situating on the fireplace in the corner (good in small rooms) or along the wall (preferable if space permits). In either case, proximity to the fire was crucial in keeping warm, with the added problem that open fires meant being 'roasted in front while freezing behind'—a complaint made by Franz Keslar when marketing his stove in the early decades of the seventeenth century.[13] Despite this, the fireplace remained vital in warming British houses well into the nineteenth century. Moreover, they were central to the ways in which comfort was conceived. In January 1812, Richard Aldworth Griffin wrote of Audley End in Essex that: 'We lived remarkably comfortable, dining & sitting in the Eating room where we had a capital fire with Carpet & curtains'.[14]

In northern and central Europe, enclosed and free-standing stoves were the norm by the eighteenth century. The Germans were particularly noted for their use of stoves. Writing to Walpole from a snowy Florence in December 1767, Horace Mann observed that 'the Germans have brought their climate with them, and say that they find no difference from that of Vienna, excepting that they are starved here from want of the comfortable stoves which they left there'.[15] In Austria and Switzerland, where the oldest models date from the twelfth century, stoves were more often made from brick and mortar and covered by tiles. These could be substantial structures and later spread to the Netherlands and elsewhere (Figure 2.1). North of the Alps, smaller cast iron stoves became increasingly common in the sixteenth century, the oldest models (from the 1490s) being box shaped, made from iron plates.[16] These cast iron stoves were generally more expensive than tiled stoves, which limited their spread down the social hierarchy before the nineteenth century.[17] They gave out an intense heat and could warm a room quickly, and their modest size meant that they could be moved between rooms or orangeries. By 1700 they were common not only across central Europe but also in Denmark and Norway.

Despite these attractions, it was the tiled stove that came to dominate in Sweden and also in eastern Europe. This comprised a tiled-covered masonry construction that stored heat from burning wood. In contrast with iron stoves, which became very hot and cooled quickly, the heat in tiled stoves radiated for a long time and at a fairly constant temperature, making it in effect a storage heater. The result was a more ambient temperature over a longer period of time and throughout the room, removing the necessity to huddle around the fire.[18] The first rooms to be fitted with tiled stoves instead of open fireplaces were often bedrooms, studies and libraries: larger country houses usually had their own supply of firewood and their owners often preferred to keep their open fireplace in the more public rooms. Regions where firewood was sparse often saw the widest deployment of tiled stoves, but personal experience was also important. The crown princess, Lovisa Ulrika, born in Berlin in 1720 and sister to Frederick the Great of Prussia, was accustomed to the tiled stoves of her homeland and insisted on having them installed in the new royal castle in central Stockholm. By the time the royal family took up residence in 1754, there were no less than 150 tiled stoves in the palace.[19]

Figure 2.1 Jan Luyken, *Drie figuren warmen zich bij een kachel* (1711): Rijksmuseum, Amsterdam, RP-P-OB-45.646

Such profusion was also a mark of lighting in elite households. Crowley places great emphasis on the comfort and luxury of artificial lighting in the early-modern home, both in Britain and America. He argues that the public use of candles to create brightly lit environments gradually spread into the home from the theatre, assembly room and coffee house.[20] Lighting became a mark of elite domestic leisure and comfort: being able to sit into the evening reading, playing cards, making music or engaging in handicrafts required significant investment in candles and lamps which both lightened the gloom and signalled the wealth of the householder. The importance of illumination is apparent from the accounts kept in the 1750s by James Leigh and Caroline Brydges of Adlestrop in Gloucestershire.[21] Whilst stores of some foods (sugar and raisins, for example) were allowed to dwindle before being replenished, a stock of at least 92 lbs of candles was always maintained. These would have been carefully stored in a designated space, perhaps like the candle room at Stoneleigh Abbey, which in 1806 contained two large and one small oak candle chests, as well as a 'quantity of soap and candles'.[22]

The need to have a good supply of candles to hand underpins the importance of conserving and managing lighting, both as stocks of commodities and as an asset to be deployed in the house. Letter-writers were often struck with the illumination of houses for special entertainments. William Lower, in his translation of a French account of the visit of Charles II to Holland in the spring of 1660, wrote of the lavish illumination of Mauritshuis in The Hague for a banquet: 'four lusters or christal candlesticks, which with many other candlesticks, arms of silver, and a great number of torches, enlightened all the corners much better than the Sun could have done at midday'.[23] One hundred years later, Lady Shelburne wrote in similarly effusive terms about her new house which, when illuminated for guests 'look'd very fine as it was very much lighted up'.[24] The importance of illumination when entertaining guests is apparent from a preprinted invitation card sent from Lady Ailesbury to Horace Walpole in the 1750s (Figure 2.2). The text is framed by a tea kettle that

Figure 2.2 Invitation card from Lady Ailesbury, 1753 or 1759: Lewis Walpole Library, Folio 49 3585 leaf 14 Box 2 (Courtesy of The Lewis Walpole Library, Yale University)

promised polite refreshment and three freshly lit candles set in elaborate rococo holders that suggested a bright interior and a long evening.

In contrast, Walpole complained in a letter to Lady Ossory that he was 'forced on Saturday to light a candle at eleven in the morning . . . to read the newspapers'.[25] This was an uncomfortable situation in terms of cost and inconvenience, but not unusual. Interiors were generally dark, with a small number of candles or lamps creating particular qualities of light. The flickering flames brought out the rich textural qualities of fabrics and wood, the reflective qualities of gold thread or cut glass on clothing or fittings, and especially the gilding of furniture and frames. It brought out the visceral qualities of many novel goods which, Maxine Berg argues, formed part of their appeal to eighteenth-century consumers.[26] At Canons Ashby, the collection includes a dark velvet suit, probably belonging to Sir John Turner Dryden and dating from the 1780s/90s. Sewn onto the coat and breeches are numerous glass beads which hang loose at the bottom. Their movement as Sir John walked or danced would have caught, reflected and refracted the candlelight. Much the same was true of jewellery, the facetted presentation of gemstones again being designed to catch the light, as Marcia Pointon makes clear.[27] Mimi Hellman goes further, arguing that the jewellery worn by wealthy Parisian women not only accented their upper bodies and framed their faces but also shaped the ways in which people looked, the eye flitting between earrings and bodice ornaments, creating the 'shifting, oblique glances of decorous looking'.[28]

The limited pools of light which characterised most homes, especially in the evenings, are all too easily forgotten in an age of electric lighting, but contemporary paintings and engravings make clear that illumination was patchy even in the homes of the wealthy. An early seventeenth-century woodcut found in Johannes de Brune's *Emblemata of Zinnerwerck* shows a bedchamber at night in which a man stands holding a baby that has apparently woken, whilst his wife lies asleep in bed.[29] The scene is lit by a single candle on the hearth; it casts a pool of light leaving most of the room in the gloom, yet the convenience of the nightlight is apparent, allowing the father to deal with a child without stumbling around in the darkness. More conventional are a set of paintings by the eighteenth-century artist William Laquy, based on earlier paintings by Gerard Dou, dating from the 1660s (Figure 2.3).[30] One shows three people around a single candle engaged in writing on a small chalkboard and with a quill on paper. In the background are a second similar group and a woman holding a candle in her hand; a fourth candle stands in a lantern in the foreground. A similar contrast of light and dark is apparent in Richard Morton Paye's self-portrait, *The Artist in his Studio* (1783).[31] Paye is pictured at his desk, preparing an engraving, with a single candle the only source of light in an otherwise dark room.

In these examples, the inconvenience of the darkness is apparent from its contrast with the bright pool of candlelight. We might see a similar

Figure 2.3 William Laquy, *Allegory of Art Training* (c.1770)—detail: Rijksmuseum, Amsterdam, SK-A-2320-B

set of concerns in the paintings of the Swedish Pehr Hilleström (1732–1816) who portrayed a range of social gatherings and encounters at night. These allowed him to demonstrate his ability to manage light and dark, but they convey something of the intimacy created by candlelight. In *The Milliner*, for example, the retailer lays out some of her wares on a table and holds others in her hands (Figure 2.4). A candle on the table provides the only light in the room, but it allows the seated customer to assess the bonnet, feathers and ribbons that she is shown. The rest of the room is in the shadows, yet the gilding around the mirror and window

Figure 2.4 Pehr Hilleström, *The Milliner* (1770s): Nationalmuseum, Stockholm, CC BY-SA 4.0

frame sparkles in the candlelight, and the impression is one of intimacy rather than an inconvenience.[32] These ideas are taken further in the pendant pair, *Before the Ball* and *After the Ball* (1735) by Jean-François de Troy. The light is more diffuse, generated by candles on the table, on the chimneypiece and in sconces on the wall, and reflected in large mirrors and on numerous polished and gilded surfaces.[33] It creates a sumptuous yet intimate atmosphere which brings together the subjects of the painting as they prepare for and return from a masquerade ball. The relative darkness of the room behind them is still apparent but it serves to focus attention onto the main scene rather than suggest inconvenience born of economy. It also plays on the idea of concealment: what can be seen in the candlelight and what is hidden in the shadows. Yet, as Hellman argues, pools of candlelight brought not just intimacy but also threw bright light onto the features of those gathered around, making any gestures and expressions very visible.[34]

These lighting patterns and artistic concerns were not culturally specific: the same contrasts are brought out by the American artist, Henry Sargent, in his painting *The Tea Party* which depicts a social gathering in early nineteenth-century New York.[35] The room at the back of the painting is well lit, but that in the foreground is much darker, borrowing much of its light from its neighbour. It is full of people arranged in small groups, mostly engaged in conversation. Some sit or stand in pools of light created by four sets of candles, augmented by the light of the open fire; they are brought together by the light and separated from neighbouring groups by the shadows. Other groups occupy these darker spaces, which create a different kind of sociability in which facial expressions and gestures are more difficult to discern. In this contrasting world of revelation and concealment, it is far from clear where comfort—in the sense of social ease—can best be found.

The importance of candlelight as a focus for activity is shown clearly in a 1783 print after Daniel Dodd which depicts a large family gathered around a table at which their father is sat, reading to them by candlelight (Figure 2.5). It is also apparent in a series of sketches and paintings produced by John Harden, a contemporary of Sargent, many of which depict his family at home at Brathay Hall near Windermere in Westmorland. Harden was a talented amateur artist, well connected with the Lakeland poets. He gained some recognition for his paintings of village life, but it is his domestic scenes which are of most interest here.[36] Although the scenes themselves lack the sharp contrasts of light and dark, they make clear the importance of limited lighting in a small country house. In one, we see three women seated on a sofa and sewing; they share the light of two candles placed on a small table in front of them, whilst opposite a man sits on a stool, reading by the light of the fire, his foot resting on the grate. Another shows a different group around a table on which stands a single candle: two are reading letters and the others are sewing

Figure 2.5 Family sitting in a parlour (1783), after Daniel Dodd: British Museum, London, 1875, 0109.193 (© The Trustees of the British Museum)

or embroidering.[37] During a visit to Brathay Hall in 1806, John Constable sketched a similar domestic scene, with two men and two women grouped at a piano, their music making illuminated by a single candle which stands on the piano (Figure 2.6). Two things are important here. The first is that it was possible for several people to engage in a range of activities, even with the light provided by just one or two candles. Large amounts of light might have been desirable, especially when entertaining company, but everyday domestic sociability was possible without such extravagant illumination. The second is that the need for light drew

Figure 2.6 John Constable, *A Music Party at Brathay Hall* (1806): British Museum, London, 1896,0821.18 (© The Trustees of the British Museum)

people together around a table or the fire in a way that was sociable and often informal—a point to which we return in the next chapter.

Harden's homely pictures make clear that a single well-placed candle in a simple candlestick was no barrier to gentility in the home, despite Benjamin Franklin's association of artificial lighting with genteel domesticity. That said, Crowley confidently asserts that 'people wanted more light',[38] tracing this desire through improvements made to wicks and new forms of candle wax (most notably spermaceti, available from 1750) which were important in producing candles that burned more brightly and reliably. This forms part of the rhetoric of modernity associated with improved lighting. Marilyn Palmer and Ian West quote Joseph Swan, a pioneer in the use of electrical lighting, reminiscing that 'the days of my youth extend backwards to the dark ages, for I was born when the rushlight, the tallow dip or the solitary blaze of the hearth were common means of indoor lighting'.[39] Swan was born in 1828, by which time there were not only improved candles but also a wide variety of lamps available; yet he chose to remember rooms as dark and houses as unenlightened.

Managing Comfort: Choices and Costs

Making the country house warm and lit was clearly a challenge: it required investing time and money, and making choices between different forms of fuel, each of which brought its own benefits and problems. Wood was the traditional form of heating fuel, but the felling of trees for industrial and domestic hearths across Europe created periodic fuel crises and significant inflation in price. In Paris, for example, the annual consumption of wood doubled between 1669 and 1725, as did the cost: for a typical *hôtel* the annual fuel bill rose from 1,320 livres in the 1690s to a crippling 6,600 livres by the turn of the nineteenth century.[40] Supplies were often stretched and periodic crises led to raids on the woods of Vincennes and Boulogne.[41] Coal was advocated as an alternative, its merits as a fuel being outlined in detail by Jean-François Clement Morand in his 1774 *Les arts des mines*: it burned hotter and longer, and most fireplaces could be adapted relatively easily. Despite this, it remained relatively unimportant as a fuel source in Paris into the nineteenth century.[42] In contrast, coal was already widely used in British domestic hearths by the middle decades of the seventeenth century, prompted by the rapid destruction of forests for shipbuilding, housebuilding and domestic and industrial fuel. Coal was particularly important in London, to which large quantities were shipped from mines in north-east England, but country-house owners were by no means insulated from the switch to coal, despite being able to draw on supplies of wood from the estate. At Woburn Abbey in Bedfordshire, the accounts from the mid-seventeenth century show an annual consumption of between 200 and 260 sacks of charcoal and about 55 chaldrons of coal.[43] Assuming that they were measured using

London chaldron, this meant that the Duke of Bedford was burning somewhere around 78 tonnes of coal per year in addition to the charcoal and, no doubt, some wood from the estate. Over a century later, it took 64 wagon loads of coal each year to heat Golden Grove, a fairly modestly proportioned house in Carmarthenshire.[44]

Thermal comfort came at a price. Sir Roger Newdigate's accounts record his spending on fuel for his country house, Arbury Hall in Warwickshire, and his London house in Spring Gardens off Whitehall (Table 2.1). These show that the cost of heating his country house was roughly double that of keeping warm in his London residence—largely a product of the relative size of the two properties—and that his overall fuel bill rose through the third quarter of the eighteenth century before declining markedly from the later 1770s. It is difficult to tease out the reasons for the rise in spending on fuel. Inflation played a part, but Gregory Clark and David Jacks estimate that pithead prices rose fairly modestly during this period, from about 2s. 7d. per tonne in the 1750s to 3s. 2d. in the 1770s (an increase of approximately 20%).[45] Newdigate's growing outlay on coal must therefore reflect the consumption of greater quantities and therefore a desire to keep more rooms warmer, both at Arbury Hall and Spring Gardens, which both saw spending roughly double during this period. The subsequent decline was a direct result of Newdigate's own collieries becoming more productive as they were linked into the Coventry Canal. Using his own coal saved him the equivalent of the annual wages for his cook and five maids.[46] These savings were specific to Arbury Hall, to which the coal could be transported relatively easily; indeed, from 1778 onwards, the only outlay recorded under this heading in the accounts is for the carriage of coal. Spending on fuel in London remained steady and probably reflected a slight decline in the quantity of coal being consumed as prices continued to rise through the 1780s and

Table 2.1 Sir Roger Newdigate's spending on fuel, 1747–93

	1747–61		1762–77		1778–93	
	Total	*Annual*	*Total*	*Annual*	*Total*	*Annual*
Coal: Arbury Hall	378-14-8	25-5-0	830-19-11	51-19-0	63-12-4	4-0-0
Coal: Spring Gardens	161-18-5	10-16-0	308-5-7	19-5-0	325-13-0	20-7-0
Charcoal	27-2-5	1-16-0	21-10-2	1-7-0	6-14-6	0-8-0
Total fuel	567-15-6	37-17-0	1160-15-8	72-11-0	395-19-10	24-15-0

Source: Warwickshire Record Office (WRO), CR136/V/156, Accounts, 1747–62; CR136/V/136, Accounts, 1763–96

1790s. Although this is not made explicit in the accounts, it seems likely that the small amounts of charcoal purchased by Newdigate were also for Spring Gardens: these purchases declined markedly after 1780 when he resigned as an MP and spent less time in London, and wood could be gathered from the estate for burning at Arbury Hall. Both the charcoal and wood would have been used for heating the principal rooms, especially when he received visitors, as they burned more cleanly, without producing pungent smoke.

Newdigate was willing and able to spend handsomely to keep his houses warm and comfortable. However, even this level of spending could not keep all rooms at an even temperature: in the winter of 1773 he noted in his diary that he 'Breakfasted dined and supped in the hall, the warmest room in the house'.[47] Smaller villas were easier to keep warm, but even then the outlay on fuel could be considerable. Between 1792 and 1799 the Honourable Mary Leigh paid bills amounting to nearly £300 for fuel to heat Grove House, her villa in Kensington Gore.[48] The bulk of this was for coal, but Samuel Kingston also sold her charcoal and very occasionally wood. One surviving bill records the delivery of a sack of charcoal every two to three days during the late autumn and winter of 1797.[49] It seems unlikely that Grove House lacked the storage capacity for large quantities of charcoal—coal was delivered and stored in much larger quantities—so it appears that Mary Leigh chose to receive and use rather than store her charcoal. As with Newdigate, it was no doubt burned in the best rooms, but Mary Leigh also made a distinction between different grades of coal, writing to her housekeeper with instructions to 'burn up all the Scotch Coal that is now in the House . . . as fast as they can be wanted, for I certainly will not use any myself'.[50]

In differentiating between types of coal and choosing to burn charcoal, Mary Leigh was attending to both physical and social comfort: not only keeping her house well heated but also conforming to social norms. The importance of the latter is apparent from Lady Strafford's withering appraisal of Mr. and Mrs. Marshall's house on St James' Street, London, which she visited in December 1712. It was 'kept the Nastiest I ever see a house'; worse still, Mrs. Marshall 'sat in the first room with the Cole fire and Tallow candles which I know was made a great jest on'.[51] As any respectable householder knew, she should have burned beeswax and wood, at least when receiving company.

Like fuel, candles were not all the same: they varied in their composition and size, in the quality of light they produced and the smell they generated. The best and cleanest candles were made from beeswax and cost the Leighs around 2*s*. 10*d*. apiece in the second half of the eighteenth century.[52] They varied in length, which determined the period for which they would burn—an important consideration for formal occasions and a measure of the time which the event might be expected to last. As the author of the 1830 *Servants' Guide* noted:

> wax candles, four in the pound, will last about eleven hours and should be used when the evening is expected to be five hours, as, in that case, each candle will serve two nights. Shorter candles, of six to the pound, are preferable when required to burn for six or seven hours.[53]

This advice is included under the heading 'Economical hints' and indicates the careful calculations that were made to ensure a balance between good lighting and good household management.

The fact that everyone knew the cost of wax candles underpinned their extravagant use in prestigious displays of wealth.[54] Sir Robert Walpole marked the visit of the Duke of Lorraine to Houghton in 1731 with 130 candles in the dining room and 50 in the saloon, the cost reportedly running to £15 per night—over twice the annual wage of a housemaid. A generation later, the Duke and Duchess of Northumberland placed in their Great Gallery four chandeliers, each with 25 candles; one their 600 guests commented that they 'light the room even more brilliantly than is necessary'.[55] Such displays tipped the comfort afforded by a well-lit room into the excess of luxury and conspicuous consumption. In general, however, economy was more evident than extravagance, even in the houses of wealthy landowners. Savings could easily be made by using tallow rather than wax candles, as they were considerably cheaper. In his *Traite contre le luxe* (1705), Jean du Pradel complained about the extravagance of burning wax candles costing 22 sous per pound compared with tallow at four sous per pound.[56] Such price differences reduced somewhat over the course of the eighteenth century but remained significant. In the 1790s, Mary Leigh was paying around 10*d.* apiece for tallow and up to 3*s.* each for the best beeswax candles.

There is no evidence of candle making at either Grove House or Stoneleigh Abbey at this time, but savings were made by part-exchanging grease from the kitchen for tallow candles: the chandler allowed £3 6*s.* against a bill of £14 19*s.*[57] Mary Leigh was also billed for rushlights, which might burn for 30 minutes, at 7*d.* apiece. Despite Crowley's suggestion that they were 'unacceptable in households with any pretension to refinement', these clearly had a place in the country house, presumably in service rooms or outbuildings.[58] Cost savings came at a price, however, as tallow candles needed more work to keep the wicks trimmed (or snuffed) and the flame burning without too much smoke; they were also smelly. As Iachimo exclaims in Shakespeare's *Cymberline:* 'Base and unlustrous as the smoky light that's fed with stinking tallow'.[59] One consequence of this was that wax and tallow marked distinctions in terms of people, spaces and occasions. Tallow candles were for servants and service rooms, for private rooms or when the family was home alone. Their use when visitors called drew the kind of acerbic comment made by Lady Strafford of the Marshalls. However, burned in the right place, and at the right time, tallow candles made sound economic sense in a well-managed household and formed the majority of candles burned in most houses. Sir Roger Newdigate's accounts suggest a ratio of between 10:1 and 20:1 in terms of spending on tallow and wax candles, and therefore much greater in terms of the number of candles being consumed. More generally, they indicate that Arbury Hall and his house in Spring Gardens were increasingly well lit, as well as being better heated.[60] His payments to the chandler rose from £20–30 per annum in the 1750s to £70–90 in the 1780s, an increase that easily outstripped the rising cost of candles, which perhaps rose by 30% over this period to judge from the evidence of bills presented to the Leighs.[61]

Newdigate's accounts also list payments to the oilman. Oil lamps had long been used in domestic settings, especially in southern Europe, where suitable vegetable oils were more readily available. They were recorded in many of the inventories from seventeenth-century Rome studied by Renata Ago, with an average of 4.7 lamps listed in houses with male heads.[62] They were undoubtedly more numerous in Newdigate's two houses: his payments for oil rising from £14 per annum in the 1740s to £45 per annum in the 1790s.[63] By this time, Mary Leigh was buying sperm oil on a regular basis. This had the same burning qualities as spermaceti candles and represented a considerable improvement on many vegetable oils. However, it must have been used sparingly in her house as she bought only modest amounts—a few gallons at a time, rather than the hundreds consumed in a few months by the Duke of Rutland at Belvoir in the winter of 1839–40.[64] Mary Leigh might have burned her sperm oil in the four 'glaboler lamps and branches' recorded in the Great Hall as early as 1749, from whence they appear to have been moved to the Picture Gallery where they are listed as 'four globe lamps' in both 1786 and 1806.[65] By this time, there were also 12 'tin lamps' in the billiard room, a reflection of the need for particularly good lighting for such activities.

Creating a warm and well-lit house involved many choices and reflected a careful balancing of the sometimes-competing priorities of comfort, economy and display. Country-house owners did not necessarily eschew cheaper forms of fuel and candle: coal and tallow were viable options for many circumstances, but their use needed to be complemented with charcoal, wood and beeswax if the boundaries of good taste were to be maintained. Thermal comfort came at a cost, but the social comfort derived from displaying taste and status could cost even more. Importantly, these choices and costs persisted over the course of the eighteenth century; they were nuanced rather than replaced by a growing array of technological innovations that offered more effective means to heat and light the country house.

Technologies of Comfort: Innovation and Adoption

Growing anxieties in many parts of Europe that the forests were fast becoming depleted because of the growing demand for wood in industrial and domestic hearths, coupled with rising fuel prices and a growing desire for warmer rooms provided a strong incentive to make fireplaces and stoves more efficient and effective.[66] A fifteenth- or sixteenth-century improvement to the open fireplace was to line the back, sides and bottom with cast iron plates (*contre feu* or *kaminplatte*).[67] A damper on the chimney also helped keep the heat inside the house. In 1614–20, the French architect Louis Savot moved the bottom and back plate out from the brick wall, thus creating a pocket of air that helped heat the room. Savot's fireplace was heated by wood, but in England coal was an option in many areas, prompting John Winter's 1658 innovation of building a grate in the form of a basket to hold the burning coals. In 1723, a German minister called Johann Georg Leutmann lifted his fireplace so that it stood on feet and added a pipe to feed in air from outside. The air intake (which could be closed) was under the grate and in front of the fire, so that the smoke was pulled up the chimney, an early version of a heat-circulating fireplace.[68]

It is into this context of incremental technological improvement that we should place the ideas of Nicolas Gauger, published as *La Mécanique du Feu* in 1713 and translated into English two years later by John Desaguliers as *Fires improved: being a new method of building chimneys*.[69] This gives a clue to one of Gauger's concerns (chimneys that efficiently drew smoke out of the room), but his chief object was creating a more efficient heating system. This involved applying the latest science to practical ends: ducts drew air into the room and channelled it into the fireplace or into an airbox at the rear. The supply of air to the fire could be regulated to maintain the desired room temperature whilst a network of pipes carried warm air throughout the room or into a neighbouring bedroom or closet, if so desired.[70] Essentially, Gauger was trying to harness more of the fire's heat before it went up the chimney, a problem that was vocalised by Lady Elizabeth Grosvenor, who wrote that 'only very close to the fire does one attain the desired object of keeping oneself warm'.[71] Gauger's improved fireplaces, with their pipework and remodelled chimneys, would have been very costly to install, but this would have been a minor concern to wealthy Parisians. It is surprising, then, that very few architects or patrons took up his ideas at a time when thermal comfort was becoming such a key concern. His legacy is better seen in the influence he had on others.

Benjamin Franklin, drawing on Gauger and Leutmann, was one of the first to argue for a more efficient design comprising a smaller, recessed fireplace on which coal rather than wood was burned.[72] His Pennsylvanian Fireplace was widely copied, with a range of decorative iron grates being produced, including Bath and Pantheon stoves. In Germany, Franklin's design for an open fireplace was combined with an iron stove (*Säulen-Kaminofen*) in 1786. The idea was to keep the heat in the room longer by leading the smoke through cast iron pipework above the fireplace before discharging it up the chimney.[73] A further refinement came from another American, Benjamin Thompson, Count Rumford, whose design comprised a shallow fireplace and widely bevelled sides which radiated heat into the room. With the additional benefit of a flue for regulating the flow of gases up the chimney, Rumford stoves and Register stoves became widespread in Britain from the 1790s.[74] Rumford stoves attracted considerable attention from contemporaries. In 1800, James Gillray produced an etching entitled 'The Comforts of a Rumford Stove' which showed Count Rumford, standing with his back to the fire and enjoying the warmth provided. Charles Williams' 1801 version, 'Luxury, or the Comforts of a Rumford Stove' satirises Gillray by replacing Thompson with a young woman in a décolleté negligee raised to leave her bottom naked; the enjoyment is more illicit and risqué, but real nonetheless.[75]

Technical improvements were also made to free-standing stoves. As early as 1619, Franz Keslar of Frankfurt-am-Main published a design for an improved stove comprising several tiers which, as he argued, afforded 'a glowing and agreeable heat'.[76] In Sweden, Count Carl Johan Cronstedt and Fabian Wrede responded to a 1767 government call for fuel-saving technologies with a new design for a tiled stove.[77] Their innovation had a smaller fireplace opening and burned in a more controlled manner; the flue channels were made more complex, winding vertically up and down to keep the heat inside the stove longer, and improvements were made to refine control of the supply of air into the stove (Figure 2.7).[78] The former made the tiled stove more effective in maintaining an even temperature; the latter made it approximately eight times more efficient. With the same amount of firewood many more rooms could be heated and used all year round, thus helping to transform domestic life. The new model spread quickly in Sweden and beyond. In 1771, Cronstedt's son presented the new stove at the *Académie royale d'architecture* in Paris, and in 1787, a few Swedish tile stoves were installed at Versailles.[79] By that time, tiled stoves had found their way into other French houses, especially in the *salle à manger*, and were fitted in many public buildings, including the town hall in Paris.[80]

As Crowley argues, these innovations spoke of a growing concern for thermal comfort: part of an enlightenment programme that sought to measure, understand and ultimately be able to influence and control the natural environment.[81] This same scientific agenda spread to the technologies of lighting. There were moves to exploit different natural oils, most importantly in the form of spermaceti, which was being used to make candles in North America from the 1740s. They were odourless and

Figure 2.7 Tile stove based on the principle of Cronstedt and Wrede: J. Cronstedt, *Beskrifning på en inrättning af Kakelugnar til Weds Besparning*
(Stockholm, 1767), courtesy of Umeå Universitetsbibliotek, Sweden

burned brightly, but problems in the supply of spermaceti and the multi-
stage manufacturing process meant that they remained expensive, limiting their use to the upper echelons of colonial society.[82] Whilst spermaceti
was exported to Europe and produced by European whalers, there is little evidence in either account books or bills of their widespread adoption
in country houses—Mary Leigh bought spermaceti oil for lamps rather
than candles. Rather different was the stearin candle, invented in 1825
by Michel Eugène Chevreul and soon after available commercially across
Europe. They were made from stearic acid, extracted from animal fats,
burned almost odourlessly and did not melt as easily as wax or tallow;
just as importantly, they were soon cheaper to make than tallow candles.
Stearin factories were quickly established all over Europe, including Berlin (1837) and Stockholm (1839).[83] By this time, however, candles were
facing competition from improved oil lamps and gaslights.

As with fireplaces, the promotion of these new lamps drew on the perceived and actual shortcomings of current technologies, and thus their
ability to enhance comfort and convenience. Thus, we see a notice placed
in *L'Avantcoureur* advertising a new type of lamp that burned olive oil

and offered a light that 'is more beneficial for vision, gives light that does not flicker at all, produces no smoke, and costs little'. Furthermore, it was asserted that they would never gutter and could be 'transported without risk of spilling anything'.[84] Others asserted the benefits of lanterns with mirrored bases. It is in this context that William O'Dea could describe the Argand lamp as the 'first significant advance in lighting technology for millennia'.[85] The key innovation was that oil was burned on a cylindrical wick whilst air was forced upwards via a double glass tube.[86] They were a considerable improvement on earlier lamps as they required little or no snuffing and—because they burned efficiently—created less smoke and smell, as well as using less oil. They were also brighter, Jefferson writing enthusiastically that they 'give light equal to that of six or eight candles'.[87]

Ami Argand had spent some time experimenting with different wicks, glass and oils, making a series of improvements before perfecting his lamp in 1780. He gained a British patent in 1784, shortly after which he entered into an agreement with Matthew Boulton and the London glassmaker, William Parker. They produced several free-standing and hanging versions, available in both sterling silver and Sheffield plate, again linking the comfort and convenience of better lighting with opportunities for display. Argand took on additional partners to meet growing demand and there were numerous infringements on his patent, to supply both factories and houses across Britain.[88] By the early nineteenth century, there were dozens of London tradesmen selling patent lamps, including James Smethurst & Co. of New Bond Street, who illustrated two different designs on their bill head: the 'Spiral Burner Patent Lamp' and the 'Hydrostatic Patent Lamp'.[89] They played on the idea that different quantities and qualities of light might be needed in different rooms by offering 'New Improved Lamps for all purposes', and they also accommodated those who needed enhanced lighting for special events, announcing 'Lamps let out on hire for Balls, Rents, Illuminations &c.'.

These improved fireplaces, stoves and lamps represented the successful application of scientific experimentation and technology to social needs and desires for enhanced domestic comfort. However, we need to be cautious in striking an overly celebratory tone: Smethurst & Co. felt it useful to assure their customers that they were the 'only house for the sale of patent lamps that burn without smoke'—hinting that this was a problem that persisted despite the introduction of new technologies. Moreover, it was one thing for technologies to be developed; quite another for them to be widely adopted and to have a transformative impact on the country house, as Gauger's experience makes clear.

Given the evident attraction and cultural currency of the improved fire grates created by Franklin, Rumford and others, it is unsurprising that such 'stoves' were installed in many English country houses. In his refurbishment of Stoneleigh Abbey in the early 1760s, Edward, fifth Baron

Leigh, kept the ornate fretwork grates installed by his father, Thomas, in most of the principal rooms, and augmented those in the Great Hall with ornate marble surrounds and overmantels (Figure 2.8). However, he put Bath stoves into the smaller family rooms at the back of the West range.[90] This balance of displaying wealth and hospitality in the key public rooms and efficiency elsewhere was carried upstairs, Bath stoves appearing in the refurbished bedrooms. Sometime in the 1790s, his sister, Mary Leigh, installed 'moveable stoves'—probably register stoves—in the first-floor New Rooms, which she appears to have converted from bedrooms into a suite of dressing rooms, complete with 'two bell lines bows & tassels'; but she left untouched most of the other fireplaces in the house.[91]

This conservative approach was typical of English landowners, the gradual and contingent nature of improvement being nicely summarised by arrangements at Wollaston Hall in Northamptonshire. A sale catalogue from 1805 records a range of different types of fireplaces, all of which were seen as removable and saleable. As at Stoneleigh Abbey, there were Bath stoves in the bedrooms and also in the housekeeper's room and servants' hall; four servants' bedrooms had simple grates, and the dining parlour, library and drawing room had 'fixed' or 'neat' stoves, the precise nature of which is unclear. These might be seen as reflecting the different status of rooms, but the register stove in the breakfast room and square cast iron stove in the billiards room indicate the application of newer technology. Indeed, the description of the latter, with its iron hearth and pipe suggest that it might have been a free-standing stove. More telling in this regard is the mix of discarded ironwork found in the room over the stables. There were two cast-iron ovens, a heater stove, three iron fenders and backs, two Bath stoves (one of them measuring 48 inches compared with the 34- or 28-inch stoves found in the house), three small stoves, a Buzaglo stove and a German stove.[92] The grates, ovens and even the Bath stoves might be seen as the by-product of newer technologies introduced by the late owner, but the presence of free-standing stoves suggests that working out the optimal method of heating rooms was no easy matter and that new technologies did not always prove satisfactory.

Tiled stoves gained little traction in English country houses, despite their obvious benefits in terms of thermal efficiency. Climate seems a poor explanation for this technological reticence, not least given the similar conditions found in England and France, where tiled stoves were being installed. More important was the type of fuel source available to householders. Stoves were capable of using coal, but most were designed for wood, chopped up into smaller pieces than would be used on a fire. The wide availability of coal in Britain no doubt made fires an easier option for many householders. Palmer and West argue that cast iron stoves were unpopular because their aesthetic 'detracted from elegance of a polite interior', but this is an argument that is hard to sustain for tiled stoves which were often highly decorative.[93] In reality, the choice appears to

Figure 2.8 Fireplace and marble overmantel, Great Hall, Stoneleigh Abbey: (photograph by author)

have been cultural, though still linked with (perceived) comfort. As one commentator put it: 'nothing is more desirable than open fire-places; they perform the part of a perpetual ventilator'.[94] This British preference for fresh air is apparent in a letter from Lady Holland to her sister, Lady Kildaire, written in November 1764. She noted that the rooms at Carton 'are not large', but then observed: 'Large rooms are I think more necessary in winter than summer; a small room with open windows and no fire does very well, but shut up they are not pleasant, when they open into one another as yours do, a door open answers the purpose of a large room'.[95] Leaving the door open allowed the circulation of air.

The English taste for fresh air was far from universal. Swedish visitors, for instance, were struck by the cold draughts that rattled through the houses in which they stayed. Travelling in England during the first decade of the nineteenth century, the writer, historian and poet, Erik Gustaf Geijer, was feeling homesick. He missed the comforts of his home in Sweden and wrote to his parents:

> I felt colder in my room here than I ever did under a Swedish roof. For when the cold arrives in this country, it can find its way through all doors and windows, and the Englishman cannot do anything, except move closer to his small pile of glowing embers, which he calls a fire.[96]

A coal fire would, of course, give out most heat when burning in this way, but Geijer was clearly used to rooms with better insulation against drafts—an environment in which stoves worked most effectively. Such precautions bemused or horrified the British, as Mark Davies makes clear in his analysis of the travel writing of British visitors to Sweden.[97] Houses were universally found to be too warm and stuffy—a quality that might be real as well as imagined, given the precautions taken to ensure that stoves could work effectively. Lord Teignmouth, writing in 1830, noted that 'the rooms they occupy are well warmed by stoves, and hermetically sealed against draughts . . . A Swedish officer of the Guards, said Bishop Heber, would sooner face the mouth of a canon than a draught'.[98] Such an environment did not suit the British. Selina Bunbury exclaimed that, even in November, 'the heat of my rooms, I found almost intolerable; in the day time I was stupefied and the nights found me awake . . . roving through the rooms, or gazing from the windows'.[99] Horace Wheelwright, meanwhile, complained bitterly about the effects on the body of Swedish interior environments: 'No one who has not experienced it, can imagine what an enervating effect so much close confinement in those stove-heated rooms (with the thermometer often 22°C. warm, double windows, and the chimney blocked up, so that not a breath of fresh air can come in) has upon the constitution'.[100]

It is significant that Wheelwright apparently had equipment for measuring the temperature of the room and was interested in doing do— something that was still relatively new at this date. Even more telling is the temperature that he recorded: 22°C may seem quite reasonable to modern eyes, but was around 8° warmer than the norm in late eighteenth and early nineteenth-century British homes.[101]

Such concerns were not exclusive to the British. French soldiers, stationed in Alsace in the winter of 1674–75 complained of the excessive heat created by stoves; the troops opened windows and officers requested that the stoves be replaced with open fireplaces.[102] Writing a century later, when stoves were growing more numerous in Parisian homes, Sebastien Mercier built on these physical objections with concerns that were more emotional. He wrote that 'the sight of a stove kills my imagination and makes me sad and melancholy. I prefer the sharpest cold to this tepid, dull, invisible heat. I like to see the fire, it stirs my imagination'.[103] If the ambient heat from a stove could be seen to seep into the body and mind, dulling the senses and the imagination, it could also wreak similar havoc with furniture. Blondel was happy to have stoves in dining rooms, but not elsewhere because 'they could not but produce much dirtiness'.[104] The 1830 *Servants' Guide* warned the householder that 'heating apartments by stoves is destructive to furniture . . . The effects even of a low stove-heat are very pernicious, especially to piano fortes and other musical instruments'.[105]

These persistent concerns help to explain why stoves spread to British houses in a slow and patchy manner, despite their obvious advantages and their use in fashionable French houses. Whilst Lady Mary Wortley Montagu wrote from Germany in 1716 about the English 'obstinacy in shaking with cold six months in the year rather than make use of stoves, which are certainly one of the great conveniences of life', there is no evidence that she acted on her vow to install one in her room at home.[106] Similar caution can be seen at Audley End. In 1779, Sir John Griffin Griffin paid Abraham Buzaglo £2 18s. 6d. for the 'Trial of a Stove in the Hall' of his London house, but did not choose to install stoves in other rooms or at Audley End, where Bath stoves predominated.[107] Sir John's successor, Richard Aldworth Griffin, was more adventurous in his use of free-standing stoves. In 1807, he made improvements to the fireplaces in various rooms, reflected in bricklayer's bills 'to Rumfordise the chimney' in one room and 'Contract the Chimney' in another.[108] Yet seven years later, he regretted that: 'tho' every room is full warm by ample fires, still long passages, a Hall of 100ft, & Staircases all without Stoves as yet . . . have made me for these last three days fret at not having expended more money in procuring warm stoves'. Accordingly, he looked into rectifying the situation, noting in the same letter not only that stoves had 'late successfully placed at Euston, &

other large houses', but also that his architect, Thomas Cundy, 'does not understand these furnaces so well as the foreigners'.[109] In the end, room stoves were overtaken by a variety of central heating systems in British houses, although open fires remained important to the heating and aesthetic of the country house.

The uptake of Argand lamps could also be slow and cautious. Sir John Griffin Griffin purchased a single lamp for his London house on New Burlington Street in February 1785; clearly pleased with the results, he acquired a further 22 over the following year.[110] Mary Leigh also acquired a single lamp from Argand & Co. in November 1790, along with 2 dozen cotton wicks, probably for her house in Kensington as it is not listed in the Stoneleigh Abbey inventories.[111] Unlike Sir John, however, she does not appear to have followed up this purchase with others. Instead, it was James Henry Leigh who introduced a significant number of Argand-style lamps into Stoneleigh Abbey. In 1813, he acquired a four-light Grecian lamp, 'cut in diamonds & splits' and with an oak leaf border; a three-light bronzed antique lamp 'highly ornamented', and a 'bronzed & gold colour Gothic Lanthorn' with a four light patent burner from Hancock, Shepherd and Rixon of Cockspur Street in London. A year later, he bought a pair of two light 'plate glass Grecian antique fountains' from the Patent Lamp and Oil Warehouse of James Smethurst & Co. of New Bond Street, and a pair of vase lights from Thomas Wicks.[112] These were important in lighting up his newly inherited house, but they were clearly decorative and impressive pieces which enhanced the aesthetic of the house and displayed his wealth and taste. They cost him a hefty £176 17s. including the chains, pulleys and silk lines needed to hang them, plus a further £16 16s. in 'Mr Shepherds and Mr Grays expenses & time going down to Stoneleigh Abbey'.[113]

The extent to which these patent lamps transformed the lighting of English country houses such as Stoneleigh Abbey and made them more comfortable or convenient is perhaps not as clear-cut as this enthusiastic spending might suggest. Patent lamps had the advantage of burning more efficiently and cleanly, which gave them an advantage over candles and meant that some of the problems associated with earlier lamps were no longer such a concern. Whereas, in 1770, the housekeeper at Woburn found the Duke's bed was 'so very black with burning of oil in the room that she thinks is proper to have it cleaned', Thomas Jefferson could enthuse in a letter to James Madison that the new lamps 'consume their own smoke—do no injury to the furniture—give more light—and are cheaper than candles'.[114] However, as Smethurst's billhead makes it clear, tradesmen could still play on consumers' concerns about smoke some 20 years after Argand took out his patent. Perhaps a bigger concern, though, was the cost of using lamps. True, they were cheaper than burning the equivalent number of candles, both in fuel and the labour of tending them. However, a single candle was a far cheaper option and, as Harden's paintings make clear, could provide sufficient light for a small family group.

There was also the cultural question of just how much light was necessary or desirable. Historians such as Witold Rybcynski have asserted that the Argand lamp 'allowed social activities such as card playing to be carried on in comfort during the evening' and contemporary notices celebrated the quality of light, which was 'infinitely more beautiful' than that of candles.[115] In a 1819 painting by Louis Dupré showing the temporary Viennese residence of King Jerome of Württemberg (the younger brother of Napoleon Bonaparte), an Astral lamp stands on a table around which sit Jerome's son and wife, along with a group of friends.[116] Just out of frame, other lamps hang over the billiard table at which Jerome is playing. The convenience of modern lighting thus enhanced the sociability of the room, not only reinforcing the grouping of people around the well-lit table but also facilitating activities elsewhere in the room. A mix of lighting was quite typical, however, both in public and domestic settings. Thomas Rowlandson's depiction of the Great Subscription Rooms at Brook's on St James' Street in London shows a central chandelier and girandoles on either side of the fireplace; there are single candles on some tables and argand-style lamps on others (Figure 2.9).[117] Significantly, the

Figure 2.9 Joseph Constantine Stadler and Thomas Rowlandson, after Augustus Charles Pugin, *Great Subscription Room at Brook's* (1808): Yale Center for British Art, Paul Mellon Collection, New Haven, CT, B1977.14.18187

lamps have shades to shield members from the glare, indicating one of the ways in which more light was not necessarily a desirable thing. Early on during the period when they were being made at the Soho works, Matthew Boulton sent an Argand lamp as a present to his son's schoolmaster in Suffolk, the Reverend Samuel Parlby. Boulton's son wrote that, whilst the Parlby's admired the lamp, they found the light too bright; nor could they be persuaded to use the lampshade provided.[118] Even candlelight might be deemed too bright and shades were sometimes deployed to protect those sitting nearby. As Hellman argues, greater illumination did not necessarily make for greater social ease or comfort—pools of light, as we have seen, could play a useful role in structuring interaction and social engagement.[119]

Similar concerns were raised about the introduction of gaslighting, which was just taking hold in Britain right at the end of our period. John Lockhart described its impact at Abbotsford, where Sir Walter Scott had recently installed gaslights into many of the principal rooms:

> at the turn of a screw, the room was filled with a splendour worthy of the palace of Aladdin; but, as in the case of Aladdin, the old lamp would have been better in the upshot. Jewelry sparkled, but cheeks and lips looked cold and wan in this fierce illumination; and the eye was wearied, and the brow ached, if the sitting was at all protracted.[120]

People may have wanted more light in their houses, but attaining this ambition might come at a cost. More light could mean discomfort as well as comfort. It is no surprise, then, that candles remained central to domestic lighting throughout the eighteenth century and beyond. This leads to a more general point. New technologies undoubtedly improved the warmth and lighting in country houses, making them more comfortable and convenient. However, increased domestic comfort was not a simple story of technological advances: not only did house owners have a range of choices available to them, but they also needed to acquire an array of other household objects in order to make their homes warm and well illuminated. As we will see, these things were also invested with other values, not least because they provided opportunities to display wealth and taste.

Enhancing Comfort: Fireside Furniture and Light Fittings

Making a fire effective in warming the occupants of a room and thus making them feel comfortable required an array of other objects and furnishings—assemblages of objects that related to each other as well as to the occupants of the room.[121] Benjamin Franklin noted that 'the cold air so nips the backs and heels of those that sit before the fire that they have no comfort till either settles or screens are provided (at considerable expense) to keep it off', and we have already seen how Richard Aldworth Griffin thought his eating room cosy because of the curtains and carpet as well as the fire.[122] Such assemblages were by no means common in seventeenth-century Europe. Taking andirons as an indication of the presence of a fire in Roman houses of this period, Renata Ago notes that they were comparatively rare outside the kitchen. Braziers might have been used, as they were in Germany and Holland, but she concludes that 'overall it seems that people made do with less warmth'.[123] Dutch houses were better equipped: large fireplaces are prominent in the numerous paintings of domestic interiors from this period, and Jan Steen's 1659–60 *Fantasy Interior* also shows the extensive use of tapestries and the way in which they were hung over doors to reduce draughts. In the room beyond, we can see window shutters, to which some householders added curtains. In late seventeenth-century France, Jean-Dieu de St Jean depicted a similar set of objects in his *Femme de qualité en deshabillée sortant du lit* (1688).[124] There are fire irons set upright with hooks, a set of highly decorative andirons to help the logs burn and mark the wealth of the owner, and a fire screen (*ecran a coulisse*) which can be adjusted in height. The over-mantle is large and showy, with a collection of vases and seated cherubs, and the doorways are covered by heavy curtains with a decorative fringe.

Such interior scenes are rare for England during this period, but inventories and paintings from the eighteenth century show the increase in range and broader deployment of an array of furniture and furnishings that would enhance the warmth of the room. This process can be seen at Colworth House in Bedfordshire, a fairly modest double pile before it was considerably extended by William Lee Antonie at the very end of the eighteenth century.[125] The inventory for 1723 records fire irons in around half and window curtains in a quarter of the rooms, including the south side parlour and south chamber which also contained two pieces of tapestry (Table 2.2). Fire screens and carpets first appear in

Table 2.2 Furniture linked to thermal comfort: Colworth House, Bedfordshire, 1723–1816

	1723		1771		1816	
	Rooms (n = 11)	% of rooms	Rooms (n = 12)	% of rooms	Rooms (n = 30)	% of rooms
Fire irons	6	55.5	9	75.0	23	76.7
Window curtains	3	27.3	7	58.3	23	76.7
Carpets			6	50.0	23	76.7
Hearth rugs					8	26.7
Fire screens					7	23.3
Folding screens					2	6.7

Source: James Collett-White (ed.), *Inventories of Bedfordshire Country Houses, 1714–1830* (Bedford: Bedfordshire Historical Society, 1995), 46–70.

the 1771 inventory. The latter were quite widely distributed across the house, including several bedrooms, but the former were restricted to the two-hand screens found in the Best Parlour. By 1816, the assemblage of a comfortable fire-side material culture was complete: there were large Brussels carpets in all of the main rooms, together with window curtains and sometimes hearth rugs. In some bedchambers, curtains and carpets offered an alternative to working fires as a way to keep warm, the servants' rooms in particular often lacking the fire irons that indicate a fire actually being used. Folding screens, to offer some protection from drafts, were confined to the new dining room and breakfast room, but pole and claw screens, to protect the sitter from the harsh heat of the fire, were found in all of the principal rooms.

These rooms resemble the interiors appearing in numerous paintings from the third quarter of the eighteenth century onwards. William Hogarth's *The Lady's Last Stake* (1758–59) shows a fire in a raised basket, fire irons resting on the hearth, a small pole screen and a richly patterned carpet; surprisingly, there are no curtains (Figure 2.10). Johann Zoffany's paintings of Sir Laurence Dundas (1769) and Mrs. Abington in *The Way*

Figure 2.10 William Hogarth, *The Lady's Last Stake* (1759): Allbright-Knox Art Gallery, Buffalo, 1945:2.1

to Keep Him (1768) both depict well-furnished rooms. The former has an Adam fireplace, illustrated closed up with a chimney board, as was common during the summer months; there are heavy moreen curtains and a large Brussels carpet, fitted to the room. In the latter, the irons stand ready by a blazing log fire, held in an ornate basket; there is a decorative fire screen, a large carpet and heavy curtains. A dozen years later, Philip Reinagle depicted Mrs. Congreave and her daughters in a remarkably similar setting. The carpet has a delicate floral pattern and the curtains are lighter; but the centrepiece is still the fire, set in a pantheon stove, with a shovel, tongs and poker neatly placed on either side.[126]

These paintings all depict reception rooms, but the Colworth inventories show how these assemblages also spread to bedchambers and even to the rooms of senior servants. The housekeeper's room contained a polished fender, carpet and hearth rug, and window curtains, and her bedchamber had a 'neat stove grate', a carpet around the bed, and chintz curtains.[127] Much the same is seen at Stoneleigh Abbey. In 1774, the housekeeper's bedchamber had a Bath stove with shovel, tongs, poker and hearth brush, and crimson damask window curtains (no doubt relocated from elsewhere in the house); 12 years later, there was also a carpet and a pair of bedside carpets. Her sitting room elsewhere in the house had a Bath stove and fire irons, to which were later added an old Turkey carpet, a small pole fire screen and a second folding fire screen.[128] Not only could her rooms be kept warm and comfortable, but she was also granted the dignity of a screen to protect her from the immediate heat of the fire.

Candles or lamps were also part of a broader array of objects that allowed them to provide enhanced light and render rooms more comfortable. To burn effectively, all candles required trimming or snuffing, a task that had to be undertaken on a regular basis—perhaps every five minutes or so with tallow candles—and often formed another burden placed on servants to make their employers more comfortable.[129] Most of the snuffers bought by the Leighs of Stoneleigh Abbey were made from steel and intended for use by servants, but they also acquired silver snuffers and trays, duly engraved with their arms, supporters and coronet.[130] Trimming candle wicks oneself enhanced privacy and convenience; as Hellman argues, it also offered opportunities for elegant bodily performances akin to those involved in pouring and serving tea.[131] Candles also required holders, which came in three broad types: candlesticks which were placed on a flat surface; sconces attached to walls, and chandeliers hung from the ceiling.[132] However, the nomenclature was varied and overlapping, depending on whether English or French terms were adopted, and there were important variations on each basic type. Thus, a candlestick might be a stemless saucer with a candle socket (in French a *bougeoirs*), designed to be carried safely from room to room, or it might have several branches and be called a candelabrum (*candelabre* in French) or a *girandole*. The latter commonly had six branches but could have fewer and be set against a mirror and mounted on a wall. Whether this was then called a sconce depended as much on the inclination of whoever was offering the description as the precise qualities of the object itself. Chandeliers were initially made of brass; those which later incorporated rock crystal or glass were called *lustres* in France—a term which was then widely adopted in England.

Many elite householders owned examples of each of these as they served different purposes and were suitable for different rooms. The range and type of holders varied across Europe but generally increased over time. Ago notes an average of 4.2 lamps or candle holders per household in seventeenth-century Rome, which suggests not only that many needed to be portable between rooms, but also that rooms were rather dimly lit at best.[133] Further north in Europe, fixed sconces with a polished tin plate which reflected the candlelight were widespread by mid-century, especially in France.[134] They were decorative as well as practical but were gradually discarded in favour of others made from carved and gilded wood, a style favoured at Fontainebleau from the 1640s. As with other gilded furniture, candlelight played on the reflective surfaces; rather than offering increased light and thus greater convenience, however, they were favoured as part of an emerging taste for the baroque. The innovation was aesthetic rather than technical.

Dutch householders favoured hanging chandeliers—important in providing additional light in what would otherwise have been rather dark interiors, especially in town houses which were lit only by windows at the front and back.[135] These were generally made from polished brass and many featured a large central globe that helped to reflect lights from the candles set in surrounding branches. They feature prominently in many paintings of Dutch interiors, set centrally in the room to provide maximum light; but this position and their inclusion in paintings also highlight their cultural and social significance.[136] Thornton suggests that these brass chandeliers were far less common in seventeenth-century France and England, although they were found at Hardwick in 1601 and feature in paintings of English interiors through the early eighteenth century. For example, Gawen Hamilton's 1732 painting of Thomas Wentworth and his family shows a brass or silver chandelier paired with a matching sconce.[137] Wealthy French householders favoured more ornate chandeliers embellished with rock crystals and later glass pendants, both of which were deployed at Fontainebleau. In addition to their showiness, the crystals reflected and refracted the light, not only increasing the luminescence of the candles but also changing the quality of light, helping to create the brilliant effect of a well-lit room noted earlier. Again, English elites followed suit, glass chandeliers becoming common in country houses from the 1740s.

Tracing these changes for particular houses reveals not only a growing level of comfort and convenience in terms of the quantity of light fittings but also a changing aesthetic. Knole in Kent was the home of the Sackvilles, who had risen rapidly in fortune and title around the turn of the seventeenth century. A 1682 inventory lists two rock crystal branch chandeliers (a sign of real wealth), three gilt sconces, two pairs of brass sconces and a total of 28 candlesticks found in various rooms. There were also a 'large branch all of wrought silver' and a further 14 candlesticks in a storeroom.[138] This impressive array of fittings was augmented sometime around 1690 with a pair of silver chandeliers, each holding six candles. In 1701, more silverware was brought from the family house at Copt Hall in Essex, including 20 silver sconces with branches and four looking glasses with stands or branches for candles, and five years later an inventory lists these, together with a large lantern hanging at the head of the main staircase. By the 1720s, the house was in possession of Lionel Sackville, the seventh Earl of Dorset, who marked his elevation to a Dukedom with a lavish gathering at which 34lbs of candles were burned.[139] Yet few additions were made to the stock of fittings: just a couple of lanterns and a lamp.

A similar transition is apparent at Colworth House, although the dates are rather later. The only candleholders appearing in the 1723 inventory are three candlesticks and six brass candlesticks kept in the kitchen. By 1771 there were two sconces and a lamp in the Hall and two glass sconces in the dining parlour, as well as five flat and six brass candlesticks in the kitchen. Things were very different following William Lee Antonie's refurbishment: the breakfast room was lit by 'two beautiful lustres', the new dining room had a pair of chandeliers, the drawing room had 'a pair of very rich and costly stands or burners for lamps, got up in the most elegant taste and fashion', together with a 'very costly and elegant chandelier', and the boudoir contained an ornamental inkstand with three sconces.[140] Not only were there considerably more lighting fixtures, but they were also qualitatively different: demonstrating Antonie's taste as well as meeting a desire for improved lighting.

Contrary to Crowley's argument, there was no inherent contradiction between furnishing for physical comfort and for displaying taste and status.[141] In 1750s' Paris, the comte d'Egmont acquired from the *marchand-mercier* Lazare Duvaux a set of elaborate light fittings which cost him a grand total of 2,370 livres. His purchases included a pair of gilt-bronze girandoles with Meissen porcelain swans that were attractive more for their decorative than their practical qualities: indeed, they would have been very difficult to use, at least without damaging the delicate ornamentation.[142] However, the six-branch chandelier of Bohemian crystal and two pairs of gilt-bronze wall lights bought at the same time were a more successful combination of taste and utility. In this, they more closely resembled the furnishings and interiors in English country houses. This is apparent in the changes seen at Colworth House but is clearer still in the refurbishment of Stoneleigh Abbey undertaken by James Henry Leigh in the 1810s. He inherited a house that had been left largely unaltered since the 1760s and spent handsomely in all parts of the house, from large items to small. We have already noted some of the additional lighting acquired by James Henry Leigh. As well as these, in August 1813 he bought from Hancock, Shepherd and Rixon a total of four cylindrical lustres, one for 16 lights, another for 12 lights, and two for 8 lights.[143] These provided the potential to illuminate the house far more brightly—certainly if all the candles were alight—but they also formed a very public display of wealth and brought the light-fittings at Stoneleigh in line with prevailing taste.

The curtains that Leigh had made for his principal rooms were both functional and decorative. Four pairs for the music room made by John Johnstone from silk already purchased cost a total of £160 17s. for the calico lining, silk lace, tassels and rope and 'gold coloured Parisian fringe'; the wooden cornice, carved with scroll foliage, cost a further £100.[144] These were highly decorative and displayed Leigh's wealth, but they would also have served to make the music room a cosy and comfortable space in which to entertain guests. Much the same is true of the screens bought from Jonathan Johnstone in 1813. The bill describes these as a pair of 'handsome carved and ornamented pole fire screens finished in burnished and mat gold and filled with your crimson silk' costing £16 16s., and 'an elegant 3 leaf folding fire screen neatly carved and finished in burnished a mat gold . . . the panels filled with your crimson silk with richly carved ad gilt ornaments in the bottom panels' at a cost of £45.[145]

Carpets were also important in reducing draughts and in offering a warm as well as a decorative covering to what were usually bare oak floorboards. Leigh acquired two green and brown Brussels carpets and five superfine Kidderminster carpets from Thomas Little of Tottenham Court Road, by then an important centre for the furnishing trade, at a combined cost of £129 15s. 6d.[146] The latter were thinner ingrain carpets, suitable for a wide variety of rooms. The former were much more expensive (James Henry's cost him over £40 apiece); their close pile allowed for intricate patterns and offered a much softer and more luxurious feel. Their ability to augment both the design and warmth of the room was heightened by the fact that many were fitted wall to wall. Hearth rugs were, in essence, practical pieces, offering wooden floors and carpets some protection against sparks, yet their aesthetic qualities were important. Leigh acquired a number of these, including three Imperial hearth rugs and two 'Extra large Superfine Hearth Rugs Leopard Pattern' from Henry Watson of Old Bond Street, London, at a combined cost of £18 17s.[147] These did much more than simply protect valued carpets; they were statements of wealth and, with their leopard patterns, signalled a taste for the exotic.

All of these luxurious fixtures and furnishings helped to enhance the comfort of Stoneleigh Abbey, and some might even be seen as necessary to the effective functioning of some new technologies; yet they all served to bring James Henry Leigh's newly inherited house in line with the latest taste. Wealthy country-house owners did not need to choose between comfort and fashion; London craftsmen and furniture dealers were perfectly capable of accommodating both requirements.

Conclusions

Eighteenth-century country-house owners sought to address the twin problems of cold and darkness through a growing array of technologies that made their homes more comfortable and convenient. Better heating allowed more rooms to be in use at any one time, facilitating the specialisation of space and allowing greater scope of movement through the house. In the innovations of Gauger, Rumford, Argand and many others, we can see the practical application of enlightenment science to everyday challenges, technological solutions being found to age-old problems. As Crowley has argued, this prioritisation of comfort in the form of heat and light appears to have experienced a step change during the period, both in terms of the development of new and adapted technologies and their installation in elite houses. If the divide between regions using stoves and those retaining (improved) fireplaces indicates a cultural fault line, there was a common desire for improvement: a comfortable house was warm and well lit, with the owner able to exercise increasing control over both temperature and light.

It is just as evident, however, that technology was not the only or even the overriding factor at play, suggesting that functionalist approaches to comfort are inadequate as explanations for domestic transformation. For one thing, houses were increasingly filled with an array of objects and furnishings which helped to provide warmth and enhance light. Some of these were mundane (coal buckets and candlesticks) whilst others were showy (rich velvet curtains, thick carpets, silver sconces and crystal chandeliers). Acquiring all these things meant the cost of keeping a large house warm and well lit went far beyond those of installing new stoves or lamps, maintaining supplies of coal, charcoal, candles and lamp oil, and paying servants to carry coal buckets, clean grates and snuff candles. Indeed, the luxurious nature of many of the fixtures and furnishings that enhanced the domestic comfort provided by a new type of fireplace or lamp meant that spending on these far exceeded that of the central source of heat or light. Naturally, this provided ample opportunities for the display of taste and wealth.

More profoundly, we are confronted with the slow uptake of Gauger's improved fireplaces, the rejection of stoves in many European countries, the importance of fuel efficiency rather than comfort as a driver for many innovations, and concerns about overly bright light from Argand lamps and especially gas lights. All these suggest that the acceptance of improved technology and the functionalist pathway to comfort was far from smooth. At the same time, a glowing fire did much more than heat the room: it provided a very tangible sign of the householder's hospitality and a focus on social interaction and sociability. In the autumn and winter evenings at Chateaubriand, the Combourg family spent much of their time in the panelled great hall:

> When supper was over and the four of us had moved from the table to the fireplace, my mother sank with a sigh on an old day-bed covered in chine. A little table with a candle on it was set before her. I sat beside the fire with Lucie. My father walked about. He was lost to view when he moved away from the fire, until he emerged from the darkness like a ghost.[148]

This was a scene repeated across Europe: it shows the centrality of the fire in the arrangement of people and the interactions between them. They gathered around its warmth and light, the mother's candle clearly offering little illumination to the rest of the room. But there are other things here as well: the day-bed into which the old lady could sink, the table set beside her and the chairs drawn up to the fire. These take us beyond the comfort of heat and light and into that of comfortable sofas, convenient tables and informal living that were also a key part of comfort by the later decades of the eighteenth century.

Notes

1. Elizabeth Gaskell, *Mary Barton* (1848; London: Chapman and Hall, 1849), 8.
2. Christina Hardyment, *Home Comforts: A History of Domestic Arrangements* (London: Viking, 1992), 144–64; Daniel Roche, *A History of Everyday Things: The Birth of Consumption in France, 1600–1900* (Cambridge: Cambridge University Press, 2000); John Crowley, *The Invention of Comfort: Sensibilities and Design In Early-Modern Britain and Early America* (Baltimore: Johns Hopkins University Press, 2001), 171–200; Joan DeJean, *The Age of Comfort: When Paris Discovered Casual and the Modern Home Began* (New York: Bloomsbury, 2009), 93–101; Alan Wilson, *Comfort, Pleasure and Prestige: Country-House Technology in West Wales, 1750–1930* (Kibworth Beauchamp: Matador, 2016), 85–105.
3. Quoted in Roche, *History of Everyday Things*, 130.
4. Frank Trentmann, *Empire of Things: How We Became Consumers, from the Fifteenth Century to the Twenty-First* (London: Allen Lane, 2016), 249–50 discusses 'functionalist comfort' in terms of kitchen apparatus, but it is the deployment of technology that lies at the heart of this concept.
5. Crowley, *Invention of Comfort*, 171–202. A similar approach is taken by Olivier Jandot, 'The Invention of Thermal Comfort in Eighteenth-Century France', in Jon Stobart (ed.), *The Comforts of Home in Western Europe, 1700–1900* (London: Bloomsbury, 2020), 73–92.
6. Emile Gérard-Gailly (ed.), *Madame de Sévigné: Lettres, 1648–1696*, vol. 3 (Paris: Gallimard, 1953–1957), 877.
7. Quoted in John Fowler and John Cornforth, *English Decoration in the Eighteenth Century* (London: Barrie and Jenkins, 1974), 226.

8. Horace Walpole, *Horace Walpole's Correspondence*, vol. 1, 328, https://walpole.library.yale.edu/collections/digital-resources/horace-walpole-correspondence: Horace Walpole to William Cole, 28 May 1774. Walpole Letters, to Cole, 28 May 1774, 328.

9. Walpole, *Horace Walpole's Correspondence*, vol. 31, 348: Horace Walpole to Hannah More, 11 September 1790.

10. Jane Austen, *Emma* (1815; London: Penguin Edition, 1985), 98.

11. Gaskell, *Mary Barton*, 66.

12. Howard Colvin and John Newman (eds.), *Of Building: Roger North's Writings on Architecture* (Oxford: Oxford University Press, 1981), 48.

13. Quoted in Roche, *History of Everyday Things*, 128.

14. Quoted in Hannah Chavasse, 'Material Culture and the Country House: Fashion, Comfort and Lineage' (Unpublished PhD thesis, University of Northampton, 2015), 141.

15. Walpole, *Horace Walpole Correspondence*, vol. 10, 575: Horace Mann to Horace Walpole, 27 December 1767, 575.

16. Peter Thornton, *Authentic Décor: The Domestic Interior, 1620–1920* (London: Weidenfeld & Nicolson, 1985), 97.

17. For discussion of their uptake in ordinary homes, see Britt Denis, 'The Spread of Comfort in Nineteenth-Century Belgium Homes', in Jon Stobart (ed.), *The Comforts of Home in Western Europe, 1700–1900* (London: Bloomsbury, 2020), 104–23.

18. Roche, *History of Everyday Things*, 127; Johanna Ilmakunnas, 'Northern Comfort and Discomfort: Spaces and Objects in Swedish Country Houses, c.1740–1800', in Jon Stobart (ed.), *The Comforts of Home in Western Europe, 1700–1900* (London: Bloomsbury, 2020), 46–53.

19. Susanna Scherman, *Den Svenska Kakelugnen* (Stockholm: Wahlström & Widstrand, 2007), 43. I would like to thank Johanna Ilmakunnas for this reference.

20. Crowley, *Invention of Comfort*, 112–15, 130–1.

21. SCLA, 18/31/548, Account of stores expended every half year, Adlestrop, 1757–61.

22. SCLA, DR18/4/43, inventory of Stoneleigh Abbey, 1774 with 1806 amendments.

23. Willam Lower, *A Relation in the Form of a Journal of the Voiage and Residence Which . . . Charles II . . . Hath Made to Holland* (The Hague, 1660).

24. Quoted in Fowler and Cornforth, *English Decoration*, 223.

25. Walpole, *Horace Walpole's Correspondence*, vol. 32, 409: Horace Walpole to Lady Ossory, 23 December 1777.

26. Peter Thornton, *Seventeenth-Century Interior Decoration* (New Haven: Yale University Press, 1978), 268; Maureen Dillon, 'Advances in Lighting Technology and the Transformation of the Domestic Interior: A Case Study of Knole, Sevenoaks, Kent', in Peter Barnwell and Marilyn Palmer (eds.), *Country House Technology* (London: Paul Watkin Publishing, 2012), 93–107; Maxine Berg, *Luxury and Pleasure in Eighteenth-Century Britain* (Oxford: Oxford University Press, 2005), 37.

27. Marcia Pointon, 'Jewellery in Eighteenth-Century England', in Maxine Berg and Helen Clifford (eds.), *Consumers and Luxury: Consumer Culture in Europe, 1650–1850* (Manchester: Manchester University Press, 1999), 120–6.

28. Mimi Hellman, 'Enchanted Night: Decoration, Sociability and Visuality After Dark', in Charissa Bremer-David (ed.), *Paris: Life and Luxury in the Eighteenth Century* (Los Angeles: Getty, 2011), 107.

29. Johannes de Brune, *Emblemata of Zinnerwerck* (1624).

30. William Laquy, *Allegory of Art Training* (c.1770), Rijksmuseum, Amsterdam, www.rijksmuseum.nl/en/search/objects?q=laquy&p=2&ps=12&st=Objects&ii=4#/SK-A-2320-C,16 (accessed 19 May 2020).

31. Richard Morton Paye, *The Artist in His Studio* (1783), National Trust, Upton House, Warwickshire, www.nationaltrustcollections.org.uk/object/446692 (accessed 11 August 2020).
32. For a fuller analysis of this painting, see Johann Ilmakunnas, 'French Fashions: Aspects of Elite Lifestyle in Eighteenth-Century Sweden', in Johanna Ilmakunnas and Jon Stobart (eds.), *A Taste for Luxury in Early Modern Europe: Display, Acquisition and Boundaries* (London: Bloomsbury, 2017), 250–2.
33. Jean-François de Troy, *Before the Ball* (1735), JPG Museum, 84.P4.668 and *After the Ball* (1735), Private Collection. These are reproduced in Hellman, 'Enchanted Night', 92–3.
34. Hellman, 'Enchanted Night', 94, 98, 101–2.
35. Henry Sargent, *The Tea Party* (c.1820), Museum of Fine Arts, Boston, https://collections.mfa.org/objects/31744.
36. See Daphne Foskett, *John Harden of Brathay Hall, 1772–1847* (Kendal: Abbot Hall Art Gallery, 1974).
37. Reproduced in Foskett, *John Harden*, Plates 25 (Reading and Sewing (1805) and 14 (Family group, Charles Lloyd reading (1804).
38. Crowley, *Invention of Comfort*, 191.
39. Marilyn Palmer and Ian West, *Technology in the Country House* (Swindon: Historic England, 2016), 74.
40. Stephane Castellucio, *L'éclairage, le chauffage et l'eau aux XVIIe et XVIIIe siècles* (Paris: Gourcuff Graden, 2016), 165.
41. Roche, *History of Everyday Things*, 131.
42. Castelluccio, *L'éclairage, le chauffage et l'eau*, 166.
43. Hardyment, *Home Comfort*, 156.
44. Wilson, *Comfort, Pleasure and Prestige*, 87.
45. Gregory Clark and David Jacks, 'Coal and the Industrial Revolution, 1700–1869', 37, https://gpih.ucdavis.edu/files/Clark_Jacks.pdf (accessed 12 August 2020).
46. Warwickshire Record Office (WRO), CR136/C646: Roger Newdigate to Christopher Gullet, 29 December 1773; WRO, CR136/V/136, Accounts, 1763–96: in 1781, his cook received £20 per annum, the laundry and housemaids between £5 and £7, the dairy and kitchen maids £6, and the 'Lady's Woman' £8.
47. WRO, CR136/A/152, Diaries of Sir Roger Newdigate, 29 December 1773.
48. See, for example: SCLA DR18/5/6129, 6254, 6349, 6398, 6423, 6481: receipted bills from Samuel Kingston. These years were particularly cold, so the quantity of fuel needed might have been higher than usual (see Peter Rowntree, 'Thomas Hughes's Temperature Record for Stroud, 1775–1795', *Weather*, 67:6 (2012), 156–61). Nonetheless, the level of spending is striking, especially given the relatively modest size of the house.
49. SCLA, DR18/5/3643, bill from Samuel Kingston, 30 December 1797.
50. SCLA, DR18/17/31/11, letter dated 24 October 1804.
51. Quoted in Hannah Greig, *The Beau Monde: Fashionable Society in Georgian London* (Oxford: Oxford University Press, 2013), 42.
52. SCLA, DR18/5/4619, bill from John Coggs, 7 April 1768; DR18/5/5849, bill from Frances Field, 29 May 1789.
53. Samuel Adams and Sarah Adams, *The Servants' Guide and Family Manual* (London, 1830), 67.
54. Quoted in Thornton, *Seventeenth-Century Interior Decoration*, 388.
55. Quoted in Fowler and Cornforth, *English Decoration*, 223.
56. Jean du Pradel, *Traite contre de Luxe* (Paris, 1705).
57. SCLA, DR18/5/5991, bill from Thomas Gibberd, 25 August 1792.

58. SCLA, DR18/5/5887, bill from James Wheble, 17 July 1790; Crowley, *Invention of Comfort*, 113.
59. William Shakespeare, *Cymberline* (1623), Act 1, Scene 6.
60. WRO, CR136/V/156, Accounts, 1747–62; CR136/V/136, Accounts, 1763–96.
61. SCLA, DR18/5/2063, 2636, 3744, 4207, 5023, 5887, 6032, 6158. This outlay matches closely the £85 per annum spent on lighting at Audley End in the 1780s—see J.D. Williams, 'The Noble Household as a Unit of Consumption: The Audley End Experience, 1765–1797', *Essex Archaeology and History*, 23 (1992), 69, 78; Chavasse, 'Material Culture', 132, presents figures for the early 1800s, when £88 16s. was spent on candles and £137 17s. 4d. on lamp oil across the three houses then owned by Richard Aldworth Griffin: Audley End, New Burlington Street, London and Billingbear.
62. Renata Ago, *Gusto for Things: A History of Objects in Seventeenth-Century Rome* (Chicago: University of Chicago Press, 2013), 160.
63. WRO, CR136/V/156, Accounts, 1747–62; CR136/V/136, Accounts, 1763–96.
64. SCLA, DR18/5/5939, bill from Frances Field, 31 December 1791; DR18/5/6392, bill from R Lewis, 29 September 1798; Fowler and Cornforth, *English Decoration*, 225.
65. SCLA, DR18/4/27, inventory of Stoneleigh Abbey, 1749; DR18/4/69, inventory of Stoneleigh Abbey, 1786; DR18/4/59, inventory of Stoneleigh Abbey, 1806.
66. See Castellucio, *L'éclairage, le chauffage et l'eau*; Roche, *History of Everyday Things*, 130–4; Cristina Prytz, 'The Improved Tiled Stove: Sweden's Contribution to Defining Comfort?', in Jon Stobart (ed.), *The Comforts of Home in Western Europe, 1700–1900* (London: Bloomsbury, 2020), 93–8.
67. Alfred Faber, *Entwicklungsstufen der häuslichen Heizung* (Oldenburg: München, 1957), 47–9.
68. Faber, *Häuslichen heizung*, 52–5.
69. See Jandot, 'Invention of Thermal Comfort'.
70. DeJean, *Age of Comfort*, 97–8.
71. Quoted in Fowler and Cornforth, *English Decoration*, 225.
72. Benjamin Franklin, *The Complete Works . . . of Dr Benjamin Franklin*, vol. 3 (London: J. Johnson, 1806), 228–9. See also Crowley, *Invention of Comfort*, 180–2.
73. Faber, *Häuslichen heizung*, 62.
74. Palmer and West, *Technology in the Country House*, 96–7; Crowley, *Invention of Comfort*, 185–90.
75. James Gilray, *The Comforts of a Rumford Stove* (1800), Science and Society Picture Library, image 10315400; Charles Williams, 'Luxury, or the Comforts of a Rumford Stove' (1801), British Museum, 1935,0522.7.12. See also Crowley, *Invention of Comfort*, 187–90.
76. Quoted in Roche, *History of Everyday Things*, 128.
77. For further details, see Prytz, 'The Improved Tiled Stove'.
78. Prytz, 'Improved Tiled Stove', Figure 3a.1; Jon Stobart and Cristina Prytz, 'Comfort in English and Swedish Country Houses, c.1670–1820', *Social History*, 43:2 (2018), 242.
79. Linnéa Rollenhagen Tilly, *Carl Johan Cronstedt: Arkitekt och Organisatör* (Stockholm: Balkong Förlag, 2017), 64–6; Jonas Nordin, *Versailles: Slottet, Parken, Livet* (Stockholm: Norstedts, 2013), 317–18. My thanks to Cristina Prytz for these references.
80. Mark Girouard, *Life in the French Country House* (London: Cassell & Co., 2000), 144–5; Roche, *History of Everyday Things*, 124.
81. Crowley, *Invention of Comfort*, 171–94.

82. Emily Irwin, 'The Spermaceti Candle and the American Whaling Industry', *Historia*, 21 (2012), 45–53.
83. Joakim Hansson, *Komfort framför allt, men även nytta och nöje* (Helsingfors: Sandelin, 2015), 116–18.
84. Quoted in Hellman, 'Enchanted Night', 96.
85. William O'Dea, *The Social History of Lighting* (London: Routledge and Paul, 1958), 1.
86. Charles Carson, *Technology and the Big House in Ireland, c.1800–c.1930* (Amherst, NY: Cambria Press, 2009), 154.
87. Quoted in Crowley, *Invention of Comfort*, 193.
88. Shena Mason, *Matthew Boulton: Selling What the World Desires* (New Haven: Yale University Press, 2009), 188–9; John Wolfe, *Brandy, Balloons and Lamps: Ami Argand, 1750–1803* (Carbondale, IL: Southern Illinois University Press, 1999), 28–40.
89. SCLA, DR18/5/7051, bill from James Smethurst & Co., 12 November 1814.
90. SCLA, DR18/4/25, inventory of Stoneleigh Abbey, 1749; DR18/4/43, inventory of Stoneleigh Abbey, 1774 with 1806 amendments. The descriptions differ somewhat from those in the 1749 inventory, which generally refers to grates rather than stoves, but it is unclear whether this reflected new technology or a shift in language. See Christopher Gilbert and Anthony Wells-Cole, *The Fashionable Fireplace, 1660–1840* (Leeds: Leeds City Art Galleries, 1985), 22.
91. SCLA, DR18/4/43, inventory of Stoneleigh Abbey, 1774 with 1806 amendments.
92. Northamptonshire Central Library (NCL), MM0005644NL/5, Wollaston Hall, 1805.
93. Palmer and West, *Technology in the Country House*, 99.
94. Quoted in Crowley, *Invention of Comfort*, 189.
95. Quoted in Fowler and Cornforth, *English Decoration*, 225.
96. Henrik Schück (ed.), *Geijers ungdomsbrev: Familjebrev av Erik Gustaf Geijer utgivna* (Stockholm: Albert Bonniers, 1920), Letter sent from Stoke Newington, 24 November 1809 to his parents: 'och jag frös mer i mitt rum, än jag någonsin gjort under svenskt tak. Ty då kölden kommer i detta land, så kan han titta in genom alla dörrar och fönster, utan att engelsmannen hittar på något annat medel däremot än att flytta sig så nära sin glödhög, som man här kallar eldbrasa'.
97. Mark Davies, *A Perambulating Paradox: British Travel Literature and the Image of Sweden c. 1770–1865* (Lund: Lund University, 2000), 138–40.
98. Lord Charles John Teignmouth, *Reminiscences of Many Years*, vol. 12 (1830; Edinburgh: David Douglas, 1878), 193.
99. Selina Bunbury, *Life in Sweden: With Excursions in Norway and Denmark*, vol. 2 (London: Hurst and Blackett, 1853), 38.
100. Llewellyn Lloyd, *Field Sports of the North of Europe; Comprised in a Personal Narrative of a Residence in Sweden and Norway, in the Years 1827–28*, vol. 2 (London: Colburn & Bentley, 1830), 66.
101. Pete Smith, 'Wollaton Hall: Technology and the Regency Country House', in Peter Barnwell and Marilyn Palmer (eds.), *Country House Technology* (London: Paul Watkin Publishing, 2012), 45.
102. Jandot, 'The Invention of Thermal Comfort', 76.
103. Quoted in Roche, *History of Everyday Things*, 128.
104. Quoted in Thornton, *Authentic Decor*, 97.
105. Adams and Adams, *Servants' Guide*, 68.
106. Robert Halsband (ed.), *Selected Letters of Lady Mary Wortley Montagu* (London: Longmans, 1970), 17 December 1716.

107. Essex Record Office (ERO), D/DBy A37/2, receipted bill. At Kedleston, the saloon was fitted with stoves in the shape of antique vases and placed in niches around the wall, a deployment also seen in the vestibule at Inveraray. At Belvoir, stoves were installed in the entrance passageway and disguised as trophies of arms—see Palmer and West, *Technology in the Country House*, 98–100; Fowler and Cornforth, *English Decoration*, 227–8.
108. ERO, D/DBy A65/1, receipted bill.
109. Quoted in Chavasse, 'Material Culture', 135: Richard Aldworth Griffin to Jenny, 8 January 1814.
110. Chavasse, 'Material Culture', 131. This was typical of Sir John Griffin Griffin's practice of trying out suppliers or goods in his London home ahead of their deployment at Audley End.
111. SCLA, DR18/5/5899, receipted bill from Argand & Co.
112. SCLA, DR18/5/6992, receipted bill from Hancock, Shepherd and Rixon; DR18/5/7051, receipted bill from Patent Lamp and Oil Warehouse; DR18/5/7067, receipted bill from Thomas Wicks.
113. SCLA, DR18/5/6992, bill from Hancock, Shepherd and Rixon.
114. Quoted in, respectively: Fowler and Cornforth, *English Decoration*, 225; Crowley, *Invention of Comfort*, 194.
115. Witold Rybcynski, *Home. A Short History* (New York: Viking, 1986), 138; *Journal de Paris* (1784), quoted in Schroder, 1969, 71.
116. Reproduced in Thornton, *Authentic Decor*, 206.
117. In a similar vein, William Heath's, *Cribbage* (c.1825–30): British Museum depicts an argand lamp on a small table at which a couple play cards.
118. Mason, *Matthew Boulton*, 189.
119. Hellman, 'Enchanted Night', 99.
120. John Lockhart, *Memoirs of the Life of Sir Walter Scott* (Edinburgh: Adam and Charles Black, 1852), 501.
121. On the importance of such non-human interactions lies at the heart of assemblage theory: see Manuel DeLanda, *Assemblage Theory* (Edinburgh: Edinburgh University Press, 2016).
122. Franklin, *Complete Works*, 228–9.
123. Ago, *Gusto for Things*, 68.
124. Jan Steen, *Fantasy Interior with Jan Steen and the Family of Gerrit Schouten* (1659–60), Nelson-Atkins Museum of Art; Jean-Dieu de St Jean, *Femme de qualité en deshabillée sortant du lit* (1688), Minneapolis Institute of Art.
125. James Collett-White (ed.), *Inventories of Bedfordshire Country Houses, 1714–1830* (Bedford: Bedfordshire Historical Society, 1995), 32–46.
126. William Hogarth, *The Lady's Last Stake* (1758–59), Albright-Knox Art Gallery, Buffalo, New York; Johann Zoffany, *Mrs Abington in 'The Way to Keep Him'* (1768), Petworth House, Sussex; Johann Zoffany, *Sir Laurence Dundas with His Grandson* (1769), Marquess of Zetland; Philip Reinagle, *Mrs Congreave and Her Daughters in Their London Drawing Room* (1782), National Gallery of Ireland.
127. Collett-White, *Inventories of Bedfordshire Country Houses*, 59, 65–6.
128. SCLA, DR18/4/43, inventory for Stoneleigh Abbey, 1774 with 1806 amendments; DR18/4/69 inventory for Stoneleigh Abbey, 1786.
129. O'Dea, *History of Lighting*, 3–5.
130. SCLA, DR18/5/4251, bill from Thomas Gilpin, 15 January 1765.
131. Hellman, 'Enchanted Night', 103.
132. Thornton, *Seventeenth-Century Interior Decoration*, 268–70; Hellman, 'Enchanted Night', 95.
133. Ago, *Gusto for Things*, 160.
134. Thornton, *Seventeenth-Century Interior Decoration*, 273–4.

135. John Loughman, 'Between Reality and Artful Fiction: The Representation of the Domestic Interior in Seventeenth-Century Dutch Art', in Jeremy Aynsley and Charlotte Grant (eds.), *Imagined Interiors: Representing the Domestic Interior Since the Renaissance* (London: V&A, 2006), 91–2.
136. Thornton, *Seventeenth-Century Interior Decoration*, 275.
137. Greig, *Beau Monde*, 37. See also Saumarez Smith, *Eighteenth-Century Decoration*, 93, 95, 103, 115.
138. Dillon, 'Advances in Lighting', 98.
139. Dillon, 'Advances in Lighting', 100.
140. Collett-White, *Inventories of Bedfordshire Country Houses*, 52–5.
141. Crowley, *Invention of Comfort*, 147–9.
142. Hellman, 'Enchanted Night', 99.
143. SCLA, DR18/5/6992, bill from Hancock, Shepherd and Rixon.
144. SCLA, DR18/5/7137, bill from John Johnstone.
145. SCLA, DR18/5/7137, bill from John Johnstone.
146. SCLA, DR18/5/7029, bill from Thomas Little.
147. SCLA, DR18/5/7087, bill from Henry Watson.
148. Quoted in Roche, *History of Everyday Things*, 129.

3 Comfortable Rooms

Sociability and the 'Modern Living Room'

Warmth and light made rooms more comfortable and opened up the country house to fuller and more flexible use, facilitating the growth in the specialist room seen across eighteenth-century Europe.[1] In the early nineteenth century, Richard Aldworth Griffin may have remained for much of the day in the Eating Room at Audley End, made cosy by its fire, carpet and curtains; but there was increased scope to use multiple rooms for socialising. Historians have noted not only how this reflected the growing specialisation of chairs, tables, desks and so on, but also how this furniture became more comfortable and convenient. From an art-historical perspective, Peter Thornton has traced the development of couches and sofas through the late seventeenth and eighteenth century, noting how they were increasingly integrated into architects' designs for fashionable interiors. More recently, Joan DeJean has stressed the importance of what she terms 'convenience furniture'—that is, small tables and desks that accompanied easy chairs and sofas, making them more convenient to use. Focusing more on furniture-makers, Akiko Shimbo has demonstrated the growing interest shown by some in the comfort afforded by their designs and the often celebratory descriptions included in publications such as Rudolph Ackermann's *Repository of Arts*.[2] But a comfortable room was more than simply a collection of comfortable and convenient objects; it reflected their arrangement and use for informal sociability. Such arrangements were outlined by Mark Girouard in what he styled the arrival of informality in the English country house in the later decades of the eighteenth century. This involved a new way of living and new spatial arrangements, both of rooms and of the furniture within rooms.[3] These ideals were promoted by architects such as Humphrey Repton who contrasted the formality of the circle with the relaxed environment of the 'modern living room'. In his usual before and after illustrations, a circle of empty chairs represents the formality of the circle as a form of elite sociability: polite and inclusive, but by Repton's time also seen as rather staid and stifling.[4] The living room, which should be understood as a room in which one lives or spends most time rather than

DOI: 10.4324/9781003206361-5

in its present-day sense, was altogether more lively—a contrast captured in the poem that accompanied Repton's illustrations:

> No more the cedar parlour's formal gloom
> With dullness chills, 'tis now the living room,
> Where guests to whim, to task or fancy true
> Scatter'd in groups, their different plans pursue[5]

More striking, perhaps, is the way in which Repton's 'modern' scene is animated with people and activities. This is something which historians of the English country house have not always been so adept at achieving: there is a tendency to view rooms as architectural set pieces or as collections of exquisite furniture, rather than spaces in which people lived.[6] This is particularly problematic in discussions of comfort, where the interaction between people and furniture is central to understanding the behaviour of the former and the form, function and arrangement of the latter. At one level, this can be conceived as bodily interaction: the physical comfort and ease offered by chairs or sofas. At another, it involves thinking about the spatiality of the room and the ways in which interior space (and arrangements of furniture) and social interactions were mutually constitutive and helped to create something that might be described as social comfort. Drawing on the ideas of Michel de Certeau and others, Daniel Roche has argued that, in the 'inter-relation of people and objects', material culture was 'defined by practices'.[7] This chimes with DeJean's account of the construction of new types of seats and tables, and their arrangement in the room; but we need to recognise the relationship was two-way, with social practices being shaped by the material culture of the room. The idea that space has an active role in shaping social action is central to the so-called spatial turn, a wide range of studies showing how the spatiality of the town shaped everything from urban protest, through leisure practices, to human creativity.[8] These ideas are implicit in many architectural analyses, for example in the enfilade of state apartments, but are brought out most fully in Tara Hamling and Catherine Richardson's analysis of the early modern house, which they approach as a series of spaces for daily routines of domestic life.[9]

This chapter draws on these ideas to trace the development of 'easy' furniture and its changing material qualities, paying particular attention to the ways in which it formed an increasing concern for country-house owners—a central tenet of John Crowley's argument about the invention of comfort.[10] Building on this, it examines the impact that such furniture had on how people sat and felt, and seeks to establish what made them comfortable (or uncomfortable) both in physical and social terms. In doing this, it looks to animate histories of the country house by occupying chairs and populating rooms. This takes us away from a teleological account of improvement and towards an experiential perspective on

comfort. Indeed, the chapter develops this further by exploring the interaction between people and material objects, both as individual pieces of
furniture and as arrangements within the room. In this way, it seeks to
link together questions of (individual) physical comfort and (collective)
social comfort; of *being* comfortable and *feeling* comfortable. Finally,
the discussion arrives at questions concerning the cultural specificity of
notions of informality and comfort. DeJean argues for the primacy of
Paris, but others have sought to distinguish the formality of 'aristocratic'
French with more 'bourgeois' English taste.[11] In this context, attention
focuses particularly on how different cultures imagined and described
their comfortable and modern living rooms, especially in relation to an
English ideal.

Improving Comfort: Easy Chairs and Sofas

There is a long history of making furniture more comfortable for the sitter, not least through the use of cushions and squabs, but the trajectory
of adjustments to the furniture itself is nicely summarised in William
Cowper's much-quoted poem *The Sofa*:

> But restless was the chair; the back erect
> Distress'd the weary loins felt no ease;
> The slipp'ry seat betray'd the sliding part
> That press'd it, and the feet hung dangling down,
> Anxious in vain to find the distant floor.
>   . . .
> Thus first necessity invented stools,
> Convenience next suggested elbow chairs,
> And luxury th'accomplished Sofa last.[12]

This progression indicates a chronological development, both in the
design of furniture and the ways in which people might want and be able
to sit. There was a shift in taste and in the posture of the sitter: a lower
and upholstered seat and an angled back made for a more comfortable
sitting position and a more relaxed sitter—a link made explicit in Andre-
Jacob Roubo's *L'Art du menuisier* of 1769.[13] As Cowper intimates, early
chairs, or back-stools as they were often called in England, had vertical
backs which kept the sitter erect, but many also had rectangular padded
seats. Peter Thornton argues that they were often deployed as dining
chairs, but could also be used for relaxing in front of the fire.[14] This
type of chair was common across seventeenth-century Europe. In Rome,
for example, chairs with upholstered seats were listed in the houses of
relatively poor widows as well as those of wealthy merchants; what distinguished these houses and their owners was the number of chairs and
quality of the coverings.[15]

Two linked developments made chairs easier for the sitter: adding arms or elbows and making the back rounded and/or angled and generally upholstered. Such innovations were part of what Daniel Roche calls 'a verit-able creative fury . . . which expresses best of all the quest for comfort and relaxation'.[16] Developments were pioneered by French furniture-makers in the mid-seventeenth century but spread quickly into other parts of Europe. They appear in Dutch interior paintings from the 1660s and 1670s, espe-cially those by Pieter de Hooch and Pieter Janssens Elinga. Some have arms but others do not and, although the backs are often only slightly raked, the seats and backs are upholstered.[17] French or elbow chairs are mentioned in England from the 1660s and were clearly intended to be comfortable and suitable for repose. When Mrs. Rich, the central figure in Mary Pix's 1700 play *The Beau Defeated*, is anticipating a lengthy lecture from her brother-in-law she calls to her maid 'an elbow-chair, Betty, I foresee Mr. Rich intends to talk me to sleep'.[18] Fifty years later, the designs in Thomas Chippendale's *Director* (1745) marked a clear difference between his 'new pattern' chairs and French elbow chairs (Figure 3.1). In addition to the arms, the latter had seats that were 2½ inches lower as well as being wider and deeper, and the backs as well as the seats were upholstered.[19]

This kind of elbow chair features in numerous paintings of English domestic interiors throughout the late seventeenth and eighteenth century and, as a sample of inventories for Bedfordshire indicates, they became increasingly numerous (see Table 3.1). Unsurprisingly, they were most

Figure 3.1 'French Elbow Chairs', Thomas Chippendale, *The Gentleman and Cabinet Maker's Director* (London, 1754 edition): plate XX

Table 3.1 Listings of easy seating in Bedfordshire inventories, 1721–1823

	1721–49 (n=5)			1761–99 (n=7)			1816–23 (n=3)		
	Invs	No.	Mean	Invs	No.	Mean	Invs	No.	Mean
Elbow chair	5	39	7.8	7	89	12.7	3	95	31.7
Easy chair	4	16	3.2	3	7	1.0	3	5	1.7
Settee	3	8	1.6	3	8	1.1	3	7	2.3
Couch	2	4	0.8	6	9	1.3	1	4	1.3
Sofa	0	0	0.0	2	7	1.0	3	16	5.3

Source: James Collett-White (ed.), *Inventories of Bedfordshire Country Houses, 1714–1830* (Bedford: Bedford Historical Record Society, 1995)

Note: 1721–49: Ampthill Park House (1737); Chicksands Priory (1721); Colworth House (1723); Leighton Buzzard Prebendary House (1749); Wrest Park (1740). 1761–79: Colworth House (1771); Hasells Hall (1761); Hinwick House (1766); Houghton House (1767); Oakley House (1772); Sharnbrook House (1786); Southill Park House (1779). 1816–23: Colworth House (1816), Ickwell Bury (1823); Melchbourne House (1817)

numerous in the large houses such as Houghton House and Southill Park, but they were found everywhere, most often in living rooms and also in bedchambers. At Houghton, and later at Colworth and Ickwell Bury, they were also found in the rooms of servants, allowing housekeepers and butlers at least to sit in their rooms in some comfort.[20]

Another important French innovation, and a form not noted by Cowper, was the *fauteuil de commodité* or easy chair. This was more accommodating than an ordinary armchair, being much larger and having a lower seat and more luxuriant upholstery. They were being made for smaller royal chateaux and the more private rooms at Versailles as early as 1672. Fifteen years later, an inventory of the royal court listed 30 *fauteuil de commodité*, all apparently with adjustable backs somewhat reminiscent of earlier invalid or sleeping chairs.[21] They appear in many contemporary pictures, including a 1680s engraving: *Femme de qualitie à sa toilette*. This shows the noblewoman seated at her toilette; one of her maids is warming her gown by the fire and another dresses her hair whilst the lady herself talks to a male friend who sits in a low-seated upholstered chair with a fashionable high back.[22] According to Roubo's retrospective analysis, easy chairs evolved in important ways in the early eighteenth century: the back was lowered, making the chairs less massive, armrests were set further backwards and the seat made more curved and potentially more suited to the sitter's body shape, thus making the chair more comfortable.[23] There was also a proliferation of variations, including the *fauteuil en confessional*, the wraparound wings of which created a sense of privacy and intimacy, and the *bergère* (shepherdess), with its encompassing arms and deeper seat (Figure 3.2). The latter were much favoured by women, the Marquise de Pompadour having 14 in her Paris house and 36 at the Chateau de Ménars in the 1730s. They remained an

Figure 3.2 Two chairs in the style of the bergères, *Cabinet des Modes ou les Modes Nouvelles*, 15 Février 1786: pl. III, Rijksmuseum, Amsterdam, BI-1959–529–9

important part of the fashionable Parisian *hôtel* and the apartments of courtesans throughout the eighteenth century.[24]

On his travels around Europe in 1696/7, Scipione Santacroce was struck by the ways in which French domestic arrangements were different from those he was used to in Rome. Amongst many other things, he noted that 'next to the bed is always a more comfortable chair, for resting'.[25] Such arrangements were common at this time, but easy chairs were increasingly deployed in public rooms as well. For instance, Jean-François de Troy's *Reading from Moliere* (c.1728) shows a group of five extremely luxurious *fauteuil de commodité* pulled together in a fashionable salon, three of them with very low seats, a style particularly favoured in the 1720s.[26] English country-house owners engaged in a similar search for more comfortable seating, though without always adopting the French terminology.[27] 'Sleeping chairs' were bought for Ham House in about 1678 and easy chairs start to appear in inventories from the early eighteenth century. In the Bedfordshire sample, they were most numerous and widespread in the first half of the century (Table 3.1). As Santacroce found in France, these were mostly placed in bedchambers and were often listed directly after the beds, suggesting a spatial or functional proximity which is underscored by their upholstery being en suite with the bed hangings and curtains in several rooms at Ampthill Park House,

Bedfordshire.[28] That said, an anonymous painting of a music party shows two substantial easy chairs set on either side of a fireplace in a crowded drawing room.[29] These appear quite plain, but descriptions from auction catalogues suggest that some were more ornate; an easy chair sold at the 1772 auction at Horton House in Northamptonshire is described as 'covered in crimson silk damask, frame carved and gilded'—similar to its French counterparts.[30] From the inventories, they appear to have been less numerous than in France, although this is in part be explained the habit of referring to them simply as armed chairs, as Mary Delany did when describing her recent acquisitions: 'I have bespoke four armed-chairs and six other stuffed . . . for the drawing-room, and seats low and easy such as we love'.[31] Significantly, those in Melchbourne House (1817) were referred to as 'lounging chairs'.[32]

According to Cowper's poem, the sofa was the ultimate in comfortable seating. This was another French innovation, seen by DeJean as a highly original form, created in the Gobelins factory in the 1670s.[33] However, the *lit de repos* that they produced echoed the day bed which had its origins in the late Middle Ages and was already a common part of domestic furniture in the early seventeenth century.[34] The precise development trajectory of the sofa is complex to trace as it transmuted from earlier pieces and took on various names and forms, including *canapées* and couches (both originally forms of day bed), which themselves were found alongside alternatives such as *duchesses* and settees (more obviously descended from chairs or benches). From an early date, however, the terms were used somewhat interchangeably: a couch usually referred to something resembling a day bed, but *canapé* was used to describe both seats that took the form of bench-like settees, with a deep and soft cushion covering the whole seat (Figure 3.3) and far more ornate and deeply upholstered sofas (Figure 3.4).

This confusion over terminology is apparent in a 1695 letter sent by Daniel Cronstrom, whilst he was assigned to the Swedish embassy in Paris; he wrote about '*les sophas ou canapée*', apparently struggling to differentiate between the two, but noted that 'there is now no room here where there is not one'.[35] Whatever they were called, the French quickly developed a taste for sofas, and furniture-makers turned out a wide variety under royal and aristocratic patronage. In part, this reflected the desire of nobles for novel items in order to keep up with the latest fashions. Sofas could thus provide the physical comfort of a well-upholstered seat whilst at the same time providing a display of taste and wealth, a priority which is reflected in their increasing ornamentation with carved and often gilded frames.[36] Madame la Duchesse had 36 sofas in the Palais Bourbon placed in many different rooms, including the salon, formal bedroom, gallery, dining room and even the bathing suite, the last reflecting Blondel's imagining of the perfect bathroom with two bathtubs and a pair of sofas.[37]

Figure 3.3 Femme de qualité sur un Canapé (1686): Rijksmuseum, Amsterdam,
RP-P-1960–170

Figure 3.4 Canapé executé pour m.r le comte de Bielenski grand m.al de la cou-
ronne de Pologne, en 1735 (1738–49): Rijksmuseum, Amsterdam,
RP-P-1998–338

Couches appeared in England from the 1630s, for example at Knole
in Kent, and retained their function as day beds as well as playing a cere-
monial function. Comfort came not only from upholstery but also from
squabs and bolsters; indeed, a cane couch in a parlour at Canons Ashby
was described in a 1717 inventory as having a 'green bed and bolster'.[38]
Clearly, it was a place for people to lie and rest during the day. Settees
appear with growing frequency in the later decades of the seventeenth
century. Their form varied, with many early examples having double
backs, as if two chairs had been joined together. By the early decades of
the eighteenth century, they were being acquired for even quite modest
country houses. At Canons Ashby, where there were already two cane
couches and a settee by 1717, Edward Dryden bought a walnut-framed
settee upholstered and covered with needlework covers from the famous
London upholsterer, Thomas Phill (Figure 3.5). It was paired with a set
of six walnut chairs 'frames of newest fashion, stufft up with lynnen' and
again with needlework covers for which Dryden paid a fairly modest

Figure 3.5 Needlework settee by Thomas Phill, Canons Ashby: 1714 (photograph by author)

£9 12s. 8d. in 1715.[39] As with sofas in France, this was tasteful as well as comfortable furniture, the 'newest fashion' referring to the innovation of cabriole legs, and it was probably intended for the withdrawing room where it appeared en suite with needlework curtains and bed hangings in later inventories.

Canons Ashby appears to have been fairly typical of more modest country houses, comparisons with the sample from neighbouring Bedfordshire indicating an average of over two couches or settees per house in the first half of the eighteenth century (Table 3.1).[40] Couches were more commonly placed in bedchambers and settees in living rooms or galleries, underlining the association of the former with sleeping or resting during the day. At Canons Ashby, the pattern was more complex, but none of the couches or settees were found in bedchambers. Settees were consistently located in the Right Hand or Best Parlour and the Withdrawing Room, and later appeared in an upstairs Dining Room. They added a more comfortable option to the chairs they were placed alongside, although many of the latter were upholstered, with stuff, hair or needlework bottoms. Couches were quickly relegated to the more private Bathing Room adjoining the Withdrawing Room on the ground floor and Long Gallery, where they were found alongside a large settee from the 1756 inventory onwards. Furnishing a long gallery in this way was fairly typical, although placing three or four large seats into what is a quite narrow room must have been quite a squeeze.

The Canons Ashby inventories also highlight the interchangeable nomenclature of these upholstered seats. In the 1819 inventory, the sofa in the upstairs Drawing Room (formerly the Dining Room) was a genuinely new acquisition, marked on the inventory as the property of Lady Dryden rather than an heirloom of the house.[41] However, the other sofas were all older pieces, previously described as settees, most notably Edward Dryden's needlework settee, acquired in 1716. As a description, 'sofa' is rare in England before 1700, although its appearance does seem to be associated with a new kind of furniture, Thornton quoting a bill presented to William III for 'a fine black soffa of a new fashion, filled up with downe, the frieze and cheeks all moulded and fringed'.[42] They are absent from the sample of Bedfordshire inventories, even into the 1740s and are still outnumbered by settees and couches into the third quarter of the eighteenth century (Table 3.1). However, a shift was evident in Chippendale's *Director*, the 1762 edition including four designs for sofas, another intended for a grand apartment and a further two with elaborate chinoiserie canopies.[43] The first of these had bolsters and pillows and the seat was set at the same height as his French elbow chairs, suggesting that they would be used en suite.

By the early nineteenth century, the Antonies at Colworth House in Bedfordshire could boast seven sofas, four couches and a settee, as well as a 'superb Grecian chair covered with rick silk'.[44] Their distribution appears not only telling of the triumph of the sofa but also marks a distinction between furniture providing physical comfort in public and private: sofas were found mostly in rooms for entertaining (the drawing room and breakfast room), couches in more private bedchambers and the boudoir, and the settee in the butler's pantry. However, a rather different picture emerges at Ickwell Bury, a rather less grand residence than Colworth, but nonetheless one that had been recently refurnished by John and Susannah Harvey. Here, we see sofas and settees set alongside one another in both the lower and presumably more private upper drawing rooms. In the former, the furniture is en suite: 'a Mahogany framed sofa stuffed in Moreen, squab and cushions, two Mahogany settees to correspond with squab cushions and three linen Covers to the same'.[45] In making themselves comfortable, the Antonies and Harveys chose different styles of seating, but all were furnished in a fashionable manner.

All this finery and comfort came at a cost. English inventories from the eighteenth century rarely give the value of goods, but the sums laid out by the Antonies were probably similar to those spent by James Henry Leigh. Certainly, the descriptions of their sofas correspond to those in bills presented to Leigh. His major refurbishment of Stoneleigh Abbey included the acquisition of five ottoman sofas, two rosewood sofas, a chaise longue, a Grecian couch and an antique sofa.[46] The largest and most expensive items were the two large ottoman sofas purchased from the upholsterer David Taylor: one 19 ft 3 in. × 14 ft 9 in. and the other 17 ft 5 in. × 5 ft 5 in., both covered with crimson silk and ornamented with gold silk lace, and costing him £147 13s. 2d. They were clearly impressive and opulent items, designed to impress his guests and display his wealth and taste; but they were also built to be comfortable, with 'thick best horsehair quilted squabs & thick back cushions'.[47] This combination was repeated with the antique sofa bought from John Johnstone for £59 8s., along with three ottomans. His bill described the former as having:

> mouldings and foliage leaves all out of the solid wood, handsome ornamented legs & on strong castors, the whole richly finished in burnished and mat gold, the ends scrolled to form bolsters double stuffed and bordered in fine brown linen, with thick double stuffed squab seat with feather cushions to the end and back.

The whole thing was covered in velvet with a silk border.[48]

This marrying of display and comfort belies Crowley's implication that people gradually switched their priorities from the former to the latter as the eighteenth century progressed.[49] It was, moreover, a combination lauded in the instructive literature, as is apparent from the monthly articles on 'Fashionable Furniture' in Ackermann's *Repository of Arts*. The piece appearing in the issue for October 1809, for example, illustrated a Grecian settee and, having described its physical appearance, noted that 'this tasteful article of furniture may be drawn from the window to any other part of the room, not only affording the highest degree of comfort and convenience, but being also an elegant and fashionable ornament'.[50] Not only did these articles bring together comfort and elegance, but they also communicated to the reader how the materiality and design of the furniture enhanced the comfort and convenience of the occupant. One of a pair of library chairs featured in the issue from August 1810 gave the gentleman the option of sitting astride the chair, facing a reading desk at the back, or 'when its occupier is tired of the first position' to move the desk around and sit sideways. This clever design offered not only flexibility but also comfort: 'the circling arms in either way form a pleasant and easy back, and also, in every direction, supports the arms'.[51] This formed part of a growing taste for ingenious furniture in the early decades of the nineteenth century, which itself created a plethora of patents, but it drew on a longer tradition of furniture-makers offering inventive and convenient designs.[52]

Sitting Comfortably

To chart the spread of these more comfortable forms of seating is straightforward enough, but what difference did it make to the ways in which people sat, how they enjoyed sitting, and how they felt? DeJean places great emphasis on the way in which sofas encouraged fashionable Parisians to 'throw off formality and adopt instead carefree, casual poses'—an entirely new aspect of comfort.[53] She argues that this shift to sitting in a relaxed and comfortable position was led by the court and in particular by the Marquise de Montespan. She was depicted half-sitting and half-lying on richly upholstered sofas or *lits de repos*—a nonchalant pose replicated in a series of engravings of fashionable French noblewomen depicted on equally fashionable sofas (see Figure 3.3).[54] They are seen again in paintings such as de Troy's *Reading from Moliere* and *The Declaration of Love* (1724) and Jean-Baptiste-Marie Pierre's *La Mauvaise Nouvelle* (1740). In the first of these, the fashionable visitors to the salon recline comfortably on their thickly upholstered easy chairs and, in the last, the woman lies back in a similarly capacious easy chair, her foot resting on a small footstool.[55] The same relaxed pose is struck in the 1774 print *La Soirée d'hyver*, where a woman lies back in a bergère, legs crossed at the ankle (Figure 3.6). Quite apart from the physical relaxation depicted, what is striking is the preponderance of women featured in these paintings and engravings, cementing the connection between the female body and the comfort, luxury and perhaps even moral decadence of the sofa. This connects with Werner Sombart's arguments about women being central to a process wherein luxury was 'objectified' into 'rich dresses, comfortable houses, and precious jewels',[56] and in some ways challenges the suggestion that comfort formed an acceptable face of luxury; or perhaps more precisely it illustrates how pushing the boundaries of comfort too far could spill over into luxury and moral decadence.[57]

The sofa in Jean-François de Troy's *The Declaration of Love* (1724) adds another dimension by placing two people on the same seat: the woman is again reclining and relaxed, her head resting against the high back of the sofa and her arm resting a large cushion; the man not only kneels before her but also rests against the sofa, taking her hand in his own. There are hints here—and in the allegorical scene in the painting hanging above the couple—of the sofa's reputation as a site of seduction.[58] This idea is repeated in works by the Swedish painter Niclas Lafrensen (1737–1807), including *Le Dejeuner en Tête a Tête* which portrays a young couple in a loving embrace on an elegant sofa upholstered in blue satin, and *L'Heureux Moment*, where a man kneels and leans forward to embrace a woman who sits on a heavily gilded sofa (Figure 3.7).[59] It also appears in many French novels and is most completely developed in Crebillon's *La Sopha* (1742), which tells of a

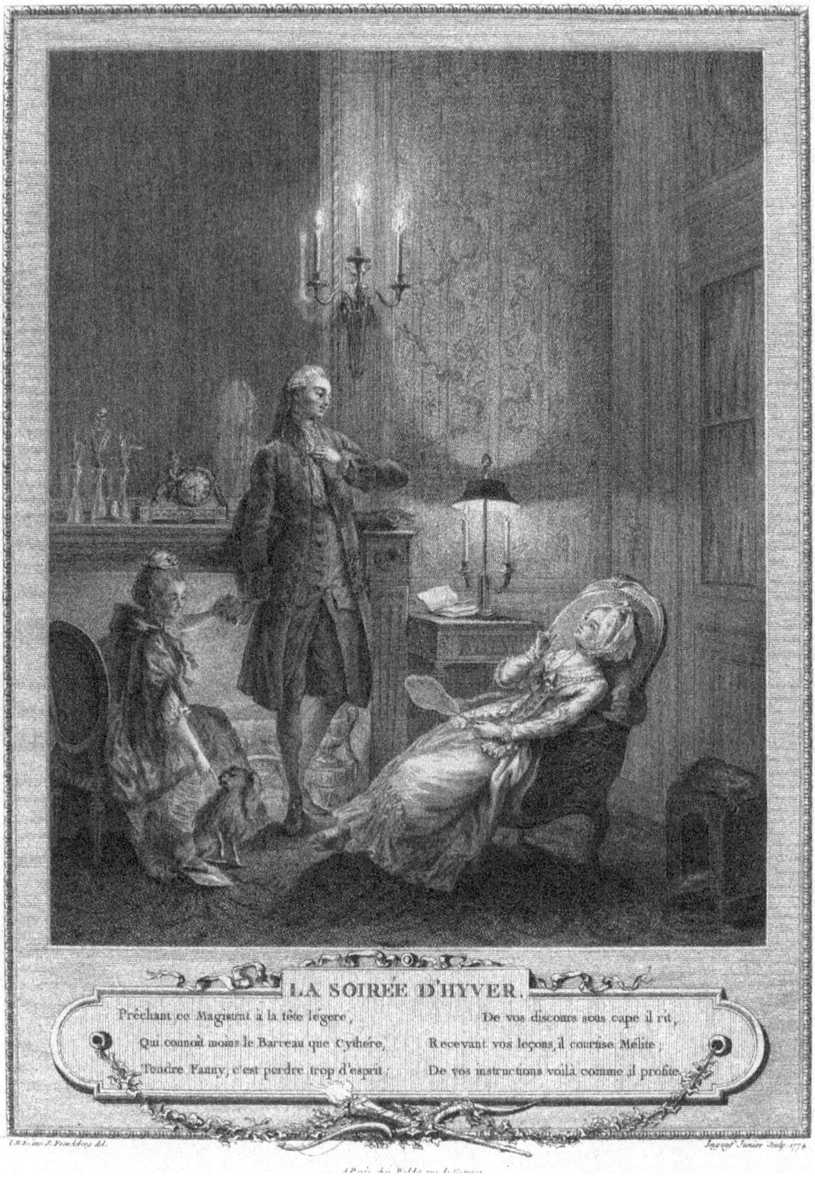

LA SOIRÉE D'HYVER.

Figure 3.6 François Robert Inguof, *La Soirée d'hyver* (1774): National Gallery of Art, Washington, DC, 1943.3.4377

Figure 3.7 Nicolas Delaunay, engraving after Niclas Lafrensen, *L'Heureux moment* (1770): Rijksmuseum, Amsterdam, RP-P-1924-482

soul forced to inhabit sofas in different situations. In one, the female owner uses the sofa to consummate her love for both a slave and a young Brahmin.[60] Although, as DeJean observes, there is little to substantiate this reputation in historical sources, the literary associations were often repeated, Walpole penning the following:

> I am so nice, who ever saw
> A Latin book on my sofa?
> You'll find as soon a Bible there,
> Or recipes for pastry-ware.
> Jesus! D'ye think I ever read
> But Crebillon or Calprenede?[61]

For DeJean, these associations made the English very nervous about having sofas in their homes, especially in public rooms where they received guests. She argues that they preferred to perch uncomfortably on upright chairs, contrasting the paintings of de Troy and François Boucher with those of Arthur Devis, specifically his portrayal of Mr. and Mrs. Bull who she dismisses as being unable to master 'the French look' (that is relaxed, almost decadent informality) because they are too stiff and formal, and too intent on display.[62]

The contradistinction between comfort and performance and display of self is also brought out in Crowley's analysis, although he marks a temporal rather than spatial shift.[63] However, the contrast between France and England may be more imagined than real. It is suggestive of an important cultural difference that French and English elites wanted to see themselves in such different lights: the former lounging on sofas or looking at them with a longing gaze, the latter with their settees half out of sight beside the fireplace. Yet this relies on a rather selective sample of French paintings: many produced in the middle decades of the eighteenth century by Charpentier and others portray families sitting in groups and poses remarkably similar to those seen in English conversation pieces.[64] Even if we read Devis as an accurate portrayer of behaviour and manners, it is quite possible that the Bulls derived a kind of social comfort from sitting in a correct manner. They were behaving or, more accurately, chose to be painted in a way that accorded with social conventions of the day; hence, they *felt* comfortable regardless of posture or upholstery.[65]

That said, English landowners were by no means so scandalised as DeJean would have us believe. On the one hand, there was no shortage of English artists happy to play on the reputation of the sofa as a site of seduction. The 1780 engraving *A Man Trap*, published by Carrington Bowles, portrays a fashionably dressed woman in a light and low-cut dress sitting in a large patterned sofa, legs crossed and hands together on her lap. Echoing the works of Lafrensen, Matthew Darly's *The Unlucky Surprise* (1773) shows a man entering a room to find his wife in her lover's embrace, both of them sat on a low-backed sofa, whilst the 1794 print *Stay me with Flagons* depicts a young beau reclining on a sofa with a prostitute (Figure 3.8).[66] Much more explicit is the erotic scene portrayed on the inside of an early nineteenth-century gold-lined tortoiseshell snuffbox:

Figure 3.8 Stay me with Flagons, printed by Laurie and Whittle (1794): Lewis
Walpole Library, Farmington, CT, 773.03.20.02 (Courtesy of The
Lewis Walpole Library, Yale University)

a woman lies on a fashionable striped sofa, her back supported by a bolster and her leg wrapped around the lover who lies on top of her.[67]

More generally, sofas could be enjoyed as fashionable and comfortable, without being luxuries that indulged the body and compromised propriety. In a 1743 letter, Horace Walpole wrote to Horace Mann that he might stir himself into writing against the government: 'because I am not quite so much at ease as on my own sofa. I could persuade myself that it is my Lord Carteret's fault, that I am only sitting in a common arm chair, when I would be lolling in a *péché-mortel*' (literally, a mortal sin, but also a wide couch which could accommodate two people).[68]

There is not only a contrast between the relative comfort of the sofa, armchair and couch, but also a moral overtone, especially given the name of the last piece of furniture—a link which ties us back to Crebillon's story. However, Walpole's own sofa seems more like a place of quiet comfort, both in a physical sense and in the mental repose that it might offer. This same sentiment resurfaces in William Cole's account of Conyers Middleton, sent to Walpole in 1750, in which he describes the deteriorating health of their mutual friend: 'what he most complained of was the uneasiness of sitting . . . and he often mentioned the comfort of a very easy sofa that would give him rest when he got home'.[69] It is also apparent in women's letters. Writing in 1783, Lady Louisa Stuart related an anecdote about a friend making a visit to the Duchess of Argyle, whom she found 'lolling in her usual nonchalante [*sic*] manner upon a settee'.[70] Twenty years earlier, Catherine Talbot noted that 'with an aching head and twitching limbs you go about the world active, useful, cheerful, and thankful—While I, plump and rosy, eating hearty, sleeping well, sit lolling in my easy chair, and not deigning even to look comfortable'.[71] Clearly, comfortable and relaxed sitting was an expected product of the easy chair and sofa, with perhaps the key distinction between the two coming in terms of their showiness rather than their comfort. As the poet Thomas Gray remarked about a friend: 'his other great chair holds open its arms to receive you, if not with all the grace, yet with as much good-will as any Duchesses quilted péché-mortel, or sofa with a triple gold fringe'.[72]

The comfort of a couch or sofa is illustrated well in a 1760s sketch by Thomas Patch of his fellow Grand Tourist Mr. Bennet, depicted reclining on a sofa reading a letter, his back propped against a cushion (Figure 3.9). A similar pose is struck by John Farr in a painting by François Xavier Vispré and by Catherine Allan in a watercolour by John Harden: both have their feet up and recline against the side of the sofa.[73] Back in France, Theodore Lebrun's *Woman in Pink Reclining on a Canape* (1819) is again pictured sitting back with her feet resting on the sofa, quietly reading her book.[74] All these sitters are taking advantage of the versatility of sofas, which Sheraton noted in writing that the cushions from the back of a sofa might 'serve at time for bolsters, being placed against the arms to loll against'.[75] Even ordinary armchairs could offer a relaxed sitting position, as is clear from a *c.*1710 sketch by J. Poitvin.[76]

Figure 3.9 Thomas Patch, *Mr. Bennet Reclining on a Sofa* (1760s): Yale Center for British Art, Paul Mellon Collection, New Haven, CT, B1977.14.309(4)

A man and woman are pictured taking tea in front of the fire, an easy-looking armchair is in the background, but it is the man's posture which is most arresting: sitting back in his chair with his legs stretched out in front of him. He looks very comfortable. Similarly, Lafrensen also depicted people seated on sofas in a most decorous manner. In *La Consolation de l'absence*—a painting paired with *La Moment Heureux*—the same woman sits on the sofa, a letter in her hand and a workbox before her on which rests a cup and a small lidded jug. She appears to be waiting for her lover to arrive, but a more innocent image is conjured by his *Lady drinking tea*, in which the female sitter sits demure and upright on a powder-blue sofa, tiny teacup in hand, a small cylinder table placed before her to hold the teapot and sugar bowl.[77]

Assemblages and Arrangements: Comfortable Informality

As with fires, stoves, candles and lamps, the use of easy chairs and sofas to create a more relaxed and comfortable domestic environment depended on both material and technical developments and a shift in attitudes and behaviours. It also relied on the acquisition of a range of related items of furniture which formed the kind of grouping conceived in assemblage theory, which explores—amongst other things—the ways in which material systems self-organise.[78] At a conceptual level, we might see the elements of these assemblages as the building blocks comprising a comfortable room and, by scaling this up, a comfortable house—they were linked together not only materially but also socially and linguistically. More pragmatically, as Girouard notes of the French country house, they brought together 'comfortable and richly appointed chairs and sofas', pictures and mirrors, games and musical instruments.[79] More specifically, sitting in sofas and easy chairs also meant deploying a range of occasional furniture. In France, these included *tables courante* and later *tables volantes*, which could be moved around the room as required, but there were also small writing tables, sewing tables, small desks, workboxes and the like. Many of these small pieces of furniture incorporated ingenuity and technical innovation within elegant and often showy exteriors. Carolyn Sargentson shows how French secretaries, jewellery boxes and writing tables made in the later eighteenth century included numerous separate draws and hidden compartments to ensure the privacy and security of their contents.[80] They also provided convenience through everything being in its rightful place: miniature versions of the well planned and convenient house discussed in Chapter 2. Mechanical devices added further convenience and were just as much a feature of the work of English furniture-makers. Thomas Sheraton, for example, published designs for a reading and writing table, the top of which could be angled for ease of reading whilst a shelf for writing came out of the end, and another for a ladies' writing table where the ink well and pen drawer would 'fly out by themselves, by the force of a common spring, when the knob on which the candle-branch is fixed is pressed'.[81] DeJean styles this convenience furniture, allowing anyone relaxing on a sofa or easy chair to read, write, take tea or engage in a handicraft without leaving their comfortable seat.[82] As assemblages, they included both human and non-human elements: the sofa, its occupants and a variety of smaller pieces. Boucher's painting of the Marquise de Pompadour shows her elegantly reclining with a small writing desk by her side: a candle sits on top, alongside a letter waiting to be sealed; the draw is open to reveal compartments for quills, pounce powder and ink, and books are piled on a shelf beneath.[83]

Furniture of this kind might be seen as part of the culture of new luxury which de Vries argues was associated less with displays of social and economic exclusivity and more with inclusive sociability.[84] Small tea tables or games tables, for example, were central to the rituals of polite sociability that characterised eighteenth-century domestic culture. The growing informality of these activities was both facilitated by and encouraged the proliferation of moveable, convenient pieces of furniture that could be set alongside sofas and easy chairs. But, of course, such furniture was not simply a convenient prop to social practices; it also displayed the owner's wealth and taste, blurring any easy distinction between old and new luxury. As Coquery's analysis of upholsterers' accounts demonstrates, the cost of these small items of furniture could vary hugely depending on materials and workmanship. The Parisian upholsterer Mathurin Law sold a cherry-wood table for a mere 2 livres and a veneered sewing table for 27 livres, but a solid mahogany desk with shelves covered in green leather, folding candleholders, an inkwell, pounce box and tray, and decorated in gold lacework supplied to the Comptesse de Champagne cost 240 livres. Much depended upon the use to which the piece would be put: a backgammon set might be had for 13 livres if it was intended for private amusement; the board comprising an ebony table ornamented with borders, rosettes and quarter circles in gilt bronze which Law sold for 264 livres was clearly a piece of prestige furniture.[85]

In England, such furniture was a regular feature of country houses by the third quarter of the eighteenth century. At Wrest Park, for example, the 1740 inventory lists a mahogany card table, a rosewood table and a small old tea table in the Little Drawing Room which also contained a settee and a variety of chairs with cushions, whilst at Stoneleigh Abbey in 1737 there were two tea tables and two cards tables spread across three rooms.[86] Only in the more private back parlour were these accompanied by obviously comfortable seating in form of an easy chair, so they were perhaps rather different in form to the low and small pieces being deployed in Parisian *salle de compagnie*. From the mid-eighteenth century, however, there was a growing emphasis on smaller, specialised and often more mobile pieces. At Houghton House in Bedfordshire, a major refurbishment in the 1760s followed quickly after the marriage of Francis, Marquis of Tavistock and son of the Duke of Bedford, to Lady Elizabeth Keppel in 1764. An inventory taken 3 years later, following the death of the Marquis from a riding accident, thus presents a house furnished in the latest taste and comfort. The drawing room contained a large carved mahogany sofa with loose cushions and bolsters covered in green mixed damask with two elbow chairs en suite; a lined card table, a ladies' writing table with a circular front, a mahogany spider-leg table, a second ladies writing desk, and a small pear-tree wood ink stand.[87]

Similar assemblages are seen in houses across the country, the profusion of specialist pieces expanding further in the early nineteenth century. Like Houghton, Melchbourne House had experienced a relatively recent makeover when its owner, Andrew St John, 13th Baron, died in 1817—possibly during his father's time but more likely following his own marriage to Louisa Rouse-Boughton. Again, then, we see a house reflecting current standards of comfort and convenience. In the drawing room, we find 'two cabriole sofas, frames gilt, stuff'd & cover'd with green stripe satin'; 12 armchairs to match, a large lounging chair with back and seat cushions, a mahogany sofa table with two draws, a mahogany Pembroke table, a mahogany Canterbury, a mahogany stand for portfolios, an oval air wood Pembroke table, a set of mahogany trio tables, and a small

Figure 3.10 'Sofa table and sofa', Thomas Sheraton, *Cabinet Dictionary* (London: W. Smith, 1803): plate 74

octagonal table.[88] Of particular note here is the sofa table (Figure 3.10), a piece described by Sheraton as being:

> used before a Sofa, and are generally between 5 and 6 feet long, and from 22 to 2 [*sic.*] feet broad; the frame is divided into two drawers, as is shewn in Plate 76, where is also a design for a sofa, that a stranger may more clearly see the use of such tables. The Ladies chiefly occupy them to draw, write, or read upon.[89]

It is significant that women are again specifically linked with the sofa and its related furniture: they would use sofa tables and thus would be occupying sofas—something that was dependent on more informal modes of dress and especially the 'narrowness of both male and female costume'.[90] It may be that these tables were replacing earlier writing and reading desks at this time. At Stoneleigh Abbey, James Henry Leigh was acquiring not just a series of large sofas and ottomans, but also an array of related pieces. In 1813, he bought from Chipchase and Proctor two circular loo tables, a backgammon table and two sofa tables, all made from rosewood inlaid with brass and costing a total of £87 3s. In the same year, Morel and Hughes supplied a set of rosewood trio tables, a lady's writing desk and a foot hassock, which cost £21 3s. Three years later, John Johnstone provided two further sofa tables and a 'Hope table' (together costing £58 12s.), alongside the three ottomans noted earlier.[91]

Convenience, like the comfort of sofas, was by no means cheaply acquired, at least if it involved pieces that were showy as well as practical. The sofa tables from Johnstone were old as much as new luxury: 'made from beautiful Amboyna wood richly inlaid and ornamented with brass and curious East India woods' this was a piece that demonstrated Leigh's wealth, taste and 'reach' as a consumer. His furniture was convenient, but it also spoke of his place in global systems of exchange married with high-quality metropolitan workmanship.

Of course, not every room was intended for comfortable and sociable living. We have already seen that architectural designs maintained a distinction between formal public rooms and others that were intended for more private and relaxed sociability. These divisions were reinforced by the different assemblages of furniture placed in these rooms and the different purposes to which they were put. At Stoneleigh Abbey, there was a clear differentiation between the furnishings in the Great Apartment and the breakfast room and dining parlour, separated by the great hall. The former retained its gilt walnut chairs and pier tables and its crimson drapery throughout the eighteenth century; it formed a very formal statement of family pedigree, the objects working together as an assemblage, almost regardless of their use by the occupants of the house.[92] The latter experienced successive changes and additions which made the rooms more comfortable and sociable spaces. In the early 1760s, Edward, fifth Baron Leigh, added music stands, a Pembroke table, an ebony inkstand, a small organ, and a mahogany box of battledores and shuttlecocks. After his death in 1786, the process was continued by his sister, Mary, who added a variety of musical instruments, several board games and an even greater variety of work and reading tables.[93]

Set in different rooms, a particular piece of furniture could take on different meanings and uses. Canapés lined up in the great public rooms of Parisian *hôtels* (that is, grand Parisian town houses) symbolised the owner's taste; those in dining rooms were mostly decorative rather than functional. As DeJean notes, it is unclear how much either was actually used.[94] In contrast, the sofas in more private rooms undoubtedly afforded their owners greater comfort and relaxation. In English houses, the same distinctions might be inferred from the groupings of furniture which accompanied sofas. At Brixworth Hall in Northamptonshire (1797), for example, the sofa in the dining room was placed alongside the dining table and chairs, a pair of sideboards, a wine cooler, knife box and so on; it would scarcely invite comfortable and relaxed sitting. In the drawing room, by contrast, a sofa with a japanned frame and chintz covers was surrounded by matching elbow chairs, a secretary writing desk, two Pembroke tables, four conversation stools, a pair of card tables and a 'work or writing table, with drawer, slider and sliding back screen', presumably to offer protection from the fire. Here, the comfort of the sofa is matched by the convenience of accompanying furniture in a manner that might encourage relaxed sitting.[95]

It was the arrangement as well as the assemblage of furniture that made a room comfortable: writing desks and tea tables were placed close to sofas and easy chairs were grouped informally, as illustrated in de Troy's *Reading of Molliere* where the low chairs are drawn together, close to the fire and shielded from the door by a folding screen. Proximity brought intimacy and companionship, something which Roubo suggested could be achieved by placing two sofas opposite each other, facilitating a relaxed conversation or companionable reading.[96] Similar arrangements were seen in English country houses, implied in the assemblages listed in inventories and sale catalogues and made clear in a growing array of pictures portraying elite domestic interiors. Augustus Pugin's (*c*.1815) depiction of the library of Cassiobury Park shows a pair of L-shaped sofas set either side of the fireplace, one paired with an easy chair and sofa table (Figure 3.11). In Lady Sophia Cecil's (1821) etchings of the drawing rooms at Burghley House, the sofas are placed facing each other, each with their own low tables, whilst in Charlotte Bosanquet's (*c*.1840) watercolour of the drawing room at Vinters, the sofas are set less formally, but still face each other a low table.[97]

Figure 3.11 Augustus Charles Pugin, 'Great Library, Cassiobury Park' (c.1815), from John Britton, *The History and Description of Cassiobury Park, 1837* (London: Chiswick Press, 1837)

These arrangements accord with the materiality of polite but more relaxed sociability outlined by Girouard and Vickery; by the third quarter of the eighteenth century, there had been a decisive shift to these sociable and comfortable settings in country houses across Europe.[98] A comfortable room was one in which one could relax and enjoy company in an informal manner. This meant acquiring particular types of furniture and creating appropriate arrangements to facilitate the right kind of informality and a willingness to deploy the pieces in this manner. Lady Louisa Stuart wrote of her experience at a party hosted by Elizabeth Montagu in 1800, where she encountered a formal circle that was very outdated at the time:

> Everything in that house, as if under a spell, was sure to form itself into a circle or semicircle. [. . .] I once saw this produce a ludicrous scene. Mrs. Montagu having invited us to a very early party, we went at the hour appointed and took our stations in a vast half-moon, consisting of about twenty or twenty-five women, where, placed between two grave faces unknown to me, I sat, hiding yawns with my fan and wondering at the unwonted seclusion of the superior sex. At length a door opened behind us, and a body of eminent personages—the chancellor, I think, and a bishop or two among them—filed in from the dining-room. They looked wistfully over our shoulders at a good fire, which the barrier we presented left them no means of approaching; then drawing chairs from the wall, seated themselves around us in an outer crescent, silent and solemn as our own.[99]

The formal arrangements of the room spoke to Montagu's control over her company and were, as Lady Stuart observed, well suited to 'a brilliant interchange . . . of pointed sentences and happy repartees. Every flash being visible, every joke distinctly heard from one end to the other', but it was 'the worst shape imaginable for easy familiar conversation'.[100] A different arrangement of furniture was needed for this: tables for reading and writing, and corners in which to settle. As she noted of Archerfield in 1799:

> all is new and nicely furnished in the most fashionable manner. It wants nothing but more furniture for the middle of rooms. I mean all is set out in order, no comfortable tables to write or read at . . . quite a contrast to the delightful gallery at Dalkeith, where you can settle yourself in any corner.[101]

The resemblance of this to Repton's portrayal of the 'modern living room' is quite striking. In his contrasting image to the traditional and formal circle, the room is arranged with a variety of different groupings of furniture and people: an easy chair beside the fire and a second in the corner, together with a footstool; an armchair by the window, and a small table and chairs in another corner. Significantly, a man lifts a chair to join the group around the table, highlighting the flexibility of these arrangements of furniture: pieces could be moved to make different groupings and to facilitate different activities.

This was linked to a shift in fashion away from having all the furniture arranged around the walls until it was needed—a practice that remained common through to the 1770s in France and England, and even later in more peripheral parts of Europe, including Sweden.[102] What Repton depicted was not simply a different arrangement, wherein furniture was permanently placed in the middle of the room, but the act of furniture being rearranged according to need. Flexibility and mobility were increasingly built into many items of furniture. Chippendale, for instance, included designs for *duchesses* and couches which could be split to make separate easy chairs and stools, allowing different arrangements and uses of the furniture.[103] Mobility was increased by making pieces smaller and lighter, but could also be achieved through the addition of handles or castors. With the former, Sheraton noted that his reading and writing table, 'being made for the convenience of moving from one room to another, there is a handle fixed on to the upper shelf'.[104] It was thus mobile, though probably only with the assistance of servants—yet again, illustrating how servants contributed to their employer's comfort and convenience. Chippendale included castors on his designs for sofas and measured the seat height to include these. That they were often supplied in this way is apparent from the bills presented to James Henry Leigh, in which the detailed descriptions of individual pieces often mention 'strong castors'. It is also seen in many contemporary illustrations. An engraving of the library at Woburn Abbey, for instance, shows the sofa, easy chair and footstool all with castors.[105] These were important because they allowed the furniture to be moved easily and without necessarily calling on the aid of footmen. That said, the large sofas and ottomans bought by James Henry Leigh were not things that were so readily moved about the room; their placement thus created more fixed arrangements for informal and small group interaction, bringing with them the need for sofa tables and other kinds of convenience furniture.[106]

Just as telling as the emergence of these room arrangements is the growing tendency of artists to draw or paint them and everyday family life, rather than set groups of people in a somewhat artificial manner on a standardised backdrop.[107] For example, a watercolour by an amateur artist shows the library at Elton Hall in Huntingdonshire in 1818.[108] As was common by this date, the library was being used as a family living room: two easy chairs and a sofa are drawn around a small table in the middle of the room; another sofa stands in the large bay window with a low table set in front, and two further sofas flank the fire, ready to be drawn out and used when needed. On a chest of draws in the foreground sit a writing set, a number of books, a chessboard, a newspaper and a workbasket. Several of these items appear to have been casually, almost carelessly placed there, probably by one of the four women who occupy the room. The scene is relaxed and informal, with furniture and smaller items arranged in a comfortable and casual manner. It resembles the drawing room at Guy's Cliffe in Warwickshire that so delighted Prince Pückler-Muskau when he visited in the 1820s. As noted in the introduction to this volume, he was struck with an interior 'fitted up with equal attention to taste and comfort', and particularly the drawing room where there 'burnt a comfortable fire; exquisite pictures adorned the walls, and many sofas of different shapes as well as tables covered with curiosities and furniture standing about in agreeable disorder made everything appear homely and charming'.[109] Such agreeable disorder was a long distance from both the luxurious and arguably rather mannered informality of the Parisian salons and the more measured arrangements of sofas and armchairs seen in mid-eighteenth-century English houses. It fits into an increasingly Europe-wide taste for informal living illustrated in engravings and amateur watercolours of houses in France, Germany, Austria, Poland and Sweden.[110]

Informality, Sociability and 'English Comfort'

The growing use of comfortable furniture and its informal arrangement within the country house was closely linked to changing patterns of social interaction which placed emphasis on sociability and informality. Although relaxed informality can be seen in the furniture and the sociability of early-eighteenth-century Paris, an emphasis on informality was increasingly associated with England and with what was termed 'English comfort'—an idea to which we return towards the end of this chapter.

Girouard has argued that the changing spatiality and material culture of the country house was a central underpinning of successive shifts in social behaviour. For him, what the social house required above all was space for staging large gatherings and the circulation of company.[111] Something of this is seen in William Hogarth's painting of an assembly at Wanstead House in Essex (1728–31). People are arranged in separate groups, sitting around card tables or an elaborate silvered tea table, but the assembly is a single group of people: if they are not playing cards or drinking tea, the company is engaged in watching these activities. Much the same is true of his depiction of the Wollaston family (1730): cards and tea are again the focus of attention and both chairs and people are arranged around tables accordingly. There is some hint of mobility at the back of this painting, with a servant moving a chair, but it appears to be aimed at helping someone to join or observe the card game.[112] That the furniture is a prop to this rather formal socialising, rather than a source of physical comfort or ease is also apparent in several accounts of assemblies given by Mrs. Lybbe Powys. At Fawley Court in Buckingham-shire, for example, she noted the sequencing of spaces for an assembly in 1777 and the way in which rooms were repurposed for the occasion: the hall was used for supper, whist the library became the entrance hall, and the drawing room and eating room were used for cards. 'The latter looked so elegant lighted up', she exclaimed, with 'two tables at loo, one quinze, one vingt-une, many whist'.[113] This focus on grandeur, elegance and taste is repeated in many of her accounts; comfort and ease are words that she seldom used to describe the places that she visited.

Whilst not in themselves occasions that allowed relaxation or com-fort in a physical sense, there was social comfort as well as kudos to be gained from the event being well staged and from correct behaviour and manners being followed. Comfort was a feeling as well as a physi-cal experience. Powys wrote of the assembly at Fawley Court that the 'general exclamation of wonder' that greeted the sight of the hall, laid out for supper, 'you may be certain, pleas'd the owners'.[114] Mr. and Mrs. Lloyd, the hosts of a party given in 1824 and attended by John Williams, brother of Mary Elizabeth Lucy of Charlecote Park, would have been far less happy with his appraisal of their efforts. The dinner was given in a 'future Greenhouse—a most sociable banqueting room upon a very cold frosty night in January—the walls damp with undried plaster and the fireplace, calculated for cinders, refusing to take in the lumps of coal that the servant was attempting to force into its throat'.[115] The physical discomfort of the setting reflected badly on the unfortunate hosts and their attempt to show off their new house—'or rather, old one patched' as Williams rather snidely observed.

A very similar round of gatherings took place in chateaux in the French countryside. During the summer, there were balls, theatre and often plenty of good company assembled in the major houses. As in England, the company might be quite mixed. The metropolitan de Frenilly wrote rather acerbically about a 'crowd of local squires' who were invited to the chateau at Monts, home to the Vicomte de la Chastre in 1789, and complained that they 'descended there in swarms, clumsy, badly turned out and still smelling of the kennel'.[116] A few years earlier, J. de Norvins wrote about the balls staged at Brienne, noting how the company danced on the ground floor whilst servants had a ballroom in the *salle d'office* in the basement. Rooms were pressed into service as needed, regardless of their usual function. In Parisian *sociétiés* or *salons*, by contrast, the setting was everything. Especially in the mid-eighteenth century, but also into the 1780s, elegant couches were lined up for the guests and the room arranged with the latest in comfortable, convenient and fashionable fur-niture. Girouard places emphasis on the 'frequently brilliant and expen-sive decoration of the room' in which these gatherings took place, often following a meal at which the atmosphere might be more relaxed and intimate.[117] The *sociétiés* themselves could be intellectual and political, or artistic, or light-hearted; they were almost always quite formal, requiring the involvement of all the company. It is questionable, then, how far the easy chairs and sofas in Parisian salons allowed their occupants to relax; they were physically comfortable, but the occasion required everyone to be attentive and to participate, preferably in a way that reflected the character of the gathering.

Whether in town or country, formal socialising in assemblies, balls and *societies* was undoubtedly pleasurable—one needs only recollect the excitement occasioned amongst the young men and women by a forthcoming ball in Jane Austen's novels to be clear about this. However, there was often discomfort to be endured, as Thomas Rowlandson's *Comforts of a Modern Gala* (1807) makes clear: stiff collars and itchy wigs, the oppressive heat and the press of the crowd.[118] Moreover, the company itself could be tiresome. Horace Walpole spoke for many when he wrote to Lady Ossory that 'latterly I have had company enough; but it is comfortable to sit at home, and see as many as one wishes—and still more comfortable *just now*, to see very few of those one dislikes'.[119] For Walpole, comfort was derived from the people and the ability to *choose* the company with whom one mixed. This was somewhat at odds with the tradition of country house hospitality: open and available to all, at least if they were of a certain standing. As Adrian Tinniswood notes, however, this was changing through the course of the long eighteenth century and there was a growing distinction between visitors, who came to see the house, and guests, who were invited by the owner.[120] Lady Oxford removed herself from Welbeck Abbey to her cottage on the estate precisely to give herself scope to avoid unwelcome visitors. Presaging Walpole's sentiment, she wrote to Lady Mary Wortley Montagu in 1755 that she enjoyed being at Welbeck but lamented that 'I must see more company than I chuse'.[121] Social discomfort could arise from being forced into unwanted sociability.

More importantly for our present discussion, these guests were increasingly entertained in a less formal manner. Mary Delany, then still Mrs. Pendarves, captured something of this in a letter written in the autumn of 1736 from Bulstrode in Buckinghamshire, where she was staying as a guest:

> We have variety of amusements, as *reading, working*, and *drawing*, in a morning, in the afternoon, the scene changes, there are billiards, looking over prints, coffee, tea, cribbage, and by way of interlude pretty Lady Betty comes upon the stage, and I can play as well at bo-peep as if I had had a nursery of my own [. . .] I forgot to tell you, that for one hour after dinner here is an assembly of old women, that we converse with; 'tis true they are a *little antiquated* but they are easy, and though they *don't say a word* they are *great helps to our conversation*.[122]

As early as the 1730s, then, there was a mix of informality through the day and formality in the evening, a combination which required different arrangements of furniture, especially with the variety of activities under-taken in the daytime. Mary Delany implies a relaxed atmosphere where people engaged in whatever pleased them most, especially in the morning when reading, working or drawing were often undertaken individually, though sometimes with everyone together in a room. A generation later, in 1778, Lady Caroline Dawson was able to write in appreciative terms about a very informal gathering of friends at her house in Portarlington in Ireland. Lord and Lady De Vesci and Sir Robert and Lady Staples were 'very pleasant people to have in the house, as they don't require to be entertained': the men went hunting during the day, and 'in the evening we have a very good whist party, and a working party at each side of the fire, which is comfortable enough'.[123]

Such informality and contentment with mundane activities are also apparent from the account written by the Revd Stotherd Abdy of his stay at Welford in Berkshire in 1770. He was part of a larger party of about ten guests who were at the house for the wedding of Jacob Houb-lon to Susannah Archer, whose parents owned Welford. Their days were filled with hunting and billiards, or walking in the park and conversing in small groups in their dressing rooms. 11 September was wet and the whole party remained indoors:

> We rummaged all the book-cases, examined the knick knacks upon the toilet, and set a parcel of shells a-dancing in vinegar. Lady Mary and Miss Archer worked; Mr Houblon gazed with admiration upon his future bride; Mrs Abdy and Mr Archer were engaged in stamping crests upon doilys with the new invented composition; and I read to the company a most excellent chapter out of the *Art of Inventing, addressed to the Patronesses of Humble Companions*.[124]

The group is assembled, but each is engaged in their own world, creat-ing a relaxed gathering where everyone felt at their ease. Their comfort came from feeling as much as being comfortable; it was social rather than physical. Abdy says little about the furniture in the room, but there must have been a variety of chairs arranged informally around the room: a work table for Lady Mary and Miss Archer and perhaps another for Mrs. Abdy and Mr. Archer, and no doubt a fire in the hearth to keep them warm. It was precisely this kind of arrangement which Humphrey Repton imagined in his modern living room: small groups of people reading, talking, playing music or inspecting prints. To quote his accompanying poem more fully, the modern living room is a place:

Where guests to whim, to task or fancy true
Scatter'd in groups, their different plans pursue.
Here politicians eagerly relate
The last day's news, or the last night's debate.
Here books of poetry and books of prints
Furnish aspiring artists with new hints
Flowers, landscapes, figures cram'd in one portfolio
There blend discordant tints, to form an olio
While discords twanging from the half tuned harp
Make dullness cheerful, changing flat to sharp.[125]

Yet we have already noted that this was not an entirely modern scene. Abdy and Delany were socialising in very similar ways one or two generations earlier and probably drew on broadly similar room arrangements of furniture—something which questions Girouard's dating of the decline of the formal circle to *c*.1780.[126] That said, it is equally apparent that the kind of studied informality being championed by Repton was being written more firmly into the fabric of the room through the growing array of comfortable and convenient furniture discussed earlier.

The idea of the house party had also spread in pre-revolutionary France. Alongside the large balls described earlier, there was a growing taste for informal and convivial gatherings such as that described by J. de Bonardi du Mesnil when visiting his father's neighbour at Auny—a chateau owned by the Nicolays, a very wealthy and well-connected Parisian family. The house itself was 'luxury at once in the grandest manner and exceedingly enjoyable', whilst the

> house-party was made up of plenty of lawyers, most of whom had plenty of wit—and plenty of well-born women, who were no longer young but still had all the charms of breeding and good manners; they had left their grand airs in Paris and brought nothing with them but their good humour.[127]

Bonardi relates that much of the day was taken up with expeditions into the surrounding countryside, which allowed for intimate moments as well as general conviviality. The style of dining probably reflected that depicted in a painting of a dinner given by the Prince of Salm in about 1770: the atmosphere is convivial and relaxed, but the company is sat around a large table, laid out formally in the French style and with livered servants waiting on the diners' needs.[128] Closer to Paris, the chateau of Le Marais was used by Madame de La Briche to stage large entertainments in the 1770s. House parties here could often run to 30 or more people and were sometimes criticised for being too grand and Parisian in style. However, a more intimate and informal atmosphere is captured in a sketch from 1819 which shows a smaller group of family and friends mostly seated around a table. Madame de La Briche herself is dividing a skein of wool with her granddaughter; others are reading or working at their embroidery; a friend is shown sketching at a small table and another is playing a harpsichord. The seats include elbow chairs, but there is no evidence of sofas or easy chairs, although these were certainly present in the house and are depicted in another amateur painting, this time by Baron du Tott. It shows the salon at the chateau of Cahville, a room sparsely furnished and occupied by six individuals, each occupying an array of low comfortable seats and each occupied in their own pursuits: reading, sketching, embroidery and sleeping.[129]

It would be a mistake, however, to assume that these informal house parties were always relaxing and pleasurable occasions. A comfortable atmosphere and a sense of ease could be hard to create and sustain, especially when guests were not those that the host might have chosen themselves. At Canons Ashby, Elizabeth Dryden drew a sharp contrast between the social comfort afforded by different guests. Mrs. Phelps and 'her three amiable Daughters', who played and sang in the evening, were welcome because they were 'well disposed and very sensible'. The days appear to have passed pleasantly if rather uneventfully, Elizabeth noting that 'we go on in the old way here with little variety, but they are always cheerful and good humoured'.[130] She could feel relaxed and comfortable with them, something that was not the case with another group that visited the following year, when she complained that 'I now have a large vulgar family with me, so unlike the Phelps!'.[131] Similar sentiments were expressed by Sybille Reventlow at Brahetrolleborg in Denmark. Her husband, Count Johann Luvig, was an influential political figure in Copenhagen and an education reformer who ran a number of schools in the neighbourhood of the manor house at Brahetrolleborg.[132] These two roles meant that there was a constant stream of guests staying at the house. In October 1790, Reventlow wrote to her sister, Louise:

> I'm writing this to you with 3 strange Gentlemen and 6 children in the room [. . .] it seems to be written in the books of destiny that we shall never be alone here. The day before yesterday, Baggesens left, and yesterday, a young Guldencrone from Jutland arrived, today a certain Otte, they both want to <u>see</u>, and apart from them, we have Professor Abildgaard from Cop[enhagen].[133]

These were not friends, but visitors who required showing around the estate and the schools as well as accommodating and feeding. They eroded the social comfort of domestic life by making the host feel unsettled and resentful, and undermined the home as a place for family and friends, especially if they outstayed their welcome. Sybille, again writing to Louise, complained that: 'Mr. Otte, who is not leaving, is starting to bore me; really I should not be, he is a good boy [. . .] but he has established himself so well here, that I fear he might stay for the winter'. Fortunately, he left after another couple of weeks, but his place was quickly filled by a head teacher from Lindenborg, who came with his wife. Again, Sybille despaired because the woman was not 'enough of a countrywoman to talk to about the household. Imagine how our conversations dry out, we are in a desert, a boredom, which I think she shares. Tonight, she retired right after the tea'.[134]

In longing to be alone with her family, Reventlow echoed Walpole's desire to sit comfortably at home and avoid unwanted company. The social comfort afforded by informal and relaxed domestic arrangements, both material and behavioural, needed to be carefully guarded. It is in the intimacy of family and a few select friends that the comfort of furnishings could combine with that of a relaxed atmosphere to create a truly comfortable domestic environment in the country house. This 'social privacy', as Francis Hart terms being only with one's closest companions, was central to a feeling of emotional ease.[135] As Jane Austen noted 'I am very snug with the front drawing-room all to myself, & would not say "Thank you" for any companion but you. The quietness of it does me good'.[136] Similar sentiments were expressed by Catherine Neville, daughter of Richard Aldworth Griffin, the owner of Audley End. Writing to her sister Mary, she reassured her that 'we jog on very comfortably', enjoying a quiet life with few formal engagements. She continued: 'I assure you I grow quite used to sitting alone; Miss Forrest or Harriet generally stay in the Saloon till two & we never want for conversation, & from two till dinner, I have as you know plenty of occupations'.[137] That said, the absence of such company could prompt complaints, Catherine writing that, after returning from church, 'I went into my little Room & very much missed you, our dinner was not brilliant the North Parlour was hotter than usual & the Evening passed in a dull manner'.[138]

The kind of intimate and relaxed atmosphere described by Catherine Neville, and the ways in which this related to the use and arrangement of furniture, are beautifully illustrated in John Harden's paintings of his family and friends at Brathay Hall.[139] In one, *Reading and sewing* (1805), we see a group of three women seated on a sofa and engaged in needlework; one has her foot resting on a small footstool. A small table with two candles has been set in front of them and an open workbox stands at the end of the sofa. Opposite, a man sits reading, his foot resting on the fender of the fireplace. The group is relaxed, each person absorbed in their own business; the furniture is comfortable, mobile and convenient. A similar combination is seen in *Backgammon* (1808), where a low armchair has been pulled up to a sofa allowing two men to play backgammon, the board set on a small round table between them. Beyond sit another three people, one on the sofa and the others on armchairs; they are half watching the game and half engaged with reading and sewing. Significantly, none of the people in these paintings could be said to be lounging. They generally sit erect, yet are clearly at their ease, comfortable with their company and with their surroundings.

These aspects of comfort were found across Europe but were particularly associated with England and the English country house. English travellers had long been critical of the showiness of French houses, which they saw as being to the detriment of their comfortableness as places to live. Frances Crewe was typical of many English people abroad, writing of France that what a traveller needed was not magnificence; rather, it was:

> Comfort, a word they have not, and all their Gilding, Glasses, bad Pictures, and Damask Curtains are not, in my Opinion, worth one Door that Shuts, or Bell that rings, or Carpet that keeps one warm, or Shutter that defends the Window: none of which Comforts are hardly ever to be met with in France or Flanders; nor do any Foreigners that I ever met with seem to think them necessary Points, as we do, towards good Accommodation in Travelling.[140]

She wrote, of course, with the traveller's typical love of home and condemnation of standards elsewhere. Moreover, we have already seen that many developments in comfortable furniture were, in fact, French innovations.[141] Nonetheless, the essentials that Frances Crewe enumerated, together with a broader set of ideals about informal room arrangements and relaxed living, were also noted by overseas visitors as something particular and praiseworthy in English domestic material culture.

Visiting Devon in 1810, a Swedish traveller, Erik Gustaf Geijer, wrote home that 'in this area there are many beautiful country houses. An English country house, in its velvet-green settings, with white sandy paths winding along under leafy trees, gives the most pleasant image of English Comfort [*Engelsk Comfort*]'.[142] In the same year, the French traveller Louis Simond was visiting Britain. He noted in his journal that 'tables, sofas, and chairs, were studiously *deranges* about the fireplaces, and in the middle of the rooms, as if the family had just left them'. There is a slight barb in his observation that this arrangement was so prevalent that 'fashionable houses look like an Upholsterer's or cabinet-maker's Shop'. He is also clear that this is a particularly English characteristic, the fashion being 'to banish everything like géne and ceremony'.[143] A decade later, the Hungarian, Baron Miklos Wesselenyi, was gushing about Welbeck Abbey: 'The beautiful castle was built in the middle of large green lawn, next to a light-coloured lake that appears like a mirror [. . .] Real country houses are only in England, and enjoying the country life to the full—only the English know how to do that'.[144]

What this enjoyment, and more broadly 'English comfort' meant was captured by the American biographer and historian, Washington Irving, who visited England in 1820:

It is in the country that the Englishman gives scope to his natural feelings. He breaks loose gladly from the cold formalities and negative civilities of town; throws off his habits of shy reserve, and becomes joyous and free-hearted. He manages to collect round him all the conveniences and elegancies of polite life, and to banish its restraints. His country-seat abounds with every requisite, either for studious retirement, tasteful gratification, or rural exercise. Books, paintings, music, horses, dogs, and sporting implements of all kinds, are at hand. He puts no constraint, either upon his guests or himself, but, in the true spirit of hospitality, provides the means of enjoyment, and leaves every one to partake according to his inclination.[145]

Material comforts abound, but it is the coupling of these with a lack of formality and constraints, and a genial hospitality, that make the English country house truly comfortable. This was not simply the stary-eyed vision of an Anglophone American. A few years later, Prince Pückler-Muskau noted that country-house living formed 'without any question the most agreeable side of English life; for there is great freedom, and a banishment of most of the wearisome ceremonies which, with us, tire both host and guest'.[146]

This growing taste for English ways of living and English houses was part of a broader shift taking place across Europe in the later decades of the eighteenth century. England offered an alternative cultural and social reference point to France, which had long dominated European taste and material culture. It was seen as less elitist and aristocratic and more accessible and a force for the democratisation of luxury.[147] The attractions of English goods was summed up in the German publication *Journal des Luxus und der Moden*, which argued in an issue from August 1793 that:

> The tasteful simplicity and solidity that England succeeded in bestowing upon all of her manufactured goods so recommends itself to and attracts us Germans that at present the word English [or] English goods already has such an irresistibly magical allure for us, and has become nearly synonymous with perfection and beauty in works of craft.[148]

There was, of course, a political element to this. Protestant northern Germany favoured English taste whilst the Catholic states in the south remained loyal to French fashions. Sweden was divided between the Hattar (hats) who favoured France and Mössor (caps) who leant towards England.[149] In this sense, identifying and favouring taste (or comfort) as English was a political statement. And in France 'English comfort' was used as a veiled criticism of aristocratic Anglomania in the early decades of the nineteenth century.[150]

It would be wrong, though, to reduce an emphasis on comfort to political posturing. The admiration for English comfort as a way of life and a set of material objects appears too widespread and is expressed too spontaneously for that. Two things are especially noteworthy here. The first is that the pleasures of 'English comfort' were apparent in many parts of Europe long before the term became widely deployed in the early nineteenth century, as is apparent from the 1785 engraving *Le Dejeuner Anglais* (Figure 3.12). This shows an informal meal being taken in a

Figure 3.12 Geraud Vidal, *Le Dejeuner Anglais* (1785) (Courtesy National Gallery of Art, Washington, DC, 1942.9.2101)

morning room. The woman is in négligé and the man, still in English riding boots, sits reading; his hat lying on a chair where it was dropped. There is a general air of relaxed informality. In this context, 'English comfort' might be seen as a convenient label for a more general shift in domestic life in the country house; albeit one that was particularly developed and visible in English houses. The second is that 'English comfort' forms perhaps the ultimate expression of Jan de Vries' notion of bourgeois 'new luxury': accessible and inclusive, linked with new forms of sociability and new material objects.[151] Comfort was an important part of this: not only the physical comfort of easy chairs and convenient furniture, but also the social comfort of the informality of room arrangements and social interaction.

Conclusions: Home Comforts

Making a house comfortable was a complex process that involved a growing array of choices in terms of furniture intended to give the body greater ease and to facilitate a more relaxed and informal mode of living. Easy chairs and sofas encouraged different ways of sitting which helped to reshape physical posture and mental attitudes: the relaxation of the body went hand in hand with the relaxation of social conventions and social practices. Lighter furniture provided greater flexibility, allowing rooms to be arranged and rearranged by their occupants, rather than relying on servants. The relationship between domestic space and social practice was therefore mutual: furniture and room arrangements were reformed in the light of new modes of living and served to shape and orchestrate practice and behaviour. It is apparent that these changes were seen across Europe, especially in the later decades of the eighteenth century; but it is also striking that they were especially associated with the English country house. Visitors were struck with the informality and ease of English living and wrote about this when they returned home in terms that make it clear that they saw it as something different and desirable.

It is important, however, that we avoid a teleological view of comfort and informality: an English ideal to which other Europeans aspired. DeJean points to the primacy of Parisian high society in many of these developments, but more important than arguments about where such furniture and modes of living first appeared is the contingency and non-linear trajectory of any domestic transformation. For one thing, form and practice were not necessarily wedded. Whilst sofas, for example, encouraged relaxed sitting, some people chose to maintain an upright and more formal posture; conversely, it was quite possible to lean back and cross one's legs when sitting in an upright chair. Similarly, mobile and flexible furniture certainly encouraged informal arrangements and sociability, but the early nineteenth century saw increasingly heavy pieces, such as the ottomans bought by James Henry Leigh. These were much harder to move and tended to be deployed in more permanent arrangements: still informal, but in a more orchestrated manner that put greater emphasis on the objects and their arrangement in moulding behaviour and social practice.

In many ways, the creation of comfort can be seen as an exercise in balancing competing imperatives: displaying status and creating physical ease; facilitating informality and remaining in tune with social norms and conventions; welcoming company and maintaining privacy. It was in creating the right balance that true comfort might best be achieved. In Jane Austen's *Emma*, Mrs. Elton famously declares that 'there is nothing like staying at home, for real comfort'. Her meaning is revealed as she continues:

> Nobody can be more devoted to home than I am. I was quite a proverb for it at Maple Grove [. . .] and yet I am no advocate for entire seclusion. I think, on the contrary, when people shut themselves up entirely from society, it is a very bad thing; and that it is much more advisable to mix in the world in a proper degree, without living in it either too much or too little.[152]

This delicate balance could best be struck when the individual was in control of events and spaces. Sybille Reventlow longed for an end to the stream of visitors about which she had little choice. Richard Aldworth Griffin, meanwhile, complained when a guest at Stowe in 1817 that 'there is always too great ease, for amongst other things there is no damn hour for dinner'; conversely, he also criticised arrangements at Henham Hall later the same year because 'we are very regular here, but the sameness is too great for perfect ease'.[153] For Aldworth Griffin there was inconvenience and discomfort in too much and too little informality; more fundamentally, he was troubled by not being able to order his surroundings and routines—something which he could only do at home. In this, he fits with Judith Lewis' argument that such control is essential to a sense of comfort and of being at home.[154] Control might be manifest in the placement of furniture, the organisation of daily routines and the ability to decide who might visit and stay; it extended further into other aspects that impacted corporeal and mental comfort including cleanliness, the quality of air, daily practices and religious rituals. It is to these concerns that we turn next.

Notes

1. John Cornforth, *Early Georgian Interiors* (New Haven: Yale University Press, 2004), 11–74; Joan DeJean, *The Age of Comfort: When Paris Discovered Casual and the Modern Home Began* (New York: Bloomsbury, 2009), 45–64; Johanna Ilmakunnas, 'Northern Comfort and Discomfort: Spaces and Objects in Swedish Country Houses, c.1740–1800', in Jon Stobart (ed.),

The Comforts of Home in Western Europe, 1700–1900 (London: Blooms-bury, 2020), 46–53.

2. Peter Thornton, *Authentic Décor: The Domestic Interior, 1620–1920* (London: Weidenfeld & Nicolson, 1985), 102–3, 155–7, 226–8; DeJean, *Age of Comfort*, 131–9; Akiko Shimbo, *Furniture-Makers and Consumers in England, 1754–1851* (Farnham: Ashgate, 2015), 82–93. See also John Crowley, *The Invention of Comfort: Sensibilities and Design in Early-Modern Britain and Early America* (Baltimore: Johns Hopkins University Press, 2001), 141–70.

3. Mark Girouard, *Life in the English Country House: a Social and Architectural History* (New Haven: Yale University Press, 1978), 213–44. See also John Cornforth, *English Interiors, 1799–1848: The Quest for Comfort* (London: Barrie & Jenkins, 1978).

4. Girouard, *English Country House*, 236–8.

5. Humphrey Repton, *Fragments on the Theory of Landscape Gardening* (London, 1840), 460.

6. See, of example, Andor Gomme, 'Abbey into Palace: A Lesser Wilton?', in Robert Bearman (ed.), *Stoneleigh Abbey: The House, Its Owners, Its Lands* (Stratford-upon-Avon: Shakespeare Birthplace Trust, 2004); Thornton, *Authentic Decor*; Cornforth, *English Interiors*. Girouard's early example of how this might be achieved has produced remarkably few further studies in a similar mould.

7. Daniel Roche, 'Gaz à tous les étages', *En attendant Nadeau*, 48 (2018), 57. I am grateful Olivier Jandot for this reference.

8. Katrina Navickas, *Protest and the Politics of Space and Place, 1789–1848* (Manchester: Manchester University Press, 2016); Jon Stobart, Andrew Hann, and Victoria Morgan (eds.), *Spaces of Consumption: Leisure and Shopping in the English Town, c. 1680–1830* (London: Routledge, 2007); Ilja Van Damme, Bert de Munck, and Andrew Miles (eds.), *Cities and Creativity from the Renaissance to the Present* (London: Routledge, 2018).

9. Tara Hamling and Catherine Richardson, *A Day at Home in Early Modern England* (New Haven: Yale University Press, 2017).

10. Crowley, *Invention of Comfort*.

11. See, for example, Michael North, *'Material Delight and the Joy of Living': Cultural Consumption in the Age of Enlightenment in Germany* (Aldershot: Ashgate, 2008).

12. William Cowper, *The Task, Book I: The Sofa* (London, 1785).

13. Andre-Jacob Roubo, *L'Art du menuisier* (Paris, 1769–75). See also Witold Rybcynski, *Home: A Short History* (New York: Viking, 1986), 94–6; DeJean, *Age of Comfort*, 109–11.

14. Peter Thornton, *Seventeenth-Century Interior Decoration* (New Haven: Yale University Press, 1978), 186–7.

15. Renata Ago, *Gusto for Things: A History of Objects in Seventeenth-Century Rome* (Chicago: University of Chicago Press, 2013), 70–82.

16. Daniel Roche, *History of Everyday Things: The Birth of Consumption in France, 1600–1800* (Cambridge: Cambridge University Press, 2000), 173.

17. See John Lougham, 'Between Reality and Artful Fiction: The Representation of the Domestic Interior in Seventeenth-Century Dutch Art', in Jeremy Aynsley and Charlotte Grant (eds.), *Imagined Interiors: Representing the Domestic Interior Since the Renaissance* (London: V&A Publications, 2006), 79, 90, 93, 96.

18. Mary Pix, *The Beau Defeated* (1700), act 2, scene 2.

19. Thomas Chippendale, *The Gentleman and Cabinet Maker's Director* (London, 1754), 7–8, plates XII–XV, XVII–XX.

20. James Collett-White (ed.), *Inventories of Bedfordshire Country Houses, 1714–1830* (Bedford: Bedford Historical Record Society, 1995). For further discussion of comfort for servants, see Jon Stobart, 'Servants' Furniture: Hierarchies and Identities in the English Country House', in Karen Lipsage and Stephen Hague (eds.), *At Home in the Eighteenth Century: Interrogating Domestic Space* (London: Routledge, 2021).
21. DeJean, *Age of Comfort*, 107–8; Thornton, *Seventeenth-Century Interior Decoration*, 195–6.
22. Reproduced in Thornton, *Authentic Decor*, 66.
23. Roubo, *L'Art du menuisier*, vol. 2, plate 223.
24. DeJean, *Age of Comfort*, 111; Kathryn Norberg, 'Goddesses of Taste: Courtesans and Their Furniture in Late-Eighteenth-Century Paris', in Dena Goodman and Kathryn Norberg (eds.), *Furnishing the Eighteenth Century: What Furniture Can Tell Us About the European and American Past* (London: Routledge, 2006), 106.
25. Quoted in Ago, *Gusto for Things*, 90.
26. Jean-François de Troy, *Reading from Moliere* (c.1728), Private Collection, https://en.wikipedia.org/wiki/File:FdeTroyLectureMoliere.jpg.
27. Cornforth, *Early Georgian Interiors*, 100–5, 209–12; Thornton, *Authentic Decor*, 102.
28. Collett-White, *Bedfordshire Country Houses*, 18–19.
29. Anon., *A Music Party* (c.1740), Reproduced in Charles Saumarez-Smith, *Eighteenth-Century Decoration: Design and Domestic Interior in England* (London: Weidenfeld & Nicolson, 1993), 162–3.
30. Northamptonshire Central Library (NCL), M0005647NL/6, Horton Hall, 1772, f.7.
31. Sarah Chauncey Woolsey (ed.), *The Autobiography and Correspondence of Mrs Delany*, vol. 2 (Boston: Roberts Brothers, 1879), 455: Mary Delany to Anne Dewes, 24 November 1754.
32. Collett-White, *Bedfordshire Country Houses*, 178–9.
33. DeJean, *Age of Comfort*, 115.
34. Thornton, *Seventeenth-Century Interior Decoration*, 172–4.
35. Roger-Armand Weigert and Carl Hernmarck (eds.), *Les relations artistiques entre la France et la Suède, 1693–1718: Nicodème Tessin le jeune et Daniel Cronström, Correspondance*, (Stockholm: Nationalmuseum, 1964), letter 7 January 1695: 'Il n'y a maintenat point de chambre ou il n'y en ait icy [sic.]'. See also Thornton, *Seventeenth-Century Interior Decoration*, 210–14.
36. Natacha Coquery, 'The Language of Success: Marketing and Distributing Semi-Luxury Goods in Eighteenth-Century Paris', *Journal of Design History*, 17:1 (2004), 85; DeJean, *Age of Comfort*, 113–17.
37. DeJean, *Age of Comfort*, 127.
38. Northamptonshire Record Office (NRO), D(CA) 901, inventory for 1717.
39. NRO, D(CA) 129, receipted bill from Thomas Phill, 30 April 1716. See Cornforth, *Early Georgian Interiors*, 101.
40. See also Michael Wilson, *The English Country House and Its Furnishings* (London: Chancellor Press, 1977), 74–9, 140–1, 169.
41. NRO, D(CA) 904, inventory of 1819.
42. Thornton, *Seventeenth-Century Interior Decoration*, 213.
43. Chippendale, *Gentleman and Cabinet Maker's Director*, 4–5, plates XXIX–XXXI.
44. Collett-White, *Inventories of Bedfordshire Country Houses*, 55.
45. Collett-White, *Inventories of Bedfordshire Country Houses*, 139.
46. Shakespeare Central Library and Archives (SCLA), DR18/5/7021, DR18/5/7022, DR18/5/7137, DR18/5/7150, DR18/5/7156, DR18/5/7158.

47. SCLA, DR18/5/7021, bill from David Taylor.
48. SCLA, DR18/5/7156, bill from John Johnstone.
49. Crowley, *Invention of Comfort*, 147.
50. Rudolph Ackermann, *Repository of Arts*, October 1809, 277.
51. Ackermann, *Repository*, August 1810, 182.
52. See E.T. Joy, 'Georgian Patent Furniture', in *Connoisseur Year Book* (London: The Connoisseur, 1962), 9–11; Carolyn Sargentson, 'Looking at Furniture Inside Out: Strategies of Security in Eighteenth-Century French Furniture', in Dena Goodman and Kathryn Norberg (eds.), *Furnishing the Eighteenth Century: What Furniture Can Tell Us About the European and American Past* (London: Routledge, 2006), 205–36; Shimbo, *Furniture-Makers and Consumers*, 82–93; Jon Stobart, 'Material Literacies of Home Comfort in Georgian England', in Chloe Wigston-Smith and Serena Dyer (eds.), *Material Literacy in Eighteenth-Century Britain: A Nation of Makers* (London: Bloomsbury, 2020), 83–98.
53. DeJean, *Age of Comfort*, 115.
54. DeJean, *Age of Comfort*, 25, 114–19, 221–2.
55. Jean-Baptiste-Marie Pierre, *La Mauvaise Nouvelle* (1740), https://madparis.fr/francais/musees/musee-nissim-de-camondo/parcours/1er-etage/l-appartement-de-moise-de-camondo-1255/la-mauvaise-nouvelle.
56. Maxine Berg, *Luxury and Pleasure in Eighteenth-Century Britain* (Oxford: Oxford University Press, 2015), 39.
57. Marie Odile-Bernez, 'Comfort, The Acceptable Face of Luxury: An Eighteenth-Century Etymology', *The Journal for Early Modern Cultural Studies*, 14:2 (2014), 3–21.
58. Jean-François de Troy, *The Declaration of Love* (1724), Metropolitan Museum of Art, New York. Reproduced in DeJean, *Age of Comfort*, colour plate opposite 120.
59. Nicolas Delaunay, engraving after Niclas Lafrensen, *L'Heureux Moment* (1777), Rijksmuseum, Amsterdam. This may depict a day bed, but other scenes by Lafrensen show lovers in what is a more clearly a bed room (*Apres le Dejeuner*) and even on a chair (*An Amorous Couple in an Elegant Interior*).
60. Claude Crebillon, *La Sopha: A Moral Tale* (1742; London: George Routledge, 1927), 29–33.
61. Horace Walpole, *Horace Walpole's Correspondence*, vol. 35, 48, https://walpole.library.yale.edu/collections/digital-resources/horace-walpole-correspondence: Horace Walpole to Chute, 12 October 1743.
62. DeJean, *Age of Comfort*, 18–19. She seems to misread the Bulls as commissioners, Devis as an artist, and the English conversation piece as a genre—see Kate Retford, 'From the Interior to Interiority: The Conversation Piece in Georgian England', *Design History*, 20:4 (2007), 291–307.
63. Crowley, *Invention of Comfort*, 141–71.
64. See, for example, Jean-Baptiste Charpentier, *The Family of the Duc de Penthievre* (c.1767), Palace of Versailles.
65. The 'wooden' appearance of figures in Devis's paintings is also linked to his use of wooden mannequins to paint from. See Anon., *Polite Society by Arthur Devis, 1712–1787: Portraits of the English Country Gentleman and His Family* (Preston: Harris Museum and Art Gallery, 1983).
66. Anon. *A Man-Trap* (1780), from a print published by Carrington Bowles: *The Connoisseur*, VII (London: Otto Limited, 1903); Matthew Darley, *The Unlucky Surprise* (1773), Colonial Williamsburg, EMuseum, 1980–226, https://emuseum.history.org/objects/29804/the-unlucky-surprise-the-bengall-minuet;jsessionid=96F2429A3E6F075E3F447862F562003A (accessed 3 August 2020).

67. Galleries Ouaiss Antqiues, www.ouaissantiquites.com/objectdetails/782556/18112/hidden-compartment-snuff-box-tortoiseshell (accessed 3 August 2020).
68. Walpole, *Horace Walpole's Correspondence*, vol. 18, 315: Horace Walpole to Horace Mann 3 October 1743.
69. Walpole, *Horace Walpole's Correspondence*, vol. 15, 313: William Cole's account of Conyers Middleton.
70. Alice Clark (ed.), *Gleanings from an Old Portfolio Containing Some Correspondence Between Lady Louisa Stuart and Her Sister, Caroline, Countess of Portarlington and Other Friends and Relatives*, vol. 2 (Edinburgh, 1895), 301: Lady Louisa Stuart to Mary Wortley Montagu Stuart, 14 September 1783.
71. Elizabeth Carter, *A Series of Letters Between Mrs Elizabeth Carter and Miss Catherine Talbot, from the Year 1741 to 1770*, vol. 3 (Rivington, 1809), 368: Catherine Talbot to Elizabeth Carter, 14 May 1762.
72. Quoted in John Gloag, *Georgian Grace: A Social History of Design, from 1660 to 1830* (London: Black, 1956), 202.
73. Reproduced in Saumarez Smith, *Eighteenth-Century Decoration*, 256–7; Daphne Foskett, *John Harden of Brathay Hall, 1772–1847* (Kendal: Abbot Hall Art Gallery, 1974), plate VI, no. 22.
74. Metropolitan Museum of Art, New York—accession 1979.510.
75. Thomas Sheraton, *Cabinet Dictionary* (London, 1803), 388.
76. See Cornforth, *Early Georgian Interiors*, 4.
77. Niclas Lafrensen, *Consolation de l'absence* (c.1775), National Gallery of Art, Washington, DC, 1942.9.2402, www.nga.gov/collection/art-object-page.3033.html (accessed 3 August 2020); Niclas Lafrensen, *Lady Drinking Tea*, https://commons.wikimedia.org/wiki/File:Lady_drinking_tea_-_Lavreince.jpg.
78. See Gilles Deleuze and Félix Guatarri, *A Thousand Plateaus: Capitalism and Schizophrenia*, trans. Brian Massumi (London: Continuum, 1987); Manuel DeLanda, *Assemblage Theory* (Edinburgh: Edinburgh University Press, 2016).
79. Mark Girouard, *Life in the French Country House* (London: Cassell & Co., 2000), 142.
80. Sargentson, 'Looking at Furniture Inside Out'.
81. Thomas Sheraton, *The Cabinet Maker and Upholsterer's Drawing Book* (London, 1794–96), 396, 389.
82. DeJean, *Age of Comfort*, 131–9.
83. François Boucher, *Marquise de Pompadour* (1756), Alte Pinakothek, Munich.
84. Jan de Vries, *The Industrious Revolution: Consumer Behaviour and the Household Economy, 1650 to the Present* (Cambridge: Cambridge University Press, 2008), 44–5, 57–8.
85. Natacha Coquery, 'Fashion, Business, Diffusion: An Upholsterer's Shop in Eighteenth-Century Paris', in Dena Goodman and Kathryn Norberg (eds.), *Furnishing the Eighteenth Century* (London: Routledge, 2007), 73–4; Coquery, 'Marketing and Distributing Semi-Luxury Goods', 87.
86. Collet-White, *Inventories of Bedfordshire Country Houses*, 255; SCLA, DR18/4/9, 1737 inventory.
87. Collet-White, *Inventories of Bedfordshire Country Houses*, 116.
88. Collet-White, *Inventories of Bedfordshire Country Houses*, 179.
89. Sheraton, *Cabinet Dictionary*, 305–6. The sofa table and sofa are depicted on Plate 74.
90. Cornforth, *English Interiors*, 15. See also DeJean, *Age of Comfort*, 186–204.
91. SCLA, DR18/5/6999, DR18/5/7100, bills from Chipchase and Proctor; DR18/5/7007, bill from Morel and Hughes; DR18/5/7056, bill from John Johnstone. All these tradesmen supplied a great many others pieces as well.

92. For an archaeological parallel, see Oliver Harris, 'More Than Representation: Multiscalar Assemblages and the Deleuzian Challenge to Archaeology', *History of the Human Sciences*, 31:3 (2018), 83–104.

93. SCLA, DR18/4/43, 1774 Inventory with 1806 annotations; DR18/4/69, 1786 inventory. See also Jon Stobart and Mark Rothery, 'Fashion, Heritance and Family: New and Old in the Georgian Country House', *Cultural and Social History*, 11:3 (2014), 385–406.

94. DeJean, *Age of Comfort*, 127.

95. NCL, M0005646NL/15, Brixworth Hall, 1797, 6–7, 14.

96. See Dejean, *Age of Comfort*, 127.

97. Cornforth, *English Interiors*, 46, 34–5, 59.

98. Girouard, *English Country House*, 234–9; Vickery, *Behind Closed Doors*, 129–65.

99. Clark, *Gleanings from an Old Portfolio*, 62–3: Lady Louisa Stuart to Lady Caroline Dawson, September 1800.

100. Clark, *Gleanings from an Old Portfolio*, 63: Lady Louisa Stuart to Lady Caroline Dawson, September 1800.

101. Clark, *Gleanings from an Old Portfolio*, vol. 2, 281: Lady Louisa Stuart to Lady Caroline Dawson, 2 November 1799.

102. Thornton, *Authentic Decor*, 102, 135, 149, 181.

103. Chippendale, *Gentleman and Cabinet Maker's Director*, 4–5.

104. Sheraton, *Cabinet Maker and Upholsterer's Drawing Book*, 396.

105. SCLA, 18/5/7137, bill from John Johnstone; H. Moses, *The Library at Woburn Abbey, Bedfordshire* (1827), reproduced in Cornforth, *English Interiors*, 42.

106. Thornton, *Authentic Decor*, 149.

107. Cornforth, *English Interiors*, 11–23; Retford, 'From the Interior to Interiority'.

108. W. Wells, *The Library at Elton Hall, Huntingdon* (1818), reproduced in Cornforth, *English Interiors*, 68. See also the water colour of the drawing room at Renishaw Hall, Derbyshire (c.1820), reproduced in the same volume.

109. Herman Pückler-Muskau, *Briefe eines verstorbenen: Ein fragmentarisches Tagebuch aus England, Wales* (Halberger, 1831), 242–3.

110. See Thornton, *Authentic Decor*, 198, 200, 230, 233, 240–1.

111. Girouard, *English Country House*, 181–244.

112. William Hogarth, *Assembly at Wanstead* (1728–31), Philadelphia Museum of Art; William Hogarth, *The Wollaston Family* (1730), Bridgeman Art Library. For fuller discussion of the former, see Hannah Armstrong, 'The Lost Landscapes and Interiorscapes of the Eighteenth-Century Estate: Reconstructing Wanstead House and Its Ground' (Unpublished PhD thesis, Birkbeck College, University of London, 2016).

113. Emily Climenson (ed.), *Passages from the Diaries of Mrs Philip Lybbe Powys* (London: Longmans, Green and Co., 1899), 186.

114. Climenson, *Diaries of Mrs Powys*, 187.

115. Warwickshire Record Office (WRO), L6/1539a, John William to Mary Elizabeth Lucy, 15 March 1824. Note that it was a servant, of course, who was feeding the fire.

116. Quoted in Girouard, *French Country House*, 182.

117. Girouard, *French Country House*, 144.

118. Thomas Rowlandson, *The Comforts of a Modern Gala* (1809), V&A: H Beard Print Collection, S.4728–2009.

119. Walpole, *Horace Walpole's Correspondence*, vol. 32, 348: Horace Walpole to Lady Ossory, 26 January 1777.

120. Adrian Tinniswood, *The Polite Tourist: A History of Country House Visiting* (London: National Trust, 1998), 91–112.
121. Quoted in Arthur Turberville, *A History of Welbeck Abbey and Its Owners* (London: Faber and Faber, 1938), 399.
122. Chauncey Woolsey, *Autobiography and Correspondence of Mrs Delany*, vol. 1, 153: Mary Delany to Miss Collingwood, 25 October 1736.
123. Clark, *Gleanings from an Old Portfolio*, vol. 1, 87: Lady Caroline Dawson to Lady Louisa Stuart, [no date] October 1778.
124. Alice Houblon, *The Houblon Family: Its History and Times*, vol. 2 (Edinburgh: Archibald Constable & Co., 1907), 119.
125. J.C. Loudon, *The Landscape Gardening and Landscape Architecture of the Late Humphrey Repton, Esq.* (London: Printed for the Author, 1840), 460.
126. Girouard, *English Country House*, 238.
127. Quoted in Girouard, *French Country House*, 184.
128. See Girouard, *French Country House*, frontispiece.
129. See Girouard, *French Country House*, 185, 195.
130. NRO, D(CA)/361, Elizabeth Dryden to Mrs Steele, [no date] 1821.
131. NRO, D(CA)/361, Elizabeth Dryden to Mrs Steele, [no date] September 1822. This echoes the complaints made by Lady Morley of Saltram in Devon, who complained in a letter to her sister-in-law about a dreadful evening in the company of the vulgar Mrs. G. see Judith Lewis, 'When a House Is Not a Home: Elite English Women and the Eighteenth-Century Country House', *Journal of British Studies*, 48 (2009), 359.
132. See Kristine Dyrmann, 'Sybille Reventlow's Sociability at Brahaetrolleborg', unpublished paper presented at the conference *A Manorial World*, Gammel Estrup, Denmark, 21–23 September 2017. I am grateful to Kristine Dyrmann for letting me quote from her paper.
133. Dyrmann, 'Sybille Reventlow's Sociability', 4.
134. Dyrmann, 'Sybille Reventlow's Sociability', 5.
135. Francis Hart, 'The Spaces of Privacy: Jane Austen', *Nineteenth-Century Fiction*, 30:3 (1975), 310.
136. Quoted in Hart, 'Spaces of Privacy', 318.
137. Flintshire Record Office (FRO), GG15, Catherine Neville to Mary Neville, 1804. For fuller discussion of comfort at Audley End, see Hannah Chavasse, 'Material Culture and the Country House: Fashion, Comfort and Lineage' (Unpublished PhD thesis, University of Northampton, 2015), chapter 4.
138. FRO, GG15, Catherine Neville to Mary Neville, 1804, 2 January 1804.
139. Foskett, *John Harden*, plates 25 and 38.
140. Michael Allen (ed.), *An English Lady in Paris: The Diary of Frances Anne Crewe, 1786* (St Leonards: Oxford Stockley Publications, 2006), 199.
141. See Odile-Bernez, 'Comfort, the Acceptable Face of Luxury', 16.
142. Erik Gustaf Geijer, *Minnen: Utrag ur bref och dagböcker* (Uppsala, 1834), 83, letter sent from Sidmouth, 1st June 1810: 'Flera vackra landtställen finnas här I nejden. En Engelsk Landtgård på sin sammetsgröna tapet, I hvilken de hvita sandgångarna orma sig kring lummiga träd, är den angenämaste bilden af Engelsk Comfort. See also A. Blanck, *Geijer I England 1809–1810* (Stockholm: A. Bonnier, 1914) 63, 182–3, 238. I am grateful to Cristina Prytz for these references.
143. Louis Simond, *Journal of a Tour and Residence in Great Britain During the Years 1810 and 1811*, vol. 2 (Edinburgh: Archibald Constable & Co., 1817), 285–6.
144. Quoted in Kristof Fatsar, ' "Enjoying Country Life to the Full—Only the English Know How to Do That": Appreciation of the British Country House

by Hungarian Aristocratic Visitors', in Jon Stobart (ed.), *Travel and the Country House* (Manchester: Manchester University Press, 2017), 157–8.

145. Washington Irving, *The Sketch-Book of Geoffrey Crayon, Gent* (1821; Philadelphia: J.B. Lippincott & Co., 1871), 90.

146. Quoted Cornforth, *English Interiors*, 19.

147. See Alida Clemente, 'Luxury and Taste in Eighteenth-Century Naples: Representations, Ideas and Social Practices at the Intersection Between the Global and the Local', in Johanna Ilmakunnas and Jon Stobart (eds.), *A Taste for Luxury* (London: Bloomsbury, 2017), 59–76; North, *Material Delight and the Joy of Living*, 45–60; Maxine Berg, 'French Fancy and Cool Britannia: The Fashion Markets of Early Modern Europe', in Simonetta Cavaciocchi (ed.), *Fiere e mercati nella integrazione delle economie Europe secc. XIII–XVIII* (Prato: Le Monnier, 2001), 540–6.

148. Quoted in Michael North, 'Fashion and Luxury in Eighteenth-Century Germany', in Johanna Ilmakunnas and Jon Stobart (eds.), *A Taste for Luxury in Early Modern Europe* (London: Bloomsbury, 2017), 102–3.

149. For fuller discussion, see Michael Roberts, *Age of Liberty: Sweden 1719–1772* (Cambridge: Cambridge University Press, 1986), 15–58, 176–84.

150. Odile-Bernez, 'Comfort, the Acceptable Face of Luxury'.

151. De Vries, *Industrious Revolution*, 44–5.

152. Jane Austen, *Emma* (1815; London, Penguin Edition, 1985), 277.

153. FRO, GG7, Richard Aldworth Griffin to Mary Glynne (née Neville), 31 July 1817 and 3 December 1817.

154. Lewis, 'When a House Is Not a Home'.

Part 2
Emotional Comfort
Feelings, Letters and Home

4 Cleanliness and Godliness
Comforts of the Body and Mind

Whilst challenges remained, the English country house was undoubtedly a more comfortable domestic environment in 1800 than it had been a century earlier. It could be kept warmer and made lighter and was furnished with a growing quantity and range of easy seating. These things had a physical and social benefit: they helped those living in country houses to be and to feel more comfortable. However, the eighteenth-century body also experienced comfort in other ways, many of which related to contemporary understandings of the body in terms of flows and humours that needed to be kept in balance to maintain well-being.[1] Country life and the country house were seen as healthy, certainly in relation to the smoke and fog of the London season. The health-giving exercises of walking, riding and hunting were linked to the fresh air and simple pleasures of country-house living, associations which were strengthened by a growing aesthetic and moral approbation of country life.[2] These were underpinned by a desire for the cleanliness of the domestic setting and the body. Beverly Lemire, for example, has written about the importance of laundering in maintaining clean bodies, aiding personal hygiene and health, and communicating the individual's morality and respectability—an idea developed more fully by Woodruff Smith.[3] In this, the physical is linked to the social and psychological, both as an ideal and a set of values shaping everyday practices within the country house and elsewhere.

The link between body and mind, physical and mental well-being, played a key part in how men and women experienced their everyday lives. The ways in which unease in the mind could create discomfort of the body are apparent in Sarah Goldsmith's analysis of homesickness as a mental state and its physical manifestation as nostalgia. She argues that, whilst Grand Tourists were susceptible to these twin malaises, they feature very little in their travel accounts, largely because such emotions and sufferings sat uneasily with the Grand Tour's role in the formation of elite masculine identities.[4] This kind of stoicism formed one of a set of elite manly virtues discussed by Henry French and Mark Rothery. They see it as part of the virtuous gentleman's ability to exercise command over his feelings and to make the most of the situation in which he finds

DOI: 10.4324/9781003206361-7

himself—an inner fortitude and strength of character that men needed to develop early in life.[5] Religion does not play a large role in their overall vision of gentry masculinity, but others have seen it as a central pillar in many people's lives: it shaped daily practices, ways of thinking and mental well-being—not only in the growing number of evangelicals and dissenters but also in ordinary church people. Brodie Waddell found ample evidence of this in the life writings of a wide range of ordinary people up and down the country, and Donald Spaeth underlines the importance that parishioners placed on an active and effective clergy, able to provide strong religious leadership.[6] What is striking when reading such texts is how often religion and faith were framed in the language of comfort—a point made clear in Michael Smith's analysis of affective communities of religion.[7] Less apparent, however, is how these sentiments impacted the emotions and actions of country-house owners and other members of the elite.

This chapter considers some of the ways in which comfort for the body and mind were conceived and described in eighteenth-century England. The starting point is to think about how bodily comfort was disrupted by smoke and dirt, even in the increasing material comfort of the country house. Houses were warmer and lighter, and the seating and ambience more relaxing, but these were all too easily compromised by a smoking fire or by dirt intruding from outside. The discussion initially focuses on how these discomforts were alleviated through the provision of fresh air and through the labour of servants engaged in routines of domestic cleaning. In line with Woodruff Smith, I argue that these were not only aids to physical comfort, but also props to the social comfort of respectability. Attention then turns to health and the body, firstly through a brief discussion of the comfort promised in advertisements for patent medicines, and in more detail through discussion of beds and bed bugs—issues that troubled elite travellers and country-house owners alike. There was a visceral concern with the softness of feathers and the injurious impact of insect infestation; but bugs, in particular, preyed on the mind, sowing seeds of discomfort in the form of anxieties about the cleanliness of beds and bedding. Such anxieties were the antonym of contentment—a mild emotion that is explored in the third part of the chapter, which argues how this was built around notions of stoicism, but more especially through the everyday activities and routines of the country house which themselves brought comfort. Finally, the chapter turns to the comforts of faith, as expounded in religious treatises and revealed in the letters and diaries of country-house owners and their families throughout the eighteenth century. Both emphasised how comfort derived from Christian duty, the daily routines of religious practice and ultimately from God. If the tribulations of earthly existence seemed too much to bear, there was also comfort to be had in the knowledge of an afterlife in heaven. This discussion removes us somewhat from the materiality of the country house, but this is exactly in line with a key argument for how the Christian faith brought comfort.

(Un)comfortable Environments: Dirt, Smoke and Air

Dirt was a growing concern for country-house owners, and indeed all respectable householders, across eighteenth-century Europe. It was given added impetus in the early decades of the century by the opportunities and challenges for washing afforded by new types of textiles (most notably calicos) and a proliferation of soaps and wash balls.[8] Yet these concerns tapped into older traditions of cleanliness and well-laundered linen as an expression of status at the table which Woodruff Smith places at the heart of his nexus of consumption and respectability.[9] Cleanliness was a virtue, both bodily and domestically: it provided the householder with social comfort, allowing them to feel contented in the knowledge that all is clean and as it should be. Dirt was therefore doubly problematic, causing discomfort in both a physical and social sense—and it was a concern that stretched across time and space.

Dirt belonged outside the home and was frequently a source of complaint and discomfort when encountered by elite travellers. At a general level, whole towns and cities could be ascribed as dirty. Rosemary Sweet notes that many of the key cities on the Grand Tour were increasingly criticised as being dirty. In part, this related to a broader critique of the degeneracy of eighteenth-century Venetian and Roman society, and the social and cultural superiority of Britain.[10] Yet, similar criticisms were made of English towns that failed to match up with expected standards of urban respectability. Touring southern England in 1748 with her husband, Sir Roger Newdigate of Arbury Hall in Warwickshire, Sophia Newdigate dismissed Waltham Abbey as 'one of the dirtiest towns in England' and complained of the accommodation at Bruton in Somerset that 'had we not been very hungry and much tired we should have found difficulty to eat or sleep'.[11] Concerns were often focused on the dirtiness of beds and bedding, a common complaint amongst fastidious grand tourists from Flanders and the Dutch Republic. It is telling that, when one early eighteenth-century traveller refused to pay for what he saw as a miserly dinner, the landlady at an inn near Paris threatened to remove the clean sheets from the bed.[12]

The discomfort of dirt could also be a problem for the owners and occupants of country houses who found themselves in longer-term lodgings. In 1786, Richard Huddlestone, the son of a landowning family in Cambridgeshire, was sent to an academy in Bruges to continue his studies. He was unhappy with his situation and complained bitterly in a letter to his father at Sawston Hall about a number of 'inconveniences' that he had to endure: the lack of a fire in his room, the sullen nature of his tutor, and 'the extreme dirtiness of the Chamber in which we sat [which] was not swept for a month together'.[13] Huddlestone was desperate to be allowed home to England and it is significant that he focuses on these domestic inconveniences as part of his argument. Yet again, dirt and discomfort are something experienced outside the home which is conceived and valorised as a place of comfort, cleanliness and good company.

It was one thing to encounter the discomforts of dirt when travelling or away from home; quite another to risk bringing it into the home. When the Swedish Count, Claes Julius Ekeblad gave away an unwanted bed in Stockholm, his wife, Brita Horn reminded him that the bedding belonged to them; if the mattress, pillows and so on had been taken and used with the bed, she feared that they would become 'as dirty as everything else in the city'.[14] As with travellers, Brita Horn's worries about dirt and disease created an unclean other with which she could contrast her home: the city was dirty and threatened to spread this into the domestic environment of their country house. There is an implication here of the moral as well as physical imperative for cleanliness, a link that is more apparent from the reaction of Elizabeth Dryden to an incident that took place at her second husband's rooms in London. They had been entrusted to the care of a woman who had 'turned a thief and robbed the house of all the linen and everything moveable'. The expense was put at £20, but the immediate concern was that a housemaid be sent to London from the family home at Canons Ashby in Northamptonshire to 'clean it sufficient for him to sleep'.[15] This cleaning no doubt involved removing any physical dirt and tidying the mess left behind, but it might also be seen as an act of purification or reclamation of the domestic space after the despoilment of theft.[16] Once again, the dirt of the outside world was especially problematic when it intruded into the home.

Both in London and at Canons Ashby, cleaning work was carried out by a maid whose daily duties included sweeping the rooms and ensuring that they were free from dirt and dust. Writing in the 1730s, Jonathan Swift satirised this task by assuring the maid that 'when you are in haste, sweep the Dust into a Corner of the Room, but leave your Brush upon it, that it may not be seen'.[17] Around the same time, Lady Grisell Baillie of Mellerstain House in the Scottish Borders exhorted her butler to 'Make the kitchin maid keep all the places you have lookt up very clean, also the kitchin, Hal and passages'.[18] In her 1776 *Housekeeping Book*, Susanna Whatman gave more detailed instructions, itemising the work necessary in each room of the house. In the drawing room, for example, they were told that 'when the fire is light and the stove cleaned, something must be laid down to prevent the carpet from being dirtied, *as it is nailed down*. The other carpets are not'. They were also forbidden to touch the girandoles or the pictures, as Whatman herself would clean these.[19] More generally, the maids were warned against using too much soap, instructed to dust the furniture regularly, and advised to use a painter's brush on frames and furniture. Similar attention to detail was repeated by the Adams in their early nineteenth-century *Complete Servant* which gave detailed instructions about rolling the hearth rug 'so that no dirt or dust may drop from it, as it is taken out to be shaken' and turning back the carpet as the ashes are removed from the fire. The carpet itself 'must generally be swept with the carpet-mop to clean off the lint and dust, but, occasionally, with the carpet broom'.[20]

As Susanna Whatman knew all too well, each task had its own routine which had to be carefully followed to ensure the house remained clean. Dirt was a constant threat to domestic comfort and respectability, and there was a growing array of specialist equipment available to the housewife to keep dirt and dust at bay, although it was generally deployed by the housemaid. For example, a bill presented by Joseph Lee to Mary Leigh of Stoneleigh Abbey in Warwickshire in 1791 itemised brushes for clothes, shoes, tables, stairs, bannisters, glazing, the dairy and the hearth.[21] Much the same was true of laundering, where the extensive list of infrastructure and expenditure was closely linked to both the arduous nature of the work and its link to virtue.

Most country houses had extensive facilities and staff for laundering household and personal linen, servants again toiling for the comfort of others. At Stoneleigh Abbey, the fifth Baron Leigh's plans for improvements included grandiose schemes for an entirely new wing, but in the end, they boiled down to the construction of a new laundry—a much more practical addition to the house and one that spoke of the importance of cleanliness.[22] This was a large, two-floor building adjoining the servants' rooms in the older part of the house and contained provision for coppers, drying racks, mangles, irons and the like. Individually, these things could cost significant amounts: the Leighs paid £10 2*s*. 8*d*. in 1792 for a new copper, although they were allowed £4 1*s*. 4*d*. for the old one.[23] Collectively, the level of regular and ongoing spending could easily approach £100 per annum when laundry maids' wages were added to bills for soap and wash balls and fuel to heat the water. Given this, it is unsurprising that there were attempts to ease the burden of washing. Advertising their 'patent machines for washing linen &c' in the 1790s, Coates and Hancock's claimed that they would 'greatly diminish the most slavish of domestick [sic] employments, the use of them must greatly add to the ease, comfort and advantage of every family'.[24] How many of these machines were sold remains uncertain. Inventories and sale catalogues from the early nineteenth century record a wide array of coppers, clothes horses, irons, boards and mangles, but few innovations like that being marketed by Coates and Hancock. Many large householders no doubt preferred to rely on the labour of laundry maids, especially when their wages were so low. In 1714, for instance, Lady Grisell Baillie noted that 'Katherine Heart [sic.] Entreated to be Laundry Maid and Washer . . . her wage in the year is 34*s*. and 4*d*. and her two pair of shoes at 2*s*. a pair'. The wages paid to his laundrymaids by Sir Roger Newdigate rose through the second half of the eighteenth century but remained a modest £7 per annum in the 1790s.[25]

To draw a firm line between a clean home and the dirty world beyond its doors would be to ignore much of the reality of domestic life, even in the country house. Open fires were a constant cause of dirt in rooms: from coals, ashes and especially smoke. Indeed, a smoking fire was seen as one of the greatest threats to domestic comfort, as is apparent in the satirical print: *The Comforts of Matrimony—A Smoky House and a Scolding Wife* (1790). Quite apart from the unease created by a dysfunctional relationship between husband and wife, it is the smoke billowing from the fire and blown around by the draught coming through the open window that undermines the man's domestic tranquillity. It is little wonder, then, that there was an unending sequence of treatises that presented various solutions to the problem. Writing in the 1680s, Roger North noted that 'the carrying of smoak, or not, . . . makes a house delightfull, or intolerable'.[26] He presented a range of causes and remedies to the problem that demonstrated a good understanding of the ways in which an efficient chimney should be built. In early eighteenth-century France, Nicolas Gauger's innovations in fireplace design (see Chapter 2) were as much about reducing smoke, which damaged furniture and clothes, as they were about increasing the efficiency of the fire.[27] This makes his lack of commercial success still more striking: the French aristocracy may have been able to shrug off the cold or the large bills for firewood, but smoke-filled rooms could ruin a social gathering. DeJean relates that, in 1750, the Marquise de Pompadour's fabulous fireplaces at the newly built Bellevue drew so poorly that smoke filled the lavish rooms and sent her guests packing.[28] Over 40 years later, the same issue was still being addressed in publications such as Robert Clavering's 1793 *Essay on the Construction and Building of Chimneys, including an Enquiry into the Common Causes of their Smoking* and John Whitehurst's *Observations on the Ventilation of Rooms* (1794), both of which offered practical solutions to the problem.[29] Into the nineteenth century, J.M. Adair made specific recommendations about fires in bedrooms, arguing that the sulphurous air from coal fires was bad for the health of the sleeper.[30]

Even allowing for the polemic of these publications, it is apparent that smoke remained a problem for English householders. Susanna Whatman noted that particular care was needed in laying fires, 'particularly in rooms where they are apt to smoak at first lighting'. She knew from experience exactly how to minimise the risk: 'cinders and round coals should be placed at [the] bottom on the grate, then pieces of wood laid hollow, over which should be a few large cinders laid lose [sic.] by this arrangement the smoke goes upwards without impediment'.[31] Smoke was less of an issue in countries where stoves were used, making it all the more problematic when it was encountered. Writing about his travels to Paris in 1773, Johann Fredrich Karl Grimm, a German physician accustomed to the comforts of his iron stoves, complained about the discomforts of French inns and particularly about the dangerous smoke from open fires: 'the constant coughing, the eyes running from smoke, and the spitting of the servants and other visitors, and then you have to taste the stench and the filth that goes with it'.[32]

Air quality was clearly an important aspect of domestic comfort across western Europe: it contributed to personal well-being and spoke of a carefully regulated domestic environment. Treatises extolled the virtues of fresh air, gradually refining the ways in which it could be safely introduced into a room. The easiest way, of course, was to open a window. In his instructions to servants, Swift satirises the timing and care with which this was done but does not question it as a means of ventilating the room. To the chambermaid, he wrote: 'When you bar the Window-shuts of your Lady's Bed-chamber at Nights, leave open the sashes to let in the fresh Air, and sweeten the Room against Morning'.[33] Quite apart from the barb against the laziness of maids, the point was that the air in sleeping rooms should be freshened once the occupants had left them in the morning, not through the night.[34] Discussing the need for the right amount of sleep in his 1812 *Essay on Diet and Regimen*, James Adair challenges this convention, noting that 'one caution, little attended to, should be mentioned, viz. The bed-chamber ought to have a free air, and close curtains are very injurious'.[35] In part, he was seeking to discourage the use of bed curtains, but he also suggests allowing the free circulation of air in the room as a whole. This argument was not new: writing in the 1680s on a wide range of issues—from the cleanliness of food and drink, through the need for 'good airs', to the problem of bed bugs—Thomas Tryon argued that: 'In the Night also you ought not to have your Window-Curtains drawn, nor your Curtains that are about your Beds; for it hinders the sweet refreshing Influences of the Air, so that the Air of all close Places becomes of a hot sulphurous Nature and Operation'.[36] It was also a sentiment echoed across Europe, despite prevalent concerns about the threat to health posed by exposure to the night air. In sixteenth-century Germany, for example, Walter Reiff advocated fresh air and convenient houses, whilst 150 years later, the Swedish pastor, Reinerus Broocman, argued for the health benefits of airing the room by opening windows.[37]

Fresh air was something to be had in moderation, as satirical prints make clear. In the *Comforts of Matrimony*, discussed earlier, the unfortunate householder suffers discomfort from the cold air rushing in through the window as well as the smoking fireplace. Similarly, James Beresford's *The Miseries of Human Life* (1806) made much of the myriad tiny ways in which domestic comforts were undermined or destroyed in a way that highlights their growing importance.[38] In one episode, later illustrated by Thomas Rowlandson, the householder comes downstairs on a cold winter's morning in search of 'warmth and comfort' in the breakfast room, only to find the grate empty, the carpet pulled back, the maid scrubbing the floor and the window wide open. The irony is that cleaning and fresh air have robbed the man of his comfort. Conversely, the same artist could mock the discomforts which people of fashion would endure for the sake of public entertainment and status. In his 1807 print *The Comforts of a Modern Gala*, Thomas Rowlandson depicts a tightly packed scene in which people are crowded into the hall waiting to gain access to the rout taking place in the rooms above. Predictably, they complain about their stiff collars, lost wigs, misplaced partners and the close proximity of strangers; but the lack of air is also an issue, with one person in the crowd crying 'Open the Ventilators'.[39]

The ideal, then, was to have fresh air circulating without creating cold draughts. Fires could achieve the former, but generally at the price of creating the latter, despite Gauger's efforts in this direction. In 1794, John Whitehurst also noted the problem and offered a solution in his *Observations on the Ventilation of Rooms*. He argued that the layout of the house and corridors should allow air to enter from outside. A comfortable circulation of air through individual rooms could then be achieved by leaving gaps between the architrave and the wall which would allow air to enter the room and circulate before being drawn out into the next. He scorned 'the multitude who . . . obstinately maintain that the same injuries are to be expected from air admitted in this manner, as from the cold streams of it which usually flow into a room through the crevices of the door or window'.[40] This was a managed circulation of air that in some ways resembled the careful arrangements made in Swedish houses to ensure the effective functioning of stoves.

A welcoming home was thus one that was airy and clean. These imperatives impacted particularly on country houses being opened up prior to the family returning after the winter season in London. Servants might be sent in advance, or notice given to those in permanent residence, to air the house and freshen the furnishings: fires might be lit to dispel any dampness and servants instructed to sleep in various beds to ensure they were not damp. Similar imperatives were important for those at the lower end of landowning classes with few pretensions to London society. The Revd William Money was a younger son who entered the church, being appointed to the family living of Yatesbury in Wiltshire. He lived on the family's 450-acre estate in the neighbouring parish of Whetham in a house that was somewhat grander than the typical Georgian rectory. The original three-gabled seventeenth-century house had been considerably extended with the addition of a large north range in the late eighteenth century, the grounds having earlier been landscaped, probably by Stephen Switzer.[41] Returning home after being away for several weeks in 1813, his servants had clearly done their work as Money wrote to his wife that 'the old place looks well & comfortable. The house is clean, &

well aired'.[42] Similarly, when contemplating a move to London in the 1810s, Elizabeth Dryden wrote from her country house in Northamptonshire to her sister-in-law in London, asking her to identify suitable houses. She was very particular in her requirements regarding not only size and layout but also the quality of air, both in the house and more generally. She praised one house that was recommended to her because it was 'well aired', but then worried 'whether I can live at all in London as the air disagrees so much with me'.[43] The problem, she argued, was that she constantly lived in fear of the dreadful colds that afflicted her in town. Much the same concern was expressed by her contemporary, Mary Huddlestone. Writing to her son, Richard, who was stationed in Kent with the militia, she hoped that he would 'take every precaution and care of yourself when you go to Camp, to keep out all Damps', a concern which she later distilled into a particular worry about the 'Kentish agues'.[44] Of her own situation, she observed that she had been suffering for some time from a cold and was resolved to leave the family seat in Cambridgeshire and 'to go to the Sea, as tis the only recourse I have, I hope to render me tolerably Comfortable'.[45] This links to the arguments made by the fictional Mr. Parker in favour of a hilltop location for their new house at Sanditon. Strong winds were preferable to the stillness of sheltered locations, he asserted, because bad air could settle out there and 'do more mischief in a valley when they *do* arise than an open country ever experiences in the heaviest gale'.[46]

Health, Happiness and Comfort

If feeling comfortable could be achieved, in part, by removing these various environmental and domestic discomforts, it was also linked more closely to the relief of bodily suffering. This was true in a general sense, with religious tracts offering guidance on praying for the comfort of the sick and treatises such as the anonymous *An Easy Way to Prolong Life* (1780) noting that 'when the stomach is weak, or lapsed by cold, a cordial may comfort and refresh it'.[47] More specifically, we see claims for the comfort afforded by a wide variety of medicines, balms and ointments that were advertised in the press.[48] These range from a notice in *Fog's Weekly Journal* (1730) for a treatment for palsy which claimed that the medicine would give 'kindly Warmth and genial Comfort to the weaken'd limbs', to a 'Pectoral Essence of Coltsfoot', promoted in the *St James Chronicle* (1790), which would give 'immediate Relief to those who through Age & Infirmity are deprived of Rest or Sleep, as it gently composes and contributes to make the Remainder of their Days comfortable and easy'.[49] Some advertisements specifically targeted the social elite, at least in their rhetoric. One such was 'Solomon's Abstergent Lotion', advertised in the Hull Packet (1810) as being 'the only cosmetic a Lady can use at her toilette with ease, comfort and safety'.[50]

Country-house owners were in a position to send for physicians and to acquire specific medicines from apothecaries, sometimes to make up cures contained in family recipe books. Sir Roger Newdigate typically paid physicians and apothecaries a combined total of between £6 and £24 per annum.[51] The variation year-on-year reflects periods of health and illness in the household, evidenced in the exceptional outlay of £47 1s. 6d. in 1773 and £85 15s. in 1774, the latter including £60 17s. for two physicians tending his wife Sophia in the last 2 months of her life. Individual bills for the Leighs of Stoneleigh Abbey were dominated by lists of ingredients, but there were also occasional purchases of kind of comforting patent medicines advertised in the press.[52] What is even more apparent is the growing association of comfort with the relief of bodily pain or suffering that is expressed in the private correspondence of country-house owners.

Ashe Windham was the eldest son of William and Katherine Windham of Felbrigg Hall. He inherited in 1689 whilst still at Eton, his mother playing an active role in the estate and in trying to manage his relationships. Windham was to marry Hester Buckworth in 1708, but she died of smallpox shortly before the marriage and he made a quick and ultimately disastrous match with Elizabeth Dobyns, a wealthy heiress.[53] Their relationship is discussed more fully in the following chapter, but much of their correspondence through the spring of 1719 concerned the well-being of their young son, William, who was living with his father whilst Elizabeth stayed with her own mother in London. Almost every letter contained an update on his health. On 8 March, Ashe Windham noted that the boy was well, despite the cold weather and dampness of the house, and on 21 March he reported that the boy had an upset stomach after eating boiled chicken, but was now recovered.[54] Things were more serious on 8 April, when he wrote about his son having a 'worm fever, which lay much in his head', causing him to 'rub his nose mightily' and return 'to his old method of calling and crying for things, and then would not have them'. Windham's choice of words is interesting, writing of the 'uneasiness' the poor child was in during this episode, again tying physical well-being with notions of comfort, although without using the term itself.[55]

Adults were also concerned with their own health and they too deployed the language of comfort to describe their conditions. George Lucy, the bachelor owner of Charlecote Park in Warwickshire, suffered from a rheumatic fever that particularly affected his hands, leaving him unable to write at times and occasioning trips to Portugal and Italy in the 1750s in search of some relief. He travelled to Bath, ostensibly for his health, but also to enjoy the company assembled there. Whilst away, he wrote to his housekeeper and companion Mrs. Phillipa Hayes, giving regular updates on his health and always asking after her own. She replied in a similar manner. Reassurance of continued good health was invariably greeted with pleasure, whereas a lack of news brought disquiet, as when Mrs. Hayes wrote in April 1755 that 'it is a most uneasy situation to be at so great a distance, and continual suspense with regard to a good friend'.[56] Health was thus linked not only to ease but also to bodily comfort, Lucy reporting with considerable candour from Naples in April 1757 that 'My bowels (I thank God) have been comfortably easy for most part of the time'.[57]

Horace Walpole and his circle were nuanced in their use of the term comfort, as we have already seen; but from the 1770s at least they also equated it with good health. Writing to Horace Mann in January 1780, Walpole complained that illness, 'takes off the edge from the enjoyment of health; and though I seem to have patience, it is rather a state of discomfort'.[58] A year later, the Revd William Cole explained the delay in replying to a letter from Walpole by noting that he had suffered a 'most uncomfortable night with the gout in one foot'.[59] Poor health brought discomfort: the body could find no ease, no rest, when afflicted with specific or general illness. Scarce surprising, then, that Walpole associated old age with the gradual erosion of comfort. In 1774, he could write cheerfully to Lady Ailesbury that 'old age is no such uncomfortable thing if one gives oneself up to it with good grace'.[60] Seventeen years later, and then aged 73, he was still sanguine, writing that 'though my eyes, ears, teeth and motion have still lasted to make life comfortable, I do not know that I should be enchanted if surviving any of them'.[61] A year later, however, his spirits had declined with his health, still being described in the language of comfort:

> I am become an indolent poor creature . . . with a chalkstone in every finger; with feet so limping that I have been but twice this summer round my own small garden, and so much weaker than I was, can I be very comfortable, but when sitting quiet and doing nothing?[62]

Returning to the correspondence between Mary Huddlestone and her son Richard, we again see how health was equated with comfort. Pleased to learn of the 'very Comfortable quiet lodgings' that his mother had taken in Southend in the summer of 1805, Richard hoped to 'to hear by a single line that you are cheerful and comfortable'—essentially an enquiry about her health. Her reply picked up this use of language and she reassured him that 'I am very Comfortable & Cheerful when I have not the Low Nervous Complaint upon me'.[63]

All these country-house owners linked physical health and bodily comfort, the connection being axiomatic by the turn of the nineteenth century. They also connected bodily rest and well-being and were keenly aware of how the nature of beds impacted upon physical ease and the role of sleep in strengthening and revitalising (that is comforting) the body.[64] Restful sleep depended on having a good bed. In England, there was a growing consensus of what comprised a well-made bed: the bed frame and hangings, a mattress and usually a feather bed, a bolster and two pillows, three blankets (one under blanket and two covering the sleeper) and a coverlet or counterpane, and two sheets and two pillow-cases. This equipage was fairly standard across all rooms in the country house: from the master's bedchamber to the maid's garret, suggesting a minimum level of comfort for everyone. At the same time, however, the comfort of a bed was socially defined: straw or flock might do for country house servants, but even they were increasingly given feather beds. Gradations then came in terms of the quality of the feathers, size and warmth of the blankets and coverlets, and fineness of the sheets. It was scarcely surprising, then, that there were frequent complaints from travellers about a lack of comfort. John Turner Dryden, for example, moaned that his accommodation in Brighton comprised a 'bad bed, hard as a stone & not room enough for a consumptive monkey'.[65] The affront of physical discomfort was compounded by the demeaning of his status caused by a lack of space. In Sweden, the lack of suitable bedrooms for guests drove Johan Gabriel Oxenstierna from his bed when his uncle, Count Carl Johan Gyllenborg, visited Skenäs in autumn 1766. The then 16-year-old Oxenstierna remarked in his diary that he did not have anything against sleeping on the floor, but he found the small space awkward because, when turning in his sleep, Oxenstierna was constantly about to knock over a chair or put his hand in the chamber pot—as the diarist remarked with dry humour.[66]

Not all occupants required the same kind of bed: their needs varied according to their health. In his 1803 *Cabinet Dictionary*, Sheraton argued that the material qualities of beds 'should be regulated by the nature of the constitution of those who are to sleep on them'. Firm beds were necessary for: 'those who are of a delicate frame, to whom scarcely anything can be more hurtful than to sink into soft down. These sorts of beds are better adapted to the robust and healthy, who can with propriety sustain the indulgence'.[67] In this way, Sheraton directly equated the material qualities of the soft feather bed with the level of comfort it would provide to different people. The invalid might also benefit from the growing array of specialist patent furniture being advertised in the early nineteenth century. Perhaps the most famous of these was William Pocock's 'Boethema or Rising Mattress', designed to raise invalids to a sitting position in bed and, as shown in Pocock's advertisement, available in the form of a sofa or a chaise longue.

Over 100 years earlier, Thomas Tryon also cautioned against assuming that feather beds would be preferable. To quote him at length:

> The Beds, I say, receive all the several Vapours and Spirits, and the same Beds are often continued for several Generations, without changing the Feathers, until the Ticks be rotten. Besides, we have many Feathers that are Imported from several Countries, which are

the Drivings of old Beds, the Uncleanness whereof is not considered. As to the Nature of Feathers, they are of a strong, hot, fulsom Quality: for Fowls, of all Creatures, are for the most part the hottest; and their Feathers contain the same Nature: Therefore the constant lying on soft Feather-beds, does not only over-heat the Back and Reins, weakning the Joynts and Nerves; but they have power also not only to receive but retain all evil Vapours and Excrements that proceed from, and are breathed forth by various Diseased People. Hence it comes to pass, that sundry Distempers are transferred from one to another, by lying upon or in such Beds, which Distempers do secretly steal on a Man by degrees, so that he cannot imagine whence the disorder proceeds, or what the Cause thereof should be.[68]

The problems are manifold: feathers made the sleeper overly hot; they were by their very nature unclean, and they harboured disease. Instead, Tryon recommended beds of straw or chaff, with ticks of canvas and woollen or flock quilts. These were cleaner, cooler and healthier; they were also firmer, avoiding another problem with feather beds, in that:

when a Man lies down, he sinks into them, as into an Hole, with Banks rising on each side of him; especially if two lie together, when first they go to Bed they lie close, and after a little time, when they begin to be hot or sweat, they are generally willing to lie a little further off, that they may cool themselves, but cannot do it without great difficulty and trouble, by reason of the softness of the Bed, and those Banks that rise on each side. [. . .] Certainly nothing is more healthy, next to Temperance in Meat and Drink, than clean hard Beds.[69]

Tryon's thinking was very much the same as Sheraton's, but his real concern was with ensuring that beds were regularly aired and cleaned, especially if they were set against a wall. Bad air, smells and the fug of sweaty sleepers was not only unpleasant but also unhealthy—as we have already seen.

The remedy for this problem was regular airing and cleaning, not just of sheets and blankets but of the beds themselves. Tryon recommended that 'All sorts of Beds, especially Feather-beds, ought to be changed, driven, or washed, at the least three or four times in a Year'.[70] The need for frequent airing is apparent in Swift's *Directions to Servants* and in Whatman's *Housekeeping Book* in which she instructs the maids that beds should be 'always well shook'.[71] In the Adams' *Complete Servant* (1825) they describe the duties of upper housemaid:

As soon as the best bed-rooms and dressing-rooms are at liberty, she repairs thither . . . throws open the windows (or the doors only, in unfavourable weather) to air the rooms and the beds; opens all the beds, throws the bed-clothes off . . . shakes up each bed, and then proceeds to her other business in the rooms, in order to give as much time as can be spared for airing the beds.[72]

In addition to frequent airing, beds and bedding also required regular maintenance and cleaning. Much could be done in situ by the housemaids, but some required treatment elsewhere or by specialist tradesmen. At Arbury Hall, Sir Roger Newdigate's accounts include several payments under the heading 'dyer and scowrer', including those in October 1747 to Edward Eyre, 15s. 6d. for cleaning a chintz bed, and to S. Taylor, £1 15s. for cleaning some green worsted hangings. Repairs were regularly undertaken and were a further burden on servants in making their employers more comfortable. At a basic level, this might involve mending sheets or turning them to prolong their life—a practice which the ever-careful Mrs. Hayes recorded in her housekeeper's book at Charlecote in the 1740s and 1750s. Other parts of the bed were also subjected to renovation. Living just outside London in the 1780s, Mary Leigh paid the upholsterers, Bradshaw and Smith, for repairs to bed frames and for 'ripping the porters bed & bolster & taking out all the feather, well waxing the tick, driving & dressing the old feathers & putting 12 lb best season'd feathers in addition, sewing up the tick'. In this way, feather beds could be given a longer life and their comfort and cleanliness renewed in a way that Tryon felt was impossible.

Writing to his housekeeper at Charlecote Park in 1758, George Lucy combined these various concerns about the nature and cleanliness of his bed. He instructed that it should be altered: 'instead of my Feather Bed, order another mattress and instead of the Cords of the bedstead, lay some flat boards the breadth of the bedstead, no matter what sort provided they are clean and free from insects'.[73] Lucy's aim was to make his bed much firmer, reflecting his constant concern for his own health; but he was also highlighting another threat to the comfort that a bed might provide. The parasitic habits of bed bugs frequently robbed people of their sleep and left them covered in painful bites. Tryon was clear about the link between bugs and cleanliness: bugs 'are bred from the fulsom Scents and Excrements that are breathed forth from the Body'.[74] This was not an argument for spontaneous generation and he clearly understood something of their habits, writing that they 'are bred in Summer: but they live all the Winter, though they are not then so troublesom. They harbour in Bedsteads, Holes, and Hangings, Nitting and breeding as Lice do in Clothes'.[75] They were a familiar problem in the seventeenth century, especially to travellers to warmer countries on the continent. In 1673, John Ray of the Royal Academy described both the habits and smell of the bugs he found in Italy and noted that 'we have these insects in some places of England, but not many, nor are they troublesome to us'.[76] Sixty years later, John Southall was not so sanguine (as we shall see) and repeated the established wisdom that they had been brought to Britain on ships. Yet there was a geography to the problem: 'not one sea-port in England is free; whereas in inland-towns, bugs are hardly known'.[77]

The attitude of seventeenth-century householders to bed bugs appears to have been equivocal. John Ray was of the opinion that they were less troublesome than was the case on the continent and Samuel Pepys seems to have treated them as an annoyance, but one that could easily be tolerated and even joked on. His travelling companion Dr. Clerke was bitten instead of him because he was 'of the eldest blood and house' (11 June 1668).[78] At the same time, though, Tryon's was just one of several treatises to make clear that bugs were a nuisance because of their biting and their stinking smell, and that they were something that people were keen to be rid of.

The well-to-do in the eighteenth century seem to have been much readier to complain about bugs and seek out ways of avoiding being bitten, rather than accept this as a fact of life. The problem was particularly apparent amongst travellers, no doubt in part because they were less able to control their sleeping environment. Writing in 1752, Horace Walpole related an anecdote that Lady Coventry, on being offered a tent bed 'for fear of bugs in the inns', exclaimed that she would 'rather be bit to death than lie one night from my dear Cov'.[79] Visiting Avignon in June 1784, Mary Berry was more practical and placed a mattress on the floor 'as all the beds were plentifully stocked with bugs'. A similar strategy was pursued in 1791 by Maria Holroyd who found that the bugs at Fontainebleau 'were a very sharp set, and were so delighted to meet with me, that, as the least evil of the two, I slept in a chair all night not in the most comfortable manner'.[80] Avoiding the bed showed awareness that bugs generally hid in crevices in the wood or seams in the hangings, coming out at night to feed on the hapless sleeper.

It is hard to know whether bed bugs were becoming more prevalent or sensibilities were changing, as Lisa Sarasohn suggests.[81] Most likely it was a combination of the two. Awareness of the habits of bugs and the ways in which they could be exterminated was certainly on the rise, especially after the publication in 1730 of John Southall's *Treatise on Bugs*.[82] This included magnified images of bed bugs, advice to those buying furniture and a prolonged account of how he came by his patent treatment for destroying them. This was a refinement of a recipe given to him by an elderly man in Jamaica, where Southall had visited when he was younger, perfected through painstaking scientific observation and experimentation. He thus served to heighten anxiety and offer a solution which drew on and wrapped him in enlightenment thinking and methodologies.[83]

A domestic and commercial bug destruction industry quickly grew. As Pennell notes, the 1732 edition of E. Smith's *Complete Housewife* included a recipe that would 'neither stain, soil, or in the least hurt to finest silk or damask bed' and a warning not to carry out the treatment by candlelight 'lest the subtility of the mixture should catch the flame as you are using it'; later editions carried both a recipe for destroying bugs and an infallible recipe for destroying bugs, which involved painting the dismantled bedstead with a mixture of quicksilver and egg white.[84] At the same time, there was a growing number of advertisements from tradesmen offering either their own version of Southall's deadly liquor or a bug-eradication service. By the 1760s, competition amongst London tradesmen was clearly intense. Mr. Muckleston announced the opening of his shop with not only an assurance that he could clean 20 beds a week, but also a warning to 'beware of imposters, who daily puff in the papers, but by woeful experience have left the bedding and furniture in little better condition than they found them'.[85] Advertisements in the provincial press were less numerous but took a similar form. William Coulton, for example, assured the residents of Leeds in 1785 that 'he has found out an effectual Remedy for Destroying BUGS, with which many Houses and Beds are infected. In Hull he has cleared upwards of 150 Houses'. Two years later Thomas Northey promoted his 'INFALLIBLE LIQUOR for destroying BUGS, in bed furniture &c' in the Chelmsford press.[86]

The success of such treatments is impossible to gauge with any accuracy, but anxiety about infestation certainly played on the minds of householders looking to buy second-hand beds and undermined any thoughts of comfort that might derive from the bed itself or the practice of good housewifely thrift. Those advertising such goods started to assure potential buyers of their cleanliness. In London, Pennell notes sales notices that assured potential buyers that the goods were safe. One offered 'near fifty second-hand feather beds, with blankets, quilts, bedsteads and curtains', the auctioneer adding that 'I warrant that all I sell from the above houses is clear of bugs'. And it is striking that even the belongings of the titled aristocracy (in this case Lady Dixie) needed to be announced as 'clean, in good condition, and free from bugs'.[87]

Bed bugs could be a problem in both town and country, but there was a particular anxiety about furniture in London, captured nicely in a letter from Elizabeth Dryden, of Canons Ashby in Northamptonshire. Contemplating a move to London in 1820, she wrote to her sister-in-law that: 'I shall send maid servant up a week before I go to air the house and beds. I have much fear of the bugs, but must be at the expense I fear of a new bed as all old furniture in London is dangerous'.[88] It seems likely that it was the unknown provenance of London furniture that heightened such concerns, but any unfamiliar pieces could arouse suspicion. Writing in 1720, the Rev Charles Lammotte noted that a Mr. Cambre, who had come to the rectory at Warkton in Northamptonshire, was causing some distress to the incumbents there: 'Mrs Vandermulens saith that they spoil her house & have brought bugs in their goods'.[89]

Bed bugs, then, engendered a range of anxieties centred on the fear of painful bites, the inconvenience of contingent measures that were necessary, the harm the treatments might do to expensive beds and furniture, and the damage that all this might do to the householder's reputation. As Woodruff Smith has argued, cleanliness was a concern that loomed ever larger for all respectable households through the eighteenth century. In addition to weekly and seasonal washing and cleaning routines, which would help to maintain the whiteness of sheets, it is apparent that anxieties about infestations of insects chipped away at the desirability of used bedding, the attraction of thrift being replaced by the anxiety of the unknown and potentially infested. Concerns could be mitigated by warrantees that furniture was free from bugs and, probably more convincingly, assurances about provenance, but the comfort of mind was increasingly sought in the new. Feeling comfortable in bed thus had physical, social and psychological elements: bodily ease had to be matched by social respectability and contentment of the mind. This invites a broader consideration of the ways in which mental comfort was conceived and experienced. What follows switches from external and physical influences, to those located within the person themselves.

Comfort From Within: Duty, Contentment and Hope

Doing one's duty could bring a sense of contentment and social comfort—of feeling comfortable in one's self and with one's actions. Something of this can be grasped from a letter written by Mary Delany to her sister, Anne Dewes, in January 1752 in which she lays out the difficulties being faced by a friend who was in dispute with her relations. Delany faced a dilemma in terms of when and whether to accompany her friend to London to help sort out her problems and settle her into a new home. She reassured her sister:

> don't let what I have said perplex or vex your mind; I have only laid before you the *worst* that *may* happen. I have made no offer yet of staying, nor shall not till I receive an answer to this letter, but we must both consider (I am sure you always have) that there *is no real comfort or happiness without performing one's duty conscientiously*, and that these self-denials are absolutely necessary to prepare us for that blissful state to which all true Christians must aspire.[90]

We come to questions of religion later; what is important here is that Delany is able to assume her sister shares an appreciation that being dutiful was an essential underpinning to any feeling of comfort or happiness. Such contentment is not typical of the feelings generally explored in histories of emotion where the focus is on more passionate feelings. Yet recent studies have attempted to examine other, less strongly felt but perhaps more enduring or invidious emotions. As French and Rothery demonstrate in the case of the younger sons of gentry families, anxiety was never far from the surface and could gnaw away, bringing with it a feeling of unsettling discomfort, even for those in materially comfortable situations.[91] In many ways, then, contentment forms anxiety's antonym: it brought calmness, satisfaction and comfort.

For some, this sense of contentment was easy to achieve. Writing in her memoir in 1800, Lady Louisa Stuart recalled 'The only blue stocking meetings which I myself ever attended were those at Mrs. Walsingham's and Mrs. Montagu's'. This led her to reflect on Montagu's character:

> Together with a superabundance of vanity—vanity of that happy, contented, comfortable kind which, being disturbed by no uneasy doubts or misgivings, keeps us in constant good-humour with ourselves, consequently with everything else—she had quick parts, great vivacity, no small share of wit, a competent portion of learning, considerable fame as a writer, a large fortune, a fine house, and an excellent cook.[92]

No doubt her material circumstances bolstered a sense of contentment, but Lady Louisa was clear that it was Mrs. Montagu's 'contented, comfortable' vanity that formed the bedrock of her sense of self and selfworth. For most people, however, contentment relied on external factors as well as internal self-assurance. In this, life in the country house could be both the source and nemesis of comfortable contentment. Writing to her friend Miss Clavering in 1809, the Scottish novelist Susan Ferrier noted 'I was interrupted by a visit from Miss Lamont, wringing her hands and turning up the whites of her eyes in black despair at being doomed to sojourn in this wilderness'. Clearly, Miss Lamont needed company and constant stimulus in order to be happy, yet Ferrier could not feel sorry for her because 'for my own part I'm quite contented so long as I have my health, my books, work, a good fire, and my faithful blear-eyed dog'.[93]

Men could also find contentment in the routines of everyday life. The Revd William Money, who occupied a position at the lower margins of the landowning class, was alone at the family home at Whetham in May 1812. In successive letters written to his wife Emma, who was away at her parents' house in London, he expressed his contentment with a seemingly monotonous existence. He was generally up by 6.00 am, walked in the garden for an hour and then said prayers. Following breakfast at 8.00 am, he spent the rest of the morning reading and writing. 'At three I dine; walk in the garden from five to six; read an hour and drink tea at seven. From then to ten, read & write, have prayers, & go to bed'. Aware of the apparent tedium of this routine, he noted that 'this might be called, by the gay, a dull and stupid existence; no better than the vegetation or a Cabbage'. However, he argued, that even a cabbage 'makes daily progress and improvement towards the purpose and end designed for it'.[94] His comfort and contentment came from a daily routine that he saw as profitable and purposeful.

Some people found little comfort in their present situation but sought it instead in their memories of the past or hopes for the future. Looking forward to a time when things would be better is apparent in the correspondence of landed families throughout our period. Through the 1670s, Ursula Clarke Venner, from a land-owning family in Somerset, kept up a regular correspondence with her brother-in-law, Edward Clarke, who owned the Chipley estate in Devon. In a letter dated 21 June 1676, she wrote at length about the health of her father and the treatment he was receiving, including bleeding, clystering and purging. Unsurprisingly, the old man was in low spirits. Ursula hoped that he would 'reach some comfort', but noted that 'he is extream melancholy & troubles at every little thing'.[95] Comfort here is conceived both in bodily terms—the absence of the physical pain that her father's illness and its treatment created—but also as the opposite of the restlessness of melancholy. This was a condition that, whilst in some senses a fashionable malady affected by the English elite in the later Georgian period, could unsettle the mind and disturb the body.[96] Ursula herself took comfort in looking forward to a time when her father would be both free from pain and more settled in his mind. Comfort came both in the resolution of the unhappy situation and in looking forward to that resolution.

Much the same sentiment is apparent in the 1807 memoirs of the early feminist writer, Mary Anne Radcliffe. She wrote that she buoyed herself up: 'with the hope, that between one thing or another, the time would soon come round, that my family would be reunited, and though not in affluence, yet in comfort and content, which the various troubles we had each experienced would contribute to heighten'.[97] Again, there is hope that troubles, this time material and financial in nature, will pass and comfort will return. For others, the horizons were less distant: husbands and wives often wrote to each other expressing their discomfort in being apart and their hope to be reunited soon. In 1812, Emma Money wrote to her husband, William, expressing her discomfort in his absence from their country home, and looking forward to his imminent return—the only thing that would bring her contentment. Her tone was a touch melodramatic, belying 4 years of marriage: 'But alas! My William, my poor heart aches sadly at our separation, for indeed I have no comfort when deprived of my beloved William [. . .] May I hope for the happiness of embracing you this evening?'.[98] There are hints here of the heightened sensibility that increasingly characterised emotions from the 1730s, but which had become somewhat clichéd by the time Emma Money was writing.[99] Nonetheless, her feelings were sincere and were expressed in a way seen in other letters from this period. In 1818, Friedrich Engels senior (father of Karl Marx's companion) was equally distressed at leaving his new wife in the country. As soon as he was in the carriage, he was already picturing her sweet, sad face under the pretty bonnet and thinking of their speedy reunion as his only solace. Back in Bremmen, his favourite activity was reflecting on the happy hours they had spent arm and arm.[100]

For Engels, reminiscing offered comfort whilst away from his wife—thinking about happy times linked a contented past to an imperfect present and gave hope for happier times in the future. Yet memories did not always bring comfort. In March 1705, Mary Jepp Clarke, a notable letter writer who was on familiar terms with John Locke, wrote from the family estate at Chipley in Devon to John Spreat. She enclosed a letter that had originally been written to her daughter, but which had lain forgotten at the bottom of her pocket. She explained to Spreat:

> I inclose it heare that you may know some of the History of my life, tho it is impossible for you or any body else to guess att the whole of it and when you have red it burn it, for I shall never be able to looke back with comfort upon evils that are past, and my difficultyes are such as can never be overcome.[101]

The nature of these difficulties is not made clear, but it is apparent that looking back was not something that offered comfort to Mary; writing to Spreat was presumably a cathartic act, but not one from which she expected to derive lasting contentment.

The Comforts of Faith

We have already touched on the importance of religious faith and practice to a sense of comfort through William Money's reflection on his daily life at Whetham. This was also apparent in the spaces and routines of country house living and in the numerous treatises published throughout our period extolling the comforts of faith. Some of these were written as practical guides or aids to religious practice: for example, Michael Sparke's *Crums of Comfort and Godly Prayers* (originally published in 1628 but reprinted throughout the seventeenth and eighteenth centuries). Others, such as William Notcutt's, *A Believer's Evidences for Heaven, or a Short Essay for Christian Comfort* (1717) and William Johnston's *The Improved Christian's Courage and Comfort from Afflictions and Death* (1771) were more concerned with providing spiritual encouragement and fortitude to the reader.[102] Together, they lay out various aspects of the relationship between faith, God and comfort; these can be summarised under five main headings.

First is the comfort derived from doing God's will. As Johnston put it 'the people of God, especially the more faithful, and improved of them, may comfortably expect they shall be free from distressing fear of evil'.[103] Like many of her contemporaries, Mary Woodforde's religious beliefs informed her thinking about family, duty and the ways in which these might bring social or spiritual comfort. She lived in the cathedral close with her husband, Samuel, who was prebendary of Winchester. The middle of their five children, also called Samuel, went up to Cambridge in June 1687 as a scholar at St. John's College. Mary recorded her hopes and fears in her journal, writing on his departure: 'may he do virtuously, and bring a great deal of honour to the name of God, and comfort to himself and his Relations'. The same mantra was repeated six months later when Samuel again left for Cambridge: 'God of his great mercy grant he may do worthily there, and bring great honour to his Holy Name, and Comfort to his Parents'.[104] Mary saw her son's duty to God and credit to the family name as being intimately linked; together, they would bring comfort in the form of honour and contentment born of dutiful and Christian behaviour. She was all too aware of the potential pitfalls of university life, asking God (through her journal writing) to 'keep him in all ways from sin, and danger and the infection of evil company'.[105]

Significantly, this compounding of religious and familial duty persisted through the eighteenth century—in some landed families at least. Richard Huddlestone had a number of disagreements with his parents over prospective brides. In a lengthy letter, written from the family seat in Cambridgeshire in June 1805, his mother Mary discussed her concerns about the latest object of his affections. She noted the difference in their fortunes, but the issue hinged on the motivation of the woman to convert to Catholicism ahead of a marriage. However, she also observed 'your Conduct has always been so dutiful & given us so much Satisfaction' and that 'your happiness seems so much to depend upon the trial'. If his prospective bride were to 'become a good Catholic', Mary continued, it would be 'a very good thing . . . for your Comfort in this World & Eternal happiness hereafter'.[106] In being a dutiful son and a dutiful Catholic, Richard would find a sense of comfort in life and contentment in the afterlife.

A clearer sense of the comfort derived from doing one's Christian duty is apparent from the diaries of Darcy, Lady Maxwell, the youngest daughter of Thomas Brisbane, Esq., of Ayrshire in Scotland. As a young lady, she spent some time with her aunt and uncle in London before returning to Scotland and marrying Sir Walter Maxwell. Widowed within 2 years, Lady Maxwell became an ardent Christian, having met John Wesley in 1764.[107] Her diaries are focused firmly on her faith and her hopes of salvation and are peppered with references to the comfort afforded by her faith. A particularly common refrain was the way in which comfort was derived from doing what she saw as her Christian duty. Importantly, this was not simply gratification for good deeds done. On 28 May 1769, she wrote:

> Felt desirous of doing something for God to-day, but had not the opportunities which I expected. Since I came hither, I have made many attempts, but as yet have seen little fruit; yet so gracious is my Lord, that upon my doing what he convinces me is my duty, he affords me comfort, for the most part independent of success.[108]

Conversely, this sense of comfort could quickly evaporate if Lady Maxwell felt that she had fallen short, a later diary entry noting:

> In the afternoon, I had cause to lament my want of a greater degree of faithfulness to the Lord. He did not deprive me of the comfort I enjoyed, immediately, but by degrees; soon after, reflecting upon my ingratitude, and seeing clearly *what* I *ought* to have done, I found it diminished. Surely there is no safe nor comfortable path to walk in, but that of duty.[109]

Importantly, this path would take the true Christian closer to God and thus better able to benefit from the comfort that faith could bring. Reflecting on such things in August 1770, she recorded: 'I can hardly see it possible how a real Christian can converse with the word of God, and also study his own heart and experience, and not be sensible, that his comfort increases or diminishes, according to his close or careless walking with God'.[110]

Lady Maxwell was driven by the zeal of evangelicalism which gave extra force to her convictions and a particular fervour to her writing. Yet even the more worldly Lady Jane Stuart Macartney was alive to the comfort deriving from doing duty to God. In 1788, she exhorted her sister, Lady Caroline Dawson, to:

> endeavour to instil into the minds of your beloved children a sense of true religion; try to secure for them this heavenly resource under all circumstances; teach them that duty to God, to their Creator and Redeemer, ought to be the first and most pleasing thought of their heart, and all other duties fulfilled thro' a sense of obedience and gratitude to Him, this steady aim will be productive of sure and certain comfort under every difficulty and distress.[111]

The promise that solace and consolation were offered to those who developed a sense of duty to God from an early age was a powerful argument that drew on older meanings of comfort (discussed in the Introduction). It is notable that it still held weight in late eighteenth-century noble families.

The routines of Christian life offered their own sense of comfort and contentment. This was a second aspect emphasised in many treatises: Sparke's *Crums of Comfort* essentially comprised a practical guide to prayer and offered a number of exemplars, to be used as need occasioned.[112] We saw earlier how times of prayer punctuated the everyday routine of William Money; his wife Emma was explicit about the benefits of such routine, remarking in a letter written in September 1818 that 'I have had great happiness this day in going to Church twice and in attending the Blessed Sacrament'.[113] Her words echo the sentiments of earlier protestants, for whom, Michael Smith argues, 'comfort was the primary affection' leading from public worship, particularly when this involved receiving the sacrament.[114] Like Emma Money, the Manchester wigmaker, Matthew Harrold, noted in his diary in 1712 that he had been to church twice and 'stayd sacrament and received of Dr. Ashton and Ainscough very comfortably'; whilst the daughter of an eminent ejected minister, Sarah Savage, described public worship as 'quickening and comforting' and found preaching could offer a 'comfortable blessing'.[115]

For all these writers, church-going brought spiritual rather than bodily comfort: no matter how well upholstered a family pew, attending two services and communion cannot have been a physically comfortable experience. Country-house owners were rather better placed and enjoyed a measure of material comfort in the galleries of their private chapels. At Stoneleigh Abbey, for instance, the fifth Baron Leigh had the chapel richly draped with crimson velvet; there were cushions of matching velvet trimmed with gold fringe, and ten upholstered back stools. Yet his total outlay of £473 10¼d. reflected a desire to display wealth and taste, rather than to provide a physically comfortable environment.[116] Even in the relatively modest setting of their new home in Ireland, Mary Delany was quite clear that her husband, the Dean of Down, would be adding a chapel to their house, but only 'when we are rich enough to finish it as we ought to do'.[117] The numerous chapels included in the fabric of country houses, and those built in the grounds of many more, were characterised by family vaults and memorials rather than material comfort. Some enjoyed the benefit of innovative heating systems, including free-standing stoves, but they were undoubtedly places where spiritual rather than bodily comfort might be sought.

There is little evidence that Leigh made regular use of his chapel, despite employing a chaplain at the house, but elsewhere the private chapel was the setting for regular services and, for some, the kind of spiritual comfort and renewal enjoyed by Money, Harrold and Savage. At Audley End, Sir John Griffin Griffin had enlisted the master builder John Hobcroft to create a gothic-style chapel in the late 1760s, later embellished with heraldic decoration, including new stained-glass windows. The family enjoyed some material comfort in the form of a Wilton carpet and a small fireplace in the family's gallery, whilst their servants sat in the organ loft or on plain oak benches. This was a place that was used: prayers were said in the chapel every day except Sunday, when the family went to the church in nearby Saffron Walden. The extent to which any of the participants gained spiritual comfort from these routines is not apparent, but Sir John's widow, Katherine, was sufficiently attached to the practices and the chaplain to argue in 1797 for their retention by his successor at Audley End, Richard Aldworth.[118] Perhaps she feared the fate of the chapel at Jane Austen's fictional Sotherton, where Fanny Price was disappointed to find that daily prayers were no longer said. Many landed families continued to use their chapels, often insisting that their servants also attended. The Lucys were typical, going every week to divine service at the old chapel in the grounds of Charlecote Park.[119]

The public performance of religion was often matched by more private practices: bible study or the reading and rereading sermons. Having returned home from the tavern and been scolded by his wife, Harrold was unable to sleep; he got up and read a sermon by Norris and 'found a great deal of comforts to my soul from it'.[120] In more elevated tones, Lady Maxwell recorded the comfort she derived from her daily routine of reading the Bible, studying sermons and saying her prayers. Her diary entry for 1 January 1769 has the tone of setting an agenda for the year ahead. 'In the morning', she wrote:

> a sermon from 'Trust ye in the Lord for ever,' comforted and strengthened me; and in the afternoon another from 'All are your's, and ye are Christ's, and Christ is God's,' excited in my heart gratitude and love to Him, who had done so much for me. In the evening while at prayer, I felt desirous of devoting myself wholly to God, and attempted to renew the dedication of all my powers to Him.

These routines became so deeply ingrained that she later noted: 'On going to bed, so many comfortable scriptures poured in upon my mind, that I fell asleep filled with the love of God'.[121] A similar conception of the comfort of God's grace derived from studying the scriptures appears much earlier in our period. In *Robinson Crusoe*, the eponymous hero finds comfort not only in food and drink, but also in his faith in God. Several months after being shipwrecked, he starts reading a Bible and is struck by the wickedness of his earlier life. He notes in his journal that 'my Soul sought nothing of God, but deliverance from the Load of Guilt that bore down all my Comfort'. His solitary life was 'of no Consideration in Comparison with this'.[122] Thereafter, this idea surfaced regularly, especially in relation to his Bible reading, which he repeatedly describes as a comfort. In this, he reflected the broader emphasis that Protestants placed on bible reading, which offered both a source of spiritual comfort and the means to express their religious affections.[123]

Crusoe had no set place for his reading and reflection, but the country house afforded several locations for such practices. As a family activity,

Bible-reading might take place in the parlour, with the assembled children gathered around their parent—a practice which formed of the daily routine at Audley End in the 1810s, when Richard Aldworth Griffin, second Lord Braybrooke, lived there with his family (see Figure 3.5).[124] For adults, reading the Bible or sermons aloud might also happen in the drawing room or the library, although this became increasingly difficult as the latter transmuted through the last quarter of the eighteenth century into a physically comfortable and very sociable dayroom.[125] Before the Reformation, the closet was often a place of private devotion—somewhere to receive mass and to say prayers. Its metamorphosis into the cabinet meant that prayers were often said privately in the dressing room or bedchamber. Figure 4.1 depicts a modest scene rather than a grand country house bedchamber, but the association of the bedchamber, solitude and prayer is readily apparent. Sometimes, the individual at prayer employed particular pieces of furniture. Mary Delany's mother reportedly died in the act of saying her prayers; she was kneeling, as she always did, at dark-wood stool with a needlework seat, probably located in her

Figure 4.1 Thomas Gaugain, *Diligence and Dissipation: The Modest Girl in Her Bed Chamber* (1797): Yale Center for British Art, Paul Mellon Fund, New Haven, CT, B1980.22.5

bedchamber.[126] Delany herself sought solitude in her cabinet, bedchamber and in the garden, where she sometimes went to read.[127]

Quite apart from the spiritual and emotional comfort gained through the routines of church attendance, reading and prayer, they were seen as part of the process through which Christians came to a more complete trust in God and the comfort which this offered. This is drawn out in many treatises and is frequently restated in people's ego writing: faith brought comfort, both in terms of inner fortitude and of looking to God as the great comforter. William Notcutt wrote in his *Believer's Evidences for Heaven* (1717) that God 'is my Life, my Food, my Riches, my Honour, my Refuge, my Comfort, my Friend, my Father, my Home, and everlasting habitation', whilst Johnston quoted psalm 23 in his 1771 *Improved Christian's Courage*: 'though I walk through the valley of the shadow of death, I will fear no evil; for thou art with my: Thy rod, and thy staff, they comfort me'.[128]

Lady Maxwell made much of what she termed the 'comforts of religion', which she defined as 'token[s] of his love, together with peace in believing'.[129] What this meant in practical terms was a sense of contentment and an emotional resource into which she could tap in times of difficulty. Time and again, she wrote how her faith and her Christian life comforted and strengthened her. Reflecting on her coming to faith, she wrote in September 1772:

> I did not then know, that the thoughts of my God towards me, even in these dispensations of almost unmingled woe, were thoughts of peace, and not of evil. Having thus brought me into the wilderness he spoke comfortably to me; drew me with the cords of love [. . .] The Lord so tempered judgement with mercy, that I was rather *drawn* than *driven:* and generally was supported, and often comforted, with hopes of obtaining all that was necessary for happiness.[130]

The language here is important: God's message to her was spoken in comforting tones and she was gently brought to faith, supported, reassured and comforted along the way. This was no bruising conversion effected through threats or worries of painful and hopeless damnation—often the trope of more vigorous evangelicalism. And yet true contentment could only be found in faith, since 'In God alone is my comfort: Jesus is the only source of my consolation'; those who sought happiness and comfort in worldly things—or, as Lady Maxwell put it, 'in the creature'—would ultimately be disappointed because 'this takes their hearts from God, and makes them drive heavily on in his ways'.[131]

These sentiments were echoed in the journals of Mrs. Margaret A—s, published in 1804 as a collection entitled *The Christian Character Exemplified*.[132] Her diary entries often take the form of prayers, giving thanks for her salvation. On 22 January 1783, she wrote that she should be thankful that 'thou hast, in some measure, weaned me from a deceitful world, and embittered the sweets of life, to make me seek my comforts in Thee!' Recovery from illness the following year prompted a similar reflection: 'I have been very poorly of late, which has reminded me of the instability of all creature comforts. Happy is that soul, whose only repose is in Christ!'[133] This was a pious Christian rejecting the material comforts offered by this world and putting full confidence in her faith as the only true source of both spiritual comfort and salvation. Such sentiments were commonplace amongst evangelicals in late eighteenth and early nineteenth-century Britain, but they were a well-established maxim, based on Biblical teaching: not to be concerned with the trials and tribulations of this world because true contentment came from the rewards reaped in the afterlife.[134] William Money sought and offered comfort in the thought that departed loved ones were now in a better place. Following his father's funeral in 1808, he was confident that the old man was now with the saints in heaven and wrote that 'this blessed reflection is a source of consolation to us all'. When his wife's father died 6 years later, he tried to reassure her that 'death was to him a happy release' and went on to ask 'What can life afford to the weary Traveller, who has trodden its rough and uneasy course for the space of eighty long years? . . . Is not heaven the only home of a Christian?'[135] Money thus offered comfort to his wife by commending the comfort of eternity with the Saviour—the ultimate goal of all Christians.

A fourth way in which religion was linked to comfort came in the form of faith as a prompt for action: an instruction to Christians to provide comfort to others, most commonly the sick or the destitute. In 1628, Sparke offered prayers for the sick or for those approaching death; nearly 200 years later, Orlando Jeary's Mr. Consolation embodied the Christian duty to offer comfort to others, in this case, the unfortunate Mr. Fearing.[136] Following from this, the faithful also asked for others to be blessed with God's comfort, often in times of physical or moral danger and most frequently in relation to illness or death. Parson Woodforde did just this, noting in his diary both the passing of parishioners and his hope that God's comfort would give solace to their families. Thus, for example, he wrote on 26 May 1783: 'I buried poor Joe Adcocks Wife this Evening aged 43. Pray God comfort the poor Man in his distress, he having buried, his Father and Mother and Wife within 6 Weeks'.[137]

Such intercessions for the comfort of others feature in letters to and from country-house owners throughout the long eighteenth century. Writing on 26 June 1676 to her brother Edward Clarke, Ursula Clarke Venner was confident of the comfort that God could provide during times of grief and bereavement. She consoled him on 'my Cozen Cusses Death' and assured him that 'I am heartily sorry & I pray for yor little boy & comfort for you & by all wch I pray God to send us'.[138] She used a similar form of words on many occasions in her letters to Edward, most often in connection with hopes for recovery from illness or pain. This was more than simply formulaic repetition; Ursula Venner saw intercession with God as a means of bringing the comfort of both bodily health and spiritual well-being. In an undated letter from 1678, for example, she wrote that she was 'very glad to heare yt my little Cozen grows soe & I pray God to continue yor & increase of my sisters health & send us all his grace & comfort'.[139] There was also a practical element to these intercessions with God. In December 1678, she offered advice on easing the pain of teething that troubled her niece, and assured her brother that 'I pray God to comfort & strengthen my poore sister'. The following year, she wrote about her father's illness and the treatment he was receiving. She doubted the efficacy of the medication, but added that 'wee will use our best indeavor & I pray God to comfort him & direct us to doe what is best for him'.[140] Two things are notable here. One is that Ursula Venner saw comfort of the body and spirit as being closely bound together, a point which echoes my earlier argument about beds and the anxiety of infestation. The other is that God's comfort not only provided fortitude to those who were ill and solace for those experiencing grief, but also prompted action on the part of those caring for the sick. It was, in short, a Christian duty to offer comfort to those less fortunate—a point made in the writings of Sparke, Notcutt, Johnston and others.

The timelessness of this imperative and the benefits that it brought is apparent in the mid-nineteenth-century novels of Elizabeth Gaskell. In *Mary Barton*, she has Jem Wilson relating a story to Mary's aunt, Esther, about an overseer of a foundry who 'has spent his Sabbaths, for many years, in visiting the prisoners and the afflicted in Manchester New Bailey; not merely advising and comforting, but putting means into their power of regaining the virtue and the peace they had lost'.[141] Christian charity—framed by Gaskell's own Unitarian convictions—demanded deeds as well as words, making comfort a practical concern. In terms of action, this links to the long-established norm of elite landowners providing charitable support for 'their' people in a form of benign (and sometimes not so benign) patrimony. This is not the place for a detailed discussion of such charitable activity, but its ingrained nature is apparent from Sir Roger Newdigate's accounts for Arbury Hall. Throughout the 1750s and 1760s, for instance, the heading *Dues* includes both his obligations in terms of the poor rate and also regular payments to the 'Charity Schoolmaster' and to the poor of various local parishes.[142] Other landowners endowed schools, disbursed donations to the poor at birthdays and even visited sick tenants in their homes—the last most often the domain of wives and daughters of the landowner. Whether these actions were born of a Christian duty or a form of *noblesse oblige* is difficult to determine, but it seems unlikely that they drew a sense of comfort of the sort imagined by Gaskell.

This links to a fifth way in which faith was linked to comfort: as a warning against becoming reliant upon creature comforts. As John MacGowan put it in his 1772 *The Canker Worm; or the Gourd of Creature Comfort Withered*: God has placed a 'worm at the root of every gourd of creature-delight and comfort; by which means he drives people to a more excellent dwelling place'.[143] This was a sentiment that ran through much of our period and is also apparent in a 1750 advertisement for the *Pious Country Parishioners* in the London press. This book, it was argued, would show people 'how to subdue their Passions, and make them a Comfort to their Friends'.[144] Here, we see a link back not only to the Christian ideal of comforting others, but also to the necessity of giving up worldly things and animal passions in order to focus on these good deeds. This links to Mrs. Margaret A—s' recognition of the 'instability of all creature comforts' noted earlier, and is an idea to which William Money returned on several occasions in the 1810s. Sometimes this was expressed as a generalised ambition. Reflecting on the sermon preached at his mother's funeral in June 1813, he wrote 'how often have I resolved to turn my back on all Worldly views, & to live unto my God alone! How often have I made up my mind to seek comfort & Joy in the paths of Religion only'.[145] However, it was an idea that could be much more focused and impact upon his actions as well as his feelings. Remarking on 'how little is the good & gracious God of Heaven known or regarded' in the bustle of London life, he was concerned how easily this indifference could spread and asserted that 'I have no peace or comfort in such a state of things'. Three years later, similar sentiments were expressed again: 'I cannot tell you, my own beloved Emma, how uncomfortable I felt at the Heathenish life we all passed at Weymouth'. This time, it seems that he took action and returned early to his Wiltshire home, leaving Emma and his children to continue their stay in the company of relatives. In effect, he turned his back on worldly comforts and pleasures to enjoy a closer 'communion with my God in thought, word, or deed'.[146]

Conclusions

Making the body comfortable and, importantly, allowing people to *feel* that their bodies were comfortable, involved a range of interventions in both the domestic environment of the country house and the ecology of the body itself. It meant removing dirt and infestation, which could cause physical, social and mental discomfort; providing fresh air and beds that were appropriate to the physiology of the occupant and furnished with the requisite bedding, and—when all else failed—using medicines and lotions that could offer relief from aches and pains, and thus afford comfort. The extent to which these concerns grew over the course of the long eighteenth century, reflecting a rising concern with bodily comfort, is less clear. On the one hand, there was a growing concern with dirt, and bed bugs in particular appear to have been increasingly viewed as problematic through the eighteenth century, giving rise to a burgeoning eradication industry and a growing distrust of second-hand beds and bedding. On the other hand, smoke, fresh air, the quality of beds and even the relief promised by patent medicines were all apparent by the opening decades of the eighteenth century, reflecting processes underway even earlier. Importantly, all these things were described in the language of comfort throughout the period: the association is apparent in the pages of *Robinson Crusoe* as much as the novels of Jane Austen.

If a concern for bodily comfort was characteristic of our period as a whole, it was being refined through the eighteenth century in ways that played on the social and psychological dimensions of comfort. Cleanliness spoke of respectability, allowing country-house owners to feel comfortable in the messages that their homes communicated about their moral character and their standing in society. Bed bugs preyed on the mind as well as the body, creating anxieties that gnawed away at any feeling of comfort and contentment with one's sleeping arrangements. In this, we see a new manifestation of comfort as something that was felt rather than experienced. This takes us into the history of emotions, but emphasises rather different and perhaps less pronounced sentiments and feelings: contentment was aligned with comfort in the minds of many eighteenth-century letter writers and diarists.

This contentment might be grounded in what French and Rothery see as elite manly virtues of stoicism and inner fortitude, although it is noticeable that women as well as men could display these characteristics. More often, it was bolstered by everyday routines. Country-house life might have been viewed as dull by some, especially those who were periodically engaged in the London season; but others found comfort in the daily practices of gardening, reading and writing. There was also comfort to be had from faith, which again formed a thread of continuity running throughout and beyond the long eighteenth century. This is another reminder, if one was needed, that religion did not disappear from social life in Georgian England, certainly not from the country house where private chapels were maintained and built, and where household prayers punctuated daily and weekly routines. Significantly, faith brought comfort not only through trust in God and in the expectation of a better life to come, but also through action: in doing charitable deeds and offering Christian comfort to others—the kind of charitable patronage long associated with the patrician classes. Comfort, then, was a shared emotion and experience, something that could be given and received; we therefore need to explore more fully how comfort shaped relationships between family and friends.

Notes

1. See, for example: Tobbias Venner, *Via Recta ad Vitam Longam, or a Plaine Philosophical Discourse* (London, 1620).
2. Mark Girouard, *Life in the English Country House: a Social and Architectural History* (New Haven: Yale University Press, 1978), 215–16.
3. Beverly Lemire, 'An Education in Comfort: Indian Textiles and the Remaking of English Homes Over the Long Eighteenth Century', in Jon Stobart and Bruno Blondé (eds.), *Selling Textiles in the Long Eighteenth Century* (Basingstoke: Palgrave Macmillan, 2014), 13–29; Woodruff Smith, *Consumption and the Making of Respectability, 1600–1800* (London: Routledge, 2002).
4. Sarah Goldsmith, 'Nostalgia, Homesickness and Emotional Formation on the Eighteenth-Century Grand Tour', *Cultural and Social History*, 15:3 (2018), 333–60.
5. Henry French and Mark Rothery, *Man's Estate: Landed Gentry Masculinities, 1660–1900* (Oxford: Oxford University Press, 2012), 69–70. See also Karen Harvey and Alexandra Shepard, 'What Have Historians Done with Masculinity? Reflections on Five Centuries of British History, Circa 1500–1950', *Journal of British Studies*, 44:2 (2005), 274–80.
6. Brodie Waddell, *God, Duty and Community in English Economic Life, 1660–1720* (Woodbridge: Boydell & Brewer Press, 2012); Donald Spaeth, *The Church in an Age of Danger: Parsons and Parishioners, 1660–1740* (Cambridge: Cambridge University Press, 2000). See also Jeremy Gregory, 'Transforming the Age of Reason into an Age of Faiths', *Journal for Eighteenth-Century Studies*, 32 (2009); Jeremy Gregory, *Restoration, Reformation, and Reform, 1660–1828: Archbishops of Canterbury and Their Diocese* (Oxford: Oxford University Press, 2000).
7. Michael Smith, 'The Affective Communities of Protestantism in North West England, c.1660–c.1740' (Unpublished PhD thesis, University of Manchester, 2017).
8. Lemire, 'An Education in Comfort'; Nancy Cox and Karin Dannehl, *Perceptions of Retailing in Early Modern England* (Aldershot: Ashgate, 2007), 118–22. On concerns about dirt more generally, see Emily Cockayne, *Hubbub: Filth, Noise and Stench in England, 1600–1770* (New Haven: Yale University Press, 2008).
9. D.M. Mitchell, 'Fine Table Linen in England 1450–1750: Ownership and Use of a Luxury Commodity' (Unpublished PhD thesis, University of London, 1999); Smith, *Consumption and the Making of Respectability*, 115–16, 130–8.
10. Roey Sweet, *Cities and the Grand Tour: The British in Italy, c.1690–1820* (Cambridge: Cambridge University Press, 2012), 140–5, 220–1.
11. Warwickshire Record Office (WRO), CR1841/7, Travel diary of Sophia Newdigate, 1748, ff.18, 47.
12. Gerrit Verhoeven, 'Feeling at Home Abroad: Comfort, Domesticity, and Social Display on the Netherlandish Grand Tour (1585–1815)', in Jon Stobart (ed.), *The Comforts of Home in Western Europe, 1700–1900* (London: Bloomsbury, 2020), 165.
13. Cambridge Record Office (CRO), 488/C2/HD196, Richard Huddlestone to Ferdinand Huddlestone, 31 January 1786.
14. Riksarkivet (RA), Ekebladska samlingen, Brita Horn to Claes Julius Ekeblad, 8 September 1779. I am grateful to Cristina Prytz for this reference.
15. Northamptonshire Record Office (NRO), D(CA)/361, Elizabeth Dryden to Mrs Steele, 28 December 1816.

16. For parallel processes of purification of pre-owned furniture, see Robin Jones, ' "Souvenirs of People Who Have Come and Gone": Second-Hand Furnishings and the Anglo-India Domestic Interior, 1840–1920', in Jon Stobart and Ilja Van Damme (eds.), *Modernity and the Second-hand Trade* (Basingstoke: Palgrave Macmillan, 2010), 111–38.

17. Jonathan Swift, *Directions to Servants*, second edition (London, 1746), 78.

18. Lady Grisell Baillie, *The House Book of Lady Grisell Baillie, 1692–1733* (Edinburgh: Scottish Historical Society, 1911), 279.

19. Susanna Whatman, *The Housekeeping Book of Susanna Whatman* (1776; London: National Trust, 2000), 39.

20. Samuel Adams and Sarah Adams, *The Complete Servant* (London, 1825), 286, 288.

21. Shakespeare Central Library and Archive (SCLA), DR18/5/5937, bill from Joseph Lee, 28 December 1791.

22. SCLA, DR630, Designs for Stoneleigh Abbey.

23. SCLA, DR18/5/6019, bill from John Walker, 31 December 1792.

24. *Woodfall's Register*, 5 October 1790.

25. Baillie, *House Book*, 151; WRO, CR136/V/156, Accounts, 1747–62; CR136/V/136, Accounts, 1763–96.

26. Howard Colvin and John Newman (eds.), *Of Building: Roger North's Writings on Architecture* (Oxford: Oxford University Press, 1981), 48.

27. Nicolas Gauger, *La Mécanique du Feu, ou l'Art d'en Augmenter les Effets et d'en Diminuer la Dépense* (Paris, 1713); Joan DeJean, *The Age of Comfort: When Paris Discovered Casual and the Modern Home Began* (New York: Bloomsbury, 2009), 96–7.

28. DeJean, *Age of Comfort*, 100.

29. Robert Clavering, *An Essay on the Construction and Building of Chimneys* (London, 1793); John Whitehurst, *Observations on the Ventilation of Rooms, on the Construction of Chimneys and on Garden Stoves* (London, 1794).

30. James Adair, *An Essay on Diet and Regimen*, second edition (London, 1812), 77.

31. Whatman, *Housekeeping Book*, 41.

32. Johann Friedrich Karl Grimm, *Bemerkungen eines reisenden, Durch Deutschland, Frankreich, England Und Holland in Briefen an Seine Freunde* (Altenburg, 1775), 268–9.

33. Swift, *Directions to Servants*, 78–9.

34. This is the instruction given to maids in Adams and Adams, *Complete Servant*, 256.

35. Adair, *Diet and Regimen*, 72.

36. Thomas Tryon, *A Treatise of Cleanness in Meats and Drinks, of the Preparation of Food, the Excellency of Good Airs, and the Benefits of Clan Sweet Beds. Also of the Generation of Bugs, and Their Cure* (London, 1682), 9.

37. Walter Reiff, *Lustgarten der Gesundheit* (1546); Håkan Tunón (ed.), *En fullständig svensk hushållsbok, Reinerus Reineri Broocman*, vol. 2 (Stockholm: Kungl, 2016), 731. My thanks to Cristna Prytz for these references.

38. James Beresford, *The Miseries of Human Life* (London, 1806). The book is discussed at length in Crowley, *Invention of Comfort*, 196–8.

39. Thomas Rowlandson, *The Comforts of a Modern Gala* (London: Thomas Tegg, 1809), V&A, H. Beard Print Collection, S.4728–2009. There is also the suggestion of another bodily comfort: one fat women drinking from a bottle declares: 'I have lost Mr Dowlass, but here is my comfort'.

40. Whitehurst, *Observations on the Ventilation of Rooms*, 19.

41. Mark Rothery and Henry French, *The Formation of Male Elite Identities in England c.1660–1900: A Sourcebook* (Basingstoke: Palgrave Macmillan,

2012); Wiiliam Brogden, *Iconographia Rustica: Stephen Switzer and the Designed Landscape* (London: Routledge, 2016), 75–8.

42. Wiltshire Record Office (WiRO), 1720/829 (transcript), 90: William Money to Emma Money, 19 December 1813.

43. NRO, D(CA)/361, Elizabeth Dryden to Mrs Steele, 30 October 1820; [no date] November 1819.

44. CRO, 488/C3/HD175, Mary Huddlestone to Richard Huddlestone: 14 June 1805; 488/CD/HD176, Mary Huddlestone to Richard Huddlestone: 30 July 1805.

45. CRO, 488/C3/HD175, Mary Huddlestone to Richard Huddlestone: 14 June 1805.

46. Jane Austen, *Sanditon* (1817; Oxford: Oxford University Press, 1998), 337.

47. Anon., *An Easy Way to Prolong Life* (London, 1780), 31.

48. See, for example: Alan Mackintosh, *The Patent Medicines Industry in Georgian England: Constructing the Market by the Potency of Print* (Basingstoke: Palgrave Macmillan, 2017); Susanna Burghartz, 'Printed Markets: The Basel Avisblatt, 1729–1845', https://avisblatt.ch/ (accessed 6 August 2020).

49. *Fog's Weekly Journal*, 4 April 1730; *St James Chronicle*, 30 January 1790.

50. *Hull Packet*, 16 October 1810.

51. WRO, CR136/V/156, Accounts, 1747–62; CR136/V/136, Accounts, 1763–96.

52. SCLA, DR18/5/5813, bill from B. Wilmer, 9 August 1788; DR18/5/5915, bill from B Wilmer, 20 August 1791.

53. For the context of this marriage and the views of Ashe's mother, Katherine Windham, see R.W. Ketton-Cremer, *Felbrigg: The Story of a House* (London: Futura, 1982), 92–100.

54. Norfolk Record Office (NoRO), WKC, 7/20/15, Ashe Windham to Elizabeth Windham, 8 March 1719, 21 March 1719.

55. NoRO, WKC, 7/20/15, Ashe Windham to Elizabeth Windham, 8 April 1719.

56. Warwickshire Record Office (WRO), L6/1439, Phillipa Hayes to George Lucy, 18 April 1755.

57. WRO, L6/1439, George Lucy to Phillipa Hayes, 25 April 1757.

58. Horace Walpole, *Horace Walpole's Correspondence*, vol. 25, 5, https://walpole.library.yale.edu/collections/digital-resources/horace-walpole-corre-spondence: Horace Walpole to Horace Mann, 4 January 1780.

59. Walpole, *Horace Walpole's Correspondence*, vol. 2, 279: William Cole to Horace Walpole, 23 July 1781.

60. Walpole, *Horace Walpole's Correspondence*, vol. 39, 209: Horace Walpole to Lady Ailesbury, 7 November 1774.

61. Walpole, *Horace Walpole's Correspondence*, vol. 11, 249: Horace Walpole to Mary Berry, 15 April 1791.

62. Walpole, *Horace Walpole's Correspondence*, vol. 39, 494: Horace Walpole to Henry Seymour Conway, 31 August 1792.

63. CRO, 488/CD/HD176, Richard Huddlestone to Mary Huddlestone, 30 July 1805; 488/CD/HD177, Richard Huddlestone to Mary Huddlestone, 3 August 1805; 488/CD/HD178, Mary Huddlestone to Richard Huddlestone, 8 August 1805.

64. Crowley, *Invention of Comfort*, 75–6. See also Sasha Handley, *Sleep in Early Modern England* (New Haven: Yale University Press, 2016).

65. NRO, D(CA)/347, John Turner Dryden's Tour of France, 21 July 1774.

66. Swedish National Archive, Tosterupsamlingen, vol. 108, Johan Gabriel Oxenstiernas journal 1766–1768, 29 August 1766, 1 September 1766 (I am grateful to Johanna Ilmakunnas for this reference). See also Johanna

Ilmakunnas, 'Northern Comfort and Discomfort: Spaces and Objects in Swedish Country Houses, c.1740–1800', in Jon Stobart (ed.), *The Comforts of Home in Western Europe, 1700–1900* (London: Bloomsbury, 2020), 58.

67. Thomas Sheraton, *Cabinet Dictionary* (London, 1803), 43–4. See also Akiko Shimbo, *Furniture-Makers and Consumers in England, 1754–1851* (Farnham: Ashgate, 2015), 88–9.
68. Tryon, *Treatise of Cleanness*, 5.
69. Tryon, *Treatise of Cleanness*, 10–11.
70. Tryon, *Treatise of Cleanness*, 11.
71. Whatman, *Housekeeping Book*, 41.
72. Adams and Adams, *The Complete Servant*, 279.
73. WRO, L6/1450, George Lucy to Phillipa Hayes, 12 June 1758.
74. Tryon, *Treatise of Cleanness*, 13.
75. Tryon, *Treatise of Cleanness*, 12.
76. John Ray, *Observations Topographical, Moral, & Physiological; Made in a Journey Through Part of the Low-Countries, Germany, Italy, and France* (London, 1673), 411.
77. John Southall, *A Treatise on Cimex Lectularius, or the Bed Bug*, second edition (1730; Ipswich: J. Bush, 1793), 34.
78. See Lisa Sarasohn, '"That Nauseous Venomous Insect": Bedbugs in Early Modern England', *Eighteenth-Century Studies*, 46:4 (2013), 513.
79. Walpole, *Horace Walpole's Correspondence*, vol. 20, 324: Horace Walpole to Horace Mann, 27 July 1752.
80. Maria Theresa Lewis (ed.), *Extracts of the Journals and Correspondence of Miss Berry from the Year 1783–1852*, vol. 2 (London: Longmans, 1908), 169: diary entry for 21 June 1784; Jane Adeane (ed.), *The Girlhood of Maria Josepha Holroyd, Lady Stanley of Alderley: Recorded in Letters of a Hundred Years Ago, from 1776 to 1796*, vol. 2 (London: Longmans, 1896), 74: Maria Josepha Holroyd Stanley to Serena Holroyd, 19 July 1791.
81. Sarasohn, '"That Nauseous Venomous Insect"'.
82. For a fuller discussion, see Sara Pennell, 'Making the Bed in Later Stuart and Georgian England', in Jon Stobart and Bruno Blondé (eds.), *Selling Textiles in the Long Eighteenth Century* (Basingstoke: Palgrave Macmillan, 2014), 39–41.
83. Sarasohn, '"That Nauseous Venomous Insect"', 523–6.
84. Pennell, 'Making the Bed', 40.
85. Quoted in Pennell, 'Making the Bed', 40.
86. *Leeds Intelligencer*, 23 August 1785; *Chelmsford Chronicle*, 20 April 1787.
87. Pennell, 'Making the Bed', 41.
88. NRO, D(CA)/361, Elizabeth Dryden to Mrs Steele, 30 October 1820.
89. Peter McKay and David Hall (eds.), *Estate Letters from the Time of John, 2nd Duke of Montagu, 1709–39* (Northampton: Northamptonshire Record Society, 2013), 55: Lamotte to Duke John, 19 March 1720.
90. Sarah Chauncey Woolsey (ed.), *The Autobiography and Correspondence of Mrs Delany*, vol. 2 (Boston: Roberts Brothers, 1879), 402: Mary Delany to Anne Dewes, 3 January 1752. Emphasis in the original.
91. Henry French and Mark Rothery, 'Male Anxiety Among Younger Sons of the English Landed Gentry', *The Historical Journal*, 62:4 (2019), 967–95.
92. Alice Clark (ed.), *Gleanings from an Old Portfolio Containing Some Correspondence Between Lady Louisa Stuart and Her Sister, Caroline, Countess of Portarlington and Other Friends and Relatives*, vol. 2 (Edinburgh, 1895), 61: Lady Louisa Stuart to Lady Caroline Dawson, September 1800.
93. John Doyle (ed.), *Memoir and Correspondence of Susan Ferrier, 1782–1854* (London: John Murray, 1898), 76: Susan Ferrier to Miss Clavering 1809.

94. WiRO, 1720/829 (transcript), 55: William Money to Emma Money, 14 May 1812.
95. Mary Jepp Clarke *et al.*, *Clarke Family Letters* (Alexandra, VA: Alexandra Press, 2003), 28.
96. See Goldsmith, 'Nostalgia, Homesickness and Emotional Formation', 346–7; Eric Gidal, 'Civic Melancholy: English Gloom and French Enlightenment', *Eighteenth-Century Studies*, 37:1 (2003), 23–45.
97. Mary Anne Radcliffe, *Memoirs of Mrs Mary Anne Radcliffe, in Familiar Letters to Her Female Friend* (Edinburgh, 1810), 131.
98. WiRO, 1720/829 (transcript), 42: Emma Money to William Money, [no date] April 1812.
99. Katrina O'Loughlin, 'Sensibility', in Susa Broomhall (ed.), *Early Modern Emotions: An Introduction* (London: Routledge, 2017).
100. Michael Knierim (ed.), *Die Herkunft des Friedrich Engels: Briefe aus der Verwandtschaft* (Trier: Karl Marx Haus1991), 345: Friedrich Engels to Elise van Haar, 3 December 1818. Thanks to Sophie Anne Overkamp for this reference.
101. Mary Jepp Clarke *et al.*, *Clarke Family Letters*, 461.
102. For a more general discussion of emotions and affections in relation to faith, see Smith, 'Affective Communities of Protestantism'; Lauren Winner, *A Cheerful and Comfortable Faith: Anglican Religious Practice in the Elite Households of Eighteenth-Century Virginia* (New Haven: Yale University Press, 2010).
103. William Johnston, *The Improved Christian's Courage and Comfort from Afflictions and Death* (London, 1771), 9.
104. Dorothy Heighes Woodforde (ed.), *Woodforde Papers and Diaries* (London: Peter Davies, 1932): Mary Woodforde's Booke, 1 June 1687, 13 October 1687.
105. Heighes Woodforde, *Woodforde Papers:* 'Mary Woodforde's Booke', 13 October 1687.
106. CRO 488/C3/HD175, Mary Huddlestone to Richard Huddlestone, 14 June 1805.
107. John Lancaster, *The Life of Darcy, Lady Maxwell . . . Compiled from Her Voluminous Diary and Correspondence* (New York, 1822), 1–32.
108. Lancaster, *Life of Darcy, Lady Maxwell*, 90–1.
109. Lancaster, *Life of Darcy, Lady Maxwell*, 153–4.
110. Lancaster, *Life of Darcy, Lady Maxwell*, 131.
111. Clark, *Gleanings from an Old Portfolio*, vol. 2, 109: Lady Jane Stuart Macartney to Lady Caroline Dawson, 27 November 1788.
112. Michael Sparke, *Crums of Comfort and Godly Prayers* (London, 1628). Smith, notes that Timothy Cragg of Chappelhouse Wrysdale in Lancashire recorded in his memoirs that his mother used to read prayers from this book, highlighting in particular that to be said in times of pestilence— Smith, 'Affective Communities of Protestantism', 80.
113. WiRO, 1720/829 (transcript), 192: Emma Money to William Money, 13 September 1818.
114. Smith, 'Affective Communities of Protestantism', 115.
115. Craig Horner (ed.), *The Diary of Edmund Harrold, Wigmaker of Manchester 1712–15* (Aldershot: Ashgate, 2008), 63; Savage is quoted in Smith, 'Affective Communities of Protestantism', 119–20. Savage's father was a casualty of the so-called Great Ejection which followed the Act of Uniformity; several thousand puritan minister were forced out of the Church of England for refusing to conform to the Book of Common Prayer.

116. Shakespeare Central Library and Archive, DR18/3/47/52/15-1765 bill from Thomas Burnett.
117. Chauncey Woolsey, *Correspondence of Mrs Delany*, vol. 1: Mary Delany to Anne Dewes, 28 June 1744.
118. Hannah Chavasse, 'Material Culture and the Country House: Fashion, Comfort and Lineage' (Unpublished PhD thesis, University of Northampton, 2015), 44–5, 87, 97, 149.
119. Jane Austen, *Mansfield Park* (1814; Oxford: Oxford University Press, 1980), 76–7; Elsie Donald (ed.), *Mistress of Charlecote: The Memoirs of Mary Elizabeth Lucy, 1803–1889* (1983; London: Orion, 2002), 81–2.
120. Horner, *Diary of Edmund Harrold*, 44, 4 November 1712.
121. Lancaster, *Life of Darcy, Lady Maxwell*, 86, 147.
122. Daniel Defoe, *Robinson Crusoe* (1719; London: Palgrave Macmillan, 1868), 98.
123. Smith, 'Affective Communities of Protestantism', 49–50.
124. Chavasse, 'Material Culture and the Country House', 153.
125. Mark Purcell, *The Country House Library* (New Haven: Yale University Press, 2017), 186–93.
126. Chauncey Woolsey, *Correspondence of Mrs Delany*, vol. 1: editor's notes, 347.
127. See, for example, Chauncey Woolsey, *Correspondence of Mrs Delany*, vol. 1: Mary Delany to Anne Dewes, 8 June 1753.
128. William Notcutt, *A Believer's Evidences for Heaven, or a Short Essay for Christian Comfort* (1717), 33; Johnston, *The Improved Christian's Courage*, 8–9. See also Spark, *Crums of Comfort*; Orlando Jeary, *A Dialogue Between Mr Fearing and Mr Consolation; or a Word of Comfort to the Fearful of Christ's Flock* (1800), 47.
129. Lancaster, *Life of Darcy, Lady Maxwell*, 118.
130. Lancaster, *Life of Darcy, Lady Maxwell*, 27–8.
131. Lancaster, *Life of Darcy, Lady Maxwell*, 135, 161.
132. John Newton (ed.), *The Christian Character Exemplified, from the Papers of Mrs. Margaret Magdalen A—s. . .* (London: Lincoln & Gleason, 1804).
133. Newton, *Christian Character*, 89, 100.
134. This is the central message of Psalm 23, quoted repeatedly in Johnston, *The Improved Christians' Courage*.
135. WiRO, 1720/829 (transcript), 29, 113: William Money to Emma Money, 14 November 1808, 26 July 1814.
136. Sparke, *Crums of Comfort*, n.p.; Jeary, *A Dialogue Between Mr Fearing and Mr Consolation*.
137. John Beresford (ed.), *The Diary of a Country Parson, 1758–1802* (Norwich: Canterbury Press, 1999), 139.
138. Clarke *et al.*, *Clarke Family Letters*, 31.
139. Clarke *et al.*, *Clarke Family Letters*, 138.
140. Clarke *et al.*, *Clarke Family Letters*, 112, 121.
141. Elizabeth Gaskell, *Mary Barton* (1848; London: Chapman and Hall, 1849), 246–7.
142. Baillie, *House Book*, 151; WRO, CR136/V/156, Accounts, 1747–62; CR136/V/136, Accounts, 1763–96.
143. John McGowan, *The Canker Worm; or the Gourd of Creature Comforts Withered* (1772), 13.
144. *London Evening Post*, 12 July 1750.
145. WiRO, 1720/829 (transcript), 87: William Money to Emma Money, [no date] June 1813.
146. WiRO, 1720/829 (transcript), 103, 147: William Money to Emma Money, 25 June 1814, 3 September 1817.

5 Family and Friends
Comfort, Consolation and Correspondence

Material comforts were central in making the country house into a home, but so too were relationships with people. As Thomas Malthus noted in his *Essay on the Principle of Population* (1803), 'the evening meal, the warm house, and the comfortable fireside, would lose half their interest, if we were to exclude the idea of some object of affection, with whom they were to be shared'.[1] Malthus, of course, was writing with a specific purpose in mind: to bring ideas of population control within the compass of the family and household. With a manageable number of children, every household might enjoy this level of material comfort and redouble its impact by being able to share it with family and friends.[2] In this, he links material ease to earlier meanings of comfort as something shared between people: an emotional response rather than a physical experience.

This ties into emotion histories which place great emphasis on family and home in framing and articulating affective relationships. There are many aspects to this, but four, in particular, are important to the present discussion. The first is the centrality of family to emotional interactions and relationships, with the ties between husbands and wives, and parents and children, being especially important. These relationships had the opportunity to grow and strengthen through regular and extended interaction, and their intensity added further to the establishment of lasting bonds.[3] Joanne Bailey has demonstrated the complexity of the parent–child relationship, with parents constructed as affectionate, tender, feeling, anxious and so on—a range of emotions that reflects the complexity of parenting and how this developed over time and over the family lifecycle. She has also shown how husbands and wives experienced a similar range of emotional relations and bonds, often diverging from ideals of conjugal bliss.[4] The second is the status of the household as an emotional community, defined by particular practices and modes of affective articulation.[5] Importantly, the household provided both a spatial setting and a social grouping that included, *inter alia*, servants as well as family, all of whom shared emotional bonds, both positive and negative.[6] This is something that has been shown in a variety of settings, from the gentleman servants of early modern elite households

DOI: 10.4324/9781003206361-8

to the apprentices accommodated in artisan households in early nineteenth-century Manchester.[7] Third, there is what Nicole Pohl refers to as a 'sentimental household' which went beyond the physical, domestic and contractual bounds of the household to encompass a wider network of emotional relations with distant family and friends. Pohl herself sees these networks in opposition to the 'texture of female subordination in contemporary family and household structures', but it is also possible to view them as complementary to the more spatially and socially bounded ties of household.[8] Often fed by regular letter writing, these relationships could bind together kin and friends who were geographically remote and nurture strong affective ties, giving them a sense of common cause and a shared emotional world.[9] Fourth is the question of how all this related to the physical structure and daily routines of the country house—a building that was a statement of power and status, a personal and domestic space, and an imagined 'home' to those distant from it.

What is remarkable in all this discussion of emotions within and beyond the household is that comfort has been entirely overlooked, despite it being a word that was frequently deployed by people through the eighteenth and early nineteenth century to describe their emotions in relation to other people. In this context, comfort was a *feeling* of well-being that arose from being in company or correspondence with family and friends, and a social and cultural *practice*: something which was sought from and offered to others, especially in times of distress.[10] Mary Delany was alive to this, writing to her sister in 1744 that 'the solitude of Bradley was really *too much* for a sociable spirit to bear' and wishing to have her closer to home, 'in a neighbourhood where you may have some conversation a little better suited to your own'. Significantly, this need for companionship was captured in the ideal of a 'comfortable house . . . a main article for happiness to those who know so well how to enjoy home and make it pleasant to your friends'.[11]

This chapter looks to unpack the complexities of the feelings and relationships captured in Mary Delany's ideal of sociability and friendship within and beyond a comfortable home. In this, we need to be attentive to the materiality of country houses and the use to which they were put by their owners. The size of the house is one factor. None of those included here were at the scale of Blenheim Palace and some were quite modest dwellings, yet all contained a number of servants as well as family members. One question, then, is how this impacted the development of close emotional bonds and perhaps the sense of a companionable home. Equally important was the extent to which the country house was occupied year-round and by whom.[12] Whilst few of the families considered in this chapter used their country houses purely as an escape from the London season, the make-up of the family often changed as the husband travelled or siblings came to stay; this changed family dynamics and influenced emotional attachments within and between households. Such considerations are woven through this chapter and the one that follows, where emotional attachment to objects is explored. Here the focus is on spaces and practices within the country house and the ways in which these were sometimes linked to bonds of emotional comfort.

The chapter begins by exploring the place of comfort in familial relationships within the home, particularly those between husbands and wives, and parents and children. Building on the argument of Bailey and others, it examines a series of tensions and resolutions, including: ideals of companionship and the problems of falling short; the experience of discomfort, anxiety and conflict; the comforts of stable family relationships, and the discomforts of a dysfunctional family. The discussion is then extended into the broader household and touches in particular on the role of servants in providing the comfort of companionship rather than simply being a prop to physical ease. Broadening the scope of enquiry still further, attention turns next to the emotional network of kin and friends, addressing the ways in which these formed a complementary or alternative set of relations, especially in situations where household relationships were problematic. Finally, the chapter focuses on the key medium through which these relationships and emotions were expressed and explores letters in terms of their physical form and, more particularly, the ways in which they communicated and offered comfort to both writer and reader. In doing this, we need to be particularly attentive to language, recognising its importance in giving voice to and being part of emotional experiences.[13]

Comforts of Matrimony

In his *Comforts of Matrimony* (1809), Thomas Rowlandson paints an idyllic picture of the assemblage of objects and people that comprised happy family life: a warming fire, a meal being prepared and a comfortable seat, plus the companionship of the marital partner and a contented group of children (Figure 5.1).[14] This was an ideal reproduced in paintings, the conduct literature, novels and short stories.[15] A loving relationship between husband and wife was central to a contented family and a comfortable domestic milieu, even amongst elites where arranged marriages remained an important way of securing dynastic alliances.[16] This love, of course, could be manifest in different ways and expressed in different languages, as is apparent from three examples, drawn from across the span of the long eighteenth century.

Richard Coffin owned a modest estate at Portledge, north Devon. He married three times, in 1644, 1648 and 1674, by which time he was 52 and already had five children. Nonetheless, he was affectionate in his courtship of Anne Prideaux. In April 1673, he wrote that 'the most sincere and ardent Affection which I have . . . makes mee very sollicitous to hear from you in whose wellness consists the Happiness of my life'.

Figure 5.1 Thomas Rowlandson, *Comforts of Matrimony* (1809): British Museum, London, 1871,0812.4497 (© The Trustees of the British Museum)

Belying his years, he went on to assert that 'the time seems tedious until that blessed houre come when that union which hath been for happiness begun between us shall be consummated by our marriage'.[17] Into married life, his ardour seems to have cooled a little and his letters were mostly focused on family affairs and the running of the estate. These, of course, were closely interrelated issues; family, house and estate were part of the same undertaking, which might be aggrandised as a dynastic project. However, Coffin still wrote to his wife in affectionate terms, addressing his letters to 'My deare Heart' and signing off as 'Your Loving Husband'. In the summer of 1684, he wrote in gratitude that his sister had been bene-fitted from Anne's presence during a difficult confinement, noting that 'shee hath had ye comfort & assistance of yr companye'. He ended the same letter desiring 'God to give you health & strength, & us a comfort-able meeting'.[18] If the language is rather formal, the sentiment is genuine: he looks forward to a safe and happy reunion. There is emotion here, but of a restrained and moderate type; it is sometimes framed by family events, but not tied into the spaces of their marital home.

From their marriage in 1743, Sir Roger Newdigate and his wife, Sophia Conyers, shared a long and happy relationship until her death in 1774—one based on mutual affection and a close personal bond. Newdigate kept her informed about his work as MP for Oxford University, including political negotiations and the business of the House, and relied heavily on Sophia for emotional support and solace during difficult times. They corresponded when Newdigate was away, mostly in London or Oxford, whilst his wife usually resided at the family seat, Arbury Hall in Warwickshire, which remained separate and at times a haven from his political life.[19] Most of his letters not only contain news of his public activities, but also more personal lines that speak of his affection. Writing from Oxford of the ceremony to mark his award of an honorary doctorate, for example, he gave an account of the other people also present and then discussed his options for travelling home. He was concerned about the uncertainty and delay in terms that revealed his affection. 'When I shall see thy dear face again I can't positively say', he wrote, adding that 'I begin already to think it long since I saw you'. Much of the rest of this letter is illegible, but he closed by confessing 'I have stolen a minute & must return, so good night. Think of me all day long & dream of me all night. Yours most entirely, RN'.[20] The tenderness of these lines belies his public reputation and reveals a sincere affection for Sophia, though it is interesting that all of these lines have been struck through sometime after the letter was written. So too was the assurance that 'I kiss my dearest Sophys pale' with which Newdigate began a letter written from his London house in November 1762.[21] The reason for these deletions is not clear, although the editor's hand seems to have targeted the more tender lines in his letters. Nonetheless, they show that Newdigate's affection was both deeply felt and far from being the infatuation of the newly wed. Indeed, the enduring character of his devotion is apparent in the late 1760s and early 1770s when her illness made him reluctant to travel. On one occasion, his loyalty to Lord North forced him to leave her in Bath, where they were staying for her health; he wrote that 'I set out with concern. I cannot help it when I turn my back on my dearest Ba [his affectionate name for Sophia] but it was no small addition that she is a convalescent & her delicate feelings can at any time tear her slender frame to pieces'.[22]

Newdigate often described his company, meals or daily routines, but the absence of Sophia's replies makes it difficult to tie their relationship into the fabric and routines of the country house. Remarkably for a renowned man of letters, the couple's close and loving relationship was expressed simply and unaffectedly in his letters. Their emotional bond was more apparent than that of the Coffins, its linguistic articulation perhaps serving to underline and strengthen the intensity of their affection.[23] Yet neither deployed the language of comfort to describe their contentment, although this is undoubtedly how they felt.

William and Emma Money made different linguistic choices to describe their shared affection and the assurance they felt in each other's love. The second son of a landed family, William Money attended Oxford and entered the church; he married Emma, the daughter of a London banker, in 1805. They lived in rather grander circumstances than most clergymen on one of the Money family estates in Whetham but were constantly concerned about having sufficient money to support their large house and growing family. William and Emma enjoyed a very close marriage that lasted over 40 years and, although they spent relatively little of that time apart, exchanged almost 1,000 letters over the course of their married life.[24] These letters make clear their loving and affectionate relationship, which was often expressed in terms of the comfort they drew from each other. Missing her absent husband in September 1807, Emma wrote to him of her troubles: 'I exclaim William, William come to my assistance, but alas no William, no friend have I to speak to, no one to comfort me'. His reply came back in kind: 'O! my Angel! Shall I tell you that I never passed so wretched a night as the last, no Emma to talk to, to comfort to cheer me, all alone in an Inn'.[25] The comfort they sought in this exchange derived from their companionship—a gentle form of love befitting a clergyman and his wife—but their lack of comfort in the absence of the other often took on a physical manifestation. Away from home shortly after their wedding, William wrote of his 'tiresome, solitary and comfortless evening', and confessed that he was constantly sighing and unable to eat. She, in turn, wrote to tell him that she had 'passed a most comfortless night for want of my dear Bed fellow, my feet, and back were almost perished' and that 'my poor heart aches sadly at our separation, for indeed I have no comfort when deprived of my beloved William'. The solution was expressed in a simple request: 'May I hope for the happiness of embracing you this evening?'[26]

In framing their mutual affection in such language, William and Emma Money drew out both mental and physical manifestations of comfort. They were also using comfort as an emotive, reinforcing their feelings by describing them to the object of their affection.[27] Indeed, the regular use of comfort in this way may have acted to intensify this feeling: repeatedly talking of their comfort—or lack of it—strengthened the idea that real comfort could only be found in each other's company. Importantly, this sentiment persisted over the course of their correspondence, Emma declaring after 12 years of marriage that: 'a newly married couple do not love each other more truly that we do each other'.[28] Unsurprisingly, the nature of their relationship shifted over the years, youthful ardour giving way to a more gentle love and quiet humour,[29] but it was regularly strengthened through remembering and celebrating their wedding anniversary. In July 1815, Emma wrote that she intended to give the children a holiday from their studies to mark the occasion and hoped that 'may our approaching <u>wedding day</u> be the <u>last</u> we are <u>ever</u> separated from each other in this world'. Sadly, this was not the case and their letters in July the following year turn on a similar theme. On 14th July, Emma wrote again about their anniversary to which William responded with matching reminiscences, before declaring that Emma was 'Heaven's choicest gift to me! Your heart is inexhaustible in love and tenderness'.[30] The theme was later picked up by their children, William junior writing a poem in 1720 'On the 16th day of July being the Wedding day of Papa and Mamma', the poem itself focusing on the enduring love his parents had for each other.[31] As both Fletcher and Bailey note, parenthood involved didactic performance, but it would be too much to reduce the emotional bond between William and Emma Money to a simple pedagogic device.[32] Their strong mutual affection was genuine and gave them a shared sense of comfort and contentment throughout their marriage.

Within their affectionate and comforting correspondence, neither William nor Emma made much reference to the spaces and routines at Whetham. They were both fond of the house, but the primary concern in their correspondence was with the emotions they felt for each other. Little is said about where they were sitting when reading or writing these letters, for instance, and there are few attempts to paint a picture of the domestic comfort to remind the absent spouse what they were missing. The domesticity that does appear in their letters is usually practical in nature: the health of their children, exhortations to 'keep good fires thro' this dreadfully damp season', and discussions about improvements and redecorations being undertaken.[33] One notable exception was the detail of the daily routine that kept William busy and contented, which was discussed in the previous chapter. Whilst this demonstrated his ability to find contentment in the mundane, it also served to forge a tangible connection between their lives when apart. Emma could imagine her husband in different parts of the house and garden—reading, eating, praying or walking—in ways that tied her back to their shared home in the country.[34]

The Moneys worked hard to make their marriage a success: communicating regularly and being flexible when the need arose for them to be apart. They lived and performed an ideal marriage that came close to the comfortable scene pictured in the *Comforts of Matrimony*, albeit in rather more prosperous circumstances. This ideal was frequently satirised, not least by Rowlandson himself. In his series of satirical prints, *Matrimonial Comforts* (1799), he depicts husbands and wives in a variety of domestic settings which highlight the dissonance and discomfort of their relationship. In *Return from a Walk*, for instance, the husband enters the room to find his young wife embracing an officer, eyes closed and blissfully unaware of his presence, whilst *Anonymous Letter* shows a wife confronting her husband with the words: 'You can't deny the letter you false man—I shall find out all your Vicked Vomen—I shall you abominable Seducer'. Both of these play on the idea of marital infidelity, with wife or husband guilty of disrupting the trust and contentment of the conjugal relationship. *A Curtain Lecture* (Figure 5.2) goes a stage further in contrasting the ideal of domestic and marital comfort with the reality of lived experience. It depicts a couple in bed, the man trying to sleep whilst his wife berates him: 'Yes, you base man you, don't you eat drink and sleep comfortably at home and still you must be jaunting abroad every night. I'll find out your intrigues, you may depend upon

Figure 5.2 Thomas Rowlandson, *Matrimonial Comforts: A Curtain Lecture* (1800), Lewis Walpole Library, Farmington, CT, 800.00.00.17 (Courtesy of The Lewis Walpole Library, Yale University)

it'.[35] In short, he should be content with his wife and home, rather than seek comfort elsewhere. There is an obvious point of connection here to Rowlandson's paired images 'At Home and Abroad' and 'Abroad and at Home' (Figure 5.3).[36] In the first, the man is at home with his large and ugly wife, yet he is not connected with her or his surroundings. She

Figure 5.3 Thomas Rowlandson, *At Home and Abroad: Abroad and at Home* (1807), Lewis Walpole Library, Farmington, CT, 807.02.28.01 (Courtesy of The Lewis Walpole Library, Yale University)

is engaged in trying to prepare some food on a smoking fire, balancing awkwardly on the edge of the bed; he is asleep in his chair, a broken pipe and dropped book on the floor beside him. He is quite clearly not 'at home' in any meaningful sense. In the second image, the man is away from home, sitting in front of a warm fire on a large sofa that he shares with his lover; they lounge together and gaze into each other's eyes. He is making himself very much at home. What makes the difference is not the location but the relationship between the two people and the ways in which this intimacy is reflected in their material surroundings.

On a similar theme, there are a large number of satirical prints depicting the domestic milieu a few short weeks after marriage. Some show violent scenes, but a more restrained and perhaps more realistic scenario is depicted in a print entitled *Three Weeks after Marriage*, published in 1822 (Figure 5.4).[37] In contrast to the happiness of the couple going hand in hand into church shown in the painting on the wall, they sit back to back, not talking to, touching or even acknowledging one another's presence. Many of the material trappings of a comfortable home are in place—a warming fire, a screen, carpet and curtains, and clean linen on the table—but it is clearly not a place of emotional contentment or comfortable companionship. Robert Sayer's *The Comforts of Matrimony—A Smoky House & Scolding Wife* takes this a stage further: the window

Figure 5.4 Anon. *Three Weeks After Marriage* (published by J.L. Marks, 1822), Lewis Walpole Library, Farmington, CT, 822.00.00.25 (Courtesy of The Lewis Walpole Library, Yale University)

blows open, the fire smokes, the child is scalded by boiling water and the wife scolds her careworn looking husband. Physical and emotional discomfort combine to make the husband (and wife) thoroughly miserable.[38] There are echoes here of the fate that befalls the rakish Willoughby at the end of Jane Austen's *Sense and Sensibility*: 'He lived to exert, and frequently to enjoy himself. His wife was not always out of humour, nor his home always uncomfortable'.[39] In short, Willoughby's home was rendered more or less comfortable by the humour of his wife.

There is humour as well as bite in all these portrayals of unhappy marriages. Yet the discomfort and emotional strain of dysfunctional relationships were all too real for many families. Ashe Windham, of Felbrigg Hall in Norfolk, had married Elizabeth Dobyns shortly after the death from smallpox of his intended bride, Hester Buckworth.[40] The reasons for their deteriorating marriage were complex, but their correspondence around this time reveals the level of antagonism and discomfort that an unhappy marriage could entail, and the way that much of this was played out through their relationships with their son, William, born in 1717.

Through to the spring of 1719, they exchanged letters that indicate a civil, if strained, relationship: they wrote about a range of social and domestic issues and about the health and development of William. In April or May that year, Ashe Windham wrote of his mounting exasperation with Billy, as he called him: 'I wish you could prevail with him to leave off biting his nails . . . My speaking to him so often as is necessary, for doing things ungentell, walking with his toes in, sloping, biting nails, &c, that he avoids being with me'.[41] Perhaps, for this reason, the boy appears to have spent more time with his mother in London, but this created additional tension, Ashe writing later in the year that: 'by one scheme or another I have lost my wife, & I am unwilling to lose my child too'.[42] Things then developed into something of a tug-of-war over where the boy would reside and who enjoyed his affection. Matters came to head in August 1720. In a letter that lay unposted for nearly 2 weeks as he determined whether or not to send it, Ashe laid bare the full misery of the situation. Elizabeth Windham had stayed some time at Felbrigg and her husband did not hold back in his condemnation of her behaviour towards Billy and by extension himself:

> I might well say, you do not care one jot for ~~my Son~~ Mr W^m or Me; when all the Pain, ~~the racks of mind,~~ & all the torment which I had the last time you was here, by your cruel usage of ~~him~~ my son, could not prevent your writing him so but the Night was fill'd with his horrid shriek, terrible to every Ear, but ~~your own~~ his Mothers; and stabbing every Breast in the family, ~~but his own Mother's~~ but your own.
>
> And yet more incredible, that tho' I may as well have seen my Son broke [. . . illegible. . .] yet all I could say, all the uneasiness it gave me, and all the intreaties I could make, signified no one farthing to

prevent it [. . .] I cannot possibly account for such behaviour to him ~~an only child,~~ unless it was out of pure hatred to me, even tho' you greatly indangered the very life of the only child, who to me is more valuable than the riches of the Universe.

I do not say this to quarrell, but the thing is Notorious, and I will not be run down in it, and tho' your Person is the most agreeable to me in the world, and your capacity excellent, yet unless you resolve and ~~promise to~~ use me for the future with some ~~sort of~~ Regard: at least to use me like a Gentleman; and my Son with ~~some~~ some sort of Humanity.[43]

Quite apart from the narrative of events presented by Ashe Windham, the many crossings out and amendments are revealing of his emotions. Following Diana Barnes, we might see these as signs of a man writing in a hurry and keen to unburden himself of his distress and anger.[44] Yet he had waited a long time before sending the letter (as a post-script makes clear) and the amendments often seem to have been made to improve the flow and the rhetorical effect, whilst leaving the original in place. Is it possible that Ashe Windham was doing this deliberately to communicate an image of writing emotionally and in the moment—perhaps as a display of what Linda Pollock calls 'constructive anger'?[45] Whatever the case, this was undoubtedly an emotional letter communicating his view that Elizabeth had no love for him or their son, and no respect for his status. In the meantime, Elizabeth had written to her husband, justifying her sudden departure from Felbrigg. She had left 'after you telling me my company will give you great afflictions . . . and that I cruelly use my child'. She protested that Ashe had been interfering in her affairs yet offered that, whenever

> you think with your ease and happiness and the good of my child I may be with you both, I shall readily obey your summons, in the mean time excuse a mothers fondness & let me beg he may take no Physick [. . .] my blessing to him. Pray God send him a better freind [sic.] if possible than his unhappy mother.[46]

From Elizabeth's perspective, she was both the loving mother, caring for her child's physical health, and the wronged wife, cast out and excluded from a husband's friendship.

How long this poisoned correspondence continued is uncertain as there is a break in the letters at this point—no doubt linked to their legal separation. When we can pick up the conversation again in 1728, the tone had changed considerably. Ashe wrote on 16 August that year that:

> Our son is a charming youth, and I always own that the fine parts of his mind are owing to you: the care of him shall be the business of

my life [. . .] and you may depend upon it that no Care, nor Expense shall be wanting in me, to make him worthy of that Esteem and Love of your's which his unhappy Father could never be posses'd of.[47]

He signed this 'with the utmost affection' and added a postscript urging that 'the Reader must forgive the Partiality of a Father'. Elizabeth's reply offered a reconciliation (that never happened), signed herself 'Your affect wife', and added that 'I think it a great blessing that I can return my dear child so much better than when you saw him'.[48] Whilst the language was affectionate and the tone conciliatory, both parties continued to portray themselves as wronged: Ashe pictured himself as unloved by his wife; Elizabeth wrote in December that it is 'in vain to say any thing in my justification to you since your hate and the malice of some of your relations for me is insurmountable . . . My only comfort is that God will clear me'.[49]

Both Ashe and Elizabeth Windham drew on emotive language to describe their feelings towards each other and their son. In doing so, they were undoubtedly seeking to communicate their emotions, as well as their actions and requests, but it seems that they were also cementing these emotions in their own minds.[50] In writing that they were uneasy, pained, fond, unhappy or comforted, they reinforced their feelings and hardened their position in relation to each other. What is particularly striking about this poisoned relationship is that their son remained the object of affection for both parents. Indeed, there was a competitive edge to their care and attention, each maintaining that they were performing the duties of parenthood better than the other. There was shared pride in his achievements and a common concern for his health and well-being, the gnawing anxiety over minor ailments giving way to pleasure and contentment at the news of his recovery. An unloving marriage did not necessarily mean neglect or a lack of love when it came to children; yet neither did the presence of a child have the power to alleviate the problems of a broken marriage—both tropes that appear in late eighteenth-century fiction. Indeed, their son became a 'weapon in marital conflict', as Bailey puts it. Ashe Windham's decision to remove the boy from his mother clearly caused her anguish and worry over a number of years; she understood it—as would later fiction and court cases—as an act of cruelty.[51] From the perspective of Ashe, bringing the boy into his own care no doubt reflected genuine affection, but it was also tied into a concern for dynastic succession, something that was critical to the long-term continuity of family estates. What is missing from both is any real feeling for how young William fitted into the routines of his parents' daily lives—as with the Moneys, the country house as a setting is largely absent from the correspondence.

In many marriages, children brought joy to their parents—a happy state of being idealised and formulated through in Jean-Jacques Rousseau's

Emile, or On Education of 1762. Central to his arguments about peda-gogy is the loving relationship between parents and children.[52] Bodily enactments of affection were held to strengthen bonds: sitting on the parental knee, being embraced in their arms or held to their bosom all providing powerful symbols and performances of comforting affection.[53] These are reproduced in numerous images of contented family life. *The Pleasures of Matrimony* (1773) by Thomas Colley is fairly typical of the genre (Figure 5.5).[54] It shows a family of four at a table: the father has his young son at his knee, apparently instructing him from the open book in the boy's hand, and the mother plays with her toddler daughter who touches her mother's chest. A sense of play is given by the presence on the floor of a battledore and shuttlecock.

Emma and William Money took great joy in their eight children, and both played an active part in their upbringing. They were both affectionate and tender parents, emotionally close to and nurturing of their offspring.[55] As with their own conjugal relationship, physical proximity to their young children was important. When Emma was staying with her mother London in the summer and early autumn of 1818, trying to recover her health, she wrote to William: 'If you feel my loss so sensibly, surrounded by all our children, pity and deplore the fate of the fondest

Figure 5.5 Thomas Colley, *The Pleasures of Matrimony* (1773), Lewis Walpole Library, Farmington, CT, 773.03.20.02 (Courtesy of The Lewis Walpole Library, Yale University)

Wife, & most affectionate of Mothers—alone—Emma'.[56] Two things are significant here. First is the way in which it was the everyday interaction with her children that Emma missed—being part of family life at Whetham House. Second is that this appears to have been a rare moment of despondency; more generally, absence made both parents keen for news of their children's well-being. Visiting his terminally ill father in November 1808, William Money noted that, already in a 'melancholy condition . . . it gave me additional uneasiness to hear that you and my darling Boy were not quite well'.[57] As with the Windhams a century earlier, these moments of anxiety were the inevitable counterpoint to the happiness that children could bring, and both Emma and William sought news of the achievements and progress of their offspring when they were away from home, again indicating a desire to be involved—even when spatially removed—in the daily routines of family life. It is telling that their correspondence about this is often expressed in terms of the comfort they derive from their receiving positive reports: anxiety is assuaged and contentment resumes.[58]

If comfort could be had from reassuring news about children's development and well-being, it also derived directly from the children themselves. In this way, the tenderness expected in parents was repaid in the solace to be found in their devotion, especially during times of trouble. Sir Roger and Sophia Newdigate had no children of their own, but this neither damaged their own marriage nor prevented their interest in their friends' offspring.[59] In the absence of an heir, he carefully nurtured the development of his protégé, Charles Parker. When the young man died in 1795, Newdigate wrote a long and affectionate letter to his widow, expressing his thanks for her 'worthy brother', who had given him 'all the comfort he could'. He then looked to console her, first with ideas of Christian fortitude, but then by suggesting that 'you have a sweet inducement to drag you back from these sublime contemplations, your little smiling brood, whom you now hang over with tears. . . . They will every day add more & more joy and comfort'.[60] Such optimism was probably not ill placed. Lady Margaret Williams, the mother of Mary Elizabeth Lucy, was devastated by the death of her husband, Sir John, in 1831 and she looked to her children for support. The old lady wrote in anguished terms to Mary, giving thanks that the Almighty had provided 'me such comforts as my children' and, in a second letter, described her 'beloved children' as blessings and 'my only comforts'.[61] The pages of both were edged with black, heightening their emotional impact.[62]

The difference between Newdigate's vision and the experience of Margaret Williams is the age of the children involved. In the first case, comfort would derive from young children and the joy their happiness would bring to their grieving mother; in the second, comfort came from adult children who were cast as more active agents with the ability to make conscious choices and act in ways intended to provide solace. This transition links to ideals of parenting and the inter-generational transfer of family values discussed by Bailey.[63] She focuses on the later Georgian period and ideas such as virtue, industriousness and filial duty, but it is clear that similar processes were at play much earlier; they also involved comfort and consolation.

Humphrey Prideaux was a renowned Oxford scholar until he left the university in 1686 to marry Bridget Bockenham. He moved first to a rural parish in Norfolk and later to Norwich, where he became Dean in 1702. He had firm beliefs about the best way to educate children, especially in terms of their morals and duties, and wrote regularly to his sister and brother-in-law, Anne and Richard Coffin of Portledge House in Devon, offering advice on the education of their sons.[64] Unsurprisingly, his advice was suffused with the obligations due from children to their parents, which he often framed in terms of comfort. In 1684, he wrote to Anne that he would be 'glad to hear how your children grow up & what hope they give of being a comfort to you'. This same message was repeated 2 years later: 'I am glad of the good health of your family and ye growing hopes of your Children. God grant that they may all prove such as may bring true Comfort unto you'.[65] Here, the provision of comfort is conceived almost as a duty, a sentiment echoed in the correspondence of Prideaux's contemporary, Elizabeth Brydges, who signed off a letter to her sister Mary by saying 'God bless thee and make thee a comfort to my dear Mother'.[66]

Neither Prideux nor Brydges make explicit the nature of this duty of comfort, nor do they describe the circumstances in which it might be expected—how it might have fitted into daily life in the country house. These things become clearer in letters received by Mary Pendarves (later Delany) when her father died in 1727. Lord Landsdowne, her uncle, wrote in emotional terms: 'It grieves me that the first time of my saluting you in this manner, should be upon so melancholy an occasion as the death of so tender a father; my heart joins with you in all the affliction you feel. Comfort your poor mother, let that be your care'.[67]

As was enacted by William Money nearly a hundred years later, children were expected to care for and console their parents at times of bereavement. Yet the duties and relationships were rendered more complex in the presence of more than one child. Writing to Mary Pendarves three weeks before Landsdowne, Sir John Stanley noted: 'I have that opinion both of your good understandings and true piety, that you will endeavor [sic.] to be easy under this stroke of Providence, which though heavy when it comes, yet we know must fall on everybody in their turn'.[68] From this position of emotional resilience, Pendarves could console her mother, but Stanley also observed that her brother's going down to the family home 'was certainly right, and so good a son and brother must be a comfort to you'.[69] Her brother then would offer consolation to both mother and sister, as a 'good' child and sibling should do. At a time of emotional crisis, the nuclear family was reunited in the family home to offer mutual support and comfort.

Many people were both parents and children, and were thus part of the multi-generational set of relationships that encompassed affection, compassion and comfort; they also formed a link between two houses.[70] Emma Money could benefit from the kindness and care of her mother at her parental home in Colney Hatch, and at the same time offer the same comforts to her own children at Whetham House. William wrote in September 1818 of his confidence that 'she [Emma's mother] will take good care of you, and keep up your spirits. I hope and trust you will make yourself comfortable and happy. The Boys here neither do nor will forget you!'[71] Comfort flowed to Emma from both directions: physical care from her mother and emotional support from the knowledge of her children's love and fidelity. Ten years before, when his own father was dying, William Money reported that his father had 'everything that can contribute to his comfort, and each individual in the family seems to vie with each other in kind attention'.[72] Here again we might see comfort being used as an emotive: William making himself feel easier because his father was comfortable, despite his illness. This becomes explicit after the old man's death, when William again wrote to Emma, expressing his grief and despondency, but then adding that he retained the 'sweet reflection . . . that I have in the course of life contributed perhaps to his happiness'. This afforded him 'in the midst of affliction, inexpressible consolation'.[73] Comfort, then, was something that could be gained from the belief that one had comforted others. This idea not only takes us back to the earlier discussion of comfort deriving from fulfilling one's duty but also highlights comfort as a shared emotion—a point to which we will return later. The death of a parent had other impacts on the emotional bonds of the family. When his mother died 5 years later, William was again filled with grief, but still enquired after the well-being of Emma and their children, noting that 'you are all, if possible, dearer to me than ever. The dissolution of one tie, serves to strengthen the other'.[74]

If children could bring joy and offer comfort to their parents, then they were also capable of engendering a range of other emotions. Hannah More's moral tale *Mr Bragwell and his two daughters* (1796) illustrates the importance of children as a source of domestic comfort. Invited to stay for a meal at the house of his friend, Mr. Worthy, Bragwell notes the 'plain but neat and good dinner' prepared by his friend's wife and is duly made to reflect on his own domestic circumstances. His daughters, we are told, are 'too genteel to do any thing so very useful' because they view such work as 'extremely vulgar and unbecoming'. He quickly concludes that 'his late experience of the little comfort he found at home, inclined him now still more strongly to suspect that things were not so right as he had been made to suppose'.[75] His domestic comfort was limited by the attitude and actions of his daughters (and also his wife), leaving him unsettled and anxious: worried that things were not as they should be. The story is a critique of social pretensions, but it is telling that these are explored, in part, through consideration of domestic familial arrangements. Bragwell might also have been anxious that he had somehow failed as a father because his daughters were unable to provide him with simple pleasures and comfort. As French and Rothery note, fathers' reputations were closed tied to the actions of their children, so his daughters' pride and apparent coldness would indeed reflect his own flawed character.[76]

Elizabeth Dryden appears to have had no such misgivings. She had married John Turner in 1781 and together they had nine children, five of them surviving into adulthood. Her relationship with these children was very difficult and went well beyond a lack of help and support into outright antagonism and vitriol. Elizabeth described her second son, Henry, as 'extravagant & wrong headed' and a 'Malignant Demon', traits that were, she claimed, inherited from their father: 'they are all complete Turners, which is saying enough'.[77] In part, this dysfunctional relationship arose from the difficulties in getting her children properly set up in life—a problem that arose from the indebtedness of the estate, which might, in turn, be traced to the extravagance of her husband. One of her younger sons, Leopold, spent some time in Tenerife, trying to make a career in trade. Dryden wrote to her sister-in-law, Mrs. Steele, in May 1812 exclaiming that 'he does not promise to turn out well, is very ungrateful to me and I believe everyone else . . . he is of that strange Turner temper that I am afraid will put him back in everything'. She continued in a similar vein, complaining that 'he will be one and twenty by the time he returns when he must provide for himself or take the ill consequences'. What comes next is especially revealing: 'indeed, I have little comfort in any of my family, they are bad dispositions'.[78]

Elizabeth Dryden clearly expected to receive comfort from her children in the form of contentment born of them being dutiful and supportive. Specifically, sons should have respect for parents and a serious attitude to their responsibilities for the estate and the family name.[79] However, Leopold was described two years later, again in correspondence with Mrs. Steele, as being 'ill tempered, extremely proud and very disagreeable'—characteristics which made Elizabeth despair of getting him a clerkship.[80] Daughters carried more of the burden of emotional support; yet Elizabeth, in a general tirade against her offspring, complained that 'my daughter [Caroline] is indeed a nuisance to me instead of a comfort, so that I cannot be very pleasantly situated. Excepting Sir Edward who behaves very friendly and well, they are a bad lot'.[81] This emotive language may have been partly an attempt to justify her position as the wronged party in these dysfunctional relationships; writing these words would surely have strengthened her own feelings. That they were addressed to her sister-in-law may have given her scope to vent her spleen rather than generate a constructive dialogue. Whatever her motivation in writing, both the emotions expressed and the language used are telling.

The discomfort Elizabeth Dryden felt with her children came to head when Canons Ashby came into Henry's possession, following the early death of the favoured Sir Edward, and prompted her to search for an escape in the form of a house in London. It is significant that ownership and occupation of the family seat at Canons Ashby should create this crisis. Writing again to Mrs. Steele in June 1819, she declared that a new house 'is a thing I much want and indeed cannot be comfortable without'.[82] If we pause for a moment, this is a remarkable phrase. The looking forward to a desired object or outcome chimes with Colin Campbell's assertion of a new consumer ethos that was emerging in the late eighteenth and early nineteenth centuries, one in which the prospect of consumption was every bit as enjoyable as the act of consumption itself.[83] Moreover, Dryden suggests that her current discomfort, which is mental rather than physical, can be resolved by a material change. In fact, this move never came—the London house remained an elusive ideal. Dryden's comfort and contentment remained rooted in her relationships with family and friends whilst she herself remained firmly ensconced at Canons Ashby. Perhaps the house held more emotional resonance for her than she cared to admit.

What emerges from these various examples is a clear reiteration of the importance of family as a key emotional community: even when expectations were disappointed, it was to marital partners and children that people looked for comfort and consolation.[84] In many cases, family provided not only a contented and comfortable milieu but also the context in which emotions and emotional bonds were shaped. That these were physically located in the family home—generally conceived and experienced as their country seat—reveals the way in which people and place were bound together in emotional webs. As Elizabeth Dryden's case makes clear, however, comfort could also be sought outside the immediate family: in a network of wider kin and friends.

Networks of Comfort: Friends and Relations

For Nicole Pohl, the sentimental household encompassed a 'whole network of human attachments'; here, I want to focus on attachments to siblings, friends and servants and explore the ways in which these broader kinship and household groupings afforded comfort.[85] Although there are problems in accessing the interior world of children, it is clear that broader networks of comfort could be wrought at an early age. A glimpse of this can be had in the correspondence of William and Emma Money, when William junior began to write to whichever parent was absent from the family group. These are sometimes formulaic, as when he signed off 'with my affectionate love to my Brothers and Nurse and a thousand kisses to yourself', and at times reflect the use of letter-writing being as a pedagogic tool.[86] Nonetheless, he also communicated honest emotions and a search for companionship in the family group. In a letter to his mother in October 1817, he asked after the health of his brothers but then turned to more personal feelings: 'I should like to see Aunt Julia's little dog and then play with it with my brothers. I find it lonely here not having anyone to play with'.[87] Quite understandably, he sought companionship amongst his siblings and in the everyday activities of domestic family life. As French and Rothery make clear, William and Emma were successful in providing a role model for their children in terms of their marital relationship and behaviour.[88] Importantly, this model also encompassed their own broader kin networks, especially their siblings, and the ways in which they offered mutual comfort and support. As is so often the case, this is brought into sharpest focus when things went wrong. In the summer of 1816, there was a disagreement amongst Emma's siblings. William's response tells us much about his view of the ideal family and the ways in which love, duty and comfort were central to this conception. He wrote to Emma saying 'I am grieved to hear of the differences which you mention between those who ought to be united in the closest bonds of duty and love. These are, indeed, sad interruptions to the comfort of a family circle'.[89] Importantly, he saw this family circle as broadly defined: brothers and sisters, even as adults, should be part of a supportive network.

This view was clearly shared by others, with women especially seeking companionship and comfort from sisters. We see this in a late eighteenth-century engraving by the Dutch printmaker, Reinier Vinkeles (Figure 5.6). Two women sit together on a fashionable sofa: one comforts the other, who is crying: she holds her hand and gazes anxiously into her face. Comfort and companionship are brought together in the text beneath: 'now, my darling, I exhort you to friendship' (*Nu mijn schat, bezweer ik u bij de Vriendship*). Such emotional bonds were sustained by regular correspondence when sisters or friends were geographically distant.[90] Something of the intricacies of such comfort is captured in the correspondence of Lady Louisa Stuart and her sister Lady Caroline Dawson. Lady Louisa was unmarried and living at her parents' house, Luton Hoo in Bedfordshire, when she wrote to her recently-married sister in July 1778:

> I am not at all surprised at your horsemanship; I always thought you would take the first opportunity to ride, and as Mr. Dawson seems to be your only companion, I suppose it is the most comfortable time you have. How do the rest of the family go on? are they grown fond of you? Does Mr. Joseph [Dawson's younger brother] open his lips oftener than he did in town, and is he kind or cruel to the lady who admires him? For my part, I am sufficiently accustomed to dumb

VII.D.pl.I.

"Nu mijn schat, bezweer ik u bij de Vriendschap,
XV. *Brief.*

Figure 5.6 Reinier Vinkeles, *A Young Woman Comforts Her Crying Friend* (1751–1816): Rijksmuseum, Amsterdam, RP-P-OB-65.458

people, for here are Frederick and William [her brothers] who speak about six words a day, and instead of being any company or comfort, only serve to give me the vapours by walking up and down the room without ceasing.

The two sisters shared a tacit understanding that Carolina Dawson's principal source of comfort and companionship would be her husband, with whom she could share activities as part of a close emotional relationship, but that she should also look to the rest of the family. Brothers were very much second best in this respect, not least because they offered poor company and little conversation. For Lady Louisa, this lack of companionship is linked into and revealed through the spaces and social practices at Luton Hoo. Her account continues:

> don't think I mean my room, for I assure you they never deign to visit that, but after tea, as my father and mother always retire to the library, I have brought down my work and sat with these two gentlemen to try if any acquaintance could be made with them, and as I tell you, I am entertained with their eternally walking backwards and forwards, or now and then flinging themselves upon the couch, yawning, and asking me questions as 'When we go to London?' 'When you come back?' 'Whether the Duchess of Portland comes here this year?' and so forth. [. . .] The rest of the day is employed as usual in trailing to the farm and dawdling to the flower garden; but bad as it is, it will be worse when they go, for they at least enliven our meals a little.[91]

Her brothers do not choose to join her in her room, so instead, she comes downstairs to join them in one of the family rooms, seeking some familial sociability. The house is thus internally differentiated on the basis of the potential for family interaction, but even in less private spaces the young men seem unable to participate in companionable discourse: they are bored and boring. Ultimately, however, Lady Louisa declares that their company is better than being left alone with her parents.

The easy and familiar tone struck in the letters between the two sisters reveals their close relationship and the comfortable companionship they shared through their correspondence. Both women, however, also looked for company in physical domestic space as well as epistolary space. Later in July the same year, Lady Louisa wrote about her sister's (un)enviable social round, noting that 'I should pity myself very much in your place, but . . . you are a more sociable creature'. Nonetheless, she longed for some company: 'My father and the men went away yesterday, so we are left quite alone, and are likely to remain so this week, unless Lady Lothian and Emily come, which would make us very comfortable'.[92] Again, we have the idea that the company of other people within the country house was important: it offered comfort in the form of companionship, enlivened the routine of daily life and created a contented domestic milieu.

There is an important contrast drawn by Louisa Stuart between society in the public sphere and the society of particular friends in a more private or domestic setting. The comfort deriving from the latter is a common trope in the correspondence of the period. From the mid-1780s, Mary Leigh spent much of the year at her villa in Kensington Gore—a relatively modest house that had been extended and improved on a number of occasions through the eighteenth century. From this base, she made frequent visits to acquaintances elsewhere in London, sometimes playing cards in small private parties; but she had a much narrower circle of friends that she entertained at home. Much of this domestic sociability took place at her country residence, Stoneleigh Abbey, where she spent the summer months and was 'wonderfully engaged in receiving and paying visits'.[93] In contrast, a much smaller circle was invited to Grove House, including her lawyer, Joseph Hill and his wife, with whom she was particularly friendly. She clearly felt comfortable with this couple, despite the social distance between them and the quasi employer–employee relationship she had with Hill. However, beyond asking after Mrs. Hill's health and the frequent exchange of small gifts, there is little in Mary Leigh's letters that tell us about the emotional depth of their relationship.

Catherine Mann has noted that 'affective relationships and emotional exchange between . . . masters and their servants, have been difficult to locate in the emotional landscape of the early modern English household', but they were nonetheless present.[94] We get a glimpse of how these relationships might develop through the unfolding narrative of Laurence Sterne's *A Sentimental Journey* (1768). Towards the start of his journey, Yorick engages a new servant, La Fleur. As might be expected, the young man offers his employer physical comfort by performing numerous menial tasks, but La Fleur also becomes a trusted companion. Their eventual parting brings sorrow to both men—a demonstration of their shared sensibility. That this kind of comfortable companionship between master and servant was not simply a literary device is apparent from the diaries of numerous Grand Tourists. Gerrit Verhoeven shows how the manservants who accompanied Dutch travellers not only 'warranted a tailormade quality standard for domestic service', but also shielded young men from the worst pangs of homesickness and offered familiarity and friendship.[95]

A more detailed picture of the ways in which servants could be part of an individual's network of comfort can be drawn from the correspondence of George Lucy of Charlecote Park in Warwickshire and his housekeeper, Mrs. Phillipa Hayes.[96] Although she was engaged ostensibly to look after the house, Hayes was no ordinary housekeeper. She had good social connections in her native Staffordshire and was treated by Lucy as a companion and social equal, rather than a servant. The precise nature of their relationship when he was resident at Charlecote is difficult to discern, but their regular correspondence during Lucy's frequent absences makes clear their close friendship. He felt comfortable in sharing detailed and often quite personal information about himself and his associates. Writing from London and Bath, he described the company in a way that makes it apparent that Hayes was familiar with the people and their situations. He also wrote in intimate detail about his health, which was often a cause for concern.[97] In return, she kept Lucy informed about local political developments and helped to maintain his social networks in Warwickshire, a role which involved receiving people at Charlecote Park, including members of Lucy's extended family. She shared a familiar companionship with these people and her letters extended this to Lucy, even though he was geographically distant. In July 1753, Hayes wrote: 'Yr cozen Dighton, his Son Frank & Daughter Bell are come to Dine with me & sit by whilst I scribble this'.[98] The intimacy and familiarity of the group are then extended to Lucy, drawing him directly into the conversation at Charlecote: 'Yr cousin Francis Dighton Esqr insists upon my telling you yt he would have you look out for a Wife at Cheltenham'. Even if this was a jest, it telling that the relationships between the Dightons and Mrs. Hayes, and between Hayes and Lucy, were close enough to feel that such a request would carry weight or the joke would be well received.

Through such intimacies, Lucy was offered a social and emotional link back to family and the routines of country-house life, which perhaps afforded him some comfort whilst away from home. Equally telling of the nature of his relationship with Hayes is the way that Lucy could openly discuss his failings. Writing from Rome, he admitted that he had been 'hunting virtu, but I had the misfortune not to look into an Old brick Wall as far as Others'. This might be read as a playful confession of his shortcomings as a classical scholar, being 'so little acquainted with past transactions'.[99] His addiction to gambling was more problematic, though never ruinous. He wrote from Bath about his success, or otherwise, at the card table. In response, Hayes offered frank advice that underlines the strength of their friendship: 'you must take your fate', she wrote, 'it is not of so great consequence as ye other, as I am persuaded you know how to set bounds to yr losses'.[100] These were again the kind of exchanges that might be seen between siblings: a brother honestly admitting that he was disinterested in classical culture and a sister chiding her errant sibling about his gambling and urging more self-control—a key gentlemanly virtue.[101] A similar tone was struck by Caroline Dawson when writing to her sister, recently settled in a house on Gloucester Place in London. This was later to become the centre of Lady Louisa's considerable circle of friends, but it seems that she was initially rather lonely and still troubled by the recent death of her mother. Dawson wrote:

> My DEAREST LOUISA—I find, by a letter from Lady Macartney, you are now settled in town, and I hope you are more comfortable there than you expected; in short, my dear, you must take pains to get the better of your feelings, and try to be happy, or at least contented with your situation . . . How happy I should be if I could make you feel as I do on this subject, and that instead of pining your life away

as you have hitherto done, you would resolve to make the best of everything, to make yourself happy by trying to make every one else about you so.[102]

The solace offered by Dawson has a sharp and purposeful edge: her sister should stop pining for their mother and get on her with life, becoming more sociable and accommodating of other people. It also ranges through a number of emotions, with the coupling together of happiness, contentment and comfort lying at the heart of the advice being given. As with Phillipa Hayes, affording solace went beyond mere sympathy to incorporate suggestions about how the situation might be resolved. Comfort could thus have a practical dimension.

When spouse or children disappointed, then, a wider network of siblings and servant-companions could thus be drawn on for solace and emotional support. Household and family were central to these relationships, but comfort and solace could also be found amongst a wider circle of friends, as is apparent from the extensive correspondence of Mrs. Howard, later Countess of Suffolk. Two examples will suffice to illustrate the more general point. Writing in 1727 from his self-imposed exile following the accession of George I, Lord Landsdowne thanked Mrs. Howard for her kindness towards his wife.[103] He noted that 'Under her present anxiety for her son, she tells me the only comfort she has is in the continuance of your friendship'. He was concerned for his wife's health and revealed that:

> Your goodness, madam, she says, is her only consolation. The pleasure of being sure of such a friend would, indeed, be a relief under any trouble. I would fain find something to say upon this subject which might explain what my heart feels. It is possible to be touched beyond what any language can reach; and this is my case.[104]

The emotion of Landsdowne's outpouring is apparent; whilst he found it hard to express in words his own gratitude, he was able to capture the benefits that his wife received from her relationship with Mrs. Howard: there was a pleasure in and comfort from the security of friendship, and consolation in her goodness.

Later in the same year, Alexander Pope, Mrs. Howard's friend (and later her neighbour in Twickenham), wrote consoling her on the appalling treatment she received at the hands of her husband.[105] His opening is striking: 'Your letter unfeignedly gives me great disquiet. I do not only *say* that I have a true concern for you: indeed, I *feel* it many times, very many, when I say it not. I wish to God any method were soon taken to put you out of this uneasy, tormenting situation'.[106] In emphasising his feelings as well as his words, Pope was heightening his emotional engagement with the situation. His choice of words, however, is telling—as is the way in which these framed and articulated the relationships he describes. His letter continues:

> as to the last thing that troubles you, (the odd usage of Mr. H. to his son) I would fain hope some good may be derived from it. It may turn him to a reflection, that possibly his mother may be yet worse used than himself; and make him think of some means to comfort himself in comforting her.[107]

Pope thus sought to console Mrs. Howard with the thought that her son might recognise her suffering in his own, and offer her comfort. In doing so, he would feel comfort himself—a link that returns us to the idea that a Christian would receive comfort from comforting others. In this way, Pope wove a web of comfort that drew together friends and family in a virtuous cycle. However, notions of comfort as consolation could be taken a step further. Writing to Mrs. Howard in April 1720, Elizabeth Molesworth confided that 'What you tell me of my Lord Dalkeith's comforting himself with another Lady Jane, I had heard before, with some wonder—not so much at him as at the lady who was content to be the comforter'.[108] The two women extend the meaning of comfort so that it became a subtle reference to sexual relations—a stretch, perhaps, but one fits with ideas of consolation.

In all these relationships, comfort was conceived in terms of companionship and consolation—long-established meanings that endured through the early nineteenth century and beyond. Comfort formed a key part of the emotional language deployed by family and friends. Whilst it is seen most frequently in correspondence from the late eighteenth and early nineteenth century, the emotional language of comfort was being deployed much earlier. It is, perhaps, ironic that we know so much about the comforts offered by family and friends because they were often written about in their absence, when a loved one was away from home or a trusted friend lived some distance away. Letters, then, are key sources, but they were also vital conduits of comfort and emotional support.

Comforting Correspondence: Letters as Emotional Channels

Historians have long been alive to the 'capacity of letters to document the lived experience of social interactions'.[109] For most people, they were the only way of maintaining regular contact with friends and family when they were apart. Letters, therefore, served a multitude of overlapping functions: they carried information that helped to feed and nurture social relations; comprised physical objects that made tangible the bonds between people, and which might be preserved and treasured, and offered comfort to both the reader and writer. However, we need to remember that letters do not provide a direct window onto a person's inner self because letter writing was a skill learnt in childhood and a performance of self and of one's place in tangled webs of emotional, social and economic relationships.[110] Yet this complexity gives letters even greater significance in the construction, expression and experience of emotional comfort.

Letters offered the opportunity to share hopes for the future or memories of the past; to bear one's soul or vent one's spleen to a trusted confidant, and to ask or offer favours. For many correspondents, however, their key attraction came in the news they contained, especially about friends and family.[111] Writing to Henrietta Howard in 1718, the rather indelicate Mrs. Bradshaw exclaimed that 'You will not expect any news, when I tell you I have been out of my castle but once since I saw you, and that was yesterday to see Lady Clarges, who is come to town'. She then proceeded to relate the latest gossip about a number of mutual acquaintances before declaring that she had 'no other comfort but what you in your bounty will afford me by letter; and in order to it, a cargo of paper shall come by the first conveyance I can get'.[112] The one consequential piece of news passed on was that Mrs. Bradshaw had met with Howard's son and could report that he was well. Despite or perhaps because of their gossipy nature, it seems that these letters were welcomed by their recipient, Bradshaw further noting that 'I wish you may not repent of your telling me to write often, for I shall certainly do it, though I am consumedly dull'. Such declarations of dullness and apologies for the lack of news were commonplace. Philip Stanhope (the future Earl of Chesterfield) wrote from Trinity Hall, Cambridge to his friend George Berkeley, who had recently gone down from university. He warned him: 'You do not know what you ask when you would have me write long letters; you would quickly be a weary on it, should I obey you: what a number of insignificant trifles must I put together to fill up this sheet of paper'.[113] As with Mrs. Bradshaw, though, Stanhope proceeded to do just that, relating the goings on of student life in a light and humorous manner. He also begged the 'comfort' of a letter in return, which, he joked, 'we will retail at proper times as our own wit'.

The distraction, indeed, the comfort of news and gossip was particularly welcomed by those who felt themselves isolated from society. They were tied into the routines of society or the family at home in the country house. In another letter to Henrietta Howard, her friend Lady Mohun lamented her situation at home in Gawsworth Hall:

> It is impossible to describe the melancholy situation of our present affairs; the weather is so bad we cannot stir abroad, nor stay at home with any comfort; for it is so cold, that large Scotch coal fires can hardly keep us warm: the neighbours we are sometimes delivered up to are more disgusting, and less conversable, than our own familiar

cattle, and an approaching visitor more formidable than any of the giants of Don Quixote; who, by the way, has hitherto been our chief entertainment; but now our books are out, and our prodigious fund of wit exhausted, no various scenes, nor ingenious correspondents from foreign parts to raise our own, we are not only grown weary of each others' repeated dullness.[114]

The poor weather and the cold house made for physical discomfort that was compounded by the unattractive nature of their neighbours, the dullness of their domestic society and the lack of entertaining news from abroad. Little wonder that Lady Mohun begged Howard for a letter to offer a distraction and some glimmer of comfort in the gloomy environment that made her daily routine at her country house in remote Cumberland.

Similar sentiments were expressed through the eighteenth century and beyond. In the 1740s and 1750s, George Lucy welcomed letters from his housekeeper, Phillipa Hayes, not only for the intelligence they contained about his estate and neighbours in Warwickshire, but also because they were entertaining. Lucy's friend and travelling companion, John Dobson, wrote commending her 'very long and very entertaining' letter and complimenting the 'Life and Spirit' with which she wrote.[115] This reflects contemporary praise for the naturalness of women's letter writing, yet what Lucy himself enjoyed most was the 'pleasure of conversing with my friends tho at a distance'.[116] Part of the pleasure was no doubt the opportunity to keep in touch with life at home whilst abroad in the world. For Lucy, this involved Hayes providing regular updates on proposed and ongoing improvements being made to the house at Charlecote. He feigned disinterest, writing in December 1753 that he would 'consent to what you shall judge most proper', but in the 1760s there was a regular correspondence between them concerning designs, colour schemes, curtain materials and ornamental china.[117] This allowed Lucy to feel involved in changes being made to his ancestral home: he was at a distance but made part of the process through the details of Hayes' letters. In effect, he could enter the world of the letter writer which was also—at other times—his own world. This is also apparent in Hayes' account of writing in a room alongside three of Lucy's wider family, which we touched on earlier. Her letter continued with a lengthy anecdote about Anne Brown, a friend of Lucy's, whose carriage was overturned by a wagon. Happily, nobody was hurt, but Hayes noted that the angry Mrs. Brown had taken the footman's whip and 'strap'd ye Waggoner heartily and when she came home served her own coachman ye same sauce, & he is run away wth ye livery & she hath sent a hue & cry after him'. Hayes closed by writing: 'Mr Dighton & his daughter have been threshing young Frank & I at Whist it is near nine & they just gone, so good night to you. you don't tell me how you sleep'.[118] Sharing the local gossip and describing the domestic routine no doubt drew Lucy closer to life back home in Warwickshire and helped to keep him entertained.

Such everyday news is what Lady Mohun was hoping for, stuck in Gawsworth Hall—something to connect her to other people and places. It is revealed again in a letter from Lady Louisa to her sister:

> Your journals are the comfort of my life. I hear and see you while I read them, and talk to you while I answer them. I dance with you, laugh with you, and ride with you; though when out of such reveries I am as sober and as serious as becomes an inhabitant of Luton.[119]

Once more, we see letters as a source of comfort in terms of the news they contained and the escape they offered: they allowed the reader to share something of their correspondent's daily life, linking them to other places as well as other people. Particularly when combined with the communication of feelings, expression of solace and offers of advice discussed earlier, the regular exchange of news helped to cement the emotional bond between correspondents.

As material objects, letters were imbued with emotions. Diana Barnes has written about the physical imprints of tears, blottings, crossings out and so on as signifying and communicating emotion beyond the actual words that appear on the page.[120] Some of these are apparent in the letters written by Ashe Windham, his deletions indicating a complex mix of careful and hurried composition. Quite apart from these considerations, however, letters formed a material connection between people who were spatially separated. Kate Smith emphasises the power of letters in linking together people over space and time: the paper, ink, seal and handwriting being physical manifestations of the distant family member or friend that could be held, kissed, treasured and carefully kept.[121]

The emotional connection between letter, writer and recipient is laid bare in the correspondence of Sir Roger Newdigate and his wife Sophia, who he often called Ba. By the early 1770s, she was suffering from serious illness and crippling rheumatism that prevented her from using her right hand. Newdigate wrote:

> What a delicious piece you have sent me today; sleep, stomach all well & the doctor writes confirming it, all but my poor dear dextra. I cannot part with that. I have a partiality to it. It gave me yourself. No, I forget, both hands did that. But it has always been my best friend in [my] absence, tho' sinistra has always done its best too.[122]

There was pleasure in receiving the letter and the good news it contained, but the deeper significance lies in Newdigate's belief that, through her letters, Sophia was able to construct and communicate herself; these letters not only articulated their relationship when apart but also maintained an intimacy that allowed Newdigate to feel emotionally close to his absent wife. Importantly, this connection was linked with the character of Sophia's handwriting, something which changed and then was lost as her rheumatism worsened.[123] It is scarcely surprising, then, that he expressed regret at their absence, though often in a light-hearted manner: 'what does the rascally postman mean?', he wrote in February 1772, 'not a scrap have I from Bath this day'. A year later he expressed dismay and mock confusion at the lack of a letter: 'I can't tell why I should have no letter from Bath today' he wrote on Lady Day 1773, 'Not Ba ill, that I won't believe—not Midge ill. I must have had a word then. No—it is the Post failed, it is the footman fail'd, some nonsense or other that vexes Ba too for my disappointment'.[124]

It is impossible to know the extent to which this tone reflected a genuine attempt to run through the possible reasons for there being no letter from his wife, but the discomfort is apparent enough; as is the pleasure and relief expressed when he does receive news: the 'delicious piece' that arrived on 2 March 1772. Yet again, we see the importance of less dramatic emotions: anxiety gave way to contentment and ease of mind.[125] Much the same can be seen in the correspondence between Phillipa Hayes and George Lucy. Although their relationship was less intense than that between husband and wife, the absence of letters was still noted with regret and anxiety about the other's well-being. In April 1755, for example, Hayes wrote asking for 'a better account of your heath, & trust in God Almighty I shall not be long without it'.[126]

Jean DeJean has argued that the regular and affordable postal service which operated briefly in Paris during the 1650s had a transformative effect on the expression of emotions through letters because of its speed and reliability.[127] What these mid-eighteenth-century correspondents were experiencing appears to be born of a similar expectation of regular and reliable deliveries. It is unsurprising, then, that habitualising the frequent exchange of letters created more anxiety and discomfort when the expectation of a letter was not fulfilled. We have seen something of this already in the letters of Sir Roger Newdigate. It is brought out more forcibly in the correspondence of William and Emma Money who exchanged letters frequently, sometimes on a daily basis, on the rare occasions when they were apart. In early 1812, Emma took the children away from the family home in Whetham because infections were rife in the area. She wrote 'how anxiously I look forward to our meeting, never to part again. Let Nothing prevent my hearing from you tomorrow, and every day. My only comfort is this prospect'.[128] Her anxiety at being apart can only be assuaged by the comfort of receiving letters from her distant husband. In this pairing of emotions, one is the response to the other, brought together in a way that was perhaps intended to express both Emma's own emotions and shape those of her husband. She had earlier taken this reasoning further, writing of her distress that no letter had arrived and offering not just reproof but also a challenge:

> There is a duty, William, you owe me as well as those you are with. Five minutes, out of the four and twenty hours, are all I ask. 'Tis hard to be denied this comfort in your absence. . . <u>William I am not well</u> and require some part of your attention.[129]

In attempting to shape her husband's emotions, she was deploying something akin to the 'constructive anger' identified by Linda Pollock as a tool in negotiating relationships in seventeenth-century letters.[130] Emma's tactic apparently backfired: William replied in a hurt tone, rejecting the accusation of neglect and reminding her of the respect he was due; she responded with an apology and an explanation: his letters had remained at the post office rather than being delivered. But perhaps her use of emotive language had worked: she got a response and the comfort of their epistolary exchange was resumed.

It is telling that Emma Money used the language of comfort in her plea for more attentive letter-writing; letters from her husband relieved anxiety and provided ease of mind, as well as entertainment. For some, letters were a welcome distraction from weightier matters. Writing in the summer of 1752 during an anxious wait for a judgement from the Lord Chancellor, Mary Delany commenced a letter to her sister with a sigh of relief: 'Oh what comfort and support are your letters!'[131] For others, this desire for comfort could be turned into an expectation and even a requirement. Like Emma Money, some letter writers berated their correspondents for failing in their duty to offer them the epistolary comfort. Frances Huddlestone, for instance, wrote to her nephew in 1752 complaining that although 'I have not had the satisfaction to hear from you, I have had that Comfort from others'.[132] Here again we see the use of emotive language in connection with comfort, pointing out one person's failings in comparison with the achievements of others and judging their capacity or perhaps willingness to afford comfort.

Significantly, not all correspondence had the same capacity to afford comfort. Horace Walpole made a distinction between those carrying bad news (which were uncomfortable) and those that brought welcome news (and were comfortable). For example, writing from Strawberry Hill in September 1796, he opened a letter to Mary Berry with the complaint: 'Though I thank you for letting me hear so often, your last night's letter by the penny post, was most uncomfortable. You had not grown better, as I hoped and expected'. By contrast, in a much earlier letter to Horace Mann, he related good news about the health of Mann's brother James, observing that 'he wrote me two very comfortable notes this week of his mending'.[133] That good or bad news could bring or take away comfort is unsurprising, although it is significant that reassurance or anxiety are expressed in the language of comfort. More striking is the way in which the content reflected on the letter itself, giving it a specific emotional agency. It is in this light that we need to read the comfort that Elizabeth Dryden received from letters. She habitually expressed gratitude for those she received from Mrs. Steele, noting on one occasion her 'thanks for your kind letter, they always do me good'.[134] More specifically, though, Elizabeth conceived the comfort afforded by letters in very similar terms to Walpole, as is apparent from the line informing her sister-in-law that 'I have had a very comfortable letter from Caroline, repenting much and apologising'.[135] The comfort described here came from the rapprochement that this signalled with her daughter who, it seems, had been repentant for what Elizabeth saw as her past misdemeanours. The letter was comfortable because it brought good news and signalled a more contented relationship with her daughter. Lady Margaret Williams's much happier relationship with her children was reflected in her finding comfort in their letters. Indeed, she was confident that her own letters afforded similar comfort, writing shortly after her husband's death that 'I will know that a few lines from me will be the greatest comfort to you—as your small letters are to me'.[136]

It is notable that such sentiments were not simply a product of the growing sensibility of the age: they were already apparent right at the start of our period and can be seen through successive generations. Writing in July 1678 about the good news of the safe delivery of her niece, Ursula Clarke Venner informed her brother that 'wee are all very glad to heare yt my sister is safely delivered of child & doe pray God to keep both her & the child well the news of ye continuance where of will be very comfortable unto us'.[137] She was pleased to receive good news, but further comfort would be gained from continued favourable reports. Similar feelings were expressed by Mary Delany in the middle decades of the eighteenth century. In another letter to Anne Dewes, she got straight to the point: 'I write, I thank God, to my dearest sister with some comfort to-day. I hope the worst is over with Lady Harriet; she is indeed a sweet creature'.[138] Thirty years later, she used a similar formulation when writing to Frances Hamilton: 'it is a cordial comfort to me to receive a good account from you of your health and prosperity'.[139] As with Walpole, she also described letters themselves as being comfortable but seems to have defined this in a slightly broader manner. For her, comfortable letters were not simply the carriers of good news, but also ones in which the author took time and trouble to write in a personal, thoughtful and engaged manner. She excused herself twice from such a task when writing to her sister. In August 1740, she apologised that 'I shall not be able to write to you a comfortable long letter till I get to Stoke, for I have my head and hands full of affairs'; in January 1744, she repeated the lament:

'I thought to have wrote you a long comfortable letter, but I find that's impossible, so take it *higgledy piggledy* as I can scrawl it'.[140]

Comfortable letters were therefore not things that simply happened: they required careful thought and the devotion of time and effort on the part of the writer. Sir Roger Newdigate could steal away for a few minutes to write some affectionate lines to his wife and Philippa Hayes could sit in the company of George Lucy's cousin and his children when writing to him about local news and family affairs.[141] However, Mary Delany clearly felt that she had to dedicate greater resources to the task. This did not necessarily make letter writing a burden. Indeed, William and Emma Money took pleasure and comfort in writing as well as receiving letters from each other. As we have seen already, they sometimes used letters as an emotional safety valve, pouring out their frustrations or working through their feelings or ideas about particular situations, from the death of a parent to the unacceptable worldliness of social life in Weymouth and London. At the same time, the act of writing brought them closer together not only through the shared medium of the letter, but also in the shared moment of writing/reading, the temporal distance of the two acts being dissolved in the words on the page—much as Smith argues.[142] In 1818, William wrote that 'having sent the Boys to Bed I sit down to enjoy a few minutes epistolary conversation with you. I need not assure you that it is the greatest pleasure I can have when absent from you'.[143] Pleasure came from writing to his absent wife and was no doubt felt by the recipient, who was connected by the letter both her to husband in the moment of his writing and the routine of family life at Whetham House. The letter was a tangible connection to people, places and practices from which she was temporarily separated.

Much the same sentiment can be seen in the correspondence between Mary Huddleston and her adult son, Richard. Writing from her summer lodgings at Southend, Mary Huddlestone set off enthusiastically, writing: 'My Dearest Richard can't imagine how much Comfort his kind letter gave me more particularly to hear you are quite well'. She then extolled the merits of sea bathing, related her own health, complained about the lack of Catholics in Southend and asked after Richard's own domestic arrangements on camp with the militia. Towards the end of her letter, she sighed, 'it gives me pleasure to write to my Family, as its the only Comfort one has at a distance'.[144] Comfort came from receiving and writing letters: from keeping in touch with family and hearing their news and of their well-being. Letters thus afforded comfort in their production as well as their consumption, just as comfort for the Christian came from offering comfort to others, though it would be wrong to see letter writing in terms of Christian duty. Nonetheless, correspondents were conscious of the power of letters to afford comfort through not only their content but also their materiality and construction.

Conclusions

This chapter has tried to identify the place of emotional comfort in the country house and to say something about the position of comfort in the history of emotions. The myth of the low affect marriage is further debunked by the love and affection apparent between husbands and wives, parents and children in aristocratic and genteel families. This affection was apparent throughout our period, from the urgent courtship of Richard Coffin to the surprising tenderness of Sir Roger Newdigate. It was increasingly described in the language of comfort—an association apparent in the letters of Emma and William Money and sufficiently engrained to be the object of numerous satirical prints which played on the comforts of married life. Such matrimonial comfort suggests contentment and ease—a gentle and reassuring affection that could be relied upon—and reminds us that emotions did not need to be extreme to be strongly felt and to be important in binding people together.[145] Indeed, the absence of this comfort from the lives of Ashe and Elizabeth Windham and Elizabeth Dryden serves to underline its importance as a stabilising force.

Notwithstanding the ongoing debate over the definition and operation of the emotional community, it is apparent that family formed an important unit in which emotional norms were produced and reproduced. Moreover, the correspondence between family members operated both as a mechanism for providing comfort and a vehicle for requesting this from others. Emma Money's requests for the comfort of a reply to her letters drew on and reinforced expected norms. We might see her outburst as constructive anger, but she also showed the importance of mutual respect and affection. Indeed, her relationship with William underlines the idea of marriage and parenthood as performance, and the central part played by comfort in that performance. Family had porous boundaries, especially as an emotional community; it could also include servants, siblings, cousins and a wider set of friends. This broader network of comfort had stronger and looser links, as Lady Louisa Stuart's relative emotional ties to her mother and father, sister and brothers demonstrate; and its constituents inevitably varied over time. Lifecourse changes produced shifts in intergenerational bonds—love and affection from parents giving way to the comfort afforded by children—and shorter-term changes occurred in response to the availability of alternatives, Lady Louisa's brothers being second best but better than nothing.

The irony in all of this is that we know most about this emotional comfort precisely when the people involved were apart. The conversations between people in the same house are largely lost; their voices emerge only in the letters written when one of them was absent. This does not mean that the country house played no part in the construction and articulation of emotional comfort. Whilst correspondents were generally intent on their relationship with people, the house cut into these relationships in a number of ways. First, most country houses afforded a range of different places in which letters could be written and read. Only rarely did correspondents make specific reference to their location in the house, but it is apparent that letter-writing could be a private affair, conducted in a few minutes and away from the company, as Sir Roger Newdigate describes; or it could be more of a group activity, set in the bustle of the drawing room and with a range of people contributing to the process—as with Philippa Hayes. Second, with their larger assemblages of family and servants, country houses often afforded a challenge to privacy and emotional intimacy, but they also provided opportunities for a greater array of emotional bonds, as the changing company enjoyed or endured by Lady Louisa makes clear. Regardless of size and composition, however, the core relationships were between parents, children and siblings—especially sisters. Third, and most profoundly, letter writers sometimes sought to draw their correspondents into the routines and spaces of daily life in the country house through accounts of everyday activities, news of the children or, more occasionally, references to locations within the house. In this way, the recipient could imagine themselves at home with their family—bedded into a web of emotional comfort that entangled people and place.

Letters provided comfort through the reassurance that they were remembered and valued (something which Emma Money sought out); through the materiality of the page (seen in Newdigate's concerns about his wife's writing hand), and above all in the contents and character of the letter itself (Walpole's definition of a comfortable letter being nuanced by Delany's emphasis on style and form). Quite apart from what this can tell us about the nature of letter writing in terms of the relationship between content, style and personality, these letters reveal much about the 'sentimental household' as a mental construct. The idealisation of home and family as the seat of comfort grew stronger when the individual was spatially removed—in both rhetoric and reality. This went beyond simple nostalgia: home was a place where emotions resided and where a person felt most comfortable. Rowlandson's satire should not detract from the deeply felt attachment experienced by many correspondents. These attachments and their links to memory are the subjects of the final chapter.

Notes

1. Thomas Malthus, *Essay on the Principle of Population* (London: John Murray, 1803), 91.
2. On this idea of comfort as a reflection of social and economic development, see Paul Slack, *Invention of Improvement: Information and Material Progress in Seventeenth-Century England* (Oxford: Oxford University Press, 2014), 215–28.

3. Susan Broomhall, 'Emotions in the Household', in Susan Broomhall (ed.), *Emotions in the Household, 1200–1900* (Basingstoke: Palgrave Macmillan, 2008), 15–19. See also Naomi Tadmor, *Family and Friends in Eighteenth-Century England: Household, Kinship and Patronage* (Cambridge: Cambridge University Press, 2001).
4. Joanne Bailey, *Parenting in England, 1760–1830* (Oxford: Oxford University Press, 2012); Joanne Bailey, *Unquiet Lives: Marriage and Marriage Breakdown in the England, 1600–1800* (Cambridge: Cambridge University Press, 2003).
5. Barbara Rosenwein, *Emotional Communities in the Early Middle Ages* (Ithaca: Cornell University Press, 2006).
6. Broomhall, 'Emotions in the Household', 17–23. This contrasts with earlier readings of family, often based on the work of Philippe Ariès, *L'Enfant et la Vie Familiale sous l'Ancien Régime* (Paris: Plon, 1960).
7. Catherine Mann, ' "Whether You Ladyship Will or ne": Displeasure, Duty and Devotion in the Lisle Letters', in Susan Broomhall (ed.), *Emotions in the Household, 1200–1900* (Basingstoke: Palgrave Macmillan, 2008), 119–43; Hannah Barker, *Family and Business During the Industrial Revolution* (Oxford: Oxford University Press, 2017), 156–95.
8. Nicole Pohl, 'Utopian Households in the Work of Sarah Scott and Sarah Fielding', in Susan Broomhall (ed.), *Emotions in the Household, 1200–1900* (Basingstoke: Palgrave Macmillan, 2008), 219–33.
9. See, for example, Kate Smith, 'Imperial Families: Women Writing Home in Georgian Britain', *Women's History Review*, 24:6 (2015), 843–60.
10. On emotions as social and cultural practice, see Sara Ahmed, *The Cultural Politics of Emotion* (London: Routledge, 2004), 8; Monique Scheer, 'Are Emotions a Kind of Practice (and What Makes Them Have a History)? A Bourdieusian Approach to Understanding Emotion', *History and Theory*, 51:2 (2010), 193–220.
11. Sarah Chauncey Woolsey (ed.), *The Autobiography and Correspondence of Mrs Delany*, vol. 2 (Boston: Roberts Brothers, 1879), 289: Mary Delany to Anne Dewes, 26 July 1744.
12. For discussion of these varied uses of the country house, see Mark Girouard, *Life in the English Country House: A Social and Architectural History* (New Haven: Yale University Press, 1978), passim; Mark Girouard, *Life in the French Country House* (London: Cassell & Co., 2000), 163–96.
13. On the importance of emotion words and emotives, see Rosenwein, *Emotional Communities*; William M. Reddy, *The Navigation of Feeling: A Framework for the History of Emotions* (Cambridge: Cambridge University Press, 2011).
14. Thomas Rowlandson, *The Comforts of Matrimony, a Good Toast* (1809), British Library, 1871,0812.4497. The family group is echoed in the cat and kitten lying by the fire.
15. See Kate Retford, *The Art of Domestic Life: Family Portraiture in Eighteenth-Century England* (New Haven: Yale University Press, 2006); Bailey, *Parenting in England*; Jennifer Popiel, 'Making Mothers: The Advice Genre and the Domestic Ideal, 1760–1830', *Journal of Family History*, 29:4 (2004), 339–50; I.H. Tague, 'Aristocratic Women and Ideas of Family in the Early Eighteenth Century', in Helen Berry and Elizabeth Foyster (eds.), *The Family in Early Modern England* (Cambridge: Cambridge University Press, 2007).
16. On love within aristocratic and gentry marriages, see, inter alia: Amanda Vickery, *The Gentleman's Daughter: Women's Lives in Georgian England* (New Haven: Yale University Press, 1998), 39–86; I.H. Tague, 'Love, Honour and Obedience: Fashionable Women and the Discourse of Marriage in the Early Eighteenth Century', *Journal of British Studies*, 40:1 (2011), 76–106; Katie Barclay, *Intimacy and Power: Marriage and Patriarchy in Scotland,*

1650–1850 (Manchester: Manchester University Press, 2011); Henry French and Mark Rothery, *Man's Estate: Landed Gentry Masculinities, 1660–1900* (Oxford: Oxford University Press, 2013), 185–220.

17. Devon Record Office (DRO), Z19/40/8a-b, Richard Coffin to Anne Prideaux, 21 April 1673.
18. DRO, Z19/40/8a-b, Richard Coffin to Anne Prideaux, 27 August 1684.
19. Writing when he was anxiously waiting to hear news of the election for the Oxford University seat, we wrote that defeat would mean 'we shall draw in our horns and retire again into our comfortable shell': Warwickshire Record Office (WRO), CR136/B1530, Sir Roger Newdigate to Dr. Thomas Burgh, 28 January 1751.
20. WRO, CR136/B1899, Sir Roger Newdigate to Sophia Newdigate: 12 April 1749.
21. WRO, CR136/B2511, Sir Roger Newdigate to Sophia Newdigate: 25 November 1762.
22. WRO, CR136/B4046[I], Sir Roger Newdigate to Sophia Newdigate: [no date] February 1772.
23. See Reddy, *Navigation of Feelings*.
24. Mark Rothery and Henry French, *The Formation of Male Elite Identities in England c.1660–1900: A Sourcebook* (Basingstoke: Palgrave Macmillan, 2012).
25. Wiltshire Record Office (WiRO), 1720/829 (transcript), 12, 15: Emma Money to William Money, September 1807; William Money to Emma Money, [no date] September 1808.
26. WiRO, 1720/829 (transcript), 2, 30, 42: William Money to Emma Money, 20 May 1805; Emma Money to William Money, [no date] 1809; Emma Money to William Money, [no date] 1812.
27. Reddy, *Navigation of Feeling*, 104–5; Scheer, 'Are Emotions a Kind of Practice'.
28. WiRO, 1720/829 (transcript), 144: Emma Money to William Money, 17 July 1817.
29. French and Rothery, *Man's Estate*, 206–7. For a brief discussion of different forms of love, see Danijela Kambaskovic, 'Love', in Susan Broomhall (ed.), *Early Modern Emotions: an Introduction* (London: Routledge, 2017), 53–6.
30. WiRO, 1720/829 (transcript), 119:, 132, 133 Emma Money to William Money, [no date] July 1815 (emphasis in the original); Emma Money to William Money, 15 July 1816; William Money to Emma Money, 17 July 1816.
31. WiRO, 1720/8.
32. Anthony Fletcher, *Growing Up in England: The Experience of Childhood, 1600–1914* (New Haven: Yale University Press, 2008), 106, 10; Bailey *Parenting in England*, 174–98.
33. WiRO, 1720/829 (transcript), 33, 110: William Money to Emma Money, [no date] 1810; William Money to Emma Money, 18 July 1814.
34. WiRO, 1720/829 (transcript), 55: William Money to Emma Money, 14 May 1812.
35. Lewis Walpole Library, 799.10.01.06, 799.10.01.05, 799.10.01.10. The theme of a curtain lecture was a common trope, with dozens of satirical prints showing similar scenes of a wife scolding her errant husband.
36. See Karen Harvey, 'Men Making Home: Masculinity and Domesticity in Eighteenth-Century Britain', *Gender and History*, 21:3 (2009), 520–2.
37. Anon., *Three Weeks After Marriage* (Published by J.L. Marks, 1822), Lewis Walpole Library, 822.00.00.25.
38. Robert Sayer, *The Comforts of Matrimony—A Smoky House & Scolding Wife* (1790), British Museum, 1985,0119.115.

39. Austen, *Sense and Sensibility* (1811; London: Penguin, 1995), 166, 322.
40. See R.W. Ketton-Cremer, *Felbrigg: The Story of a House* (London: Futura, 1982), 92–100.
41. Norfolk Record Office (NoRO), WKC, 7/20/15, Ashe Windham to Elizabeth Windham, [no date] 1719.
42. NoRO, WKC, 7/20/17, Ashe Windham to Elizabeth Windham, [no date] 1719.
43. NoRO, WKC, 7/20/21, Ashe Windham to Elizabeth Windham, 19 August 1720.
44. Diana Barnes, 'Emotional Debris in Early Modern Letters', in Stephanie Downes, Sally Holloway, and Sarah Randles (eds.), *Feeling Things: Objects and Emotions Though History* (Oxford: Oxford University Press, 2018), 129.
45. Linda Pollock, 'Anger and the Negotiation of Relationships in Early Modern England', *The Historical Journal*, 47:3 (2004), 567–90.
46. NoRO, WKC, 7/20/22, Elizabeth Windham to Ashe Windham, 4 August 1720.
47. NoRO, WKC, 7/20/25, Ashe Windham to Elizabeth Windham, 16 August 1728.
48. NoRO, WKC, 7/20/26, Elizabeth Windham to Ashe Windham, 19 August 1728.
49. NoRO, WKC, 7/20/27, Elizabeth Windham to Ashe Windham, 6 December 1728.
50. Reddy, *Navigation of Feeling*.
51. Bailey, *Parenting in England*, 23.
52. See Hugh Cunningham, *Children and Childhood in Western Society Since 1500*, second edition (London: Routledge, 2005), 58–72.
53. Bailey, *Parenting in England*, 48–60.
54. Thomas Colley, *The Pleasures of Matrimony* (1773), Lewis Walpole Library, 773.03.20.02. For other examples, see Bailey, *Parenting in England*, 24–5.
55. See Bailey, *Parenting in England*, 26–33.
56. WiRO, 1720/829 (transcript), 184: Emma Money to William Money, 31 August 1818.
57. WiRO, 1720/829 (transcript), 25: William Money to Emma Money, 8 November 1808.
58. For a discussion of anxiety as an emotion, see Henry French and Mark Rothery, 'Male Anxiety Among Younger Sons of the English Landed Gentry, 1700–1900', *Historical Journal*, 62:4 (2019), 967–95.
59. The lack of a child was often seen as damaging to marriages—see Helen Berry and Elizabeth Foyster, 'Childless Men in Early Modern England', in Helen Berry and Elizabeth Foyster (eds.), *The Family in Early Modern England* (Cambridge: Cambridge University Press, 2007).
60. WRO, CR136/B/2014, Sir Roger Newdigate to Mrs Parker, 29 April 1795.
61. WRO, L6/1536a, L6/1537, Lady Margaret Williams to Mary Elizabeth Lucy, no dates.
62. See Barnes, 'Emotional Debris'.
63. Bailey, *Parenting in England*, 174–98. See also French and Rothery, *Man's Estate*, 39–84.
64. French and Rothery, *Man's Estate*, 89–91.
65. Devon Records Office (DRO), Z19/40/8a-b: 13 August 1684, 5 October 1686.
66. SCLA, DR672/59, letter from Elizabeth Brydges to Mary Brydges, 15 August 1682.
67. Chauncey Woolsey, *Correspondence of Mrs Delany*, vol. 1, 50: Lord Landsdowne to Mrs Pendarves, 31 December 1727.
68. Chauncey Woolsey, *Correspondence of Mrs Delany*, vol. 1, 50: Sir John Stanley to Mrs Pendarves, 10 December 1727.

69. Chauncey Woolsey, *Correspondence of Mrs Delany*, vol. 1, 50: Sir John Stanley to Mrs Pendarves, 10 December 1727.
70. For a broader discussion of these changing family relationships, see Bailey, *Parenting in England*, 222–44; French and Rothery, *Man's Estate*, esp. 185–234.
71. WiRO, 1720/829 (transcript), 190: William Money to Emma Money, 9 September 1818.
72. WiRO, 1720/829 (transcript), 20: William Money to Emma Money, [no date] September 1808.
73. WiRO, 1720/829 (transcript), 27: William Money to Emma Money, 12 November 1808.
74. WiRO, 1720/829 (transcript), 86: William Money to Emma Money, 22 June 1813.
75. Hannah More, Mr Bragwell and his Two Daughters (1797), 12.
76. French and Rothery, *Man's Estate*, 222–30.
77. Northamptonshire Record Office (NRO), D(CA)/361, Elizabeth Dryden to Mrs Steele, 26 September 1809, 20 October 1814; D(CA)/361, Elizabeth Dryden to Mrs Steele, 28 January 1814.
78. NRO, D(CA)/361, Elizabeth Dryden to Mrs Steele, 26 May 1812.
79. See French and Rothery, *Man's Estate*, 185–234.
80. NRO, D(CA)/361, Elizabeth Dryden to Mrs Steele, 20 October 1814.
81. NRO, D(CA)/361, Elizabeth Dryden to Mrs Steele, 20 October 1814.
82. NRO, D(CA)/361, Elizabeth Dryden to Mrs Steele, 2 June 1819.
83. Colin Campbell, 'The Desire for the New: Its Nature and Social Location as Presented in Theories of Fashion ad Modern Consumerism', in Roger Silverman and Eric Hirsch (eds.), *Consuming Technologies: Media and Information in Domestic Spaces* (London: Routledge, 1992), 93–105.
84. Barbara Rosenwein, 'Problems and Methods in the History of Emotions', *Passions in Context: Journal of the History and Philosophy of the Emotions*, 1:1 (2010); Andrew Lynch, 'Emotional Community', in Susan Broomhall (ed.), *Early Modern Emotions: An Introduction* (London: Routledge, 2017), 3–6.
85. Pohl, 'Utopian Households', 220.
86. WiRO, 1720/829 (transcript), 151: William Money junior to William Money, [no date] September 1817. On letter-writing as a pedagogic device, see Carolyn James, 'What's Love Got to Do with It? Dynastic Politics and Motherhood in the Letters of Elenora of Aragon and Her Daughters', *Women's History Review*, 24:4 (2015), 528–47; Johanna Ilmakunnas, 'Life-Stage, Work and Daily Routines of the Eighteenth-Century Swedish Elite: Johan Gabriel Oxenstierna's Diaries', in Gudrun Andersson and Jon Stobart (eds.), *Daily Lives and Daily Routines in Eighteenth-Century Europe* (London: Routledge, 2021), 62–81.
87. WiRO, 1720/829 (transcript), 166: William Money junior to Emma Money, 12 October 1817.
88. French and Rothery, *Man's Estate*, 215.
89. WiRO, 1720/829 (transcript), 136: William Money to Emma Money, [no date] July 1816.
90. See: Susan Whyman, *Sociability and Power in Late-Stuart England: The Cultural Worlds of the Verneys 1660–1720* (Oxford: Oxford University Press, 1999).
91. Alice Clark (ed.), *Gleanings from an Old Portfolio Containing Some Correspondence Between Lady Louisa Stuart and Her Sister, Caroline, Countess of Portarlington and Other Friends and Relatives*, vol. 2 (Edinburgh, 1895), 36–7: Lady Louisa Stuart to Lady Caroline Dawson, 21 July 1778.
92. Clark, *Gleanings from an Old Portfolio*, vol. 2, 40–1: Lady Louisa Stuart to Lady Caroline Dawson, 26 July 1778.

93. SCLA, DR671, Mary Leigh to Joseph Hill, 12 September 1791. For further discussion see Jon Stobart, '"So Agreeable and Suitable a Place": The Character, Use and Provisioning of a Late Eighteenth-Century Suburban Villa', *Journal for Eighteenth-Century Studies*, 39:1 (2016), 89–102.

94. Mann, '"Whether You Ladyship Will or ne"', 121. On the emotional attachment between masters and servants, see Tim Meldrum, *Domestic Service and Gender, 1660–1750* (Harlow: Pearson, 2000), 89–90.

95. Gerrit Verhoeven, 'Feeling at Home Abroad: Comfort, Domesticity and Social Display on the Netherlandish Grand Tour, 1585–1815', in Jon Stobart (ed.), *The Comforts of Home in Western Europe, 1700–1900* (London: Bloomsbury, 2020), 168. On the discomforts of homesickness, see Sarah Goldsmith, 'Nostalgia, Homesickness, and Emotional Formation on the Eighteenth-Century Grand Tour', *Cultural and Social History*, 15:3 (2018), 333–60.

96. See Jon Stobart, 'Housekeeper, Correspondent and Confidante: The Under-Told Story of Mrs Hayes of Charlecote Park, 1744–73', *Family and Community History*, 21:2 (2018), 96–111.

97. WRO, L6/1439, George Lucy to Philippa Hayes, 25 April 1757.

98. WRO, L6/1373, Philippa Hayes to George Lucy, 30 July 1753.

99. WRO, L6/1436, George Lucy to Philippa Hayes, 27 December 1756; WRO, L6/1447, George Lucy to Philippa Hayes, 12 April 1758.

100. WRO, L6/1367, Philippa Hayes to George Lucy, 17 July 1749. Lucy appears to have become more cautious in later life, noting in a letter from Bath that he was refraining from cards because they 'play so deeply that I don't care to meddle'—WRO, L6/1453, George Lucy to Philippa Hayes, 9 February 1760.

101. M. Cohen, '"Manners" Make the Man: Politeness, Chivalry and the Construction of Masculinity', 1750–1830', *Journal of British Studies*, 44 (2005), 312–29; French and Rothery, *Man's Estate*, 56–67.

102. Clark, *Gleanings from an Old Portfolio*, vol. 2, 244: Lady Louisa Stuart to Lady Caroline Dawson, 16 February 1795.

103. Lord Landsdowne was a strong Tory, made a peer during Queen Anne's reign and opposed the Hanoverian accession. Mrs Howard was the wife of Charles Howard, 9th Earl of Suffolk, and the mistress of the Prince of Wales, later George II. The letter therefore has political as well as personal meanings.

104. Henrietta Howard, *Letters to and from Henrietta, Countess of Suffolk, and Her Second Husband, the Hon. George Berkley; from 1712 to 1767*, vol. 2 (London: John Murray, 1824), 228–9: Lord Landsdowne to Mrs Howard: 8 April 1727.

105. Charles Howard was a compulsive gambler and beat his wife.

106. Howard, *Letters to and from Henrietta, Countess of Suffolk*, vol. 1, 272–3: Alexander Pope to Mrs Howard, [no date] October 1727.

107. Howard, *Letters to and from Henrietta, Countess of Suffolk*, vol. 1, 272–3: Alexander Pope to Mrs Howard, [no date] October 1727.

108. Howard, *Letters to and from Henrietta, Countess of Suffolk*, vol. 1, 52–3: Elizabeth Molesworth to Mrs Howard, 1 April 1720.

109. Carolyn James, 'Letters', in Susan Broomhall (ed.), *Early Modern Emotions: An Introduction* (London: Routledge, 2017), 121.

110. See James, 'What's Love Got to Do with It?'; Pollock, 'Anger and the Negotiation of Relationships'; Gary Schneider, 'Affecting Correspondence: Body, Behaviour and the Textualization of Emotion in Early Modern English Letters', *Prose Studies*, 23 (2000), 31–62.

111. For fuller discussion of the role of letters in articulating social worlds, see: Whyman, *Sociability and Power*; Rebecca Earle (ed.), *Epistolary Selves: Letters and Letter-Writers, 1600–1945* (Aldershot: Ashgate, 1999); Clare Brant, *Eighteenth-Century Letters and British Culture* (Basingstoke: Palgrave Macmillan, 2006); Kate Smith, 'Imperial Families: Women Writing Home in Georgian Britain', *Women's History Review*, 24 (2015), 843–60.

112. Howard, *Letters to and from Henrietta, Countess of Suffolk*, vol. 1, 26–7: Mrs Bradshaw to Mrs Howard, 29 June 1718.

113. Howard, *Letters to and from Henrietta, Countess of Suffolk*, vol. 1, 1–2: Philip Stanhope to George Berkeley, 25 June 1711.

114. Howard, *Letters to and from Henrietta, Countess of Suffolk*, vol. 1, 95: Mrs Mohun to Mrs Howard, July 1722.

115. WRO, L6/1481, John Dobson to Philippa Hayes, no date, 1755.

116. WRO, L6/1439, George Lucy to Philippa Hayes, 25 April 1757. On women's natural abilities in letter writing, see Brant, *Eighteenth-Century Letters*, 18–19 and, more generally, N. Clarke, *The Rise and Fall of the Woman of Letters* (London: Routledge, 2004).

117. WRO, L6/1432, George Lucy to Philippa Hayes, 7 December 1753; L6/1467, George Lucy to Philippa Hayes, 18 April 1762; L6/1471, George Lucy to Philippa Hayes, 17 April 1763.

118. WRO, L6/1373, Philippa Hayes to George Lucy, 30 July 1753.

119. Clark, *Gleanings from an Old Portfolio*, vol. 2, 26: Lady Louisa Stuart to Lady Caroline Dawson, 26 July 1778.

120. Barnes, 'Emotional Debris'.

121. Smith, 'Imperial Families'. I discuss the retention of letters in chapter 7.

122. WRO, CR 136/B4046[M], Sir Roger Newdigate to Sophia Newdigate, 2 March 1772.

123. On the importance of the hand in letter writing, see: Barnes, 'Emotional Debris', 122–4; James Daybell, *The Material Letter in Early Modern England: Manuscript Letters and the Culture and Practices of Letter-Writing, 1512–1635* (Basingstoke: Palgrave Macmillan, 2012), especially 85–108.

124. WRO, CR136/B4046[H], Sir Roger Newdigate to Sophia Newdigate, 25 February 1772; CR136/B4046[E], Sir Roger Newdigate to Sophia Newdigate, 25 March 1773.

125. On the ability of letters to create or alleviate anxieties, see Susan Whyman, ' "Paper Visits": the Post-Restoration Letter as Seen Through the Verney Family Archive', in R. Earle (ed.), *Epistolary Selves: Letters and Letter-Writers, 1600–1945* (Aldershot: Ashgate, 1999), 21–22. See also French and Rothery, 'Male Anxiety'.

126. WRO, L6/1375, Mrs Hayes to George Lucy, 7 April 1755.

127. Joan DeJean, '(Love) Letters: Madeleine de Scudéry and the Epistolary Impulse', *Eighteenth-Century Fiction*, 22:3 (2010), 399–414.

128. WiRO, 1720/829 (transcript), 42: Emma Money to William Money, [no date] 1812; emphasis in the original.

129. WiRO, 1720/829 (transcript), 36–7: Emma Money to William Money, 15 January 1811, emphasis in the original.

130. Pollock, 'Anger and the Negotiation of Relationships'.

131. Chauncey Woolsey, *Correspondence of Mrs Delany*, vol. 1: Mary Delany to Anne Dewes, 20 August 1752.

132. Cambridgeshire Record Office (CRO), 488/C1/HD47, from Frances Huddlestone, August 1752.

133. Horace Walpole, *Horace Walpole's Correspondence*, vol. 12, 212, https://walpole.library.yale.edu/collections/digital-resources/horace-walpole-

correspondence: Horace Walpole to Mary Berry, 7 September 1796; vol. 20, 523: Horace Walpole to Horace Mann, 25 January 1756.

134. NRO, D(CA)/361, Elizabeth Dryden to Mrs Steele, 29 October 1822.

135. NRO, D(CA)/361, Elizabeth Dryden to Mrs Steele, 13 January 1819.

136. WRO, L6/1536a, Lady Margaret Williams to Mary Elizabeth Lucy, no date.

137. Mary Jepp Clarke *et al.*, *Clarke Family Letters* (Alexandra, VA: Alexandra Press, 2003), 79: Ursula Clarke Venner to Edward Clarke, 17 July 1768.

138. Chauncey Woolsey, *Correspondence of Mrs Delany,* vol. 1, 463: Mary Delany to Anne Dewes, 31 January 1755.

139. Chauncey Woolsey, *Correspondence of Mrs Delany,* vol. 1, 61: Mary Delany to Mrs Frances Hamilton, 3 September 1785.

140. Chauncey Woolsey, *Correspondence of Mrs Delany,* vol. 1, 193: Mary Delany to Anne Dewes, 29 August 1740; 267: Mary Delany to Anne Dewes, 28 January 1744.

141. WRO, CR136/B1899, 12 April 1749; WRO, L6/1373, Mrs Hayes to George Lucy, 30 July 1753. Mrs Hayes experience questions an older view of letter writing as a solitary and introspective activity—see Rebecca Earle, *Epistolary Selves: Letters and Letter-Writers, 1600–1945* (Aldershot: Ashgate, 1999), 6–8.

142. Smith, 'Imperial Families'.

143. WiRO, 1720/829 (transcript), 177: William Money to Emma Money, [no date] 1818.

144. CRO, 488/C3/HD178, Mary Huddlestone to Richard Huddlestone, 8 August 1805.

145. See French and Rothery, 'Male Anxiety'; Whyman, 'Paper Visits'.

6 Home Comforts
Objects and Memories

Domestic spaces and material objects were central to creating a relaxing, informal and comfortable living environment, and the company of friends and family was vital to emotional well-being. Yet, as Judith Lewis has argued, a home depended on more than material trappings; it also involved a sentimental connection between things, place and people. It was these associations that allowed at least some women to feel 'at home' in what might otherwise be luxurious but uncomfortable country houses.[1] The importance of viewing objects as imbued with meaning has become standard fare in recent years. This has sometimes followed the route of cultural theory, objects being seen as disembodied systems of signs and symbols. However, as part of the so-called material turn, historians have increasingly sought to emphasise the materiality of objects and think about how this impacted on their use, their symbolic value and their place in the home.[2] More recently, there has been growing interest in the 'broad range of emotions, which themselves materialize in human interactions with objects'.[3] Viewed in this way, things are not only inscribed with meanings and associations, they also serve to mediate emotional transactions between people and thus bind together people through affective bonds. We can see this in a wide variety of settings: from the scraps of cloth left with babies at the London Foundling Hospital, to the array of pictures and objects displayed over soldiers' beds in Victorian barrack rooms.[4] As Tara Hamling has noted, this emotional agency makes things 'good for thinking and feeling with'; but they were also good for remembering with.[5] Sarah Churchill, the wife of the Duke of Marlborough, was given a life interest in Blenheim Palace and the freedom to dispose of her own property. This prompted her to make an inventory of the palace, distinguishing goods belonging to her from those which were heirlooms of the estate. One mechanism that she used in doing this was to note the biographies of certain objects—a process which revealed not only an astonishing ability to recall the provenance and use of household goods, but also the ways in which these things were woven into her own history.[6]

DOI: 10.4324/9781003206361-9

Marius Kwint has argued that objects serve memory in three ways: they furnish memory by constituting an often very vivid picture of the past (memories of a mother's dress or a favourite toy); they stimulate memory by bringing back dormant or forgotten experiences (a particular food transporting the person back to an earlier time), and they form records of memory that go beyond individual experience, linking people across time and space (a photograph album or a door frame marked with children's heights).[7] In each case, Kwint connects people, objects and memory, which we might conceptualise as a triangular relationship. Thinking of home as a place of sentiment and sensibility situates it at the heart of this three-way interaction in a way that closely connects with Gaston Bachelard's notion of 'home' as a palimpsest of personal memories, at once comprising and spatially organising recollections of events, people and objects.[8]

The aim of this chapter is to examine some of the ways in which memory was bound up with specific objects and domestic spaces, helping to shape their meaning and use, and contributing in important ways to the construction of the country house as home. It begins by considering various ways in which objects became personal for their owners, for example through practices of making or gifting, and assesses both the ability of the maker or giver to instil meaning in the material object and the extent to which these were gendered practices. Possessions are then examined as collections or assemblages that resulted from choices about what to keep and how to store and display them. Building on Grant McCracken's ideas about curatorial consumption and Daniel Miller's analysis in *The Comfort of Things*,[9] the discussion focuses on paintings and letters as objects that were, in many different ways, curated in order to maintain or construct a link with the past, particularly within the country house. These were special possessions, yet many of the material objects to which country-house owners developed sentimental attachments were quotidian items. Attention, therefore, turns to how ownership and especially use was linked to processes of remembering, tying this to the idea of objects having 'emotional value'.[10] This involves understanding more fully the ways in which the material richness of the domestic environment was linked to emotional attachment to goods and assemblages of goods.[11] Moving up the spatial scale, the chapter then considers how rooms and whole houses were used in acts of memorialisation, both for individuals and the diachronic family in general. Finally, attention turns to the tangled relationship between memory, contentment, comfort and the home, thinking in particular about the ways in which such a gentle emotion was linked not only to the materiality but also to the memories contained in the country house as a family dwelling.

Making Objects Personal: Crafting and Gifting

To become personal and cherished, objects and spaces needed to develop associations with people, creating a special subject–object relationship—one that goes beyond the utility or non-utility emphasised in Thing Theory.[12] One key way in which this might be achieved was through the process of making material objects in the home. Amanda Vickery has highlighted the importance of women's handicrafts and their incorporation into the domestic interior of elite as well as middling houses. This is an important counterpoint to a longer historiography that has dismissed such craftwork as a quaint amusement or condemned it as part of the confinement of women to the domestic realm and a waste of their time.[13] Vickery places emphasis on the practical and social aspects of needlework in particular, and on the moral worth of handicrafts more generally. The emotional resonance of the products of this labour is less prominent, although she does note that 'the frequency with which handicrafts were given as gifts suggests both the prestige wrought upon them and the power they had to connect women'.[14] Sophia Newdigate embroidered a total of 12 seat covers for the family seat at Arbury Hall in Warwickshire. Instead of the usual flowers or classical motifs, she depicted an array of everyday objects including a scarf, a fan and lace shawl, an almanac, a hat with a ribbon, an opera score, a garden book (with a strawberry being attacked by a wasp) and a hawking net of dead birds. Margaret Jones argues that this odd choice of subjects was the result of her untidiness, her husband, Sir Roger Newdigate, urging her to depict whatever she had left lying on a chair at the time.[15] Whether or not this is true, the emotional connection between the maker, the object and its recipient is readily apparent, following the pathway described by Guy Fletcher: as highly personal creations, they gained their meaning from and helped to materialise the relationship between wife and husband, and with their home.[16]

Things might also accrue special significance through gifting. Sally Holloway has described how mothers and their female friends and relatives crafted a variety of objects to celebrate the birth of a child. Pincushions became increasingly popular as gifts from the 1760s. They were practical and decorative, often carrying embroidered messages such as 'Health to the Little Stranger' or 'God Bless the Babe and May It Live, and a Deal of Comfort May it Give'—the latter linking closely with ideals of parent–child relations discussed in the previous chapter.[17] Such gifts were exchanged between the occupants of country houses. Mary Delany was already giving pincushions as gifts to expectant mothers, including her own sister, in the second quarter of the eighteenth century. Writing to Anne Dewes in 1729, she noted that she had a pincushion for Mrs. Dashwood junior, who was 'as well as can be expected considering her condition'.[18] Twelve years later, she sent her sister a box of textiles and haberdashery to make things for her expected child. It included: 'Four yards of coarse long lawn, and two yards finer for the little night-caps, etc.; I suppose you will line the cradle with dimity or white calico, *quilted*. Let me know if you want anything of the kind or any other, and I will bring it with me'. These things were presumably commissioned by Anne Dewes because Delany added that 'the bandbox, basket, and pincushion you must be so good as to accept of from me'.[19] Mary Delany may have bought these pincushions, but she made others, sometimes deploying her skills in quilting to create elaborate double-sided cushions. Quilts were also common gifts and, as Holloway notes, were subsequently passed down the generations, reflecting not only the investment of time and craftsmanship but also the emotional value of these objects. Mary Delany only once alludes to quilting—a project that remained unfinished, in part because it took second-place to her painting and paper-cutting.[20]

If birth prompted gifting, so too did death. Whilst Lena Cowen Orlin cautions that the scope for individuals to sentimentalise objects through bequests was conditioned by the conventions of will-making, bequeathing was a key mechanism for imparting memorial significance onto an object.[21] This has been seen as a particularly female activity, Maxine Berg arguing that women were keen to preserve and mark bonds of kinship and household community.[22] The goods were not necessarily of high monetary value, but they marked and carried important sentimental associations.

Such practices were well established by the early eighteenth century. Alice Dolan notes the 1720 will of William Gooden in which he gave his son two pairs of sheets 'to keep in Remembrance of his late mother'.[23] Later in the eighteenth century, we see a similar positive relationship between people being memorialised in objects which both mark and perpetuate emotional affinity. Mrs. Phillipa Hayes had been the housekeeper, correspondent and confidante of the lifelong bachelor George Lucy of Charlecote Park in Warwickshire for about 30 years when she died in 1772. By this time, she constituted the closest thing that Lucy had to family.[24] She appointed him as her executor and gave him 'out of the great regard I have for him, my cornelian seal, and desire he will accept my buff tabby to cover his easy chair'.[25] These two objects have particular significance. Cornelian seals were often held on a ring, so Mrs. Hayes may have worn hers as an item of jewellery and most likely used it to seal her letters. It was thus a potent symbol of their long epistolary relationship and a reminder to Lucy of their correspondence and the enjoyment that he had in reading her letters. The buff tabby was most likely a piece of dress fabric and had perhaps had an afterlife covering her own chair; passing it on to be used in the same manner would again have encouraged Lucy to remember his old friend and thus attain some comfort in her absence. Every time he sat in his easy chair, he would have come into contact with her cloth and through it with memories of her. Through everyday material objects that were loaded with personal associations, Mrs. Hayes thus offered George Lucy ways of remembering their friendship in much the same way that Sarah Churchill recalled past relationships through a range of material objects at Blenheim Palace.[26]

The Honourable Mary Leigh, chatelaine of Stoneleigh Abbey in Warwickshire, used bequests in a similar way, reinforcing relationships through material objects. In the absence of any close family, she made dozens of cash bequests and marked particular friendships and kinship bonds with gifts of rings and brooches bought for the occasion from William Makepeace, the London silversmith. These were more than the simple mourning rings typically distributed after funerals, some being fitted with gemstones or pearls. Most cost 5 guineas, but four brooches decorated with brilliants (i.e. diamonds) cost £50 apiece.[27] Such jewellery could have been worn by the recipient and, as with Mrs. Hayes' cornelian seal, would have acted as a reminder to the wearer of their relationship with Mary. In giving these rings, Mary likely wished to signal and memorialise an affective bond with the recipients; it was the occasion (her death) that gave these things their emotional resonance, but they symbolised relationships established and maintained over a lifetime.

More emotionally charged were things that Leigh herself had owned and had formed part of the material culture of Stoneleigh Abbey. She noted that 'I desire all the legacys I have received may be returned to the familys from whence I had them'.[28] Specifically, this meant returning to Mrs. Yorke's family an amber egg and gold spoon, to Lady Howard a painting of Tintern Abbey by Turner, and to the Dolben family a silver model of St Paul's. That Mary Leigh could recall who these things were from suggests that they held emotional importance for her; giving them back would have added another layer of significance: memories of Mary as well as the person who had originally gifted the egg, painting or model to her. However, the most poignant reminders of Mary's relationship with family are the picture of Admiral Craven—which she desired to be hung up at the Craven's house, Coombe Abbey—and the 'miniature picture of William, Lord Craven, dated 1786' which she gave to William's daughter Mary Craven.[29] William Craven was her cousin and had been responsible, along with Mary Leigh, for the maintenance and management of the Stoneleigh estate during the long period of mental illness that prevented her brother, Edward, fifth Baron Leigh, from managing his own affairs; 1786 was the year in which Edward died. In transferring a painting from one country house to another, Mary could maintain the emotional bonds between the two families. Moreover, family tradition has it that she had tender feelings for her cousin, William, so the miniature would have held layers of complex emotional resonance for Mary. Passing it to his daughter served to continue the memory of this close relationship onto the next generation of these neighbouring families, much as Fletcher argues.[30]

Women's post-mortem gifting practices have received most attention in the literature, but men also passed on personal bequests. Edward, fifth Baron Leigh, was a talented musician and his violins went with him when he was taken to London and then Lincolnshire for treatment for his mental illness which had become increasingly apparent from the late 1760s.[31] In his will of 1786, he instructed that three of these were to be given to William Craven, forming another memorial of the close bond between the two families.[32] He gave a fourth violin to his friend and neighbour Sir Watkins Williams Wyn, along with a picture from the dining parlour and another by Teniers; a second painting from the dining parlour and a depiction of Don Quixote by Hayman was given to Lord Willoughby de Brooke, and William Grove received a study clock, a small picture of a church and a 'little picture of cats singing catches painted by Brughel'.[33] These were items that clearly held particular sentimental meaning for Leigh and formed a point of connection between him and his close friends within the neighbourhood. Transferring his violins, clock and paintings in effect placed part of one country house, and home, into another.

Gifts made during an individual's lifetime could also sentimentalise objects, sometimes in a manner that quite explicitly sought to frame and communicate the subject–object relationship. The most obvious occasion for such meaningful gift-giving was a wedding. Following the 1823 marriage of George Hammond Lucy of Charlecote Park and Mary Elizabeth Williams, the couple went to London. Mary Elizabeth recalled in her memoirs that they 'went shopping and my husband gave me endless beautiful and useful things . . . in fact anything I expressed the slightest wish for'. However, the most significant gift in terms of its ability to accumulate family memories was a harp, bought at Errard's. As Mary Elizabeth noted years later, this was 'the very harp which my children and now my Grandchildren play on'.[34] Initially desired because of its links to the music in her childhood home at Boddlewydden in north Wales, then treasured as a wedding present, it gathered meaning as it was 'warmed' and given associations of home through use by generations of the family.[35] Indeed, the instrument had already gained a sufficiently special place in Lucy's construction of home that they took it with them when decamping to Coppington near Stratford-upon-Avon whilst building work was carried out at Charlecote. Mary Elizabeth noted in her journal, the temporary accommodation was 'made most comfortable', the harp being accompanied by 'a Sofa, Arm Chairs, and lots of Flowers and pretty things to make our rooms look nice'.[36] Sentimental objects and material ease were combined to create domestic comfort even in the temporary accommodation of a country-house owner.

Further down the social scale, Ellen Weeton was the daughter of a merchant sea captain working in the West Africa trade. The family struggled to make a living after his death at sea in 1782 and Ellen eventually worked for a succession of families as a governess, before entering a disastrous marriage. Her later life was spent writing memoirs, taking modest walking holidays and trying to maintain contact with her daughter, Mary.[37] In 1824, she wrote to the 9-year-old Mary, enclosing with the letter a parcel of textiles that she was passing on to the little girl. As Ellen Weeton explained:

> I have inclosed 4 different kinds of Gimp, of 4 and 2 yds length as you may perceive when you measure it (my mother once had gowns trimmed with it—perhaps 60 years ago) [. . .] The Green ribbon is part of a box-full my mother (your grandmother Weeton) once had; they were taken in a prize, which my father captured during the American war.[38]

These items are accompanied by their respective biographies which tied them, and by extension the girl, to her grandparents. Memories were kept alive through the objects and through narrating their stories, transferring emotional meanings down the generations. Importantly, Ellen is quite clear about her purpose:

> I am thus minute, my Mary, that you might know something of the history of your mother's family [. . .] The piece of patchwork is of an old quilt, I made it above 20 years ago; it may serve as a pattern. The Hexagon in the middle was a shred of our best bed hangings, they were Chintz, from the East Indies, which my father brought home with him.[39]

She wanted to keep her daughter connected with her maternal family after separating from her husband and chose to do this through material objects, no doubt hoping that, in touching these textiles, her daughter would remember these stories and come closer to her family.

Ellen Weeton was consciously deploying household objects as records of memory which could then serve to stimulate remembering of family and home. Not everyone was so deliberate, but the power of household objects to store memories and carry emotions could impinge on people almost despite themselves. Mary Delany, writing to Anne Dewes shortly before departing for Dublin, informed her sister that: 'I have got an old broken Indian chest for you, some scrub chairs, a sofa and couch—(the couch is precious because covered with a gift of my mother's, but it is so lumbering a thing I can't take it with me)—a clock, and a few pictures'.[40] Only the couch is singled out as holding any particular significance amongst these assorted objects because it was a link back to their mother. Although the connection is made in aside and almost brushed off with a dismissal of the couch as large and unwieldy, Mary perhaps hoped to pass on a loyalty to the piece as a family heirloom.

Collecting and Keeping: Curating Family Through Pictures and Letters

The process of acquiring things might serve to make them significant within the home, but it was in owning them and placing them into the domestic environment that they were most powerful in making a house into a home. Such curated collections and identities are perhaps most evident in the use of family portraits. These were often deployed in explicitly dynastic terms, sometimes to trace the descent of title and sometimes to map out a broader family tree of connections. This was a key part of any visit to a country house; visitors expected to see portraits of ancestors and to be able to use these to trace the pedigree of the family. Mrs. Lybbe Powys invariably commented on such things, noting at Knole House, for instance, the 'portraits of family for many generations'.[41]

Perhaps the most famous attempt to orchestrate family portraits in this way was undertaken by Henrietta Cavendish at Welbeck Abbey in Nottinghamshire in the years following the death in 1741 of her husband, Edward Harley, second Earl of Oxford.[42] Along with numerous improvements made to the house itself, she set about assembling and organising over 200 portraits of her and her husband's family lines. They were hung in different rooms at Welbeck, primarily according to the branch of the family they depicted. Some were annotated with inscriptions to clarify the identity of the person depicted and their relationship to Henrietta or Edward, or to underline great deeds or royal connections. This huge display of portraits formed what Kate Retford has termed a 'pictorial family tree' which left the visitor with no doubt about the pedigree and good connections of the Cavendish family: it memorialised and celebrated family.[43] Much the same can be seen in country houses across Europe. At Lövstabruk in Uppland, Sweden, for example, Charles de Geer inherited the estate and ironworks in 1730. The new house that he built included a formal dining room in which a series of family portraits were fitted into the wooden panelling. As with Henrietta Cavendish, these were carefully labelled with the identity of the sitter and their place in the de Geer family tree.[44] Such practices were sufficiently ingrained that James Ogden could create a fictional *Ahnengallerie* (or gallery of ancestors) for William III's house at Het Loo as part of his 1790 poem *The Revolution*, which celebrated the events of 1688.[45] This imagined picture gallery contained William's illustrious ancestors, the 'Nassovian Heroes', and explicitly linked these both to the foundation of the Dutch Republic and the house itself. The fact that the real picture gallery bore little resemblance to this fiction was of little concern to either Ogden or his readers: what mattered was that lineage could be traced and celebrated through portraits, whether created by the artist's brush or the writer's pen.

Some found the effect of this kind of conscious memorialising a little overbearing. Mary Delany noted of Welbeck that 'everything displays the antiquity of the noble race from whence the owners are descended . . . but there is a glare of grandeur'.[46] A decade earlier, in 1743, the bluestocking Miss Catherine Talbot wrote to her friend, Mrs. Carter, complaining about the pedantry and ostentation of such exhibitions of pedigree. Her principal target was the 'History of the Family of Yvery': 'two thick volumes which are really filled with circumstances of as little importance to any of its readers [. . .] an enumeration of the various misspellings of the name of Percival, engrosses half a page to prove the antiquity of the family'.[47] However, this kind of pretension was pricked by relating a story about Lord Chesterfield, who:

> has treated this sort of family vanity very whimsically. A vertuoso [sic.] of his acquaintance this winter at an auction bought a very old picture of a man and woman and two boys, and with great joy observed the Stanhope arms at one corner of it. This he presented to my lord, imagining he would be greatly pleased and delighted to have such a proof of the antiquity of his family; and to prevent all disputes of precedency for the future, my lord has inscribed under the figures, Adam Stanhope of Eden garden Egypt, and Eve Stanhope his wife, with their two sons Cain Stanhope and Abel Stanhope; his genealogy would have been indisputable, if he had put Seth Stanhope instead of Cain; but the humour was really a good one, as you may see I thought it, by writing you such a long story about it.[48]

Clearly not one to celebrate pedigree in this way, Lord Chesterfield parodied the labelling of paintings seen at Welbeck and Lövstabruk; significantly, he also linked family to residence, in this instance in the Garden of Eden.

Such use of family portraits within the country house suggests little room for sentiment attachment: they created a diachronic narrative rather than an emotional connection and, in Judith Lewis' terms, were about the house rather than home. Elsewhere, however, paintings were deployed in a way that gave them greater sentimental significance, helping to create a sense of belonging and perhaps comfort. Individual portraits could be heavy with an emotional meaning, something which was apparent to Lady Mary Coke, the widow of Edward, Viscount Coke of Holkham Hall in Norfolk. Writing in her journal in January 1767, she noted that 'Ly Dal. wrote me word the Picture of her Son (who she lately lost) is arrived from Paris, & that it was the greatest comfort to her imaginable'.[49] When emotions were this raw, portraits could offer consolation to the grieving mother and help to sustain the bond between them. We do not know where Lady Dalkeith chose to hang the picture of her son, but it seems likely to have occupied a place in her personal rooms where its emotional resonance would be most powerful.

Even away from the intensity of such loss, portraits could be used to sustain sentimental ties with family. The collection of family pictures at Stoneleigh Abbey was largely assembled by Thomas, fourth Baron Leigh, in the 1730s and 1740s with a substantial number also coming to Stoneleigh from Leighton Buzzard Prebendary House—the property of his uncle, Charles Leigh, who died just a few months prior to Thomas in 1749.[50] The collection included paintings of Sir Thomas Leigh (d.1571), who acquired the Stoneleigh estate when the original monastery was dissolved, and his wife Alice. However, the majority depicted more recent descendants and various branches of the synchronic family, including the Honourable Lady Rockingham, the mother of Eleanor, wife of the second Baron Leigh; Thomas Holbech, the father of the third Baron Leigh's wife, Mary; the Honourable Miss Verney, an aunt of the fourth Baron Leigh, and Mary Isham, a cousin who married into the Ishams of Lamport Hall in Northamptonshire. Numbering about 30 pictures in total, these portraits are listed in the 1749 inventory as hanging in the Picture Gallery. The separate collections of Charles and Thomas had been amalgamated into a single assemblage that demonstrated both the Leigh's family lineage and their broader kinship networks—a curated embodiment of family identity that formed a small-scale version of the pictorial family tree created by Henrietta Cavendish.

Upon Thomas' death, the house was unoccupied for the next 15 years until his son, Edward, came of age and began an extensive programme of refurbishment. This included a reorganisation of his pictures, partly prompted by his own purchases, partly through further additions from Leighton Buzzard, but mostly as a result of a rather different set of curation practices. Edward Leigh relocated 15 family pictures to the Breakfast and Dining Parlour (which formed the main rooms for entertaining in the house); he also hung four in the Brown Parlour and one in the Drawing Room (within the more formal Great Apartment), and a further five in private family rooms at the back of the house; two were placed in his own dressing room.[51] This redistribution seems to have reflected personal choices rather than dynastic posturing. The family pictures in the breakfast and dining rooms were hung alongside landscapes and historical pieces; those in the private family rooms were put in the place of a series of racing prints bought by his father, which Edward Leigh rehung in the picture gallery. Dispersed in this way, the portraits could no longer constitute a meaningful family tree; a better analogy might be the family album, with different rooms forming different pages in the book. In the absence of information about which portraits were located in which rooms, it is impossible to know for certain, but Leigh may well have been grouping pictures in a manner that reflected his emotional rather than dynastic association with the family. If so, this suggests a different relationship between subject and object, one in which the object had taken on a rather more active role.[52]

Miniatures were particularly important in the comfort they afforded to the owner. The form as well as the subject of the painting was significant because miniatures might be displayed on the wall, but could equally be kept in a drawer or set on a box. They were mobile and could be carried in a pocket or worn as a locket, and they could be handled as well as gazed upon, bringing memories of their subject physically close. Lady Mary Coke recognised both this mobility and the emotional resonance of miniatures. In May 1767, she noted in her journal a visit to Ranelagh where:

> there was more company than I like, yet we found seats. The Duke of York & the Duke of Gloucester were both there. Lord Pembroke and the Duke de Fronsac came up to Us. The latter had a very pretty snuff Box, with the picture of his Duchess, who is lately dead, upon the outside, his two little Sons on the inside, & his Sister, Madam D'Egmond, at the bottom.[53]

As with Lady Dalkeith, the image of a recently deceased loved one no doubt afforded some consolation to the Duke de Fronsac, but what is more striking is the way in which the snuffbox acted as a portable family album with pictures of his wife, children and sister all contained within its compass. His motivation in showing it to Mary Coke and others is not recorded. There was a thirst for novelty and ingenuity in such pieces,[54] but it seems likely that the subjects of the paintings were just as important to the Duke's carrying the box with him and showing it to others. It had emotional rather than simply cultural value.[55] The strength of emotion and attachment that could be carried by such objects is apparent from the reaction of William Fitzgerald, Marquis of Kildare, to the gift of a snuffbox bearing the image of his mother. He was away on an extended Grand Tour and extremely homesick, missing his mother in particular, in part because difficulties with her eyesight made it hard for her to write to him.[56] Fitzgerald wrote to his mother in December 1766 of the happiness that it brought to him and a few weeks later noted the pleasure it afforded 'to think I have you in my pocket'.[57] It was a reminder not only of his mother but also of home—a place to which he longed to return—and thus brought him considerable comfort.

The comfort, and the connection to home and family, that could be derived from physical interaction with pictures is apparent in the correspondence of William and Emma Money, who lived on the modest family estate at Wharton in Wiltshire. Early in their married life, William was away from home for several weeks in the autumn of 1808, in part to be with his father who was seriously ill. On 28 September, he wrote 'I miss you my love, every moment of the day. I kiss your dear picture constantly, and dwell on you in my thoughts'.[58] A few days later, he added a postscript to a lengthy letter that repeated the sentiment: 'I kiss your sweet picture constantly & think incessantly of my Emma'.[59] As with Fronsac and Fitzgerald, the picture formed a reminder and a tangible link to an absent loved one: kissing the image enacted the affective bond between them, whilst describing these actions in a letter offered comfort and reiterated the emotional bond between them. Emma reciprocated, both in actions and words. In July 1817, she wrote that 'I am this moment kissing my wedding ring, put on by your dear hand this day eleven years'.[60] It is easy to see that a wedding ring and the pictures could represent a strong affective tie—and it is no coincidence that Emma Money's actions were a way of marking their anniversary—but she could also derive comfort from more mundane objects belonging to William. In September 1808, and apparently in response to her husband's lines about kissing her picture, she wrote that 'I make a point every night of going into your dressing room & kissing either your old hat, shoes or Boots, then praying God to bless & preserve you I undress'.[61] Three things are notable here: one is the way that his clothes form a proxy for the absent William; the second is that this formed part of her daily routine of preparing for bed (a normally shared experience repeated in his absence), and the third is that the action is located in the intimacy of his dressing room. Objects, spaces and memories come together to offer comfort and to underscore a feeling of a shared home, especially important during a period of absence.

William and Emma Money were using objects to substantiate their relationship when spatially removed from the family home: their memories were generally of things and events only a few days or weeks in the past. Objects became particularly powerful when they held memories over a longer time period. Again, pictures were important in this regard. Mary Elizabeth Lucy of Charlecote Park in Warwickshire had eight miniatures painted by the Liverpool-based artist Thomas Hargreaves when she married in 1823 and left her parents' home, Boddlewyddan in north Wales. There was one of herself, one of each of her parents and her four sisters, and one of her old nurse, Catherine Hughes. Looking at these paintings brought back vivid memories of the person depicted. Writing of the time when Hughes had recently died, Lucy recalled having commissioned the miniature and noted that 'I always look at it with the most affectionate pleasure, and almost fancy I can hear her speak, it is such an admirable likeness'.[62] As Kwint argues, these were things that prompted memories and remembering: object, person and memory were intertwined in a way that not only linked Mary Elizabeth back to an earlier time but also took her to a different place.[63] Looking at the miniatures, her memory of Catherine is so vivid that the old lady almost comes alive. This carries Mary Elizabeth back in time and links her present marital home at Charlecote with her past childhood home at Boddlewyddan. No doubt similar emotions and memories were prompted when she gazed at the tiny paintings of her mother, father and sisters; keeping a similar picture of herself within her collection of miniatures may have helped to symbolically lock herself in her family; if so, it is notable that this was a partial reconstruction, her three brothers apparently being omitted from the virtual family group. This reminds us that family, as well as family pictures, could be curated in different ways: as dynasty or as a family of current kinship ties. It also shows that blood was just as potent as cohabitation in creating and maintaining emotional bonds, and that conceptions of the family home did not simply change over the life course as a person moved from parental to marital home.[64]

Mary Elizabeth Lucy's miniature paintings were central in maintaining an emotional bond to different homes, built up over her life; but she also drew on letters as tangible links to the past and to home. We discussed the content and exchange of letters more fully in the previous chapter, but letters were also material objects, the physical nature of which should not be ignored. As Kate Smith has argued, the materiality of letters drew people together over space through shared experience: touching the same paper and tracing the words on the page.[65] The letter's value was thus raised as 'an object of affection, equivalent to other gifts'.[66] To preserve letters was thus to preserve the link to other people, other places and other times, because—of course—the connection could be temporal as well as spatial.

Mary Elizabeth Lucy kept the letters she received from family and friends, noting on some the special significance that they held. One from her mother, Lady Margaret Williams, is annotated with the note: 'The first letter received from my beloved Mother after my marriage on Dec. 3 1823'.[67] There is no record of where these letters were stored, but Mary Elizabeth clearly had them to hand when writing her memoirs in 1889, using them and her journals as points of reference in telling the story of her life.[68] This is very different from the preservation of letters as part of a family archive, but both processes involved selection in what to write and what to keep: curation was an active process, not simply a question of preserving everything. Mary Delany highlights one of the key motivations here, writing to her sister Anne Dewes in 1744 that:

> I believe I have burnt this week an hundred of your letters: *how unwillingly* did I commit to the flames those testimonies of your tender friendship! but I *have preserved* more than double their number, which I shall take with me as so many charms. I thought it prudent to destroy letters that mentioned particular affairs of particular people, or family business.[69]

So, letters containing sensitive topics are destroyed, but far more are preserved as a reminder of friendship and a source of entertainment and comfort. Letters were clearly emotionally charged objects, yet they could be carefully curated to compartmentalise sentiments and relationships, and to obscure if not erase those that might cause distress or embarrassment. As agents of emotion they were potentially hazardous; managing the objects gave some measure of control over emotions and memory.

Not everybody was interested in family or sought to keep and preserve memories and attachments in this way. Elizabeth Dryden of Canons Ashby seems to have felt a little sentimental or practical attachment to her family papers. In 1817, she noted in a letter that: 'All the family writings which I have are in a long box bound with Hair with my Grand-fathers initials, sometimes in the Brown Gallery & sometimes in the Storeroom, but ought to be in Sir Edward Drydens custody, as he has the greatest interest in them, not having any myself'.[70] This, of course, reflected her eldest son's then ownership of the estate, but it also suggests a disregard for family history that is remarkable in itself. Bachelard might write about the significance of a cask that 'contains the things that are unforgettable', but Elizabeth Dryden apparently had little desire to know or remember the things contained in this box.[71] In this, she was the exception: most country-house owners were careful to preserve at least a selection of the letters they received and many were engaged in actively curating family through objects such as paintings. These practices were not culturally specific: they were common practice across space and time. Linking family, objects and memory in domestic settings helped to cement a sense of identity and belonging, but a much wider array of goods was deployed in making houses into homes.

Owning and Remembering: Making a House Into a Home

As Daniel Miller has argued in the context of modern Britain, it is everyday household objects that most commonly carry and communicate the identity of their owners.[72] Often, these are natural accretions which build up over time, layering identities and memories. As with letters, though, there is the possibility of curating these things—a process explored by Grant McCracken in his account of the curatorial consumption of Lois Roget. He highlights the significance to the family of a small number of key objects, including a 'family seat' and the deeds to the property.[73] However, it is the array of everyday objects, inherited from a large number of relatives, which makes the family home distinctive. It is these things that make it a home, McCracken noting:

> Lois often looks up from a book to gaze at a table or a chair and recalls the ancestor who owned it [. . .] The constant presence of this visual archive make the family history ever present and ubiquitous [. . .] The relatives are so well represented I felt that she was reading me the family tree instead of showing me her living room.[74]

The Roget family is exceptional in the completeness of this material archive, but the importance of everyday objects in evoking emotions and memories is apparent in many eighteenth-century families. These things made emotions tangible, as Jules Prown argues, but they also made memories tangible, bringing to mind other people, places and times.[75] Their presence in the house made them instrumental in shaping people's construction of and relationship with home.[76]

As we noted earlier, Sarah Churchill was able to recall detailed biographies of a range of household objects at Blenheim Palace. In one room, there was a: 'yellow Damask Bed lined with white Sattin Embroidered and a very old suit of tapestry hangings wch the Queen gave me to furnish part of my lodgings at Windsor Castle which afterwards I sent to St. Albans and afterwards to Blenheim'. In her own bedchamber, she identified a valance 'of a very rich embroidery which was made of the duchess of Marlborough's cloathes'.[77] These biographies were not only a reflection of her ability to remember the provenance and life story of household objects; they also showed the power of these things to carry and prompt memories, and thus provide some comfort through recollecting people and places from her past. Their stories were interwoven with her own: goods coming from Queen Anne and taken along as she moved from house to house. What is striking, though, is that the emotional and memorial significance of these objects did not rub off onto Blenheim. She felt no affection for the house and it never became comfortable in the same way as Holywell, her childhood home where she had lived when first married. In effect, Blenheim remained a house, not a home; in the language of the anthropologists, Amber Epp and Linda Price, the whole house was a 'cold' space in which goods held emotional significance despite rather than because of their setting.[78]

Further down the social scale, we can see a similar concern with the biography of things and with how they made relationships and memories tangible. Elizabeth Forth was the daughter of a wealthy Yorkshire grocer, Robert Woodhouse, and married the Reverend John Forth in 1791.[79] They inherited a wide array of household goods from both sets of parents as well as acquiring pieces of their own and lived in some style at Ganthorpe near Castle Howard. An inventory taken in 1806 notes the provenance of many of these objects, the contents of a cupboard being especially rich in biographical detail:

> 1 large silver sauce boat marked EW which belonged to Mrs Forth's mother, the gift of Mrs Williamson
> 1 small silver cream or sauce boat marked REW—which belonged to the same & the gift of the same
> One silver soup ladle the gift of Mrs Wright
> 1 compleat set of white and Gold tea China the gift of Mrs Woodhouse
> 2 Foreign Blue and White China tea pots and one Cream pot, one of the tea pots and Cream Pot the gift of Mrs Woodhouse and the Tea pot the Gift of Mrs Wright[80]

This itemisation of gifts and family connections underlines the importance of objects as able to 'do duty as persons' as Alfred Gell puts it.[81] However, we can go further than this. These things not only stood as proxies for the people who had gifted them, materialising and perpetuating the relationship they had with the Forths; they also acted as prompts for memories and associations that were central in the construction of a home. Their substantial house, like the one imagined by Bachelard, was stuffed with reminders of dead friends and relatives, the importance of which is apparent from their careful itemisation on the inventory.[82] Perhaps the appraisers were being followed round the rooms by Mrs. Forth, telling them the biography of each object and urging them to write them down; or perhaps Mrs. Forth herself had the pen in her hand and recorded the personal provenance of each thing she listed. Whatever the precise mechanism, the inventory is remarkable because it carries the web of person–object relationships beyond the recollections of an individual and onto the written pages of an inventory. Text and object thus went together in carrying memories of previous ownership and family ties on to subsequent generations.

Around the same time that this inventory was being drawn up for the Forths, Mary Mackenzie was engaged in refurbishing the family seat, Brahan Castle in Ross-shire. She had inherited the property at the death of her father in 1815 and was busy impressing her taste and character on her Scottish residence for the next 20 years or so.[83] Mary was married to Vice-Admiral Hood and had travelled with him to Madras when he was appointed commander-in-chief in the East Indies in 1811, returning home shortly after his death in December 1814. As with many families who had East India Company connections, she used Indian goods to mark a particular attachment to place, notions of home being characterised by a blend of colonial and British material culture.[84] For Mackenzie, this meant not only a large set of drawings that she had commissioned in India, but also inlaid and japanned cabinets, shawls, porcelain jars, carpets and curiosities including a stuffed leopard. Ellen Filor shows that, at Brahan, these were concentrated into certain rooms which consequently held particular significance for Mackenzie. Principal amongst these was the *Botany Bay Room*—a private boudoir leading directly from the main bedroom. This was rendered a 'warm' space by its contents, which stood in marked contrast to the martial Highland/imperial character of the public rooms. It subsequently took on a special significance for Mackenzie, defining Brahan as *her* home through its material and emotional connection with her life in India.[85] It is telling that, when subsequently negotiating to rent out the house, she insisted that the *Botany Bay Room* remain shut up because of the significance of the objects it contained.

Unsurprisingly, Elizabeth Dryden again challenges our easy assumptions about natural attachment to personal belongings and the comfort that they might afford. In an inventory drawn up in 1819, Dryden went through the house, distinguishing things that belonged to her from those that were 'Heir Looms of the Mansion of Canons Ashby'—much as Sarah Churchill had done 100 years earlier.[86] The circumstances in which she found herself must have shaped Elizabeth's feelings towards these belongings. She was being pursued by her dead husband's creditors and had a fractious relationship with her children, especially her second son Henry, who had inherited the estate the previous year. She therefore had an interest in downplaying the monetary value of the estate as opposed to her own property, but may also have viewed objects with particular familial associations with a somewhat jaundiced eye. Whatever the cause, Elizabeth made few emotional links with the contents of what had been her home for over 60 years as daughter, wife and now dowager. The Canons Ashby inventory contains none of the associations and narrative seen in that drawn up for Elizabeth Forth, and only twice does Elizabeth Dryden's correspondence betray any notion that the contents of the house held any memories of family. In 1822, when contemplating the acquisition of a seaside residence, she wrote that 'I must have a good house & my comforts about me'.[87] Yet even here there is ambivalence: these comforts may have been objects with emotional meanings, but they might also have been her dogs, mentioned with affection in the previous sentence, or a general sense of material well-being. More telling, in the same letter in which she dismisses the family papers, she notes 'Two small Cabinet Pictures purchased by my Uncle are in good preservation & hang on each side of the best Cabinet in the Drawing Room'.[88] The quality and familial association of these paintings are noted, and the location is carefully recorded. They are situated in the 'warm' space of the drawing room: a much-frequented place that would help to imbue objects with associations and meanings.[89] Yet these were not her things, they appear under heirlooms in the 1819 inventory, listed as '1 pair of small pictures by G Houet of Venus and Cupid', and she made no particular claim to them in her letter.[90]

For Elizabeth Dryden, then, household objects appear to have held few (positive) associations or memories. This challenges any easy assumptions about the emotional power of things, but two broad points remain. The first is that the emotional link between people and objects, and the importance of this is constructions of home, was a gendered process: notwithstanding Dryden's seeming detachment, women particularly engaged in recording their emotional attachment to things. The second is that the spatial location of things was important in shaping their sentimental significance, their power as carriers of associations and materialisations of relationships, and their role in making the home a place of emotional comfort. This links back to our earlier discussion of the location and meaning of paintings, but it also ties into the broader role of different rooms in carrying memories and making homes.

Memorialisation: Fixing Family Into Home

An ancient house spoke of an equally ancient lineage, both in its overall appearance and the detail of its decoration. In France, there were plenty of chateaux that retained something of their original form and decorative schemes. The sophisticated Parisian eye of the diplomat and politician, François-Auguste De Frénilly, picked out the old-fashioned character of Monts, the country residence of the Vicomte de al Chastre. Writing in 1789, he noted that it was a 'vast Gothic chateau, approached through three great courts, bristling with towers and turrets' inside of which was 'an immense salon with a beamed ceiling, hung with tapestries'.[91] However, it was not until the middle decades of the nineteenth century that these features were accorded particular value as noble families began to restore their old chateaux. The ducs de Rohan restored the interiors of their chateau at Josselin and the fourteenth-century chateau of Roquetail-lade was lavishly refurbished in a re-imagination of medieval interiors. This marked a shift in taste, drawing heavily on English developments earlier in the century rather than a sentimental attachment to the house itself.[92]

Much the same was true of many English country houses being Jaco-beanised or Gothicised in the early decades of the nineteenth century, but there were some houses where decorative taste was matched by familial connections and memorialisation. One such house was Charlecote Park in Warwickshire. Here, an American visitor, Washington Irving, noted the great hall in 1820, which 'still retains much of the appearance it must have had in the days of Shakespeare', and also the stained glass in the windows emblazoned with the Lucy arms, which traced the family line back to medieval times.[93] Not satisfied with this evocation of the past, George Hammond Lucy (the husband of Mary Elizabeth) set about re-edifying the interiors in a broadly Jacobean style, with new ceilings, fireplaces and a range of Elizabethan and Jacobean furniture—either original or reproduction.[94] Such decorative schemes were in keeping with the prevailing taste of the 1820s and 1830s, but Lucy was constructing more than simply a fashionable house. He was fascinated with heraldry and with tracing the history of his family. He commissioned a pedigree book from the Heralds' College, had the stained glass in the hall repaired and reset (with meticulous care being taken about colours and dates) and commissioned from Thomas Willement a whole new set of armorial glass which traced 'the descent of Sir John Lucy Knight who built Charlecote House in the reign of Queen Elizabeth'.[95] Together with carefully chosen furniture, his aim was to create not only a house with a Jacobean spirit but also one that memorialised both the Lucy family and the historic associations of Charlecote. In 1837, he bought a suite of ebony furniture that was reputed to have been a present from Queen Elizabeth to Robert Dudley, Earl of Leicester, and had originally been at nearby Kenilworth Castle. This made them of particular interest because Elizabeth had visited Charlecote when staying with Dudley at Kenilworth; they were given an additional layer of meaning because the needlework upholstery was worked by Mary Elizabeth Lucy. Past and present were thus stitched together in the fabric of the house.[96]

The connection between house and family that was manifest in the built fabric and carefully retained or assembled collections of objects was sometimes reinforced through text. Richard Neville (later Griffin), third Lord Braybrooke, was an antiquarian and like George Hammond Lucy he was intent on remodelling his house, Audley End, in an authentic manner. Rather than looking elsewhere for 'genuine' Jacobean objects, however, Neville took inspiration from surviving aspects of the house itself, restoring original features and reproducing extant decorative schemes elsewhere in the house. Yet this search for authenticity was tempered with a respect for the changes made by his predecessor: the Adam rooms remained untouched as did a new suite of first-floor rooms fitted out after Sir John Griffin Griffin's peerage was granted.[97] Richard Neville clearly made a close association between the house and his ancestors: it was a memorial to their endeavours and achievements. In this, the materiality of the house was underpinned through the pages of Neville's *History of Audley End*, published in 1836. As well as detailing the development of the house, this told the story of its owners; a critical tone was struck when discussing the misdemeanours of early owners but was largely celebratory when it came to his immediate predecessors. Hannah Chavasse rightly stresses that Neville was actively managing the family image, but he was also memorialising family and its link to the house. On occasions, this was rendered through detailed biographies of particular objects: two volumes of Pliny, for example, bore the autograph of Sir Henry Neville (Ambassador to France, d.1615), whilst the south library contained curtains made from Florentine damask given to another Henry Neville by the third Grand Duke of Tuscany 'with whom, from letters still extant in the family, he appears to have lived in habits of intimacy'.[98] Family papers and objects as heirlooms are thus drawn together both in the surviving materiality of the house and the pages of Neville's history.

The link between family and the fabric of buildings was often most apparent in state apartments. Originally conceived as the rooms in which visiting royalty would stay, this function became redundant as Hanoverian monarchs eschewed tours of their kingdom and they increasingly became vested as symbols of rank and lineage.[99] At Stoneleigh Abbey in Warwickshire, Edward, third Baron Leigh, had a large extension built onto a house that largely comprised buildings that were part of the former Cistercian monastery. The Great Apartment—comprising a drawing room, parlour and state bedchamber—was typical of such apartments. Edward wrote his family status into the fabric of the rooms, his coronet and arms being carved into the capitals of the pilasters. He also commissioned a set of seven walnut chairs embroidered with scenes from classical mythology and again with his coronet and arms painted in full colour in a gilded panel at the top of the chair backs—as was common for hall chairs at this time. The armchair also includes a panel at the base of the backrest with the monograms of Edward and his wife Mary Holbech. In this way, the traditional badges of rank and pedigree are given a personal touch, linking husband and wife to their linear family. What is perhaps most striking about these rooms and their furnishings is the way that they were preserved, largely unaltered, through successive improvements made by subsequent generations of the Leighs. Other rooms demonstrated their fashionable taste and sociability; the Great Apartment was preserved as a marker of family lineage.

Continuity with earlier generations and a sense of the family belonging in the house can also be seen in the naming of rooms. Of course, it was quite typical for rooms to retain the name of the last occupant. At Stoneleigh Abbey, the 1806 inventory still noted 'His Lordship's Bed Chamber' and his dressing room, even though the last Baron Leigh had died some 20 years earlier.[100] This continuity is perhaps understandable in terms of the status of these rooms. At Canons Ashby, an inventory taken when Edward Dryden died in 1717 identified several rooms by the names of the one-time occupant.[101] 'Mr Wyche's Room', 'Joseph Garner's Room', 'Thomas Garner's Room' and 'Christopher's Room' were named for the servants who occupied them, but two were identified by reference to family members. 'Sir E. Dryden's Room' was named for Edward's father, Erasmus (who had inherited the family title and periodically lived at Canons Ashby, looking after the house and estate for his son) and may have been the room in which he slept when at the house. 'Late Sir Robert's Room' referred to the third baronet, who had bequeathed the estate to Edward in 1708, may again reflect the former use of the room as Sir Robert's bedchamber—the silk damask bed hangings certainly suggest that it had been a room of note. What is more telling than these carry-overs from a previous generation is that, whilst any association with Erasmus is quickly dropped, Sir Robert's name remained attached to his room through three subsequent owners. It was by no means an exceptional room in terms of its furniture (an unremarkable bed, a few chairs and tables and, in 1770, 42 gooseberry bottles) yet the name remained as a link to the individual who had given the estate to this branch of the family.

There are echoes here of the suite of rooms, preserved in memory of the long-dead Mrs. Tilney, that so fascinated Catherine Morland at Northanger Abbey. Prevented from visiting them on her initial tour of the house, she imagines that they contain some dark secret. Returning later, on her own, she is intensely disappointed to find a 'large well-proportioned apartment, an handsome dimity bed . . . a bright Bath stove, mahogany wardrobes and neatly-painted chairs'.[102] Reality failed to match Catherine's gothic imagining, but the rooms were nonetheless a place that held memories of Mrs. Tilney—they had been shut up and left untouched following her demise. Such memories can be found in the pages of Mary Elizabeth Lucy's memoirs of her life at Charlecote Park. These often situate the unfolding story of her life and family in the interior spaces of the house, particularly the bedchambers where her children were born and where she watched several of them die. She sometimes noted her place by their side in a little bed placed there especially. In this way, the family home resembled Gaston Bachelard's imaging of a dwelling in which 'a great many of our memories are housed, and if the house is a bit elaborate, if it has a cellar and a garret, nooks and corridors, our memories have refuges that are more clearly delineated'.[103]

The ways in which memories could reside in every corner of a house are important in the emotional bonds which people might feel with home and the comfort that they might derive from its rooms and contents. For Mary Elizabeth, the space in which her memories were most sharply delineated was the church on the grounds of the estate. At one level, this was a straightforward memorial to the Lucy pedigree containing, as it did, the funerary monuments of the builder of the house, his son and grandson. Her decision to rebuild it as a memorial to her dead husband followed a similar practice of memorialisation, as did the windows inserted into the new structure, one for each of her children. Wider family was also commemorated, Mary Elizabeth's sister and brother-in-law, Lord Willoughby de Brooke, donating a new stone font.[104] Yet the great irony in all this is that the old church held so many memories of the family: it was where she had worshipped each week for many years, together with her husband and children. Its destruction, therefore, stimulated remembering:

> The last Sunday that Divine Service was performed in the old church I could not help feeling very sorrowful as it contained memories dear to my very soul. How many times since I had been a wife and a mother (now 26 years) with husband and children I had prayed in that old family pew with its large oak desk around which we knelt together, there in the plain ancient Norman font all our children had been Christened. Before that Altar we had received 'the bread of life', and the old church bell had rung its remorseless toll four different times and the burial service had been read for my beloved husband and three beloved sons, and once had rung merrily and the marriage service had been read for my dearest Emily. The recollection of these things kindled at my heart and caused my tears to fall fast on the old building as it fell to the ground and there was not one stone left upon another.[105]

All of the weekly routines and the most significant events in her family life were held in the fabric of the church and all are recalled as the building is pulled down. The loss of the building not only prompts remembering but also signals a loss of the material imprint of those memories.

Memory and Contentment: The Comforts of Home

We have seen how the rooms making up a house could hold and stimulate memory. They were also crucial in holding and shaping memories of family and past events that helped to make the house into a home. Csikszentmihalyi and Rochberg-Halton have suggested that: 'few English words are filled with the emotional meaning of the word "home". It brings to mind one's childhood, the roots of one's being, the security of a private enclave where one can be free and in control of one's life'.[106] We see something of this sentiment in the letters written to Mary Elizabeth Lucy by her brother John Williams. He lived in London with his wife Emily and sent regular letters to Charlecote Park. In 1824, he recorded his pleasure in his sister's happiness in the 'domestic bliss' of her new home in Warwickshire—a theme to which he returned frequently over the next 20 years, often mixed with joy in his sister's growing family.[107] Writing when she had just returned from an extended family tour of the continent in 1844, he opined:

> How refreshing to find yourself in easy slippers running from one flower bed to another . . . little toes relaxed on the turf after the hard flags of London. How delicious to pick a strawberry & smell a rose & kiss the sweet cheeks of your chicks & turn about in ease and comfort.[108]

All this was very different from his 'artificial life' in London, which provided 'insight into the ways of the Gay world', but which did not allow for relaxation or ease. For Williams, home was a place with happy memories and familial associations: a place of comfort and contentment that was very different from a fashionable yet seemingly rather shallow metropolitan existence.

Milder emotions have only recently begun to be explored by historians, perhaps because it is more difficult to extract them from the historical record.[109] Yet contentment is an emotion that occurs over and again in people's writing about home. Something of this can be seen in the way that Lady Louisa Stuart contrasted the main family seat at Luton Hoo in Bedfordshire with their private residence at Wharncliffe in Yorkshire. Writing to her sister, Lady Caroline Dawson, she noted that:

> you have no idea . . . how compleatly uncomfortable I feel in this great house, after being so much the contrary in our dear little clean, neat cottage at Wharncliff, where we really lived in quite a pastoral

manner. I never think of it but as the abode of peace and content, for it is exactly the retirement you sometimes see described in a romance, where travellers driven in by a storm find a happy family and a place that they think a paradise. 'Tis true we are quite solitary and quiet enough here, but it is with a mixture of melancholy and stateliness, while there we seemed to be in a retreat from all care and anxiety, just what poets are always talking of, though I never saw their descriptions realised before.[110]

Luton Hoo was quiet, but oppressive in its stateliness and a melancholy house, whereas Wharncliffe was a place of peace and contentment—the kind of retreat from the world found in romantic fiction. This notion of home as a haven echoes the sentiments of John Williams and comes through particularly strongly in William Money's description of his domestic routine at home in Yatesbury, especially as an escape from the 'Heathenish life' in Weymouth and London.[111] Simple routines provided contentment and built up a bank of happy memories linking family and home.

Given such sentimental attachment to home as a physical and emotional place, it is unsurprising that people missed this comfort when away from home. Sons sent away to school often expressed feelings of homesickness or its physical manifestation as nostalgia.[112] They missed not only the physical comforts of home but also the familiarity of domestic routines and the emotional comfort of family. Sent to a small Catholic academy in Bruges after a very unhappy year in Antwerp, the young Richard Huddlestone was not only removed to the alien environment of school but was also away from England. Writing to his father, Ferdinand Huddlestone, in the winter of 1786, he noted that:

I was always very low & sometimes extremely melancholy, but besides this when the winter came on so far from having a fire in my own room which my Dear Mama would be glad to know in her letter, what we had below stairs could scarce be called a fire, so that I never suffered so much cold in my Life, which together with other Inconveniences such as Mr Hubertte's morose & sullen temper at times, the extreme dirtiness of the Chamber in which we sat was not swept for a month together, & the Windows never being opened gave me such a disgust of it that I did not doubt but were my Dear Papa & Mama to know these particulars they would be the first to have me moved.[113]

Physical and emotional discomfort compound in making the young man long for home as the antithesis of his present plight. He yearned for the creature comforts of not only a warming fire and domestic cleanliness, but also the contentment of being with family and in familiar surroundings.

Boys and young men expressed these longings with an intensity at least partly born of a hope that they would be allowed to escape their exile and return to the family home. The most frequent response from parents was to refuse any such requests, the separation being seen as important in building character, self-reliance and independence.[114] In February 1800, Juliana Mary Buxton wrote to her son, John Jacob, that his complaint about the cold at his school in Middlesex 'is rather a proof that too much tenderness at home is a bad thing as it makes school seem the more hard . . . good sense will help you get the better of these little things'.[115] She thus problematised the comforts of home: not only had physical and emotional tenderness made him soft, but his hardships—and by implication the comforts with which they were contrasted—were 'little things', unimportant in the grander scheme of life. Her aim, of course, was to cultivate an appropriate manly stoicism, yet generations of public schoolboys went on to create, with the help of their wives, just the kind of domestic contentment and comfort that John Jacob so sorely missed.

Much the same was true of young men travelling on the Grand Tour, who, as Goldsmith makes clear, often expressed feelings of homesickness. They missed both the physical comforts of home and the familiarity of domestic routines, and the emotional comfort of family.[116] For Grand Tourists, notions of home were layered with home country, with its familiar norms and customs. In this context, small reminders of home and family were extremely important; William Fitzgerald, for instance, treasured a miniature of his mother, noting the comfort it afforded 'to think I have you in my pocket'.[117] Grown men, with many of these virtues firmly established in their character, could express similar discomfort at being away and a longing to return home. As we have already seen, this was a recurrent theme in the correspondence of William and Emma Money. When travelling, he longed for not only a comfortable bed (free from bugs) but also the comfort of companionship.[118] In contrast, when visiting his brother James at Homme House in Herefordshire, he commended the improvements which had rendered it modern and convenient, and wrote approvingly of the vicarage in which their friends Mary and Ernle 'seem to live very comfortably', looked after by five servants. Crucially, he also noted that 'nothing can be more delightful than the harmony which appears to prevail between these two families'.[119] A comfortable and happy home depended on physical ease and emotional contentment.

If people temporarily removed from home could express feelings of discomfort, it is unsurprising that those permanently leaving homes in which they had spent many happy years should try to maintain something of those memories and associations. At Audley End, Sir John Griffin Griffin's widow, Katherine, felt the loss of her husband deeply and expressed this in terms of her experience of daily routines and spaces.[120] She wrote in June 1797 to her husband's successor, Richard Aldworth, that her loss was 'felt acutely to day as I have recommenced our usual morning Duty in the Chapel & breakfasted in the Saloon Window'.[121] When she moved out a few weeks later, she wrote again to Aldworth, wishing 'comfort to yourself & affectionate recollection' of those 'who have inhabited it with so much delight for such a number of years'.[122] The end of this happiness came both with her husband's death and with having to move out of Audley End, sentiments that echoed those expressed 14 years by her stepmother, Louisa Clayton. When required to give up Harleyford in favour of the next generation, she had written of 'the sad sensation of which my coming from a place which I have known such true & contented happiness coud not fail of exciting'.[123] Katherine could at least find some comfort in Aldworth's reassurances of continuity in the domestic regimen, writing that it was 'a real consolation to my mind to find you speak in such terms of a place I must ever dearly love & of faithful servants to whom I owe sincere regard'.[124]

Conclusion

Home is made of emotional attachments to objects and people as well as the material trappings of physical ease. It was constructed around relationships with objects that held emotional significance, often because of the associations they carried of other people and other places. This much is clear from the growing literature on emotions and things. What I have highlighted in this chapter are the ways in which memory and remembering played a huge part in cementing these affective connections between things, people and spaces, and thus in the construction of home. Neither Henrietta Cavendish's pictorial family tree nor George Hammond Lucy's armorial stained glass turned their houses into homes, but the de Geer portraits, collected together at Lövstabruk may have done more to link them with their immediate ancestors and Mary Elizabeth Lucy's collection of miniatures were certainly charged with emotional memories of family and home. Memory materialised in everyday objects underpinned the role of diachronic as well as wider kin in building emotional bonds and offering comfort. The association of things and people was often powerful and enduring, especially when object biographies were retold to self and others. Household objects could be kept 'warm', to use in Epp and Price's language, through a repeated narration of their personal and familial significance as well their everyday use. At the same time, objects could help to carry memory across time and space, especially as they were gifted or bequeathed. They not only stimulated remembering but also went beyond the individual: memory, like the goods themselves, passing down generations and tying one home to another.

As was noted at the start of this chapter, things are good for not only feeling with, but also remembering with; they had memorial as well as emotional value. Things, people and memory were thus entangled in webs that spread over space and time, but it is in their association with or collection in a particular place that they helped to produce feelings of home. This links to Bachelard's assertion that the house and its various spaces formed containers of memories. Ellen Weeton's work basket, Mrs. Forth's cupboard, the old church at Charlecote or the material and written house created by Richard Neville were all receptacles holding memories of family in the material objects they contained. Conceived in this way, home was a lived space, occupied by family and friends who offered social and emotional comfort. It was also a place of memories and sentimental attachment and lay at the centre of a web of people–object–place relationships that were not only about the present but also about the past.

Notes

1. Judith Lewis, 'When a House Is Not a Home: Elite English Women and the Eighteenth-Century Country House', *Journal of British Studies*, 48 (2009), 336–63. See also Terence Dooley, Maeve O-Riordan, and Christopher Ridgway (eds.), *Women and the Country House in Ireland and Britain* (Dublin: Four Courts Press, 2018).
2. See, for example: Grant McCracken, *Culture and Consumption: New Approaches to the Symbolic Character of Consumer Goods and Activities* (Bloomington and Indianapolis: Indiana University Press, 1988); Jennifer Germann and Heidi Strobel (eds.), *Materializing Gender in Eighteenth-Century Europe* (London: Routledge, 2016); Johanna Ilmakunnas and Jon Stobart (eds.), *A Taste for Luxury in Early Modern Europe* (London: Bloomsbury, 2017); Tara Hamling and Catherine Richardson, *A Day at Home in Early Modern England* (New Haven: Yale University Press, 2017).
3. Stephanie Downes, Sally Holloway, and Sarah Randles (eds.), *Feeling Things: Objects and Emotions Through History* (Oxford: Oxford University Press, 2018), 4. See also Daniel Millar, *The Comfort of Things* (Cambridge: Polity Press, 2011).
4. John Styles, *Threads of Feeling: The London Foundling Hospital's Textile Tokens, 1740–1770* (London: The Foundling Hospital Museum, 2010); Rowena Willard-Wright, 'Home from Home? Making Life Comfortable in Victorian Barracks', in Jon Stobart (ed.), *The Comforts of Home in Western Europe, 1700–1900* (London: Bloomsbury, 2020), 191–6.
5. Tara Hamling, 'Household Objects', in Susan Broomhall (ed.), *Early Modern Emotions: An Introduction* (London: Routledge, 2017), 135. See also Ann Rosalin Jones and Peter Stallybrass, *Renaissance Clothing and the Materials of Memory* (Cambridge: Cambridge University Press, 2000); Ariane Fennetaux, 'Sentimental Economics: Recycling Textiles in Eighteenth-Century Britain', in Ariane Fennetaux, Amelie Junqua, and Sophie Vasset (eds.), *The Afterlife of Used Things: Recycling in the Long Eighteenth Century* (London: Routledge, 2015), 122–41.
6. Lewis, 'When a House Is Not a Home'.
7. Marius Kwint, 'Introduction: The Physical Past', in Marius Kwint, Christopher Breward, and Jeremy Aynsley (eds.), *Material Memories* (Oxford: Oxford University Press, 1999), 2. See also Stephanie Downes, Sally Holloway, and Sarah Randles, 'A Feeling for Things, Past and Present', in Stephanie Downes, Sally Holloway, and Sarah Randles (eds.), *Feeling Things:*

Objects and Emotions Through History (Oxford: Oxford University Press, 2018), 8–23.

8. Gaston Bachelard, *The Poetics of Space* (London: Penguin, 1964). See also Yannis Hamilakis, 'Sensorial Assemblages: Affect, Memory and Temporality in Assemblage Thinking', *Cambridge Archaeological Journal*, 27:1 (2017), 169–82.

9. McCracken, *Culture and Consumption*, 44–56; Miller, *Comfort of Things*.

10. Downes *et al.*, 'A Feeling for Things', 13.

11. See Hamilakis, 'Sensorial Assemblages'.

12. Bill Brown, 'Thing Theory', *Critical Inquiry*, 28:1 (2001), 1–22. Brown argues that objects become things when they stop working for people; as their normal role in daily life is interrupted, the relationship between object and subject is transformed, highlighting the way in which the thing refers less to an object and more to a particular subject–object relation.

13. Amanda Vickery, *Behind Closed Doors: At Home in Georgian England* (New Haven: Yale University Press, 2009), 231–57. See also John Fowler and John Cornforth, *English Decoration in the Eighteenth Century* (London: Barrie and Jenkins, 1974), 253; Anne Bermingham, 'Elegant Females and Gentlemen Connoisseurs: The Commerce in Culture and Self-Image in Eighteenth-Century England', in John Brewer and Anne Bermingham (eds.), *The Consumption of Culture, 1660–2800: Image, Object, Text* (London: Routledge, 1995), 489–513; Johanna Ilmakunnas, 'Embroidering Women and Turning Men: Handiwork, Gender, and Emotions in Sweden and Finland, c. 1720–1820', *Scandinavian Journal of History*, 41:3 (2016), 306–31.

14. Vickery, *Behind Closed Doors*, 246.

15. Margaret Jones, 'A Cure for Untidiness?', *Country Life*, 28 March 1957.

16. See Guy Fletcher, 'Sentimental Value', *Journal of Value Inquiry*, 43:1 (2009), 55–65.

17. Sarah Holloway, 'Materializing Maternal Emotions: Birth, Celebration and Renunciation in England, c.1688–1830', in Stephanie Downes, Sally Holloway, and Sarah Randles (eds.), *Feeling Things: Objects and Emotions Through History* (Oxford: Oxford University Press, 2018), 162. See also, Hamling, 'Household Objects'.

18. Sarah Chauncey Woolsey (ed.), *The Autobiography and Correspondence of Mrs Delany*, vol. 2 (Boston: Roberts Brothers, 1879), 97: Mary Delany to Anne Dewes, [no date] 1729.

19. Chauncey Woolsey, *Autobiography and Correspondence of Mrs Delany*, vol. 1, 220: Mary Delany to Anne Dewes, 23 April 1741.

20. Chauncey Woolsey, *Autobiography and Correspondence of Mrs Delany*, vol. 1, 379, note 162.

21. Lena Cowen Orlin, 'Empty Vessels', in Tara Hamling and Catherine Richardson (eds.), *Everyday Objects: Medieval and Early Modern Material Culture and Its Meanings* (Farnham: Ashgate, 2010), 299–308; Alice Dolan, 'Touching Linen: Textiles, Emotion and Bodily Intimacy in England c.1708–1818', *Cultural and Social History*, 16:2 (2019), 145–64.

22. Maxine Berg, 'Women's Consumption and the Industrial Classes of Eighteenth-Century England', *Journal of Social History*, 30 (1996), 415–34.

23. Dolan, 'Touching Linen', 151.

24. Jon Stobart, 'Housekeeper, Correspondent and Confidante: The Under-Told Story of Mrs Hayes of Charleocte Park', *Family and Community History*, 21:2 (2018), 96–111.

25. Alice Fairfax-Lucy, *Charlecote and the Lucys* (London: Victor Gollanz Ltd, 1990), 221.

26. Lewis, 'When a House Is Not a Home'.
27. Shakespeare Central Library and Archives (SCLA), DR 671 56 List of rings and brooches given by Mary Leigh.
28. The National Archives (TNA), PROB 11/1448/37: will of The Honourable Mary Leigh of Stoneleigh Abbey, 5 August 1806.
29. TNA, PROB 11/1448/37.
30. Fletcher, 'Sentimental Value'. See also Berg, 'Women's Consumption'.
31. Mairi Macdonald, 'Not Unmarked by Some Eccentricities: The Leigh Family of Stoneleigh Abbey', in Robert Bearman (ed.), *Stoneleigh Abbey: The House, Its Owners, Its Lands* (Straford-upon-Avon: Shakespeare Birthplace Trust, 2004), 150–1.
32. TNA, PROB 11/1144/223, will of The Right Honourable Edward, Lord Leigh, Baron of Stoneleigh, 22 July 1786.
33. Edward Leigh was a member of the Catch Club in London—dedicated to promote and perform the singing of catches and glees.
34. Elsie Donald (ed.), *Mistress of Charlecote: The Memoirs of Mary Elizabeth Lucy, 1803–1889* (1983; London: Orion, 2002), 32.
35. On the processes through which household objects could be "warmed" with associations of family and home, see Amber Epp and Linda Price, 'The Storied Life of Singularized Objects: Forces of Agency and Network Transformation', *Journal of Consumer Research*, 36:5 (2010), 820–37.
36. Quoted in Fairfax-Lucy, *Charlecote and the Lucys*, 262.
37. Amanda Vickery, *The Gentleman's Daughter: Women's Lives in Georgian England* (New Haven: Yale University Press, 1998), 381–2.
38. Ellen Weeton, *Miss Weeton's Journal of a Governess, 1807–1825*, vol. 2 (Oxford: Oxford University Press, 1939), 325. This incident is also discussed in Fennetaux, 'Sentimental Economics', 134.
39. Weeton, *Miss Weeton's Journal of a Governess*, 326.
40. Chauncey Woolsey, *Autobiography and Correspondence of Mrs Delany*, vol. 1, 465: Mary Delany to Anne Dewes, 10 March 1744.
41. Emily Climenson (ed.), *Passages form the Diaries of Mrs Philip Lybbe Powys* (London: Longmans, Green and Co., 1899), 54.
42. Kate Retford, 'Patrilineal Portraiture? Gender and Genealogy in the Eighteenth-Century English Country House', in John Styles and Amanda Vickery (eds.), *Gender, Taste and Material Culture in Britain and North America, 1700–1830* (New Haven: Yale University Press, 2006), 315–44.
43. Retford, 'Patrilineal Portraiture', 327.
44. Karl Johan Eklund, 'Husen och miljön', in Ann-Charlotte Ljungholm (ed.), *Lövstabruk: Ej Sin Like I Hela Riket* (Uppsala: Stiftelsen Leufsta, 2011), 27–36.
45. See Hanneke Ronnes, 'A Sense of Heritage: Renewal Versus Preservation in the English and Dutch Palaces of William III in the 18th Century', in Jon Stobart and Andrew Hann (eds.), *The Country House: Material Culture and Consumption* (Swindon: Historic England, 2016), 78–9.
46. Chauncey Woolsey, *Autobiography and Correspondence of Mrs Delany*, vol. 2,: Mary Delany to Anne Dewes, 7 September 1756.
47. Elizabeth Carter, *A Series of Letters Between Mrs. Elizabeth Carter and Miss Catherine Talbot, from the Year 1741 To 1770*, vol. 4 (London: F. C. And J. Rivington, 1809), 32–3: Catherine Talbot to Elizabeth Carter, 23 May 1743.
48. Carter, *A Series of Letters*.
49. Mary Coke, *The Letters and Journals of Lady Mary Coke, vol. 1, 1756–1767* (1889, reprinted, Bath: Kingsmead Reprints, 1970), 112: January 1767.
50. SCLA, DR18/31/903 Inventory of Leighton Buzzard, 1749; DR18/4/27 Inventory of Stoneleigh Abbey, 1749.

51. SCLA, DR18/4/43, Inventory of Stoneleigh Abbey 1774, with amendments in 1806.
52. Brown, 'Thing Theory'.
53. Coke, *The Letters and Journals of Lady Mary Coke*, vol. 1, 245: 22 May 1767.
54. Arianne Fennetaux, 'Toying with Novelty: Toys, Consumption and Novelty in Eighteenth-Century Britain', in Bruno Blondé, Natacha Coquery, Jon Stobart, and Ilja Van Damme (eds.), *Fashioning Old and New: Changing Consumer Patterns in Western Europe (1650–1900)* (Turnhout: Brepols, 2009), 17–28; Jenni Dixon, 'The Toyshop, the Cabinet and Eighteenth-Century Curiosity', *History of Retailing and Consumption*, 5:3 (2019), 205–27.
55. See Downes *et al.*, 'A Feeling for Things'.
56. Sarah Goldsmith, 'Nostalgia, Homesickness and Emotional Formation on the Eighteenth-Century Grand Tour', *Cultural and Social History*, 15:3 (2018), 345.
57. Quoted in Goldsmith, 'Nostalgia', 345: letters dated 16 December 1766 and 3 February 1767.
58. Wiltshire Record Office (WiRO), 1720/829 (transcript), 16: William Money to Emma Money, [no date] September 1808.
59. WiRO, 1720/829 (transcript), 21: William Money to Emma Money, [no date] September 1808.
60. WiRO, 1720/829 (transcript), 144: Emma Money to William Money, 17 July 1817.
61. WiRO, 1720/829 (transcript), 18: Emma Money to William Money, 28 September 1808.
62. Donald, *Mistress of Charlecote*, 56.
63. Kwint, 'Introduction'.
64. Katie Barclay, 'Family and Household', in Susan Broomhall (ed.), *Early Modern Emotions* (London: Routledge, 2017), 244–6.
65. Kate Smith, 'Imperial Families: Women Writing Home in Georgian Britain', *Women's History Review*, 24 (2015), 843–60.
66. Goldsmith, 'Nostalgia', 345. See also Susan Whyman, *The Pen and the People: English Letter Writers, 1660–1800* (Oxord: Oxford University Press, 2009), 226–7.
67. Warwickshire Record Office (WRO), L6/1532, Lady Margaret Williams to Mary Elizabeth Lucy, no date, December 1823.
68. See Donald, *Mistress of Charlecote*.
69. Chauncey Woolsey, *Autobiography and Correspondence of Mrs Delany*, vol. 1, 275: Mary Delany to Anne Dewes, 3 April 1744.
70. Northamptonshire Record Office (NRO), D(CA) 903b: Elizabeth Dryden to Mrs Steele, 13 January 1817.
71. Bachelard, *Poetics of Space*, 105.
72. Miller, *Comfort of Things*.
73. McCracken, *Cultures of Consumption*, 45.
74. McCracken, *Cultures of Consumption*, 45–6.
75. Jules Prown, 'The Truth of Material Culture', in Jules Prown and Kenneth Haltman (eds.), *American Artefacts: Essays in Material Culture* (East Lansing, MI: Michigan State University Press, 2000), 1–19.
76. See Lewis, 'When a House Is Not a Home'; Vickery, *Behind Closed Doors*, 207–30; Ellen Filor, '"No Lady Could Do This": Navigating Gender and Collecting Objects in India and Scotland, c.1810–50', in Jon Stobart (ed.), *Travel and the British Country House: Cultures, Critiques ad Consumption in the Long Eighteenth Century* (Manchester: Manchester University Press, 2017), 206–24.
77. Quoted in Lewis, 'When a House Is Not a Home', 347.
78. Epp and Price, 'Storied Life of Singularized Objects'.

79. Vickery, *Behind Closed Doors*, 224–5.
80. Quoted in Vickery, *Behind Closed Doors*, 225.
81. Alfred Gell, *Art and Agency: A New Anthropological Theory* (Oxford: Oxford University Press, 1998), 16.
82. Bachelard, *Poetics of Space*, 30.
83. Filor, ' "No Lady Could Do This" ', 214–21.
84. Margot Finn and Kate Smith, *The East India Company at Home, 1757–1857* (London: UCL Press, 2017).
85. Filor, ' "No Lady Could Do This" ', 215–17.
86. NRO, D(CA) 904, Inventory of Canons Ashby, 1819.
87. NRO, D(CA) 361, Elizabeth Dryden to Mrs Steele, 29 October 1822.
88. NRO, D(CA) 903b, Elizabeth Dryden to Mrs Steele, 13 January 1817.
89. Epp and Price, 'Storied Life of Singularized Objects'.
90. NRO, D(CA) 904, Inventory of Canons Ashby, 1819.
91. Quoted in Mark Girouard, *Life in the French Country House* (London: Cassell & Co., 2000), 182.
92. Girouard, *French Country House*, 299–300.
93. Quoted in Fairfax-Lucy, *Charlecote and the Lucys*, 239.
94. Clive Wainwright, *The Romantic Interior* (New Haven: Yale University Press, 1989), 225–40.
95. WRO, L6/1144, Thomas Willement to George Lucy, [no date] 1837. See also Wainwright, *Romantic Interior*, 219–25.
96. Wainwright, *Romantic Interior*, 228–9. In reality, they were seventeenth-century products of Indian workshops, but this does little to detract from their ability to memorialise past events.
97. Hannah Chavasse, 'Material Culture and the Country House: Fashion, Comfort and Lineage' (Unpublished PhD thesis, University of Northampton, 2015), 200–9.
98. Richard Griffin, Lord Braybrooke, *The History of Audley End: To Which Are Appended Notices of the Town and Parish of Saffron Walden in the County of Essex* (London: Samuel Bentley, 1836), 118. See also Chavasse, 'Material Culture and the Country House', 217–18.
99. John Cornforth, *Early Georgian Interiors* (New Haven: Yale University Press, 2004), 13–19.
100. SCLA, DR18/4/59, inventory of Stoneleigh Abbey, 1806.
101. NRO, D(CA) 901, inventory of Canons Ashby, 1717.
102. Jane Austen, *Northanger Abbey* (1818; Oxford: Oxford University Press, 1980), 149, 155.
103. Bachelard, *Poetics of Space*, 30.
104. Fairfax-Lucy, *Charlecote and the Lucys*, 286. The author is quite scathing about the new chapel, describing it as a pastiche replacing a genuinely old and meaningful structure.
105. Donald, *Mistress of Charlecote*, 81–2.
106. Mihaly Csikszentmihalyi and Eugene Rochberg-Halton, *The Meaning of Things: Domestic Symbols and the Self* (Cambridge: Cambridge University Press, 1981), 121.
107. WRO, L6/1539a, John Williams to Mary Elizabeth Lucy, 15 March 1824.
108. WRO, L6/1545, John Williams to Mary Elizabeth Lucy, 23 June 1844.
109. See, for example, Henry French and Mark Rothery, 'Male Anxiety Among Younger Sons of the English Landed Gentry', *The Historical Journal*, 62:4 (2019), 967–95.
110. Alice Clark (ed.), *Gleanings from an Old Portfolio Containing Some Correspondence Between Lady Louisa Stuart and Her Sister, Caroline,*

Countess of Portarlington and Other Friends and Relatives, vol. 2 (Edinburgh, 1895), 18: Lady Louisa Stuart to Lady Caroline Dawson, 15 July 1778.

111. WiRO, 1720/829 (transcript), 103, 147: William Money to Emma Money, 25 June 1814, 3 September 1817.

112. Henry French and Mark Rothery, *Man's Estate: Landed Gentry Masculinities, 1660–1900* (Oxford: Oxford University Press, 2012), 52–74, 143–54; Goldsmith, 'Nostalgia'.

113. Cambridge Records Office, 488/C2/HD196, Richard Huddlestone to Ferdinand Huddlestone, 31 January 1786.

114. French and Rothery, *Man's Estate*, 67–74.

115. Quoted in French and Rothery, *Man's Estate*, 68.

116. Goldsmith, 'Nostalgia'; French and Rothery, *Man's Estate*, 67–74.

117. Quoted in Goldsmith, 'Nostalgia', 345: letter dated 3 February 1767.

118. WiRO, 1720/829 (transcript), 2, 15, 16: William Money to Emma Money, 20 May 1805, [no date] September 1808, [no date] September 1808.

119. WiRO, 1720/829 (transcript), 157: William Money to Emma Money, 26 September 1817.

120. For a more general discussion, see Chavasse, 'Material Culture and the Country House', 164–7.

121. Essex Record Office (ERO) D/DBy C40: Katherine Griffin Griffin to Richard Aldworth Griffin, second Lord Braybrooke, 9 June 1797.

122. ERO, D/DBy C40: Katherine Griffin Griffin to Richard Aldworth Griffin, second Lord Braybrooke, 25 June 1797.

123. Quoted in Chavasse, 'Material Culture and the Country House', 164: Louisa Clayton to William Clayton, 10 August 1783.

124. ERO, D/DBy C6/6: Katherine Griffin Griffin to Richard Aldworth Griffin, second Lord Braybrooke, 29 September 1797. See also Kate Smith, 'Warfield Park, Berkshire: Longing, Belonging and the British Country House', in Margot Finn and Kate Smith (eds.), *The East India Company at Home, 1757–1857* (London: UCL Press, 2018), 175–90.

Conclusions
House and Home

In September 2020, a property on Air B&B advertised itself as providing 'country house comfort'; the same promise was made by a hotel in Perthshire, whilst another in Somerset offered the opportunity to 'experience luxury and comfort' in a 'luxurious Georgian country house'.[1] All these elide the country house with ideas of superior material comfort and imply that this association is both unproblematic and axiomatic. This contrasts sharply with the experiences and complaints of many country-house owners in the eighteenth century, and the arguments of John Crowley, Jean DeJean and others, who have highlighted the concerted effort by wealthy householders in Britain, America and France to make their houses more comfortable places to live.[2] This book has sought to highlight the country house as a place where physical and emotional comfort came together and were combined with ideas of social comfort to produce a particular domestic milieu. In doing so, it has tried to take a different view of the country house—one that gives more weight to the ways in which people interacted and felt about their surroundings—and has argued that home was important to a highly mobile elite as an ideal that linked them to place and people as well as things. The emotions and needs that they expressed in terms of comfort had deep roots and broad implications: basic human needs remained remarkably constant over space and time, even for a wealthy elite. They may have made their houses more convenient and comfortable, but they retained the need for solace and support, and to feel a sense of belonging.

Being and Feeling Comfortable

For many country-house owners, comfort meant physical and material well-being. The scale and form of many country houses—even those of relatively modest proportions—brought particular challenges in this regard, and it is possible to see the eighteenth century as a period when being comfortable became a key priority for many householders, much as Crowley argues. Adequate heating was a particular concern as cold brought discomfort and discontent, as the complaints of Horace Walpole

DOI: 10.4324/9781003206361-10

and many others make clear Lighting drew fewer negative comments, despite the dark interiors revealed in many paintings; it was the brilliance of a well-lit room that excited more interest. This might reflect the inconvenience rather than the discomfort of traditional forms of lighting: candles created pools of light and required frequent snuffing, and fires often failed to provide adequate heat for anyone beyond their immediate glow. The emphasis that is often placed on technological solutions to these problems serves to bring the comfort of the domestic realm into the sphere of Enlightenment science. Certainly, there was the widespread adoption of Rumford-style stoves in many English country houses in the final third of the eighteenth century, the thermal benefits of which should not be underestimated. However, the more radical and arguably more efficient system proposed by Gauger had little traction, and free-standing stoves were rarely installed in English country houses, despite their efficiency and efficacy.

Much the same might be argued of Argand lamps. They were bought by many house owners around the turn of the nineteenth century, but candles remained the key light source, even after major refurbishments such as that undertaken at Stoneleigh Abbey in the 1810s by James Henry Leigh. The rejection of stoves because of the nature of the heat and the airless atmosphere they created points to cultural differences across Europe in the level and quality of heat that was desirable. The English were not exceptional in their desire for well-ventilated as well as warm rooms: similar preferences were apparent in France. However, their attachment to the fireplace, albeit modified and burning coal, not only reflects different cultural norms but also questions functionalist approaches to comfort. Being comfortably warm meant different things to different people, as the mutual incomprehension of English and Swedish travellers confirms. It also relied on the presence of a wide array of other domestic objects, from carpets and curtains to chandeliers and lamp stands. Importantly, investment in these allowed householders the opportunity to augment their comfort and display their status. James Henry Leigh undoubtedly made his rooms more convenient by improving the level of lighting, but he also displayed his wealth and taste.

That comfort augmented rather than replaced gentility as a cultural and material priority is also apparent in changing attitudes to furniture. The trajectory of bodily comfort traced by William Cowper was perhaps a little too simplistic; but the spread of armed chairs, easy chairs and sofas is apparent from paintings and inventories. Rooms were transformed by the acquisition of such furniture, as is apparent from the inventories for Colworth House and Stoneleigh Abbey, where the pace of change quickened by the early nineteenth century. So too were the ways in which people sat and interacted with others. There was a direct link to physical posture in which we might argue for the agency of objects in shaping human action. Just as profound, however, is the way that assemblages of the furniture helped to transform social practice. Arrangements of furniture in a room made for comfort and convenience, especially when sofas were combined with low tables, workboxes and mobile writing desks, as is apparent from paintings of Elton Hall, Cassiobury and elsewhere. Arrangements of rooms in the house, especially when linked by corridors and back stairs, increasingly enhanced convenience and privacy, and facilitated the specialisation of rooms, as the writings of Roger North, Jacques-François Blondel and others attest. In this, we can see something of the scaling of assemblages theorised by Deleuze and Gutarri (objects in a room and rooms in a house), a point to which we return later.[3]

Tensions between aesthetics and taste on the one hand, and convenience on the other, were apparent at the scale of both the house and the room, and they persisted through the eighteenth century and beyond. The well-known debates over how best to make classical (or gothic) houses conform with architectural principles whilst providing convenient accommodation were repeated at the scale of the room in terms of balancing the visual and aesthetic impact of a sofa with the desire for flexible and informal arrangements. This tension played out on the pages of Ackermann's *Repository* and in the furniture bought by James Henry Leigh in the 1810s: both combined large immobile and fashionable pieces (Grecian sofas and ottomans, for instance), with others that were small, versatile and ingenious (library chairs or writing desks).

Beds could be rendered more comfortable through the use of better-quality feathers, but this reflected status distinctions as much as bodily requirements; only with the invalid or infirm did comfort take priority, with a range of patent furniture being developed, especially in the early nineteenth century. Bodily comfort was certainly a growing priority when it came to bed bugs, which were increasingly seen as an intolerable discomfort rather than an inevitable inconvenience. Here, Southall's 1730 treatise was important both in highlighting a problem and providing a solution through the commercial provision of fumigation treatments. In many respects, however, he reinforced rather than revolutionised a concern with hygiene and the proper airing of beds and rooms. Servants' guides throughout the eighteenth century were clear on this point and on the role of servants in facilitating the comfort of their employers through their labour in cleaning rooms and washing linen. From the householder's perspective, the housekeeping book of Susanna Whatman and the correspondence of Elizabeth Dryden and others make clear that furnishings, rooms and houses needed to be properly cleaned and aired.

Here again, we can see how an emphasis on comfort did not preclude other concerns. A clean bed meant greater bodily comfort: a restful night's sleep and the absence of painful and unsightly bites. It also signalled respectability and thus the ability to feel comfortable and at ease, as well to be comfortable in a physical sense. This is what I have called social comfort and forms an important aspect of what comfort meant to country-house owners. At one level, social comfort equated to a general sense of material well-being—a comfortable living—but, more specifically, it involved house owners matching expected norms and feeling at one with their situation. As Woodruff Smith noted, cleanliness was tied not only to virtue but also to notions of a well-run household, as seen in the concern shown by Elizabeth Dryden following the theft from her husband's London house, and elsewhere in studies by Harvey, Whittle and Griffiths, and others.[4]

The parameters of social comfort shifted over the course of the long eighteenth century as the priorities of cleanliness and virtue were increasingly overlain with those of informality.[5] However, there was also a tension between the two. Informal room arrangements and sociability made the country house feel comfortable in comparison with more rigid physical and social regimens that persisted in other parts of Europe and in London society. This contrast was most apparent to those coming to the English country house from elsewhere and is exemplified in the reaction of foreign visitors such as Pückler-Muskau and Washington Irving. That said, the reaction of English people encountering unfamiliar formality is telling: Lady Louisa Stuart's disappointment at the room arrangements at Archerfield in 1799 contrasts with the Revd Stotherd Abdy's unaffected account of informal and ad hoc sociability at Welford in 1770. Yet informality could also be challenging. Sofas, it seems, were not an appropriate prop for the subjects of Arthur Devis' mid-eighteenth-century paintings, in which they are pushed to the margins, the sitters feeling more socially comfortable being portrayed on upright or elbow chairs. Into the early nineteenth century, by which time informality held sway, Richard Aldworth could still lament the lack of structure to the daily routine at Stowe, even in terms of mealtimes.

One way of understanding this tension and the anxieties that informality could bring is to recognise the importance of control in giving a sense of comfort. At one level, this involved control of emotions and links to elite masculine ideals as discussed by French and Rothery. At another, it is about control of the domestic domain. We can see this in the discomfort of Sybille Reventlow that arose from her lack of control over who stayed as guests in her house at Brahetrolleborg and in Aldworth Griffin's frustration at Stowe. It is also apparent in the growing and persistent desire for privacy. The ultimate in controlled access, privacy and thus social comfort came in the form of the villa, but it ties more generally to notions of home as a place to relax and escape from the world—an ideal to which Horace Walpole was very much alive. Within the country house, controlling access allowed for privacy in bedchambers or dressing rooms and, when moving through the house, allowed one to avoid both servants and guests, as Roger North observed. The removal of such privacy made even the enthusiastic Pückler-Muskau despair: he felt obliged to write his letters in the public rooms, but sometimes longed to escape to his bedchamber.

Feeling comfortable was intimately tied up with emotions in ways that connected to older-established meanings of comfort as solace and consolation. Comfort derived from other people: friends and especially family. The ideals and parodies of satirical prints highlight the interrelationship between physical and emotional comfort, and the centrality of marriage to a comfortable and contented domestic life. Importantly, a loving marriage was key to domestic comfort throughout the eighteenth century; the language of comfort shaped the way that husbands and wives communicated their feelings. From Richard Coffin in the 1680s to William and Emma Money in the 1810s, married couples often described and declared their relationships in terms of comfort. In this sense, comfort might be viewed as a gentle emotion, but its absence could bring disappointment and disillusion, even anger. This was most apparent in terms of the comfort expected from children. Whilst Sir Roger Newdigate could point a grieving mother to the consolation of her children, Elizabeth Dryden railed about the lack of comfort she was afforded by her miscreant offspring. This, and the poisoned relationship of Ashe and Elizabeth Windham in the 1710s, show how failure and dysfunction can serve to highlight the human relationships that were central to a comfortable marriage and home, much as Rowlandson's turn of the century satirical prints suggest.

The country house was the physical setting for these relationships. Felbrigg Hall became an unwelcome and uncomfortable place for Elizabeth Windham, and Elizabeth's Dryden's troubled relationship with her children was intimately bound up with ownership, occupation and control of the family seat at Canons Ashby. In most cases, however, the country house offered myriad spaces for familial interaction and a large pool of family, friends and servants from whom comfort and solace might be sought. The provision of mutual affection, comfort and contentment made family an important emotional community—one that could be consciously created through the reproduction of behavioural norms within the country house, as is apparent from the ways in which William and Emma Money raised their children. This places the focus on the modern nuclear family, but the construction of a community of comfort frequently drew in a wider circle of family and friends. Sisters emerge as more important and perhaps more reliable sources of comfort than were brothers, a finding which confirms the kinds of fraternal relationships described by French and Rothery.[6] The role of servants in this respect is perhaps more surprising, but significant nonetheless. Phillipa Hayes was exceptional in her social proximity to her employer, but Mary Leigh also drew comfort from her relationship with the family lawyer, and Grand Tourists drew heavily on servants for both physical and emotional comfort.

Letters were crucial in articulating these emotional communities and communicating comfort between family and friends. At one level, of course, they replaced the everyday interaction and small acts of affection and comfort that could pass between people living in the same country house. As such, the receipt of letters was, in itself, a source of comfort; conversely, their absence was a cause of distress and discomfort, as Sir Roger Newdigate, Emma Money and many others made clear to their correspondents. Letters were emotional channels, communicating affection and fidelity, and reinforcing affective bonds strained by the distance between people. Comfort also came from the content of letters. The provision of everyday news kept the recipient up-to-date and maintained their position within the affective group—hence we see Louisa Stuart and Lady Mohun, for example, revelling in the minutiae of daily life. In this, the country house could become an emotional resource with which those away from home could associate. This happened in a number of different ways. Being kept informed of the well-being of children and parents linked both William and Emma Money into family life in their marital and parental homes; updates on building work or programmes of redecoration involved them in the processes through which the fabric of the building was moulded to current needs and tastes—an interest which George Lucy clearly maintained, despite his protests of indifference; and information on daily routines helped them feel part of the emotional community which the country house embodied and contained, as is apparent from the correspondence of Louisa Stuart, Mary Delany and many others. Whilst there was a difference between comfortable and uncomfortable letters—the distinction was marked by the nature of the news they contained and the impact they had on the recipient—all had the power to connect the writer and reader, bringing together through mutual correspondence the chairs, rooms and houses that they respectively occupied.

The materiality of letters could also be a source of comfort. As Kate Smith has argued, they formed a tangible link between distant family or friends—one that was sustained by the durability of paper and ink. Letters were thus a source of comfort at the moment of receipt and reading, when reread later and when carefully stored as an embodiment of the relationship that created them. Mary Delany may have burnt some sensitive letters, but she kept many more because of their emotional significance. Importantly, this durability meant that letters could link people and offer comfort across time as well as space. They not only articulated syncretic relationships but also drew together family in a diachronic sense. The importance of lineage and pedigree to the titled owners of country houses is commonplace, but emotional bonds with diachronic family could also be powerful. We see this in the arrangement of pictures at Stoneleigh Abbey, but perhaps more profoundly in the memorialisation of family at Charlecote Park. The collection of miniatures commissioned and gazed on by Mary Elizabeth Lucy and her recollection of family events and relationships through the private chapel in the grounds at Charlecote both point to the significance of family and the emotional power and comfort deriving from material objects. Significantly, it was the memory of family as much as their synchronic presence that was important to Mary Elizabeth Lucy.

This points to the wider importance of things being good for remembering with and for reinforcing family bonds. The process of telling her daughter something of her family history through material objects was important to Ellen Weeton in maintaining her relationship with a girl she seldom saw; she also derived comfort from touching the things and retelling the stories. These processes of looking, touching and remembering resemble the actions of Sarah Churchill as she surveyed the material environment at Blenheim Palace, but the grouping of objects created by Ellen Weeton also signals the additional emotional power of assemblages. As goods gain meaning and emotional significance from their context and setting—the process of 'warming' described by Epp and Price—assemblages could carry additional affective meaning and offer greater comfort.[7]

Much the same might be argued of behaviour. Comfort could be had from small everyday actions, but the accretion of these into routines offered a greater sense of contentment and comfort. This is seen in William Money's account of his daily life at his home in Whetham; it is equally apparent in the routines of religious life described by his wife, Emma, and by many others, from the artisan Matthew Harald to the titled evangelical, Lady Maxwell. All drew comfort from the routine of church services, Bible reading and prayer, but country-house owners were also in a position to mould the routines of others, most commonly in the form of daily prayers and weekly services in which family, servants and sometimes guests were expected to participate. They could also inscribe religion and faith into the country house in the form of chapels and, more occasionally, spaces for private devotion. The comfort derived from these spaces and practices could be found in the routines themselves, but more particularly in their ultimate purpose: a closer bond with God as the ultimate source of comfort. For the faithful, this was the ultimate prize; earthly discomforts might be tolerated in the expectation of eternal comfort in the presence of God. This was often used as a way of comforting those recently bereaved, and clearly offered some solace to both William and Emma Money when their parents died. Yet faith also spurred action, and comfort could be derived from doing one's Christian duty. Importantly, this was equally apparent in the behaviour of country-house owners at the start of our period and at the end: from Ursula Clarke Venner in the late seventeenth century to Lady Maxwell in the early nineteenth century.

For country-house owners, their families and their guests, comfort was complex and multifaceted, encompassing physical, social and emotional dimensions. Sometimes, these coalesced around a particular form or set of practices, most obviously in the informality and ease of what was often referred to by foreign visitors as 'English comfort'. The admiration expressed by Erik Gustaf Geijer and Pückler-Muskau, amongst others, can be seen as symptomatic of the spread of English ideas and English modes of living into continental Europe. It is not always clear what this idealisation comprised in the mind of the individual, and Odile-Bernez argues that, in France at least, it carried a veiled criticism of the French elite and their Anglomania.[8] Nevertheless, English comfort was something to be admired and replicated, not least because it was far from an exclusive and aristocratic form of comfort: informality and social ease could be recreated in the bourgeois living room, thus carrying ideals of comfort out of the country house and into a broader array of dwellings.

Comfort: Invention, Ideal and Impetus

It is perhaps too easy to be carried along with this enthusiasm and to view comfort, in its various forms, as all pervasive. It is certainly a word, an idea and an ideal that was frequently deployed across the long eighteenth century. But it is important to consider the extent to which comfort was a genuinely new idea and a driving force for change in the country house and beyond, and to consider what it might add to our understanding of the country house or ideas of home.

Taking these questions in turn, the quest for comfort in a material sense lies at the heart of Crowley's thesis and is central to many other studies of comfort in the houses of the elite. The evidence explored here confirms that English country houses undoubtedly became more comfortable as places in which to live during the eighteenth century. They had more effective (if still surprisingly inadequate) heating systems and were better lit; they had a growing array of easy seating and convenience furniture, along with increasing numbers of carpets, curtains, rugs and screens, and enjoyed the convenience and privacy afforded by corridors and back stairs. These things did not happen by accident; they reflected the investment of considerable amounts of time and money from owners who were clearly concerned with how their bodily comfort could be enhanced, even if it was only for the few months that they spent at their country houses. However, we should be wary of assuming that comfort overshadowed other concerns. The array of furniture and lights bought by James Henry Leigh in the 1810s certainly made Stoneleigh Abbey more comfortable, but they also symbolised his wealth and taste. Comfort and taste/gentility should not be seen as competing priorities: the material trappings of comfort could themselves be fashionable—for example an elegant sofa or a handsome chandelier—as could their consciously informal arrangement.

Conscious attempts to make the country house a place of emotional comfort are more difficult to trace, although applying the rhetoric of home is significant in this regard because it suggests an affective tie between people and place. In this, emotional attachment to objects played a crucial role, as Judith Lewis has argued.[9] Yet we need to look beyond these to consider relationships between people and how they were conceived and described in terms of comfort. It is unsurprising that feeling comfortable was a desirable state for a wide range of country house residents, from Ursula Clarke Venner to Mary Delany to William Money. It is perhaps more striking that they all used the word 'comfort' to describe their emotions and relationships with others, despite being separated by well over 100 years. Moreover, comfort was not simply a description; it was also deployed rhetorically as an important emotive that shaped how others felt—something which Emma Money did on numerous occasions.

A key question running through this book is whether a concern with—or indeed a quest for—comfort becomes more apparent over time. Again, Crowley and DeJean are clear that the eighteenth century witnessed the invention or the age of comfort. The former suggests a conscious project and the alignment of material comfort with Enlightenment scientific and technological endeavour: the invention of new fireplaces, stoves and lamps. There was certainly a proliferation of technologies, especially in the last quarter of the eighteenth century, but physical comfort was far from being the child of a technological revolution. There were certainly important shifts in the expectation of physical comfort: country-house owners wanted their houses to be warmer and lighter; they sought out seating that was more forgiving and relaxing, and they were less tolerant of things that disrupted their comfort, such as bed bugs. In these ways, comfort was clearly an objective that drove decisions and behaviours, but there is a danger of viewing things in a teleological manner. Comfort (like luxury) is a cultural construct and so is shaped by norms and expectations that vary across time and space. It is easy to see developments as progressive, leading to ever greater levels of comfort, whereas in reality houses were becoming more comfortable through contingent, partial and often fragmented processes. The acquisition of new furniture, for instance, often took place at key life events (marriage or inheritance) which might delay a move to more comfortable seating; country houses were an amalgamation of inherited and new furniture and room arrangements, making some pieces and spaces more comfortable than others; individual rooms could be made warmer, but corridors and staircases remained cold and draughty.

A desire for emotional comfort is again not unique to this period. The myth of the low affect early modern family has long since been exploded, and it is apparent that country-house owners in the late seventeenth century were just as concerned with giving and receiving comfort and consolation as their counterparts in the early nineteenth century. There was, however, a greater tendency to pepper their correspondence with 'comfort' in its varied guises, and to use it as a rhetorical device. This does not constitute a fundamental shift in the nature or language of emotional comfort, but it does indicate that it was something that was considered and discussed more frequently. If comfort tripped more easily from the tongue or the pen, then this suggests that it was how people conceived and articulated their relationships with others.

More profound changes came in terms of social comfort, not least because the behaviours which this enacted reflected shifting social norms. This is most apparent in the move to greater informality and the related shift to what Jan de Vries terms new luxury. This is not to argue that comfort was a way of representing luxury in a way that was less loaded in moral terms, as Odille-Benez has argued. It is true that comfort carried meanings of material well-being, but there is little in the evidence presented here to suggest that eighteenth-century landowners were eliding luxury with comfort. Only on rare occasions are worldly or creature comforts presented negatively, and then it is in contrast with the more enduring comforts afforded by an afterlife spent in heaven—a point made in religious treatises and the correspondence of William Money. More generally, comfort was aligned with the acquisition of the material trappings and behavioural norms of a more inclusive and certainly less formal polite sociability—a process which de Vries too readily associates with a rising bourgeoisie. For country-house owners and their families and guests, this involved shifts in how and where one might sit and interact with others—changes that are apparent from Louisa Stuart's discomfort in the formal circle she encountered at Mrs. Montagu's house. Physical, social and emotional comfort were bound together in this incident: distance from the warming fire, awkwardness in the stilted conversation and the desire for consolation in sharing the unhappy experience with her correspondent.

Given the growing importance, if not novelty, of comfort in the eighteenth century, what does a focus on comfort add to our understanding of the country house and elite domestic milieux more generally? First, comfort can be viewed as an ideal that provided the motivation to create new spaces within country houses, to acquire new technologies and new furniture, to organise these things in different assemblages and arrangements, and to interact with others in particular ways. As such, we can see the search for comfort as a way of understanding changes in the form, function, appearance and use of rooms, and of the country house as a whole. This does not mean jettisoning ideas of taste, status and pedigree; indeed, it would be wrong to do so, given what we have already seen about the ways in which taste and comfort were often intertwined. However, it does provide a different explanatory framework that challenges easy assumptions about the country house as cultural capital: a statement of power, taste and wealth. Importantly, because the parameters of material and social comfort were relative and shifting, it provides a dynamic reading of the country house.

Second, since comfort is derived from behaviour as well as material objects, it serves to animate the house. Focusing on comfort as practice means populating rooms with men and women engaged in their everyday routines or in social gatherings, be they the quiet domestic scenes at Brathay Hall, the informal sociability described by the Revd Abdy or unexpected encounter with the formality of the circle that surprised Louise Stuart. Moreover, as being comfortable meant assembling and using an array of furniture and fittings, we need to view the country house as a lived space, created through the everyday practices of sociability and comfortable daily life. This means combining histories of the architecture, spatial organisation and furniture of houses with those of elite social practice and (familial) relationships in a way that goes beyond Girouard's marrying of form and function. Rendering a house or a room comfortable meant more than simply organising the sequence of rooms or assembling material objects; it was an ongoing process of social and material interaction—sitting on sofas, talking with friends and family, lighting and snuffing candles, writing and reading letters. This again confronts us with a country house that was dynamic and changing, rather than simply a static backdrop.

Third, and closely related to this, is the idea of viewing the country house as a series of assemblages. Comfort was enhanced through particular arrangements of rooms in the house, furniture in a room, and component parts of a bed, fireplace or sofa. We do not need to adopt the full conceptual framework of assemblage theory to recognise how organising and reorganising these arrangements would impact how the country house was experienced as a lived space. Two things are important here: that comfort derived from assemblages that nested into one another, and that objects as well as humans had agency. The latter can be readily seen in the ways in which sofas encouraged different sitting postures and the arrangement of chairs into small groups encouraged informal and multiple groupings within the room (in contrast to the formal circle). The first enhanced physical and the second social comfort. Some care is necessary, of course, because it was people who ultimately determined the selection and arrangement of furniture in a room, and people could decide to move furniture about, making object–agency contingent.

Fourth, thinking further about these assemblages and arrangements offers a route into the knotted question of what, if anything, made the English country house distinctive. Rather than address this question in terms of architectural styles or the relationship between house and garden— important though both considerations might be—it is useful to think of modes of living and their associated assemblages. English comfort, as identified and appreciated by foreign visitors, had both behavioural and material dimensions, both of which revolved around notions of informality and ease. Such ideas were by no means unique to England, yet the association and the model were clear: the English lived in their country houses in a particular way, one that required both adjective (English) and noun (comfort), even when the latter carried only its new, imported meaning.

Physical and, to a lesser extent, social comfort is derived from the tangible, material interaction between people and objects. However, we have seen that objects could also carry emotional attachments, serving to link a person to other people, other places and other times. This is my fifth point: objects were good for feeling with and remembering with, and could bring emotional comfort to those who owned, handled or gazed on them. This has important implications for how we approach the country house, not least the need to be cognisant of the processes through which objects acquired—or were imbued with—emotional meaning. Given the importance of gifting and bequeathing in this process, there is the need to reappraise the ways in which provenance is studied, complementing an art historical approach with one that focuses on object biographies. Objects could also acquire meaning from their context and setting, placing additional emphasis on understanding the ways in which assemblages of objects were created and modified, and how this might impact on the meaning and emotional resonance of particular items or the assemblage as a whole. This links to Grant McCracken's notion of curatorial consumption and the active role of the owner in assembling, ordering and presenting objects, be they pictures, letters, porcelain or scraps of fabric.

Sixth, as emotional comfort derived from people as well as things, viewing the country house through the lens of comfort means focusing much more on people and the ways in which they related to each other. This means situating families, friends and servants in their spatial context and thinking about how their emotional well-being was shaped by presence and absence; memories and hopes for the future; love and conflict; affection and indifference. It should certainly involve exploring dysfunction and discomfort, which formed the reality for some, just as others enjoyed the contentment of a happy marriage. At a more general, historiographical level, this ties the country house more firmly to the history of emotions. At present, there are too few studies that attempt to draw on the immense and growing literature on emotions to explore the workings of the country house and elite domestic life, especially in the eighteenth century. Comfort provides an important route through which this connection might be made, not least because exploring the emotional comfort of elite householders throws the spotlight on a set of milder emotions hitherto explored only patchily in the literature: the work of French and Rothery on anxiety amongst younger sons is a useful first step in this direction.[10] Whilst lacking the drama of emotions like love, anger and melancholy, or the intellectual fascination of sensibility, comfort and contentment emerge from numerous letters as a desirable state of emotional well-being for many country-house owners.

Finally, there is the question of how the various dimensions of comfort coalesced in making a country house into a home. For Lewis, the key was an emotional attachment to the house, constructed and articulated through a similar attachment to objects and assemblages held within it. The evidence explored here suggests a rather more complex picture: one that portrays home as a nexus of material, social and emotional comfort. As Jane Austen's Robert Ferrars notes of the cottage ideal, home needed to contain at least an acceptable level of material well-being; but it also needed to offer seclusion—an escape from the outside world and the ability to control access and interaction. This agency was crucial because it allowed the owner to regulate both who came into the home and the behaviours, routines and norms that shaped the domestic milieu. It was thus a place of social comfort. Layered onto this, home was a place where objects held particular meanings and memories which connected them (and their owner) to other people, places and times. And it was the focus for relationships with other people, most obviously family, that gave emotional comfort and a feeling of contentment. The absence of any one of these elements undermined the feeling of being at home, as is apparent in the detachment of Sarah Churchill from Blenheim or the attitude of Elizabeth Dryden to Canons Ashby when inherited by her son.

Physical, social and emotional comforts were thus manifest in the complex assemblage of spaces, objects, people that comprised the country house. Yet neither the country house nor notions of comfort can be fully understood without giving due regard to the connections between these things. This means attending not simply to the tangible, but also the web of relationships, actions, feelings, choices and memories that bound them together.

Notes

1. www.airbnb.co.uk/rooms/10798625?source_impression_id=p3_16013999 08_rknnYWkqrHsmf4H8; www.mikegerrard.com/country-house-comfort-in-perthshire/; www.thecountrycastlecompany.co.uk/property/Somerset-country-house (All accessed 29 September 2020).
2. See John Crowley, *The Invention of Comfort: Sensibilities and Design in Early-Modern Britain and Early America* (Baltimore: Johns Hopkins University Press, 2001); Joan DeJean, *The Age of Comfort: When Paris Discovered Casual and the Modern Home Began* (New York: Bloomsbury, 2009).
3. Gilles Deleuze and Félix Guatarri, *A Thousand Plateaus: Capitalism and Schizophrenia*, trans. Brian Massumi (London: Continuum, 1987).
4. Woodruff Smith, *Consumption and the Making of Respectability, 1600–1800* (London: Routledge, 2002); Karen Harvey, *The Little Republic: Masculinity and Domestic Authority in Eighteenth-Century Britain* (Oxford: Oxford University Press, 2012); Jane Whittle and Elizabeth Griffiths, *Consumption*

and Gender in the Early Seventeenth-Century Household: The World of Alice Le Strange (Oxford: Oxford University Press, 2012).

5. Mark Girouard, *Life in the English Country House: A Social and Architectural History* (New Haven: Yale University Press, 1978), 213–44.

6. Henry French and Mark Rothery, *Man's Estate: Landed Gentry Masculinities, 1660–1900* (Oxford: Oxford University Press, 2013).

7. Amber Epp and Linda Price, 'The Storied Life of Singularized Objects: Forces of Agency and Network Transformation', *Journal of Consumer Research*, 36:5 (2010), 820–37.

8. Marie Odile-Bernez, 'Comfort, the Acceptable Face of Luxury: An Eighteenth-Century Etymology', *Journal for Early Modern Cultural Studies*, 14:2 (2014), 16–17.

9. Judith Lewis, 'When a House Is Not a Home: Elite English Women and the Eighteenth-Century Country House', *Journal of British Studies*, 48:2 (2009), 336–63.

10. Henry French and Mark Rothery, 'Male Anxiety Among Younger Sons of the English Landed Gentry', *The Historical Journal*, 62:4 (2019), 967–95.

Bibliography

Archival Sources

Cambridge Record Office

Frances Huddlestone: 488/C1/HD47, August 1752.
Mary Huddlestone to Richard Huddlestone: 488/C3/HD175, 14 June 1805; 488/CD/HD176, 30 July 1805; 488/CD/HD178, 8 August 1805.
Richard Huddlestone to Ferdinand Huddlestone: 488/C2/HD196, 31 January 1786.
Richard Huddlestone to Mary Huddlestone: 488/CD/HD177, 3 August 1805.

Devon Record Office

Richard Coffin to Anne Prideaux: Z19/40/8a-b, 21 April 1673, 13 August 1684, 27 August 1684 October 1686.

Essex Record Office

Katherine Griffin to Richard Aldworth Griffin, Second Lord Braybrooke: D/DBy C40, 9 June 1797, 25 June 1797; D/DBy C6/6, 29 September 1797.
Receipted Bills: D/DBy A37/2; D/DBy A65/1.

Flintshire Record Office

Catherine Neville to Mary Neville: GG15, 2 January 1804.
Richard Aldworth Griffin to Mary Glynne (née Neville): GG7, 31 July 1817, 3 December 1817.

The National Archives

PROB 11/1144/223, Will of the Right Honourable Edward, Lord Leigh, Baron of Stoneleigh, 22 July 1786.
PROB 11/1448/37: Will of the Honourable Mary Leigh of Stoneleigh Abbey, 5 August 1806.

Norfolk Record Office

Ashe Windham to Elizabeth Windham: WKC, 7/20/15, [no date] 1719, 8 March 1719, 21 March 1719, 8 April 1719; WKC, 7/20/17, [no date] 1719; WKC, 7/20/21, 19 August 1720; WKC, 7/20/25, 16 August 1728.

Elizabeth Windham to Ashe Windham: WKC, 7/20/22, 4 August 1720; WKC, 7/20/26, 19 August 1728; Norfolk RO, WKC, 7/20/27, 6 December 1728.

Northamptonshire Central Library

Auction Catalogues: MM0005644NL/5, Wollaston Hall, 1805; M0005646NL/15, Brixworth Hall, 1797; M0005647NL/6, Horton Hall, 1772.

Northamptonshire Record Office

Correspondence Between John Scattergood and William Hanbury: H(K) 183.

Elizabeth Dryden to Mrs Steele: D(CA) 903b, 13 January 1817; D(CA)/361, 26 September 1809, 26 May 1812, 28 January 1814, 20 October 1814, 28 December 1816, 8 January 1819, 13 January 1819, [no date] April 1819, 2 June 1819, [no date] October 1819, [no date] November 1819, 30 October 1820, [no date] 1821, [no date] September 1822, 29 October 1822.

Inventories for Canons Ashby House: D(CA) 901, Inventory for 1717; D(CA) 904, Inventory for 1819.

John Turner Dryden's Tour of France: D(CA)/347, 21 July 1774.

Receipted Bill from Thomas Phill: D(CA) 129, 30 April 1716.

Riksarkivet, Stockholm

Ekebladska samlingen: Brita Horn to Claes Julius Ekeblad, 8 September 1779.

Shakespeare Central Library and Archive

Accounts: DR18/31/548, Account of Stores Expended Every Half Year, Adlestrop, 1757–1761; DR18/31–656 — Day Book for Grove House, 1793–1798.

Elizabeth Brydges to Mary Brydges: DR672/59, 15 August 1682.

Inventories: DR18/4/9, Inventory of Stoneleigh Abbey, 1737; DR18/4/27 Inventory of Stoneleigh Abbey, 1749; DR18/31/903 Inventory of Leighton Buzzard, 1749; DR18/4/43, Inventory of Stoneleigh Abbey, 1774 with 1806 Amendments; DR18/4/69, Inventory of Stoneleigh Abbey, 1786; DR18/4/59, Inventory of Stoneleigh Abbey, 1806; DR 671 56 List of Rings and Brooches Given by Mary Leigh, 1806; DR18/4/46, Inventory of China, 19 July 1806; DR18/4/47, Plate Sent Down by Mr Hill from Grove House.

Mary Leigh to Joseph Hill: DR18/671, 11 February 1791; DR18/671, 27 March 1791; DR671, 28 January 1792; DR18/17/31/11, 24 October 1804.

Plans and Designs: DR630, Designs for Stoneleigh Abbey; DR671/33/25: General Plan of the House; DR671/33/11, The Chamber Plan.

Receipted Bills: DR18/5/5899, Argand & Co; DR18/5/6122, Barnet & Mason; DR18/3/47/52/15, Thomas Burnett; DR18/5/6999, 7100, Chipchase and

Proctor; DR18/5/4207, 4619, John Coggs; DR18/5/5023, John Davis; DR18/5/5849, 5939, Frances Field; DR18/5/6129, James Fisher; DR18/5/6032, 6158, John Gardner; DR18/5/5991, Thomas Gibberd; DR18/5/4251, Thomas Gilpin; DR18/5/4408, William Gomm; DR18/5/6992, Hancock, Shepherd and Rixon; DR18/5/7056, 7137, 7156, 7158, John Johnstone, DR18/5/6254, 6349, 6398, 6423, 6481, Samuel Kingston; DR18/5/5937, Joseph Lee; DR18/5/6392, R. Lewis; DR18/5/7029, Thomas Little; DR18/5/5809, Thomas Makepeace; DR18/5/3744, Thomas Minchin; DR18/5/7007, Morel and Hughes; DR18/5/6130, Joseph Naylor; DR18/5/7022, 7150, George Oakley; DR18/5/7051, Patent Lamp and Oil Warehouse; DR18/5/6124, Thomas Poole; DR18/5/2063, 2636, Thomas Smith; DR18/5/6019, John Walker; DR18/5/6123, M. Storer; DR18/5/7021, David Taylor; DR18/5/7087, Henry Watson; DR18/5/6125, Thomas Watts; DR18/5/5684, Josiah Wedgwood; DR18/5/6126, John Weston; DR18/5/5887, James Wheble; DR18/5/7067, Thomas Wicks; DR18/5/5813, 5915, B Wilmer.

Swedish National Archive

Tosterupsamlingen vol. 108, Johan Gabriel Oxenstiernas Journal 1766–1768.

Warwickshire Record Office

NEWDIGATE FAMILY PAPERS

Accounts for Arbury Hall: CR136/V/156, Accounts, 1747–62; CR136/V/136, Accounts, 1763–96.

Journals and Diaries: CR136/A/152, Diaries of Sir Roger Newdigate; CR1841/7, Travel diary of Sophia Newdigate, 1748.

Roger Newdigate to Christopher Gullet: CR136/C646, 29 December 1773.

Roger Newdigate to Mrs Parker: CR136/B/2014, 29 April 1795.

Roger Newdigate to Sophia Newdigate: CR136/B1899, 12 April 1749; CR136/B2511, 25 November 1762; CR136/B4046[I], February 1772; CR136/B4046[H], 25 February 1772; CR 136/B4046[M], 2 March 1772; CR136/B4046[E], 25 March 1773.

LUCY FAMILY PAPERS

George Lucy to Mrs Hayes: L6/1436, 27 December 1756; L6/1439, 25 April 1757; L6/1447, 12 April 1758; L6/1450, 12 June 1758; L6/1453, 9 February 1760.

John Dobson to Mrs Hayes: L6/1481, [no date] 1755.

John Williams to Mary Elizabeth Lucy: L6/1539a, 15 March 1824; L6/1545, 23 June 1844.

Margaret Williams to Mary Elizabeth Lucy: L6/1532, [no date] December 1823; L6/1536a, [no date]; L6/1537, not date.

Mrs Hayes to George Lucy: L6/1367, 17 July 1749; L6/1373, 30 July 1753; L6/1375, 7 April 1755; L6/1439, 18 April 1755.

Thomas Willement to George Lucy: L6/1144, [no date] 1837.

Wiltshire Record Office

Emma Money to William Money (Transcript—1720/829): [no date] September 1807, 28 September 1808, [no date] 1809, 15 January 1811, [no date] April 1812, [no date] 1812, [no date] July 1815, 15 July 1816, 17 July 1817, 31 August 1818, 13 September 1818.

William Money Junior to Emma Money (Transcript—1720/829): 12 October 1817.

William Money Junior to William Money (Transcript—1720/829): [no date] September 1817.

William Money to Emma Money (Transcript—1720/829): 20 May 1805, [no date] September 1808, 8 November 1808, 12 November 1808, 14 November 1808, 14 May 1812, [no date] June 1813, 22 June 1813, 19 December 1813, 25 June 1814, 26 July 1814, [no date] July 1816, 17 July 1816, 3 September 1817, 26 September 1817, [no date] 1818, 9 September 1818.

Paintings and Engravings

Anon. *A Man-Trap* (1780), from a Print Published by Carrington Bowles, *The Connoisseur*, vol. VII (London: Otto Limited, 1903).

Anon. *Stay with Me Flagons* (1794), Printed by Laurie and Whittle, Lewis Walpole Library.

Anon. *Three Weeks After Marriage* (Published by J.L. Marks, 1822), Lewis Walpole Library.

Boucher, François. *Marquise de Pompadour* (1756), Alte Pinakothek, Munich.

Charpentier, Jean-Baptiste. *The Family of the Duc de Penthievre* (c.1767), Palace of Versailles.

Colley, Thomas. *The Pleasures of Matrimony* (1773), Lewis Walpole Library, 773.03.20.02.

Constable, John. *A Music Party at Brathay Hall* (1806), British Museum, 1896,0821.18.

Darley, Matthew. *The Unlucky Surprise* (1773), Colonial Williamsburg, EMuseum, 1980–226, https://emuseum.history.org/objects/29804/the-unlucky-surprise-the-bengall-minuet;jsessionid=96F2429A3E6F075E3F447862F562003A (accessed 3 August 2020).

de Brune, Johannes. *Emblemata of Zinnerwerck* (1624).

Delaunay, Nicolas: Engraving After Niclas Lafrensen. *L'Heureux Moment* (1777), Rijksmuseum, Amsterdam.

de St Jean, Jean-Dieu. *Femme de qualité en deshabillée sortant du lit* (1688), Institute of Art, Minneapolis.

de Troy, Jean-François. *Reading from Moliere* (c.1728), Private Collection, https://en.wikipedia.org/wiki/File:FdeTroyLectureMoliere.jpg.

de Troy, Jean-François. *The Declaration of Love* (1724), Metropolitan Museum of Art, New York.

de Troy, Jean-François. *After the Ball* (1735), Private Collection.

de Troy, Jean-François. *Before the Ball* (1735), JPG Museum.

Gaugain, Thomas. *Diligence and Dissipation: The Modest Girl in her Bed Chamber* (1797), Yale Center for British Art.

Gilray, James. *The Comforts of a Rumford Stove* (1800), Science and Society Picture Library.

Galleries Ouaiss Antqiues, www.ouaissantiquites.com/objectdetails/782556/18112/hidden-compartment-snuff-box-tortoiseshell (accessed 3 August 2020).

Harden, John. *Family Group: Charles Lloyd Reading* (1804), Reproduced in Foskett, *John Harden of Brathay Hall*, plate IV.

Harden, John. *Catherine Allan* (1805), Reproduced in Foskett, *John Harden of Brathay Hall*, plate VI.

Harden, John. *Reading and Sewing* (1805), Reproduced in Foskett, *John Harden of Brathay Hall*, plate V.

Harden, John. *Backgammon* (1808), Reproduced in Foskett, *John Harden of Brathay Hall*, plate X.

Heath, William. *Cribbage* (c.1825–30), British Museum.

Hilleström, Pehr. *The Milliner* (1770s), Nationalmuseum, Stockholm.

Hogarth, William. *Assembly at Wanstead* (1728–31), Philadelphia Museum of Art.

Hogarth, William. *The Wollaston Family* (1730), Bridgeman Art Library.

Hogarth, William. *The Lady's Last Stake* (1759), Albright-Knox Art Gallery.

Inguof, François Robert. *La Soirée d'hyver* (1774), National Gallery of Art.

Lafrensen, Niclas. *Consolation de l'absence* (c.1775), National Gallery of Art, Washington, DC, www.nga.gov/collection/art-object-page.3033.html (accessed 3 August 2020).

Lafrensen, Niclas. *Le Dejeuner en Tête a Tête* (c.1775), Musée de Louvre, https://commons.wikimedia.org/wiki/File:Le_d%C3%A9jeuner_en_t%C3%A Ate_%C3%A0_t%C3%AAte.jpg.

Lafrensen, Niclas. 'Lady Drinking Tea', https://commons.wikimedia.org/wiki/File:Lady_drinking_tea_-_Lavreince.jpg.

Laquy, William. *Allegory of Art Training* (c.1770), Rijksmuseum, Amsterdam, www.rijksmuseum.nl/en/search/objects?q=laquy&p=2&ps=12&st=Objects &ii=4#/SK-A-2320-C,16 (accessed 19 May 2020).

Luyken, Jan. *Drie figuren zich bij een kachel* (1711), Rijksmuseum, Amsterdam.

Moses, H. *The Library at Woburn Abbey, Bedfordshire* (1827), Reproduced in Cornforth, English Interiors, 42.

Patch, Thomas. *Mr Bennet Reclining on a Sof*a (1760s), Yale Centre for British Art.

Paye, Richard Morton. *The Artist in His Studio* (1783), National Trust, Upton House, Warwickshire, www.nationaltrustcollections.org.uk/object/446692 (accessed 11 August 2020).

Pierre, Jean-Baptiste-Marie. *La Mauvaise Nouvelle* (1740), Le Musée Nissim de Camondo, Paris, https://madparis.fr/francais/musees/musee-nissim-de-camondo/parcours/1er-etage/l-appartement-de-moise-de-camondo-1255/la-mauvaise-nouvelle.

Pugin, Augustus Charles. 'Great Library, Cassiobury Park' (c.1815), from John Britton, *The History and Description of Cassiobury Park, 1837* (London: Chiswick Press, 1837).

Reinagle, Philip. *Mrs Congreave and Her Daughters in Their London Drawing Room* (1782), National Gallery of Ireland.

Rowlandson, Thomas. *Matrimonial Comforts: Anonymous Letter* (1800), Lewis Walpole Library.

Rowlandson, Thomas. *Matrimonial Comforts: A Curtain Lecture* (1800), Lewis Walpole Library.

Rowlandson, Thomas. *Matrimonial Comforts: Return from a Walk* (1800), Lewis Walpole Library.

Rowlandson, Thomas. *At Home and Abroad; Abroad and at Home* (1807), Lewis Walpole Library.

Rowlandson, Thomas. *Great Subscription Room at Brook's* (1808), Lewis Walpole Library.

Rowlandson, Thomas. *The Comforts of a Modern Gala* (London: Thomas Tegg, 1809), V&A, H. Beard Print Collection.

Rowlandson, Thomas. *The Comforts of Matrimony, a Good Toast* (1809), British Library.

Sargent, Henry. *The Tea Party* (c.1820), Museum of Fine Arts, Boston, https://collections.mfa.org/objects/31744.

Sayer, Robert. *The Comforts of Matrimony—A Smoky House & Scolding Wife* (1790), British Museum.

Steen, Jan. *Fantasy Interior with Jan Steen and the Family of Gerrit Schouten* (1659–60), Nelson-Atkins Museum of Art.

Vidal, Geraud. *Le Dejeuner Anglais* (1785), Nationalmuseum, Stockholm.

Vinkeles, Reinier. *A Young Woman Comforts Her Crying Friend* [no date], Rijksmuseum.

Wells, W. *The Library at Elton Hall, Huntingdon* (1818), Reproduced in Cornforth, English Interiors.

Williams, Charles. *Luxury, or the Comforts of a Rumford Stove* (1801), British Museum,

Zoffany, Johann. *Mrs Abington in 'The Way to Keep Him'* (1768), Petworth House, Sussex.

Zoffany, Johann. *Sir Laurence Dundas with his grandson* (1769), Marquess of Zetland.

Printed Primary Sources

Newspapers and Journals

Ackermann, Rudolph. *Repository of Arts.*
Chelmsford Chronicle.
Fog's Weekly Journal.
Hull Packet.
Journal des luxus und der Moden.
Leeds Intelligencer.
London Evening Post.
St James Chronicle.
Woodfall's Register.

Journals, Diaries and Correspondence

Adeane, Jane (ed.). *The Girlhood of Maria Josepha Holroyd, Lady Stanley of Alderley: Recorded in Letters of a Hundred Years Ago, from 1776 to 1796*, vol. 2 (London: Longmans, 1896).

Allen, Michael (ed.). *An English Lady in Paris: The Diary of Frances Anne Crewe, 1786* (St Leonards: Oxford Stockley Publications, 2006).

Andrews, C. Bryun, and John Beresford (eds.). *The Torrington Diaries: Containing the Tours Through England and Wales of the Hon. John Byng (Later Fifth Viscount Torrington) Between the Years 1781 and 1794*, vol. 4 (London: Eyre and Spottiswoode, 1934).

Baillie, Lady Grisell. *The House Book of Lady Grisell Baillie, 1692–1733* (Edinburgh: Scottish Historical Society, 1911).

Beresford, J. (ed.). *The Diary of a Country Parson, 1758–1802* (Norwich: Canterbury Press, 1999).

Blanck, Anton. *Geijer I England 1809–1810* (Stockholm: A. Bonnier, 1914).

Bunbury, Selina. *Life in Sweden: With Excursions in Norway and Denmark*, vol. 2 (London: Hurst and Blackett, 1853).

Carter, Elizabeth. *A Series of Letters Between Mrs Elizabeth Carter and Miss Catherine Talbot, from the Year 1741 to 1770* (London: F. C. and J. Rivington, 1809).

Chapple, John, and Arthur Pollard (eds.). *The Letters of Mrs Gaskell* (Manchester: Manchester University Press, 1966).

Chauncey Woolsey, Sarah (ed.). *The Autobiography and Correspondence of Mrs Delany*, vol. 2 (Boston: Roberts Brothers, 1879).

Clark, Alice (ed.). *Gleanings from an Old Portfolio Containing Some Correspondence Between Lady Louisa Stuart and Her Sister, Caroline, Countess of Portarlington and Other Friends and Relatives*, vol. 2 (Edinburgh, 1895).

Climenson, Emily (ed.). *Passages form the Diaries of Mrs Philip Lybbe Powys* (London: Longmans, Green and Co., 1899).

Coke, Mary. *The Letters and Journals of Lady Mary Coke, Vol. 1, 1756–1767* (1889; Bath: Kingsmead Reprints, 1970).

Collett-White, James (ed.). *Inventories of Bedfordshire Country Houses, 1714–1830* (Bedford: Bedford Historical Record Society, 1995).

Donald, Elsie (ed.). *Mistress of Charlecote: The Memoirs of Mary Elizabeth Lucy, 1803–1889* (1983; London: Orion, 2002).

Doyle, John (ed.). *Memoir and Correspondence of Susan Ferrier, 1782–1854* (London: John Murray, 1898).

Geijer, Erik Gustaf. *Minnen: Utrag ur bref och dagböcker* (Uppsala: Palmblad, 1834).

Gérard-Gailly, Emile (ed.). *Madame de Sévigné: Lettres, 1648–1696*, vol. 3 (Paris: Gallimard, 1953–1957).

Grimm, Johann Friedrich Karl. *Bemerkungen eines reisenden, Durch Deutschland, Frankreich, England Und Holland in Briefen an Seine Freunde* (Altenburg, 1775).

Halsband, Robert (ed.). *Selected Letters of Lady Mary Wortley Montagu* (London: Longmans, 1970).

Heighes Woodforde, Dorothy (ed.). *Woodforde Papers and Diaries* (London: Peter Davies, 1932).

Horner, Craig (ed.). *The Diary of Edmund Harrold, Wigmaker of Manchester 1712–15* (Aldershot: Ashgate, 2008).

Howard, Henrietta. *Letters to and from Henrietta, Countess of Suffolk, and Her Second Husband, the Hon. George Berkley; from 1712 to 1767*, vol. 2 (London: John Murray, 1824).

Irving, Washington. *The Sketch-Book of Geoffrey Crayon, Gent.* (1821; Philadelphia: J.B. Lippincott & Co., 1871).

Jepp Clarke, Mary *et al. Clarke Family Letters* (Alexandra, VA: Alexandra Press, 2003).

Knierim, Michael (ed.). *Die Herkunft des Friedrich Engels: Briefe aus der Verwandtschaft* (Trier: Karl Marx Haus, 1991).

Laing, Samuel. *Journal of a Residence in Norway, During the Year 1834, 1835 and 1836; Made with a View to Inquire into Moral and Political Economy of That Country, and the Condition of Its Inhabitants* (London: Longmans, 1839).

Lancaster, John. *The Life of Darcy, Lady Maxwell . . . Compiled from her Voluminous Diary and Correspondence* (New York: N. Bangs and T. Mason, 1822).

Lewis, Maria Theresa (ed.). *Extracts of the Journals and Correspondence of Miss Berry from the Year 1783–1852*, vol. 2 (London: Longmans, 1908).

Lloyd, Llewellyn. *Field Sports of the North of Europe; Comprised in a Personal Narrative of a Residence in Sweden and Norway, in the Years 1827–28*, vol. 2 (London: Colburn & Bentley, 1830).

Lockhart, John. *Memoirs of the Life of Sir Walter Scott* (Edinburgh: Adam and Charles Black, 1852), 501.

Lower, William. *A Relation in the Form of a Journal of the Voiage and Residence Which . . . Charles II . . . Hath Made to Holland* (The Hague, 1660).

McKay, Peter, and David Hall (eds.). *Estate Letters from the Time of John, 2nd Duke of Montagu, 1709–39* (Northampton: Northamptonshire Record Society, 2013).

Pückler-Muskau, Herman. *Briefe eines verstorbenen: Ein fragmentarisches Tagebuch aus England, Wales* (Stuttgart: Halberger, 1831).

Radcliffe, Mary Anne. *Memoirs of Mrs Mary Anne Radcliffe, in Familiar Letters to Her Female Friend* (Edinburgh: Printed for the Author, 1810).

Schück, Henrik (ed.). *Geijers ungdomsbrev: Familjebrev av Erik Gustaf Geijer utgivna av Henrik Schück* (Stockholm: Albert Bonniers, 1920).

Simond, Louis. *Journal of a Tour and Residence in Great Britain During the Years 1810 and 1811*, vol. 2 (Edinburgh: Archibald Constable & Co., 1817).

Stiernström, Gustaf (ed.). *Dagboks-anteckningar åren 1769–1771* (Uppsala: Svenska Litteratursällskapet, 1881).

Teignmouth, Lord Charles John. *Reminiscences of Many Years*, vol. 12 (1830; Edinburgh: David Douglas, 1878).

Tessin, Carl Gustaf. *Framledne riks-rådet, m.m. grefve Carl Gustaf Tessins dagbok, 1757* (Stockholm: Gustf Adolf Montgomery, 1824).

Walpole, Hoarce. 'Horace Walpole's Correspondence', https://walpole.library.yale.edu/collections/digital-resources/horace-walpole-correspondence.

Weeton, Ellen. *Miss Weeton's Journal of a Governess, 1807–1825*, vol. 2 (Oxford: Oxford University Press, 1939).

Weigert, Roger-Armand, and Carl Hernmarck (eds.). *Les relations artistiques entre la France et la Suède, 1693–1718: Nicodème Tessin le jeune et Daniel Cronström, Correspondance* (Stockholm: Nationalmuseum, 1964).

Treatises, Dictionaries and Directors

Adair, James. *An Essay on Diet and Regimen*, second edition (London: James Ridgway, 1812).

Adams, Samuel, and Sarah Adams. *The Complete Servant* (London: Knight and Lacey, 1825).

Adams, Samuel, and Sarah Adams. *The Servants' Guide and Family Manual* (London, 1830).

Anon. *An Easy Way to Prolong Life* (London, 1780).

Arnold, Theodor. *A Compleat Vocabulary, English and German* (Züllichau: M. Johann Bartholomäus Rogler, 1784).

Beresford, James. *The Miseries of Human Life* (London: William Miller, 1806).

Chambers, William. *A Treatise on Civil Architecture* (London: J. Haberkorn, 1759).

Chippendale, Thomas. *The Gentleman and Cabinet Maker's Director* (London: Printed for the Author, 1754).

Clavering, Robert. *An Essay on the Construction and Building of Chimneys* (London: I. and J. Taylor, 1793).

Crunden, John. *Convenient and Ornamental Architecture* (London: Isaac Taylor, 1767).

de Bray, Salomen, and Cornelis Danckerts. *Architectura moderna ofte Bouwinge van onsen tyt* (Amsterdam, 1631).

du Pradel, Jean. *Traite contre de Luxe* (Paris, 1705).

Franklin, Benjamin. *The Complete Works . . . of Dr Benjamin Franklin*, vol. 3 (London: J. Johnson, 1806).

Furttenbach, Joseph. *Architectura Civilis* (Ulm, 1628).

Furttenbach, Joseph. *Architectura Privata* (Ulm, 1641).

Gauger, Nicolas. *La Mécanique du Feu, ou l'Art d'en Augmenter les Effets et d'en Diminuer la Dépense* (Paris: Jacques Estienne and Jean Jombert, 1713).

Gerard, Alexander. *An Essay on Taste* (London: A. Millar, 1759).

Gilpin, William. *Observations on the Western Parts of England* (London: T. Cadell and W. Davies, 1798).

Griffin, Richard, Third Lord Braybrooke. *The History of Audley End: To Which Are Appended Notices of the Town and Parish of Saffron Walden in the County of Essex* (London: Samuel Bentley, 1836).

Halfpenny, William. *New and Complete System of Architecture* (London: John Brindley, 1749).

Halfpenny, William. *Rural Architecture in the Chinese Taste* (London: Robert Sayer, 1750).

Halfpenny, William. *Rural Architecture in the Gothic Taste* (London: Robert Sayer, 1752).

Home, Henry, Lord Kames. *Elements of Criticism*, vol. 3 (London: A. Millar, 1762).

Hume, David. *A Treatise of Human Nature: Being an Attempt to Introduce the Experimental Method of Reasoning into Moral Subjects*, vol. 3 (London: John Noon, 1739–40).

Jeary, Orlando. *A Dialogue Between MrFearing and MrConsolation; or a Word of Comfort to the Fearful of Christ's Flock* (1800).

Johnson, Samuel. *A Dictionary of the English Language*, vol. 2 (London, 1755–56).

Johnson, Samuel. *The History of Rasselas, Prince of Abissinia* (1759; Oxford: Oxford University Press, 1988).

Johnston, William. *The Improved Christian's Courage and Comfort from Afflictions and Death* (London: Printed for the Author, 1771).

Kent, Nathaniel. *Hints to Gentlemen of Landed Property* (London: J. Dodsley, 1775).

Kersey, John. *A New English Dictionary* (London, 1713).

Laing, David. *Hints for Dwellings: Consisting of Original Designs for Cottages, Farm-House, Villas &c., Plain and Ornamental* (London: J Taylor, 1800).

Littré, Emile. *Dictionnaire de la langue francaise* (Paris: Librairie Hachette, 1872–77).

Loudon, J.C. *The Landscape Gardening and Landscape Architecture of the Late Humphrey Repton, Esq.* (London: Printed for the Author, 1840).

Malthus, Thomas. *Essay on the Principle of Population* (London: John Murray, 1803).

McGowan, John. *The Canker Worm; or the Gourd of Creature Comforts Withered* (London, 1772).

Newton, John (ed.). *The Christian Character Exemplified, from the Papers of Mrs. Margaret Magdalen A—s...* (London: Lincoln & Gleason, 1804).

Penther, Johann Friedrich. *Ausführliche Anleitung zur bürgerlichen Bau-Kunst* (Augsburg, 1745).

Phillips, Edward. *The New World of Words or Universal English Dictionary* (London: J. Phillips, 1706).

Plaw, John. *Sketches for Country Houses, Villas and Rural Dwellings* (London: S. Gosnell, 1800).

Pocock, William Fuller. *Architectural Designs for Rustic Cottages, Picturesque Dwellings, Villas, & C.* (London: J. Taylor, 1807).

Ray, John. *Observations Topographical, Moral, & Physiological; Made in a Journey Through Part of the Low-Countries, Germany, Italy, and France* (London: John Martyn, 1673).

Reiff, Walter. *Lustgarten der Gesundheit* (1546).

Repton, Humphrey. *Sketches and Hints on Landscape Gardening* (London: Printed for W. Bulmer and Co., 1794).

Repton, Humphrey. *Fragments on the Theory of Landscape Gardening* (London: Printed for J. Taylor, 1816).

Richardson, Charles. *New Dictionary of the English Language* (London: William Pickering, 1836).

Roubo, Andre-Jacob. *L'Art du menuisier* (Paris: L.F. Delatour, 1769–75).

Schwan, Chretien F. *Nouveau Dictionnaire de la Langue Francoise* (Mannheim: C.F. Schwan and M. Fontaine, 1787).

Sheraton, Thomas. *The Cabinet Maker and Upholsterer's Drawing Book* (London: Thomas Bensley, 1794–96).

Sheraton, Thomas. *Cabinet Dictionary* (London: W. Smith, 1803).

Southall, John. *A Treatise on Cimex Lectularius, or the Bed Bug*, second edition (1730; Ipswich: J. Bush, 1793).

Sparke, Michael. *Crums of Comfort and Godly Prayers* (London, 1628).

Sturm, Leonhard Christoph. *Vollständige Anweisung Innerer Austheilung der Gebäude* (Augsburg, 1720).

Swift, Jonathan. *Directions to Servants*, second edition (London, 1746).

Tessin, Nicloas. *Observationer angående så wähl pubiqve som priuate huus byggnaders starkheet, bekqwämligheet och skiönheet, in rättade, efter wår Swänska climat och oeconomie* (republished; Stockholm: Byggfölaget, 2002).

Tryon, Thomas. *A Treatise of Cleanness in Meats and Drinks, of the Preparation of Food, the Excellency of Good Airs, and the Benefits of Clan Sweet Beds. Also of the Generation of Bugs, and Their Cure* (London, 1682).

Venner, Tobbias. *Via Recta ad Vitam Longam, or a Plaine Philosophical Discourse* (London, 1620).

von Schwerin, Martina. *Småsaker af en nybegynnare*, vol. 4 (Lund: Gleerup, 1840).

Walpole, Horace. *Description of the Villa of Mr Horace Walpole* (London: Printed for the Author, 1784).

Whatman, Susanna. *The Housekeeping Book of Susanna Whatman* (1776; London: National Trust, 2000).

Whitehurst, John. *Observations on the Ventilation of Rooms, on the Construction of Chimneys and on Garden Stoves* (London: W. Bent, 1794).

Wijnblad, Carl. *Ritningar på fyratio våningshus* (Stockholm: Rekolid, 1755).

Wood, John. *A Series of Plans, for Cottages or Habitations of the Labourer, Either in Husbandry, or the Mechanic Arts, Adapted as well to Towns, as to the Country* (Bath: Hooper and Keenes, 1788).

Wotton, Henry. *The Elements of Architecture* (London: John Bill, 1624).

Novels and Poems

Anon. *Letters of Miss Riversdale* (London, 1803).

Austen, Jane. *Mansfield Park* (1814; Oxford: Oxford University Press, 1980).

Austen, Jane. *Northanger Abbey* (1818; Oxford: Oxford University Press, 1980).

Austen, Jane. *Emma* (1815; London: Penguin Edition, 1985).

Austen, Jane. *Sense and Sensibility* (1811; Oxford: Oxford University Press, 1970).

Austen, Jane. *Sense and Sensibility* (1811; London: Penguin, 1995).

Austen, Jane. *Sanditon* (1817; Oxford: Oxford University Press, 1998).

Austen, Jane. *Pride and Prejudice* (1813; Oxford: Oxford University Press, 2004).

Burney, Fanny. *Evelina: The History of a Young Lady's Entrance into the World* (1778; London: Harrison, 1861).

Cowper, William. *The Task, Book I: The Sofa* (London: J. Johnson, 1785).

Crebillon, Claude. *La Sopha: a Moral Tale* (1742; London: George Routledge, 1927).

Defoe, Daniel. *Robinson Crusoe* (1719; London: Palgrave Macmillan, 1868).

Defoe, Daniel. *The Fortunes and Misfortunes of the Famous Moll Flanders* (1722; Oxford: Oxford University Press, 1971).

Gaskell, Elizabeth. *Mary Barton* (1848; London: Chapman and Hall, 1849).

More, Hannah. *Mr Bragwell and His Two Daughters* (London, 1797).

Pix, Mary. *The Beau Defeated* (1700).

Scott, Walter. *Ivanhoe* (1820; Oxford: Oxford University Press, 1996).

Shakespeare, William. *Cymberline* (1623).

von Goethe, Johann Wolfgang. *Die Wahlverwandtschaften* (Tübingen, 1809).

von Goethe, Johann Wolfgang. *Die Leiden des Jungen Werthers* (1774, The Works of Johann Wolfgang von Goethe, vol. 3, New York: International Publishing Company, 1901).

Secondary Sources

Adams, Christine. *A Taste for Comfort and Status: A Bourgeois Family in Eighteenth-Century France* (Philadelphia: Penn State University Press, 2000).

Ago, Reneta. *Gusto for Things: A History of Objects in Seventeenth-Century Rome* (Chicago: University of Chicago Press, 2013).

Ahmed, Sara. *The Cultural Politics of Emotion* (London: Routledge, 2004).

Anon. *Polite Society by Arthur Devis, 1712–1787: Portraits of the English Country Gentleman and His Family* (Preston: Harris Museum and Art Gallery, 1983).

Archer, John. *The Literature of British Domestic Architecture, 1715–1842* (Cambridge, MA: MIT Press, 1985).

Ariès, Philippe. *L'Enfant et la Vie Familiale sous l'Ancien Régime* (Paris: Plon, 1960).

Armstrong, Hannah. 'The Lost Landscapes and Interiorscapes of the Eighteenth-Century Estate: Reconstructing Wanstead House and Its Ground' (Unpublished PhD thesis, Birkbeck College, University of London, 2016).

Arnold, Dana. *The Georgian Country House: Architecture, Landscape and Society* (Stroud: Alan Sutton, 2003).

Bachelard, Gaston. *The Poetics of Space* (London: Penguin, 1964).

Bailey, Joanne. *Unquiet Lives: Marriage and Marriage Breakdown in the England, 1600–1800* (Cambridge: Cambridge University Press, 2003).

Bailey, Joanne. *Parenting in England, 1760–1830* (Oxford: Oxford University Press, 2012).

Barclay, Katie. *Intimacy and Power: Marriage and Patriarchy in Scotland, 1650–1850* (Manchester: Manchester University Press, 2011).

Barclay, Katie. 'Family and Household', in Susan Broomhall (ed.), *Early Modern Emotions* (London: Routledge, 2017), 244–6.

Barczewski, Stephanie. *Country Houses and the British Empire, 1700–1930* (Manchester: Manchester University Press, 2014).

Barker, Hannah. *Family and Business During the Industrial Revolution* (Oxford: Oxford University Press, 2017).

Barnes, Diana. 'Emotional Debris in Early Modern Letters', in Stephanie Downes, Sally Holloway, and Sarah Randles (eds.), *Feeling Things: Objects and Emotions Though History* (Oxford: Oxford University Press, 2018), 114–52.

Barnwell, Peter, and Marilyn Palmer (eds.). *Country House Technology* (London: Paul Watkin Publishing, 2012).

Beard, Geoffrey. *Georgian Craftsmen and Their Work* (London: Country Life, 1966).

Beckett, John. 'The Pattern of Landownership in England and Wales, 1660–1800', *Economic History Review*, 37 (1984), 1–22.

Beckett, John. *The Aristocracy in England, 1660–1914* (Oxford: Blackwell, 1986).

Berg, Maxine. 'Women's Consumption and the Industrial Classes of Eighteenth-Century England', *Journal of Social History*, 30 (1996), 415–34.

Berg, Maxine. 'French Fancy and Cool Britannia: The Fashion Markets of Early Modern Europe', in Simonetta Cavaciocchi (ed.), *Fiere e mercati nella integrazione delle economie Europe secc. XIII–XVIII* (Prato: Le Monnier, 2001), 540–6.

Berg, Maxine. *Luxury and Pleasure in Eighteenth-Century Britain* (Oxford: Oxford University Press, 2005).

Bermingham, Anne. 'Elegant Females and Gentlemen Connoisseurs: The Commerce in Culture and Self-Image in Eighteenth-Century England', in John Brewer and Anne Bermingham (eds.), *The Consumption of Culture, 1660–2800: Image, Object, Text* (London: Routledge, 1995), 489–513.

Berry, Helen, and Elizabeth Foyster. 'Childless Men in Early Modern England', in Helen Berry and Elizabeth Foyster (eds.), *The Family in Early Modern England* (Cambridge: Cambridge University Press, 2007).

Bold, John. 'Privacy and the Plan', in John Bold and Edward Chaney (eds.), *English Architecture, Public and Private: Essays for Kerry Downes* (London: Hambledon Press, 1993), 107–19.

Brant, Clare. *Eighteenth-Century Letters and British Culture* (Basingstoke: Palgrave Macmillan, 2006).

Brogden, William. *Iconographia Rustica: Stephen Switzer and the Designed Landscape* (London: Routledge, 2016).

Broomhall, Susan. 'Emotions in the Household', in Susan Broomhall (ed.), *Emotions in the Household, 1200–1900* (Basingstoke: Palgrave Macmillan, 2008), 15–19.

Brown, Bill. 'Thing Theory', *Critical Inquiry*, 28:1 (2001), 1–22.

Burghartz, Susanna. 'Printed Markets: The Basel Avisblatt, 1729–1845', https://avisblatt.ch/ (accessed 6 August 2020).

Campbell, Colin. 'The Desire for the New: Its Nature and Social Location as Presented in Theories of Fashion ad Modern Consumerism', in Roger Silverman and Eric Hirsch (eds.), *Consuming Technologies: Media and Information in Domestic Spaces* (London: Routledge, 1992), 93–105.

Carson, Charles. *Technology and the Big House in Ireland, c.1800–c.1930* (Amherst, NY: Cambria Press, 2009).

Castellucio, Stephane. *L'éclairage, le chauffage et l'eau aux XVIIe et XVIIIe siècles* (Paris: Gourcuff Graden, 2016).

Chavasse, Hannah. 'Material Culture and the Country House: Fashion, Comfort and Lineage' (Unpublished PhD thesis, University of Northampton, 2015).

Christie, Christopher. *The British Country House in the Eighteenth Century* (Manchester: Manchester University Press, 2000).

Clark, Gregory, and David Jacks. 'Coal and the Industrial Revolution, 1700–1869', https://gpih.ucdavis.edu/files/Clark_Jacks.pdf (accessed 12 August 2020).

Clarke, N. *The Rise and Fall of the Woman of Letters* (London: Routledge, 2004).

Clemente, Alida. 'Luxury and Taste in Eighteenth-Century Naples: Representations, Ideas and Social Practices at the Intersection Between the Global and the Local', in Johanna Ilmakunnas and Jon Stobart (eds.), *A Taste for Luxury* (London: Bloomsbury, 2017), 59–76.

Cockayne, Emily. *Hubbub: Filth, Noise and Stench in England, 1600–1770* (New Haven: Yale University Press, 2008).

Coffin, David. *The Villa Life of Renaissance Rome* (Princeton, NJ: Princeton University Press, 1979).

Cohen, Deborah. *Household Gods: The British and Their Possessions* (New Haven, CT: Yale University Press, 2006).

Cohen, M. ' "Manners" Make the Man: Politeness, Chivalry and the Construction of Masculinity, 1750–1830', *Journal of British Studies*, 44 (2005), 312–29.

Colvin, Howard, and John Harris (eds.). *The Country Seat: Studies in the History of the British Country House* (London: Allen Lane, 1970).

Colvin, Howard, and John Newman (eds.). *Of Building: Roger North's Writings on Architecture* (Oxford: Oxford University Press, 1981).

Coquery, Natacha. 'The Language of Success: Marketing and Distributing Semi-Luxury Goods in Eighteenth-Century Paris', *Journal of Design History*, 17:1 (2004), 71–89.

Coquery, Natacha. 'Fashion, Business, Diffusion: An Upholsterer's Shop in Eighteenth-Century Paris', in Dena Goodman and Kathryn Norberg (eds.), *Furnishing the Eighteenth Century* (London: Routledge, 2007), 63–78.

Cornforth, John. *English Interiors, 1799–1848: The Quest for Comfort* (London: Barrie & Jenkins, 1978).

Cornforth, John. *Early Georgian Interiors* (New Haven: Yale University Press, 2004).

Coutu, Joan, Peter Lindfield, and Jon Stobart (eds.). *Houses of Politicians* (Montreal: McGill University Press, forthcoming 2022).

Cowen Orlin, Lena. 'Empty Vessels', in Tara Hamling and Catherine Richardson (eds.), *Everyday Objects: Medieval and Early Modern Material Culture and Its Meanings* (Farnham: Ashgate, 2010), 299–308.

Cox, Nancy, and Karin Dannehl. *Perceptions of Retailing in Early Modern England* (Aldershot: Ashgate, 2007).

Crowley, John. *The Invention of Comfort: Sensibilities and Design in Early-Modern Britain and Early America* (Baltimore: Johns Hopkins University Press, 2001).

Crowley, John. 'From Luxury to Comfort and Back Again: Landscape Architecture and the Cottage in Britain and America', in Maxine Berg and Elizabeth Eger (eds.), *Luxury in the Eighteenth Century: Debates, Desires and Delectable Goods* (Basingstoke: Palgrave Macmillan, 2003), 135–50.

Csikszentmihalyi, Mihaly, and Eugene Rochberg-Halton. *The Meaning of Things: Domestic Symbols and the Self* (Cambridge: Cambridge University Press, 1981).

Cunningham, Hugh. *Children and Childhood in Western Society Since 1500*, second edition (London: Routledge, 2005).

Davies, Mark. *A Perambulating Paradox: British Travel Literature and the Image of Sweden c. 1770–1865* (Lund: Lund University, 2000).

Davrius, Aurélien. *Jacques-François Blondel, architecte des Lumières* (Paris: Classiques Garnier, 2018).

Davrius, Aurélien. 'Masters and Servants: Parallel Worlds in Blondel's *maisons de plaisance*', in Jon Stobart (ed.), *The Comforts of Home in Western Europe, 1700–1900* (London: Bloomsbury, 2020), 39–44.

Daybell, James. *The Material Letter in Early Modern England: Manuscript Letters and the Culture and Practices of Letter-Writing, 1512–1635* (Basingstoke: Palgrave Macmillan, 2012).

DeJean, Joan. *The Age of Comfort: When Paris Discovered Casual and the Modern Home Began* (New York: Bloomsbury, 2009).

DeJean, Joan. '(Love) Letters: Madeleine de Scudéry and the Epistolary Impulse', *Eighteenth-Century Fiction*, 22:3 (2010), 399–414.

DeLanda, Manuel. *Assemblage Theory* (Edinburgh: Edinburgh University Press, 2016).

Deleuze, Gilles, and Félix Guatarri. *A Thousand Plateaus: Capitalism and Schizophrenia*, trans. by Brian Massumi (London: Continuum, 1987).

Denis, Britt. 'The Spread of Comfort in Nineteenth-Century Belgium Homes', in Jon Stobart (ed.), *The Comforts of Home in Western Europe, 1700–1900* (London: Bloomsbury, 2020), 104–123.

de Vries, Jan. *Industrious Revolution: Consumer Behaviour and the Household Economy, 1650 to the Present* (Cambridge: Cambridge University Press, 2006).

Dillon, Maureen. 'Advances in Lighting Technology and the Transformation of the Domestic Interior: A Case Study of Knole, Sevenoaks, Kent', in Peter Barnwell and Marilyn Palmer (eds.), *Country House Technology* (London: Paul Watkin Publishing, 2012), 93–107.

Dixon, Jenni. 'The Toyshop, the Cabinet and Eighteenth-Century Curiosity', *History of Retailing and Consumption*, 5:3 (2019), 205–27.

Dolan, Alice. 'Touching Linen: Textiles, Emotion and Bodily Intimacy in England c.1708–1818', *Cultural and Social History*, 16:2 (2019), 145–64.

Dooley, Terence, Maeve O-Riordan, and Christopher Ridgway (eds.). *Women and the Country House in Ireland and Britain* (Dublin: Four Courts Press, 2018).

Downes, Stephanie, Sally Holloway, and Sarah Randles. 'A Feeling for Things, Past and Present', in Stephanie Downes, Sally Holloway, and Sarah Randles (eds.), *Feeling Things: Objects and Emotions Through History* (Oxford: Oxford University Press, 2018), 8–23.

Dyrmann, Kristine. 'Sybille Reventlow's Sociability at Brahaetrolleborg', unpublished paper presented at the conference *A Manorial World*, Gammel Estrup, Denmark, 21–23 September 2017.

Eacott, Jonathan. *Selling Empire: India in the Making of Britain and America, 1600–1830* (Chapel Hill: University of North Carolina Press, 2016).

Earle, Rebecca (ed.). *Epistolary Selves: Letters and Letter-Writers, 1600–1945* (Aldershot: Ashgate, 1999).

Edwards, Clive. *Turning Houses into Homes: A History of the Retailing and Consumption of Domestic Furnishings* (Aldershot: Ashgate, 2005), 4.

Eklund, Karl Johan. 'Husen och miljön', in Ann-Charlotte Ljungholm (ed.), *Lövstabruk: Ej Sin Like I Hela Riket* (Uppsala: Stiftelsen Leufsta, 2011), 27–36.

English, B., and J. Saville. 'Family Settlement and "the Rise of the Great Estates"', *Economic History Review*, 33 (1980), 556–8.

Epp, Amber, and Linda Price. 'The Storied Life of Singularized Objects: Forces of Agency and Network Transformation', *Journal of Consumer Research*, 36:5 (2010), 820–37.

Faber, Alfred. *Entwicklungsstufen der häuslichen Heizung* (Oldenburg: München, 1957).

Fairfax-Lucy, Alice. *Charlecote and the Lucys* (London: Victor Gollanz Ltd, 1990).

Fatsar, Kristof. ' "Enjoying Country Life to the Full—Only the English Know How to Do That": Appreciation of the British Country House by Hungarian Aristocratic Visitors', in Jon Stobart (ed.), *Travel and the Country House* (Manchester: Manchester University Press, 2017), 147–67.

Fennetaux, Arianne. 'Toying with Novelty: Toys, Consumption and Novelty in Eighteenth-Century Britain', in Bruno Blondé, Natacha Coquery, Jon Stobart, and Ilja Van Damme (eds.), *Fashioning Old and New: Changing Consumer Patterns in Western Europe (1650–1900)* (Turnhout: Brepols, 2009), 17–28.

Fennetaux, Ariane. 'Sentimental Economics: Recycling Textiles in Eighteenth-Century Britain', in Ariane Fennetaux, Amelie Junqua, and Sophie Vasset (eds.), *The Afterlife of Used Things: Recycling in the Long Eighteenth Century* (London: Routledge, 2015), 122–41.

Filor, Ellen. ' "No Lady Could Do This": Navigating Gender and Collecting Objects in India and Scotland, c.1810–50', in Jon Stobart (ed.), *Travel and the British Country House: Cultures, Critiques ad Consumption in the Long Eighteenth Century* (Manchester: Manchester University Press, 2017), 206–24.

Finn, Margot, and Kate Smith. *The East India Company at Home, 1757–1857* (London: UCL Press, 2017).

Fletcher, Anthony. *Growing Up in England: The Experience of Childhood, 1600–1914* (New Haven: Yale University Press, 2008).

Fletcher, Guy. 'Sentimental Value', *Journal of Value Inquiry*, 43:1 (2009), 55–65.

Foskett, Daphne. *John Harden of Brathay Hall, 1772–1847* (Kendal: Abbot Hall Art Gallery, 1974).

Fowler, John, and John Cornforth. *English Decoration in the Eighteenth Century* (London: Barrie and Jenkins, 1974).

French, Henry, and Mark Rothery. *Man's Estate: Landed Gentry Masculinities, 1660–1900* (Oxford: Oxford University Press, 2013).

French, Henry, and Mark Rothery. 'Male Anxiety Among Younger Sons of the English Landed Gentry', *The Historical Journal*, 62:4 (2019), 967–95.

Gell, Alfred. *Art and Agency: A New Anthropological Theory* (Oxford: Oxford University Press, 1998).

Gerhold, Dorian. 'London's Suburban Villas and Mansions, 1660–1830', *The London Journal*, 34:3 (2009), 233–63.

Germann, Jennifer, and Heidi Strobel (eds.), *Materializing Gender in Eighteenth-Century Europe* (London: Routledge, 2016).

Gidal, Eric. 'Civic Melancholy: English Gloom and French Enlightenment', *Eighteenth-Century Studies*, 37:1 (2003), 23–45.

Gilbert, Chrisopher, and Anthony Wells-Cole. *The Fashionable Fireplace, 1660–1840* (Leeds: Leeds City Art Galleries, 1985).

Girouard, Mark. *Life in the English Country House: A Social and Architectural History* (New Haven: Yale University Press, 1978).

Girouard, Mark. *Life in the French Country House* (London: Cassell & Co., 2000).

Gloag, John. *Georgian Grace: A Social History of Design, from 1660 to 1830* (London: Black, 1956).

Gloag, John. *Victorian Comfort: A Social History of Design from 1830–1900* (Basingstoke: Palgrave Macmillan, 1961).

Goldsmith, Sarah. 'Nostalgia, Homesickness and Emotional Formation on the Eighteenth-Century Grand Tour', *Cultural and Social History*, 15:3 (2018), 333–60.

Gomme, Andor. 'Stoneleigh After the Grand Tour', *The Antiquaries Journal*, 68 (1988), 265–86.

Gomme, Andor. 'Abbey into Palace: A lesser Wilton?', in Robert Bearman (ed.), *Stoneleigh Abbey: The House, Its Owners, Its Lands* (Stratford-upon-Avon: Shakespeare Birthplace Trust, 2004).

Gow, Ian. 'The Edinburgh Villa Revisited: Function Not Form', in Dana Arnold (ed.), *The Georgian Villa* (Stroud: Sutton, 1996), 144–55.

Gregory, Jeremy. *Restoration, Reformation, and Reform, 1660–1828: Archbishops of Canterbury and Their Diocese* (Oxford: Oxford University Press, 2000).

Gregory, Jeremy. 'Transforming the Age of Reason into an Age of Faiths', *Journal for Eighteenth-Century Studies*, 32:3 (2009), 287–305.

Greig, Hannah. *The Beau Monde: Fashionable Society in Georgian London* (Oxford: Oxford University Press, 2013), 42.

Habakkuk, John. 'Marriage Settlements in the Eighteenth Century', *Transactions of the Royal Historical Society*, fourth series, 32 (1950), 15–30.

Habakkuk, John. *Marriage, Debt and the Estate System: English Landownership 1650–1950* (Oxford: Oxford University Press, 1996).

Hague, Stephen. *The Gentleman's House in the British Atlantic World, 1680–1780* (Basingstoke: Palgrave Macmillan, 2016).

Hamilakis, Yannis. 'Sensorial Assemblages: Affect, Memory and Temporality in Assemblage Thinking', *Cambridge Archaeological Journal*, 27:1 (2017), 169–182.

Hamlett, Jane. *Material Relations: Domestic Interiors and Middle-Class Families in England, 1850–1910* (Manchester: Manchester University Press, 2010).

Hamling, Tara. 'Household Objects', in Susan Broomhall (ed.), *Early Modern Emotions: An Introduction* (London: Routledge, 2017), 135–40.

Hamling, Tara, and Catherine Richardson. *A Day at Home in Early Modern England* (New Haven: Yale University Press, 2017).

Handley, Sasha. *Sleep in Early Modern England* (New Haven: Yale University Press, 2016).

Hansson, Joakim. *Komfort framför allt, men även nytta och nöje* (Helsingfors: Sandelin, 2015).

Hardyment, Christina. *Home Comforts: A History of Domestic Arrangements* (London: Viking, 1992).

Harris, John. *The Design of the English Country House* (London: Trefoil Publications, 1985).

Harris, Oliver. 'More Than Representation: Multiscalar Assemblages and the Deleuzian Challenge to Archaeology', *History of the Human Sciences*, 31:3 (2018), 83–104.

Hart, Francis. 'The Spaces of Privacy: Jane Austen', *Nineteenth-Century Fiction*, 30:3 (1975), 305–33.

Harvey, Karen. 'Men Making Home: Masculinity and Domesticity in Eighteenth-Century Britain', *Gender and History*, 21:3 (2009).

Harvey, Karen. *The Little Republic: Masculinity and Domestic Authority in Eighteenth-Century Britain* (Oxford: Oxford University Press, 2012).

Harvey, Karen, and Alexandra Shepard. 'What Have Historians Done with Masculinity? Reflections on Five Centuries of British History, Circa 1500–1950', *Journal of British Studies*, 44:2 (2005), 274–80.

Hellman, Mimi. 'Enchanted Night: Decoration, Sociability and Visuality After Dark', in Charissa Bremer-David (ed.), *Paris: Life and Luxury in the Eighteenth Century* (Los Angeles: Getty, 2011), 91–113.

Holloway, Sarah. 'Materializing Maternal Emotions: Birth, Celebration and Renunciation in England, c.1688–1830', in Stephanie Downes, Sally Holloway, and Sarah Randles (eds.), *Feeling Things: Objects and Emotions Through History* (Oxford: Oxford University Press, 2018), 154–71.

Houblon, Alice. *The Houblon Family: Its History and Times*, vol. 2 (Edinburgh: Archibald Constable & Co., 1907).

Howard, Deborah. 'The Italian Renaissance Villa: The Reconciliation of Nature and Artifice', in Dana Arnold (ed.), *The Georgian Villa* (Stroud: Alan Sutton, 1996), 1–10.

Ilmakunnas, Johanna. 'Embroidering Women and Turning Men: Handiwork, Gender, and Emotions in Sweden and Finland, c. 1720–1820', *Scandinavian Journal of History*, 41:3 (2016), 306–31.

Ilmakunnas, Johanna. 'French Fashions: Aspects of Elite Lifestyle in Eighteenth-Century Sweden', in Johanna Ilmakunnas and Jon Stobart (eds.), *A Taste for Luxury in Early Modern Europe: Display, Acquisition and Boundaries* (London: Bloomsbury, 2017), 250–2.

Ilmakunnas, Johanna. 'Northern Comfort and Discomfort: Spaces and Objects in Swedish Country Houses, c.1740–1800', in Jon Stobart (ed.), *The Comforts of Home in Western Europe, 1700–1900* (London: Bloomsbury, 2020), 46–53.

Ilmakunnas, Johanna. 'Life-Stage, Work and Daily Routines of the Eighteenth-Century Swedish Elite: Johan Gabriel Oxenstierna's Diaries', in Gudrun Andersson and Jon Stobart (eds.), *Daily Lives and Daily Routines in Eighteenth-Century Europe* (London: Routledge, 2021).

Ilmakunnas, Johanna, and Jon Stobart (eds.), *A Taste for Luxury in Early Modern Europe* (London: Bloomsbury, 2017).

Irwin, Emily. 'The Spermaceti Candle and the American Whaling Industry', *Historia*, 21 (2012), 45–53.

Jackson-Stops, Gervase (ed.). *The Treasure Houses of Britain: Five Hundred Years of Private Patronage and Art Collecting* (New Haven and London: Yale University Press, 1985).

James, Carolyn. 'What's Love Got to Do with It? Dynastic Politics and Motherhood in the Letters of Elenora of Aragon and Her Daughters', *Women's History Review*, 24:4 (2015), 528–47.

James, Carolyn. 'Letters', in Susan Broomhall (ed.), *Early Modern Emotions: An Introduction* (London: Routledge, 2017), 121.

Jandot, Oliver. 'The Invention of Thermal Comfort in Eighteenth-Century France', in Jon Stobart (ed.), *The Comforts of Home in Western Europe, 1700–1900* (London: Bloomsbury, 2020), 73–92.

Jones, Ann Rosalin, and Peter Stallybrass. *Renaissance Clothing and the Materials of Memory* (Cambridge: Cambridge University Press, 2000).

Jones, Margaret. 'A Cure for Untidiness?', *Country Life*, 28 March 1957.

Jones, Robin. ' "Souvenirs of People Who Have Come and Gone": Second-Hand Furnishings and the Anglo-India Domestic Interior, 1840–1920', in Jon Stobart and Ilja Van Damme (eds.), *Modernity and the Second-hand Trade* (Basingstoke: Palgrave Macmillan, 2010), 111–38.

Joy, E.T. 'Georgian Patent Furniture', in *Connoisseur Year Book* (London: The Connoisseur, 1962), 9–11.

Kambaskovic, Danijela. 'Love', in Susan Broomhall (ed.), *Early Modern Emotions: An Introduction* (London: Routledge, 2017), 53–6.

Ketton-Cremer, R.W. *Felbrigg: The Story of a House* (London: Futura, 1982).

Kuiper, Yme. 'The Rise of the Country House in the Dutch Republic: Beyond Johan Huizinga's Narrative of Dutch Civilisation in the Seventeenth Century', in Jon Stobart and Andrew Hann (eds.), *The Country House: Material Culture and Consumption* (Swindon: Historic England, 2016), 11–23.

Kwint, Marius. 'Introduction: The Physical Past', in Marius Kwint, Christopher Breward, and Jeremy Aynsley (eds.), *Material Memories* (Oxford: Oxford University Press, 1999), 1–16.

Lawrence, Roderick. 'What Makes a House a Home?', *Environment and Behaviour*, 19:2 (1987), 154–68.

Lemire, Beverly. 'An Education in Comfort: Indian Textiles and the Remaking of English Homes Over the Long Eighteenth Century', in Jon Stobart and Bruno Blondé (eds.), *Selling Textiles in the Long Eighteenth Century* (Basingstoke: Palgrave Macmillan, 2014), 13–29.

Lewis, Judith. 'When a House Is Not a Home: Elite English Women and the Eighteenth-Century Country House', *Journal of British Studies*, 48:2 (2009), 336–63.

Lindahl, G. 'En arkitektkarriär i maktens följe', in M. Snickare (ed.), *Tessin: Nicodemus Tessin d.y. Kunglig arkitekt och visionär* (Stockholm: Nationalmuseum, 2002).

Lindfield, Peter. *Georgian Gothic: Medievalist Architecture, Furniture and Interiors, 1730–1840* (Woodbridge: Boydell and Brewer, 2016).

Lippert, Hans-Georg. 'Das Haus in Architekturtraktaten zwischen 1450 und 1950', in Joachim Eibach and Inken Schmidt-Voges (eds.), *Das Haus In Der Geschichte Europas* (Köln: Böhlau, 2015).

Lougham, John. 'Between Reality and Artful Fiction: The Representation of the Domestic Interior in Seventeenth-Century Dutch Art', in Jeremy Aynsley and Charlotte Grant (eds.), *Imagined Interiors: Representing the Domestic Interior Since the Renaissance* (London: V&A Publications, 2006).

Lynch, Andrew. 'Emotional Community', in Susan Broomhall (ed.), *Early Modern Emotions: An Introduction* (London: Routledge, 2017), 3–6.

MacArthur, Rosie. 'Material Culture and Consumption on an English Estate: Kelmarsh Hall 1687–1845' (Unpublished PhD thesis, University of Northampton, 2010).

Macdonald, Mairi. 'Not Unmarked by Some Eccentricities: The Leigh Family of Stoneleigh Abbey', in Robert Bearman (ed.), *Stoneleigh Abbey: The House, Its Owners, Its Lands* (Straford-upon-Avon: Shakespeare Birthplace Trust, 2004).

Mackintosh, Alan. *The Patent Medicines Industry in Georgian England: Constructing the Market by the Potency of Print* (Basingstoke: Palgrave Macmillan, 2017).

Mann, Catherine. ' "Whether You Ladyship Will or ne": Displeasure, Duty and Devotion in the Lisle Letters', in Susan Broomhall (ed.), *Emotions in the Household, 1200–1900* (Basingstoke: Palgrave Macmillan, 2008), 119–43.

Mason, Shena. *Matthew Boulton: Selling What the World Desires* (New Haven: Yale University Press, 2009).

McCracken, Grant. *Culture and Consumption: New Approaches to the Symbolic Character of Consumer Goods and Activities* (Bloomington and Indianapolis: Indiana University Press, 1988).

McDowall, Stephen. 'Imperial Plots? Shugborough Chinoiserie and Imperial Ideology in Eighteenth Century British Gardens', *Cultural and Social History*, 14:1 (2017), 17–34.

Meldrum, Tim. *Domestic Service and Gender, 1660–1750* (Harlow: Pearson, 2000).

Metcalfe, Helen. 'The Social Experience of Bachelorhood in Late-Georgian England, c.1760–1830' (Unpublished PhD thesis, University of Manchester, 2017).

Miller, Daniel. *The Comfort of Things* (Cambridge: Polity Press, 2011).

Mingay, Gordon. *English Landed Society in the Eighteenth Century* (London: Routledge & Kegan Paul, 1963).

Mitchell, D.M. 'Fine Table Linen in England 1450–1750: Ownership and Use of a Luxury Commodity' (Unpublished PhD thesis, University of London, 1999).

Musson, Jeremy. *Up and Down Stairs: The History of the Country House Servant* (London: John Murray, 2009).

National Trust. *Kedleston Hall* (London: National Trust, 1999).

Navickas, Katrina. *Protest and the Politics of Space and Place, 1789–1848* (Manchester: Manchester University Press, 2016).

North, Michael. *Material Delight and the Joy of Living': Cultural Consumption in the Age of Enlightenment in Germany* (Aldershot: Ashgate, 2008).

North, Michael. 'Fashion and Luxury in Eighteenth-Century Germany', in Johanna Ilmakunnas and Jon Stobart (eds.), *A Taste for Luxury in Early Modern Europe* (London: Bloomsbury, 2017), 102–3.

Notcutt, William. 'A Believer's Evidences for Heaven, or a Short Essay for Christian Comfort', *Johnston, the Improved Christian's Courage* (1717), 33, 8–9.

O'Dea, William. *The Social History of Lighting* (London: Routledge & Paul, 1958).

Odile-Bernez, Marie. 'Comfort, the Acceptable Face of Luxury: An Eighteenth-Century Etymology', *The Journal for Early Modern Cultural Studies*, 14:2 (2014): 3–21.

O'Loughlin, Katrina. 'Sensibility', in Susa Broomhall (ed.), *Early Modern Emotions: An Introduction* (London: Routledge, 2017).

Ottenheym, Konrad, and Krista De Jonge (eds.). *The Low Countries at the Crossroads: Netherlandish Architecture as an Export Product in Early Modern Europe (1480–1680)* (Tournhout: Brepols, 2013).

Page, Norman. *The Language of Jane Austen* (Oxford: Oxford University Press, 1972).

Palmer, Marilyn. 'The Social Impact of Technological Innovation in the English Country House', in Peter Barnwell and Marilyn Palmer (eds.), *Country House Technology* (London: Paul Watkin Publishing, 2012), 1–21.

Palmer, Marilyn, and Ian West. *Technology in the Country House* (Swindon: Historic England, 2016).

Pennell, Sara. 'Making the Bed in Later Stuart and Georgian England', in Jon Stobart and Bruno Blondé (eds.), *Selling Textiles in the Long Eighteenth Century* (Basingstoke: Palgrave Macmillan, 2014), 30–45.

Phillipps, Kenneth. *Jane Austen's English* (London: Deutsch, 1970).

Pohl, Nicole. 'Utopian Households in the Work of Sarah Scott and Sarah Fielding', in Susan Broomhall (ed.), *Emotions in the Household, 1200–1900* (Basingstoke: Palgrave Macmillan, 2008), 219–33.

Pointon, Marcia. 'Jewellery in Eighteenth-Century England', in Maxine Berg and Helen Clifford (eds.), *Consumers and Luxury: Consumer Culture in Europe, 1650–1850* (Manchester: Manchester University Press, 1999), 120–26.

Pollock, Linda. 'Anger and the Negotiation of Relationships in Early Modern England', *The Historical Journal*, 47:3 (2004), 567–90.

Popiel, Jennifer. 'Making Mothers: The Advice Genre and the Domestic Ideal, 1760–1830', *Journal of Family History*, 29:4 (2004), 339–50.

Prown, Jules. 'The Truth of Material Culture', in Jules Prown and Kenneth Haltman (eds.), *American Artefacts: Essays in Material Culture* (East Lansing, MI: Michigan State University Press, 2000), 1–19.

Prytz, Cristina. 'The Improved Tiled Stove: Sweden's Contribution to Defining Comfort?', in Jon Stobart (ed.), *The Comforts of Home in Western Europe, 1700–1900* (London: Bloomsbury, 2020), 93–98.

Purcell, Mark. *The Country House Library* (New Haven: Yale University Press, 2017).

Reddy, William M. *The Navigation of Feeling: A Framework for the History of Emotions* (Cambridge: Cambridge University Press, 2011).

Retford, Kate. *The Art of Domestic Life: Family Portraiture in Eighteenth-Century England* (New Haven: Yale University Press, 2006).

Retford, Kate. 'Patrilineal Portraiture? Gender and Genealogy in the Eighteenth-Century English Country House', in John Styles and Amanda Vickery (eds.), *Gender, Taste and Material Culture in Britain and North America, 1700–1830* (New Haven: Yale University Press, 2006), 315–44.

Retford, Kate. 'From the Interior to Interiority: The Conversation Piece in Georgian England', *Design History*, 20:4 (2007), 291–307.

Retford, Kate. *The Conversation Piece: Making Modern Art in Eighteenth-Century Britain* (New Haven: Yale University Press, 2017).

Roberts, Michael. *Age of Liberty: Sweden 1719–1772* (Cambridge: Cambridge University Press, 1986).

Roche, Daniel. *A History of Everyday Things: The Birth of Consumption in France, 1600–1900* (Cambridge: Cambridge University Press, 2000).

Roche, Daniel. 'Gaz à tous les étages', *En attendant Nadeau*, 48 (2018).

Rollenhagen Tilly, Linnéa. *Carl Johan Cronstedt: Arkitekt och Organisatör* (Stockholm: Balkong Förlag, 2017).

Ronnes, Hanneke. 'A Sense of Heritage: Renewal Versus Preservation in the English and Dutch Palaces of William III in the 18th Century', in Jon Stobart and Andrew Hann (eds.), *The Country House: Material Culture and Consumption* (Swindon: Historic England, 2016), 78–9.

Rosenwein, Barbara. *Emotional Communities in the Early Middle Ages* (Ithaca: Cornell University Press, 2006).

Rosenwein, Barbara. 'Problems and Methods in the History of Emotions', *Passions in Context: Journal of the History and Philosophy of the Emotions*, 1:1 (2010).

Rothery, Mark, and Henry French. *The Formation of Male Elite Identities in England c.1660–1900: A Sourcebook* (Basingstoke: Palgrave Macmillan, 2012).

Rowntree, Peter. 'Thomas Hughes's Temperature Record for Stroud, 1775–1795', *Weather*, 67:6 (2012), 156–61.

Russell, Francis. 'The Hanging and Display of Pictures, 1799–1850', in Jackson Stops *et al.* (eds.), *The Fashioning and Functioning of the British Country House* (New Haven: Yale University Press, 1989), 133–53.

Rybcynski, Witold. *Home: A Short History of an Idea* (New York: Viking, 1986).

Sambrook, Pamela. *Keeping Their Places: Domestic Service in the Country House* (Stroud: Alan Sutton, 2009).

Sambrook, Pamela, and Peter Brears (eds.). *The Country House Kitchen, 1650–1900* (Stroud: Alan Sutton, 1996).

Sarasohn, Lisa. ' "That Nauseous Venomous Insect": Bedbugs in Early Modern England', *Eighteenth-Century Studies*, 46:4 (2013), 513–30.

Sargentson, Carolyn. 'Looking at Furniture Inside Out: Strategies of Security in Eighteenth-Century French Furniture', in Dena Goodman and Kathryn Norberg (eds.), *Furnishing the Eighteenth Century: What Furniture Can Tell Us About the European and American Past* (London: Routledge, 2006), 205–36.

Saumarez-Smith, Charles. *Eighteenth-Century Decoration: Design and Domestic Interior in England* (London: Weidenfeld & Nicolson, 1993).

Scheer, Monique. 'Are Emotions a Kind of Practice (and What Makes Them Have a History)? A Bourdieusian Approach to Understanding Emotion', *History and Theory*, 51:2 (2010), 193–220.

Scherman, Susanna. *Den Svenska Kakelugnen* (Stockholm: Wahlström & Widstrand, 2007).

Schneider, Gary. 'Affecting Correspondence: Body, Behaviour and the Textualization of Emotion in Early Modern English Letters', *Prose Studies*, 23 (2000), 31–62.

Selling, G. *Svenska Herrgårdshem under 1700-talet* (Stockholm: Stockholm College, 1937).

Shimbo, Akiko. *Furniture-Makers and Consumers in England, 1754–1851* (Farnham: Ashgate, 2015).

Slack, Paul. *Invention of Improvement: Information and Material Progress in Seventeenth-Century England* (Oxford: Oxford University Press, 2014).

Sloboda, Stacey. *Chinoiserie: Commerce and Critical Ornament in Eighteenth-Century England* (Manchester: Manchester University Press, 2014).

Smith, Kate. 'Imperial Families: Women Writing Home in Georgian Britain', *Women's History Review*, 24:6 (2015), 843–60.

Smith, Kate. 'Warfield Park, Berkshire: Longing, Belonging and the British Country House', in Margot Finn and Kate Smith (eds.), *The East India Company at Home, 1757–1857* (London: UCL Press, 2018), 175–90.

Smith, Michael. 'The Affective Communities of Protestantism in North West England, c.1660–c.1740' (Unpublished PhD thesis, University of Manchester, 2017).

Smith, Pete. 'Wollaton Hall: Technology and the Regency Country House', in Peter Barnwell and Marilyn Palmer (eds.), *Country House Technology* (London: Paul Watkin Publishing, 2012), 37–57.

Smith, Woodruff. *Consumption and the Making of Respectability, 1600–1800* (London: Routledge, 2002).

Spaeth, Donald. *The Church in an Age of Danger: Parsons and Parishioners, 1660–1740* (Cambridge: Cambridge University Press, 2000).

Stobart, Jon. 'Inventories and the Changing Furnishings of Canons Ashby, Northamptonshire, 1717–1819', *Regional Furniture*, XXVII (2013), 1–43.

Stobart, Jon. *Sugar and Spice: Grocers and Groceries in Provincial England, 1650–1830* (Oxford: Oxford University Press, 2013).

Stobart, Jon. ' "So Agreeable and Suitable a Place": A Late Eighteenth-Century Suburban Villa', *Journal of Eighteenth-Century Studies* (2016), 89–102.

Stobart, Jon. 'Making an English Country House: Taste and Luxury in the Furnishing of Stoneleigh Abbey, 1763–1765', in Johanna Ilmakunnas and Jon Stobart (eds.), *A Taste for Luxury in Early Modern Europe* (London: Bloomsbury, 2017), 143–60.

Stobart, Jon. 'Housekeeper, Correspondent and Confidante: The Under-Told Story of Mrs Hayes of Charlecote Park, 1744–73', *Family and Community History*, 21:2 (2018), 96–111.

Stobart, Jon. 'Material Literacies of Home Comfort in Georgian England', in Chloe Wigston-Smith and Serena Dyer (eds.), *Material Literacy in Eighteenth-Century Britain: A Nation of Makers* (London: Bloomsbury, 2020).

Stobart, Jon. 'Servants' Furniture: Hierarchies and Identities in the English Country House', in Karen Lipsage and Stephen Hague (eds.), *At Home in the Eighteenth Century: Interrogating Domestic Space* (London: Routledge, 2021).

Stobart, Jon, Andrew Hann, and Victoria Morgan. *Spaces of Consumption: Leisure and Shopping in the English Town, c. 1680–1830* (London: Routledge, 2007).

Stobart, Jon, and Cristina Prytz. 'Comfort in English and Swedish Country Houses, c.1670–1820', *Social History*, 43:2 (2018), 234–58.

Stobart, Jon, and Mark Rothery. 'Fashion, Heritance And Family: New and Old in the Georgian Country House', *Cultural and Social History*, 11:3 (2014), 385–406.

Stobart, Jon, and Mark Rothery. *Consumption and the Country House* (Oxford: Oxford University Press, 2016).

Styles, John. *Threads of Feeling: The London Foundling Hospital's Textile Tokens, 1740–1770* (London: The Foundling Hospital Museum, 2010).

Summerson, John. *Architecture in Britain 1530–1830* (1953; New Haven: Yale University Press, 1993).

Sweet, Roey. *Cities and the Grand Tour. The British in Italy, c.1690–1820* (Cambridge: Cambridge University Press, 2012).

Tadmor, Naomi. *Family and Friends in Eighteenth-Century England: Household, Kinship and Patronage* (Cambridge: Cambridge University Press, 2001).

Tague, I.H. 'Aristocratic Women and Ideas of Family in the Early Eighteenth Century', in Helen Berry and Elizabeth Foyster (eds.), *The Family in Early Modern England* (Cambridge: Cambridge University Press, 2007), 184–208.

Tague, I.H. 'Love, Honour and Obedience: Fashionable Women and the Discourse of Marriage in the Early Eighteenth Century', *Journal of British Studies*, 40:1 (2011), 76–106.

Thompson, F.M.L. *English Landed Society in the Nineteenth Century* (London: Routledge & Kegan Paul, 1963).

Thornton, Peter. *Seventeenth-Century Interior Decoration* (New Haven: Yale University Press, 1978).

Thornton, Peter. *Authentic Décor: The Domestic Interior, 1620–1920* (London: Weidenfeld & Nicolson, 1985).

Tinniswood, Adrian. *Life in the English Country Cottage* (London: Weidenfeld Nicholson, 1995).

Tinniswood, Adrian. *The Polite Tourist: A History of Country House Visiting* (London: National Trust, 1998), 91–112.

Townshend, Dale. 'Convenience, Utility and Comfort in British Architecture of the Long Eighteenth Century', in Jon Stobart (ed.), *The Comforts of Home in Western Europe, 1700–1900* (London: Bloomsbury, 2020), 19–38.

Trentmann, Frank. *Empire of Things: How We Became Consumers, from the Fifteenth Century to the Twenty-First* (London: Allen Lane, 2016).

Tunón, Håkan (ed.). *En fullständig svensk hushållsbok, Reinerus Reineri Broocman* (Stockholm: Kungl, 2016).

Turberville, Arthur. *A History of Welbeck Abbey and Its Owners* (London: Faber and Faber, 1938).

Tyack, Geoffrey. *Warwickshire Country Houses* (Chichester: Phillimore, 1994).

Vahlne, Bo. *Frihetstidens inredningar på Stockholms Slott: Om bekvämlighetens och skönhetens nivåer* (Stockholm: Balkong Förlag, 2012).

Van Damme, Ilja, Bert de Munck, and Andrew Miles (eds.). *Cities and Creativity from the Renaissance to the Present* (London: Routledge, 2018).

Verhoeven, Gerrit. 'Feeling at Home Abroad: Comfort, Domesticity, and Social Display on the Netherlandish Grand Tour (1585–1815)', in Jon Stobart (ed.), *The Comforts of Home in Western Europe, 1700–1900* (London: Bloomsbury, 2020), 160–80.

Vickery, Amanda. *The Gentleman's Daughter: Women's Lives in Georgian England* (New Haven: Yale University Press, 1998).

Vickery, Amanda. 'An Englishman's Home Is His Castle? Thresholds, Boundaries and Privacies in the Eighteenth-Century London Home', *Past and Present*, 199:1 (2008), 274–301.

Vickery, Amanda. *Behind Closed Doors: At Home in Georgian England* (New Haven: Yale University Press, 2009).

Waddell, Brodie. *God, Duty and Community in English Economic Life, 1660–1720* (Woodbridge: Boydell & Brewer Press, 2012).

Wainwright, Clive. *The Romantic Interior: The British Collector at Home, 1750–1850* (New Haven: Yale University Press, 1989).

Walvin, James. *Fruits of Empire: Exotic Produce and British Taste, 1660–1800* (New York: New York University Press, 1997).

Whittle, Jane, and Elizabeth Griffiths. *Consumption and Gender in the Early Seventeenth-Century Household: The World of Alice Le Strange* (Oxford: Oxford University Press, 2012).

Whyman, Susan. ' "Paper Visits": The Post-Restoration Letter as Seen Through the Verney Family Archive', in R. Earle (ed.), *Epistolary Selves: Letters and Letter-Writers, 1600–1945* (Aldershot: Ashgate, 1999), 15–36.

Whyman, Susan. *Sociability and Power in Late-Stuart England: The Cultural Worlds of the Verneys 1660–1720* (Oxford: Oxford University Press, 1999).

Whyman, Susan. *The Pen and the People: English Letter Writers, 1660–1800* (Oxford: Oxford University Press, 2009).

Willard-Wright, Rowena. 'Home from Home? Making Life Comfortable in Victorian Barracks', in Jon Stobart (ed.), *The Comforts of Home in Western Europe, 1700–1900* (London: Bloomsbury, 2020), 187–207.

Williams, J.D. 'The Noble Household as a Unit of Consumption: The Audley End Experience, 1765–1797', *Essex Archaeology and History*, 23 (1992), 67–78.

Wilson, Alan. *Comfort, Pleasure and Prestige: Country-House Technology in West Wales, 1750–1930* (Kibworth Beauchamp: Matador, 2016).

Wilson, Michael. *The English Country House and Its Furnishings* (London: Chancellor Press, 1977).

Wilson, Richard, and Alan Mackley. *Creating Paradise: The Building of the English Country House, 1660–1880* (London: Hambledon Continuum, 2000).

Winner, Lauren. *A Cheerful and Comfortable Faith: Anglican Religious Practice in the Elite Households of Eighteenth-Century Virginia* (New Haven: Yale University Press, 2010).

Wolfe, John. *Brandy, Balloons and Lamps: Ami Argand, 1750–1803* (Carbondale, IL: Southern Illinois University Press, 1999), 28–40.

Woodward, Ian. 'Domestic Objects and the Taste Epiphany', *Journal of Material Culture*, 6:2 (2001), 115–36.

Index